*Democracy
in the
Caribbean*

Democracy
in the
Caribbean

Myths and Realities

Edited by *CARLENE J. EDIE*

PRAEGER

Westport, Connecticut
London

Library of Congress Cataloging-in-Publication Data

Democracy in the Caribbean : myths and realities / edited by Carlene
J. Edie.
    p.   cm.
  Includes bibliographical references and index.
  ISBN 0–275–94595–2 (alk. paper)
    1. Caribbean Area—Politics and government—1945– 2. Democracy—
Caribbean Area. 3. Representative government and representation—
Caribbean Area. I. Edie, Carlene J.
JL599.5.A2D46 1994
321.8'098—dc20   93–5397

British Library Cataloguing in Publication Data is available.

Library of Congress Catalog Card Number: 93–5397
ISBN: 0–275–94595–2

First published in 1994

Praeger Publishers, 88 Post Road West, Westport, CT 06881
An imprint of Greenwood Publishing Group, Inc.

Printed in the United States of America

The paper used in this book complies with the
Permanent Paper Standard issued by the National
Information Standards Organization (Z39.48–1984).

10 9 8 7 6 5 4 3 2 1

Copyright Acknowledgments

The author and publisher gratefully acknowledge permission to quote the following material:

Selwyn Ryan (1992), "The Survival of Liberal Democracy in the Commonwealth Caribbean," *Caribbean Affairs* vol. 4, no. 1 (January–March): 43–60.

Chapter 2 is adapted from Carlene J. Edie, *Democracy by Default: Dependency and Clientelism in Jamaica*. Copyright © 1991 by Lynne Rienner Publishers, Inc. Reprinted with permission of the publisher.

Chapter 10 is adapted from Carmen Gautier-Mayoral, "The Puerto Rican Socio-Economic Model: Its Effect on Present Day Politics and Plebiscite," *Radical America* vol. 23, no. 1 (1990): 21–32.

Chapter 11 is adapted from *The Problem of Democracy in Cuba: Between Vision and Reality* by Carollee Bengelsdorf. Copyright © 1993 by Oxford University Press, Inc. Reprinted by permission.

For the women in my family—
Vidah, Ena, Ivy, Pearl,
Myrtle, Joy, and Khadija

Contents

Tables

Acknowledgments

This book emerged from a panel on "Democracy in the Caribbean" at the Annual Meeting of the American Political Science Association held in San Francisco, CA, August 28–September 1, 1990, and another panel on "Democracy and Human Rights in the Caribbean" at the Annual Meeting of the Caribbean Studies Association held in Port of Spain, Trinidad and Tobago, May 23–26, 1990.

The book consists of a collection of fifteen original analytical essays and an introduction. The authors are largely political scientists and sociologists from the Caribbean. Many of the chapters in this volume have benefited from the comments of other conference participants. However, responsibility for the opinions, findings, and conclusions rests solely with the authors.

I am grateful to all my fellow contributors who made this book possible. Special thanks are also due to several others with whom I discussed the project at one time or another: Ladipo Adamolekun, John Brigham, Kofi Hadjor, Julius Nyangor'o, Gloria Waite, Michael West, and Howard Wiarda. I also want to thank Beverly Labbee, and Donna Dove of the Political Science Department at the University of Massachusetts at Amherst who did all the revisions and the final typing, and Linda Chatfield (formerly of UMass) who helped with the typing when the book was at the conceptual stage. I want to thank my close friends who provided emotional support over all the years I have spent in the United States: Corine Williams, Winnie Harding, Lorna Schloss, Ruth Brown, Sëgun and Funmi Oyekunle, and Debbie Madison. My parents have always given my academic projects enthusiastic support. For this I am especially appreciative. Finally, I want to thank my husband, Mohamed Diakité, for being supportive, and my daughter, Khadija, for bearing with me as I worked on this volume and sometimes missed her bedtime stories.

Abbreviations

ABDM	Antigua-Barbuda Democratic Movement
ACDC	Action Committee of Dedicated Citizens
ALP	Antigua Labour Party
ATLU	Antigua Trades and Labour Union
BDF	Belize Defence Force
BEP	Bosneger Eenheid Partij (the Maroon Party)
BET	Barbados External Telecommunications
BITU	Bustamante Industrial Trade Union
BLP	Barbados Labour Party
BNP	Barbados National Party
BPL	Barbados Progressive League
C 47	Centrale of 47 Unions (Federation of 47 unions)
CARICOM	Caribbean Common Market
CBI	Caribbean Basin Initiative
CDU	Caribbean Democratic Union
CDWA	Colonial Development and Welfare Act
CIDA	Canadian International Development Agency
CLC	Caribbean Labour Congress
COMECON	Council for Mutual Economic Assistance
CP	Congress Party
CPE	Center for Popular Education
DA '91	Democratic Alternative '91
DAC	Democratic Action Congress
DEA	Drug Enforcement Agency

DFM	Democratic Freedom Movement
DFP	Dominica Freedom Party
DLP	Dominica Labour Party
DNA	De Nationale Assemblee (the National Assembly)
DOM	Departments D'Outremer (France)
DUPP	Dominica United Peoples Party
EC	European Community
EEZ	Exclusive Economic Zone
EPZs	Export Processing Zones
FPP	First-Past-the-Post
FRONT	Front for Democracy and Development
GDP	Gross Domestic Product
GMMWU	Grenada Manual and Mental Workers Union
GNP	Gross National Product
GNP	Grenada National Party
GPD	Gross Public Debt
GULP	Grenada United Labour Party
HEART	Human Employment and Resource Training
IADB	InterAmerican Development Bank
ICAIC	Instituto Cubano de Artes y Industria Cinematografo (Cuban Film Institute)
IDEA	Institute Diocesain d'Education des Adultes (Diocese-Supported Institute for Adult Education)
IMF	International Monetary Fund
JC	Jungle Commando
JCTC	Jamaica Commodity Trading Corporation
JDP	Jamaica Democratic Party
JEWEL	Joint Endeavour for Welfare, Education and Liberation
JLP	Jamaica Labour Party
JUCEPLAN	Junta Central de Planificacion (Central Planning Commission)
KTPI	Kaum Tani Persatuan Indonesia (Javanese Farmer's Party)
LDCs	Less Developed Countries
MAA	Maritime Areas Act
MAP	Movement for the Assemblies of the People
MLP	Montserrat Labour Party
MOP	Mouvement Ouvrier Paysan (Peasant Labor Movement)
MWPP	Montserrat Workers Progressive Party
NAR	National Alliance for Reconstruction
NDC	National Democratic Congress
NDP	National Democratic Party
NDP	New Democratic Party (St. Vincent)
NF	New Front
NGO	Nongovernment Organization

NICs	Newly Industrialized Countries
NJM	New Jewel Movement
NL	Nationaal Leger (National Army)
NLM	National Labour Movement
NMR	National Military Council
NNP	New National Party
NPP	New Progressive Party
NPS	National Party of Suriname
NRP	Nevis Reformation Party
NWO	National Women's Organization
NWU	National Worker's Union
NYO	National Youth Organization
OAS	Organization of American States
OECS	Organisation of Eastern Caribbean States
OGV	Organisatie Voor Gererchtigheid en Vrede (Organization for Justice and Peace)
ONR	Organization for National Reconstruction
ORS	Old Representative System
OWTU	Oilfield Workers Trade Union
PAC	Political Affairs Committee
PALU	Progressive Arbeidess en Landbouwers Unie (Progressive Union of Workers and Peasants)
PAM	Peoples Action Movement
PCP	Progressive Conservative Party
PDP	Progressive Democratic Party (Montserrat)
PDP	Peoples Democratic Party (Trinidad and Tobago)
PDP	Popular Democratic Party (Puerto Rico)
PFU	Progressive Farmer's Union
PLD	Partido de la Liberacion Dominicano (Dominican Liberation Party)
PLM	Progressive Labour Movement (Antigua and Barbuda)
PLM	Peoples Liberation Movement (Montserrat)
PNC	Peoples National Congress
PNM	Peoples National Movement
PNP	Peoples National Party
PNR	Party of the National Republic
PPG	Political Progress Group
PPP	Peoples Progressive Party (Guyana)
PPP	Peoples Political Party (St. Vincent)
PR	Proportional Representation
PRA	Peoples Revolutionary Army
PRD	Partido Revolucionario Dominicano (Dominican Revolutionary Party)

PRG	Peoples Revolutionary Government
PSP	Parti Socialiste Populaire (Popular Socialist Party)
PSU	Public Service Union
PUP	Peoples United Party
RGA	Representative Government Associations
RMC	Revolutionary Military Council
SDPE	Sistema de Direccíon y Planificación de la Economía (Economic Management and Planning System)
SIS	Security and Intelligence Service
SLP	Surinamese Labor Party
SPEAR	Society for the Promotion of Education and Research
SVLP	St. Vincent Labour Party
THM	Tapia House Movement
TNCs	Transnational Corporations
TNP	The National Party (Grenada)
TUC	Trade Union Congress
TWA	Trinidad Workingmen's Association
UDP	United Democratic Party
UF	United Force
UJC	Union de Jovenes Comunistas (Union of Young Communists)
ULF	United Labour Front
UNC	United National Congress
UNCHR	United Nations High Commission for Refugees
UNDP	United National Democratic Party
UP	United Party
UPM	United People's Movement
USAID	United States Agency for International Development
UWP	United Workers Party
VAT	Value Added Tax
VHP	Verenigde Hervormings Partij (United Reform Party)
VP	Volks Partij (Peoples Party)
VVV	Verenigde Volks Vergadering (United Peoples Congress)
WFP	Workers and Farmers Party
WLL	Workers Liberation League
WPA	Working People's Alliance
WPJ	Worker's Party of Jamaica

*Democracy
in the
Caribbean*

Introduction

Carlene J. Edie

Among developing nations, the Caribbean has the largest number of liberal democracies. The Commonwealth Caribbean states (hereafter English-speaking Caribbean), with a few exceptions, have maintained competitive parliamentary democracies for over three decades and have largely escaped the kinds of social and political upheaval apparent in many parts of the Third World. Over the past decade, there has been renewed interest in democracy in developing nations, dispelling the pessimistic view of the previous decades that democracy could not be achieved in the socioeconomic environment that prevailed in those states. Despite the longevity of democratic institutions there, Caribbean states have not been frequently analyzed as have other regional clusters. The recent comprehensive series *Democracy in Developing Nations*, edited by Larry Diamond, Seymour Lipset, and Juan Linz, did not include the Caribbean, with the exception of the Dominican Republic.

The Caribbean encompasses virtually every type of democratic experience in developing nations. Since independence, some nations have had relatively stable democracies (Jamaica, Barbados, Belize); some have persisted in the face of crises and lapses (Trinidad and Tobago, Grenada, Antigua); some have cycles of democratic attempts and military interventions (Haiti, Suriname); and there is one case of a failed democracy that consolidated into authoritarian rule, with the potential of democratic rebirth (Guyana). A volume such as this one is a contribution to knowledge of a diverse Caribbean that is not well understood, and one that could serve as a foundation for a comparative theory of democracy in developing nations.

In this volume, democracy refers to a system of government in which there is meaningful and extensive political competition for positions of government power, at regular intervals, among individuals and organized groups, especially political parties. This contention for power usually takes place without the use of force. In a democracy, there usually is a high degree of popular political participation in the selection of leaders and policies, through free and fair elections. There must also be freedoms of speech, association, petition, and religion, as well as respect for the rule of law and an independent judiciary. Democracy also extends beyond these values to include social justice.

The authors are concerned not only with the well-known institutional features of a democratic political system, but also with the way in which democracy has been operationalized in the Caribbean. Democracy in the English-speaking Caribbean has often been idealized by external observers.[1] While there is considerable political freedom throughout that part of the region (with a few exceptions), rights are guaranteed, the rule of law prevails, elections are held at regular intervals, and so on, the economic conditions of the majority of the people have forced them to give consent to the political system. Their basic liberties as citizens have thereby been compromised. The authors take seriously the strengths and weaknesses of democratic theory as it has been applied to the realities of contemporary Caribbean political economy. The collection is diverse, with some of the authors supporting traditional notions of democracy, and others challenging existing assumptions and traditions.

This is not the first book on the subject of democracy in the Caribbean, but it is one of the few that provide comparative cases between the so-called Commonwealth Caribbean and other Caribbean nations. There are case studies from the English-speaking Caribbean (Jamaica, Guyana, Trinidad and Tobago, Barbados, Grenada, and Belize) and the Hispanic Caribbean (Dominican Republic, Puerto Rico, and Cuba), a case study from the Francophone Caribbean (Haiti), and one from the Dutch Caribbean (Suriname). While the bulk of the book is on the English-speaking Caribbean, other areas are included to see if there are comparable patterns and trends in the region. There are significant developments in Dominica, St. Vincent, Antigua, St. Lucia, Martinique, and Guadeloupe, but because of constraints on time and space I was unable to include them.

The political differences between the English-speaking nations, with largely liberal democracies today, and the others are quite apparent. Historically, Caribbean societies were all authoritarian and the postcolonial state inherited at independence was decidedly antidemocratic. I have decided to include case studies from various colonial traditions that were initially authoritarian to try to give us a comparative understanding of the varied political fortunes of the region. The reference point for the comparison lies in where each country fits on the democratic continuum: from political and economic liberalization in Jamaica and Barbados to the extreme of Cuba, where both phenomena are still absent. The book includes the Caribbean in the discussion of a worldwide trend toward political and economic liberalization.

The chapters on the English-speaking nations are collectively concerned with the following five themes. The first theme concerns the expansion of the postcolonial state during the period of decolonization (1944–1960) and its subsequent domination by the educated middle classes. Throughout the decolonization and postindependence periods, statist organization has resulted in oligarchic control by the middle classes. Percy Hintzen's chapter on "Democracy and Middle-Class Domination in the Anglophone Caribbean" orients the reader to what is undertaken in the six chapters which follow. It reassesses the conventional approaches to the study of democracy which restrict it to procedures rather than substance. It explores the links among the Caribbean state, democratic forms, and civil society, arguing that the representatives of the educated elite employ their control of the state as their source of power. While he notes differences in ideologies and leadership styles, he argues that, without exception, power is exercised for the regimentation of the lower classes into political parties and labor unions. Political party leaders and elites have all been unwilling to foster mass participation in the political and social development of their countries, viewing this participation as potentially disruptive to the social order.

This argument is extended in my chapter on Jamaica, where my study of the political processes suggests to me that the driving force of that democracy is clientelism—the exchange of goods and services for political support. The basis of this domestic system of clientelism lies overseas, whereby foreign actors provide resources necessary to enhance the patronage-granting capacity of the state. The lower classes and the poor (constituting the majority of the population) have become locked into patron-client relationships with elected officials as goods and services continue to be exchanged for support of the political system. The democratic process (of which elections are the cornerstone) provides a convenient environment for state domination by the educated middle classes (see also Premdas, Chapter 3; Hintzen, Chapters 1 and 4; Espinal, Chapter 9).

A second related theme that runs through the chapters concerns the relationship between Caribbean people and elections. All of the authors are clear in their position that ordinary people take electoral politics very seriously, making all kinds of sacrifices in casting their votes, often risking family divisions, violence, intimidation, and death. Elections in the Caribbean, like in many other parts of the Third World, are never free and fair; rigging and official manipulation and stealing of ballots are the norm, rather than the exception (Edie, Chapter 2; Premdas, Chapter 3). According to Ralph Premdas, accountability was nonexistent for most of the years of the Burnham Peoples National Congress (PNC) regime in Guyana. While elections clearly provided some means for mass participation, the voices of the majority classes were often only heard through contact between elected officials and constituencies, as in Jamaica, Trinidad and Tobago, Grenada, Barbados, Guyana, the Dominican Republic, and others. For the poor and majority classes, only the state-controlling party elites can provide services for life-sustaining functions. Those functions can and have been used by politicians and their allies to manipulate voters and to maintain vulnerable voters and to maintain high voter turnout. Patrick Emmanuel (Chapter 15) provides some descriptive statistics about voting patterns and parties in the English-speaking Caribbean that are useful comparative data and evidence of the increasingly high voter turnout in the postindependence period.

A third theme concerns the issue of racial politics within a competitive democratic parliamentary framework. Premdas and Hintzen both argue that middle-class political leaders in Guyana and Trinidad and Tobago benefited from racial politics. Both chapters illustrate the problems of democracy in unintegrated multiethnic states imposed by colonial powers. The PNC, claiming the mantle of socialism, used the state as an instrument to maintain black middle-class power and to prevent ethnic and class domination by the East Indians. The consequences of this have been repression, violence, decay, and an antidemocratic racist state. The recent defeat of the PNC under Desmond Hoyte raises questions concerning the prospects for human rights and democratic rebirth under the newly elected Peoples Progressive Party (PPP).

Economic decline and the impact this has on the democratic process is a fourth theme explored by several authors. Neville Duncan (Chapter 5) carefully describes the recent economic democracy movement that has rocked the normally peaceful polity of Barbados and the impact this has had on its citizens. He suggests that the present economic crisis will precipitate a crisis for democracy, especially if the democratic process is not broadened to include greater and more meaningful participation by the majority classes. Similarly, Jamaican democracy faces serious challenges as the Peoples National Party (PNP) government struggles to deal with the decline of the economy, and the decline in the external aid on which Jamaica depends so heavily, and at the same time maintain support for the party system in light of the decline in revenues for patronage. The conclusions Duncan and I reached regarding the challenges to democracy may be controversial. Other analysts will want to examine more closely recent elections in Jamaica (in March 1993) to see the extent to which support has been lost for democratic political institutions over an extended period of time. The same must be done for Barbados.

"Dependency" is a concept that is little used today in analyses of Caribbean politics. Although the concept may be seen as out of fashion by many Third World analysts, several authors in this volume believe that "dependency" still remains an important consideration in Caribbean politics. The International Monetary Fund (IMF) has become central to many Caribbean economies, dependent on IMF loans to rescue them from economic collapse (Chapters 2 and 5). IMF loans, with their conditions, have led to many austerity programs, including government retrenchment involving the termination of many civil servants. Dependence on IMF loans and U.S. capital sources gives Western governments (especially the United States) a continuing role in the internal affairs of many Caribbean countries. This dependency is seen as a negative one, providing little benefit for the population.

U.S. involvement in the politics of the Caribbean is a reality. Pedro Noguera analyzes the U.S. invasions of Grenada and Panama. This chapter allows comparisons between states within the region and allows us to examine the continuing military impact of the United States. The United States invaded Grenada and Panama and destabilized Nicaragua. Its stated objective was the establishment of democratic governments. These regimes, seen as unfriendly to the United States, are all gone now, but how successful have these states been in developing democratic institutions? Can democracy still continue to be a convenient pretext for the United States to extend its power in the Caribbean? Many Caribbean residents ponder this question.

The chapters from the non-English-speaking Caribbean provide some interesting similarities and important differences. Traditionally, the English-speaking nations are discussed separately, and are often seen as a model of political development from which the others may extract lessons. It is my view that the latter may provide lessons for the English-speaking Caribbean, particularly the very poignant reminder that they too could degenerate into authoritarianism and political decay. Cuba provides a study in contrast in many ways, not only in the Caribbean, but in the world. Cuba is bucking the trend toward political and economic liberalization that has engulfed the world. By its own declaration, it is the only Marxist-Leninist state in the world today. Despite Cuba's nonappearance on the democratic continuum, Cuba is significantly advanced in the area of human development, providing superior social amenities for its population. Many observers of Cuban politics believe that it is only a matter of time before the Castro regime collapses, as its longevity has been accorded to sustained Soviet aid which has been terminated with the demise of the Soviet Union. It is not known if and when the Castro regime will fall. Carollee Bengelsdorf (Chapter 11) points to the dangers of U.S. attempts to strangle Cuba by isolating it and of forcing it to move toward political and economic liberalization. She suggests that as a result of the dire economic crises gripping Cuba, there has been an opening to the outside world, not only in economic terms, but in intellectual and political terms as well. She explores the limited political space that exists outside of the state, and the boundaries imposed by the regime in its effort to control any democracy movement that may emerge in Cuba.

Suriname and Haiti are close to Cuba on the democratic continuum. However, there is no redeeming factor in the former nations such as advancement in the area of human development. Haiti remains a nation that is synonymous with poverty and destitution and continues to be classified among the world's poorest nations. Kenneth Boodhoo and Betty Sedoc-Dahlberg raise important issues about the difficulties of implementing democracy in Haiti and Suriname, where the military has had a history of being central to politics and represents the single greatest obstacle to any attempts at democracy. Despite the difficulties, democracy movements emerged in both nations and have made progress. The fact that Father Jean-Bertrand Aristide was democratically elected in 1991 by a majority of the population is an important achievement. With his overthrow, democracy faltered, but attempts are now being made to try to restore his regime to power. Under an Organization of American States (OAS)–United Nations brokered agreement he signed with Army Chief Raoul Cedras on July 3, 1993, the deposed president is to be reinstated on October 30, 1993. That agreement was followed by a July 17, 1993 pact in which Haiti's political parties agreed to refrain for a six-month period from any actions that would hamper the country's return to democratic rule. There is definitely a desire for democracy in Suriname and Haiti, and the people there are as fascinated with the idea of elections as they are in the English-speaking Caribbean. Elections might be seen as a means to ensure continued supply of foreign aid (Sedoc-Dahlberg, Chapter 8), but they cannot be dismissed simply because they are often a distorted medium for the government to hear the voice of the people. Surinamese democracy is very fragile, and the existing government has elements of the old administration which precipitated the 1980 coup d'état. The presence of this old guard certainly suggests that there are forces that can still work against the institutionalization of democracy.

Puerto Rico and the Dominican Republic can be situated appropriately between the English-speaking Caribbean on the one hand, and Haiti, Suriname, and Cuba on the other hand. Political and economic liberalization exists in both countries, although questions have been raised about the appropriateness of the democratic label for these nations. The Dominican Republic has had a long history of authoritarianism, and only the past three decades of its history can be loosely described as "democratic." Rosario Espinal (Chapter 9) explains the tenuous and uncertain nature of the present regime in the Dominican Republic. While it may not revert to its authoritarian tradition, its future is not certain. Puerto Rico has long been identified as the model of economic development for developing nations in the post–World War II period. Economic liberalization has been entrenched there as a result of Puerto Rico's special relationship with the United States. Because of Puerto Rico's political status as a "colony" of the United States, many hesitate to identify it as a democracy. Carmen Gautier-Mayoral (Chapter 10) enters this debate and suggests that Puerto Rico has a "limited democracy." The question at issue is whether one can talk about democracy in the context of a society that has not yet experienced decolonization and does not yet have the right to self-determination. There is definitely a need for further research and discussion of the desire for decolonization on the part of the Puerto Rican people and how the decolonization process can lead to the construction of a democratic political order that is not determined by an external power.

This volume will achieve its primary goal if it contributes to a better understanding of the nature of Caribbean democracies, and of the factors that have led to durable democracy in some nations, and authoritarianism and decay in others. This volume is only a very preliminary step in the direction of generating a theory of democracy in developing nations. The wealth of information provided by all the authors should make a contribution toward meeting this challenge. There are many unanswered questions that can provide the basis for future research. For example, with the election of Cheddi Jagan's PPP in Guyana, are we likely to witness the disappearance of ethnic politics? Will economic liberalization lead to the regrouping of ethnic and racial groups in Guyana? Will democracy be given another chance in Haiti? Can the factors that have sustained democracy in the English-speaking Caribbean take root in Haiti, Suriname, or Cuba? Will political and economic liberalization in Jamaica reduce political violence? With the decline in patronage resources, can democratic politics survive in states such as Jamaica, Trinidad and Tobago, and the Dominican Republic? Can intra-party succession in the Jamaica Labour Party occur without damage to the political system? How will the North American Free Trade Agreement affect Puerto Rico's "special relationship" with the United States? How will Puerto Rico eventually resolve its status question? Will Cuban communism survive? If not, will Cuba be able to maintain its social achievements if political and economic liberalization occurs? What will be the consequences of IMF stabilization programs for stability in the region if vulnerable groups cannot be protected? With the cooling of tensions between the United States and the former Soviet Union, and a new Democratic administration in Washington, are we likely to see an end to U.S. intervention in the affairs of Caribbean nations? These and similar questions are likely to be prominent in future debates on democracy in the Caribbean.

NOTE

1. An exception to this trend is Norman Graham and Keith Edwards, *The Caribbean Basin to the Year 2000* (Boulder, CO: Westview Press, 1984). The authors suggest that democracy may decline in the region as the economies falter.

1

Democracy and Middle-Class Domination in the Anglophone Caribbean

Percy C. Hintzen

After an all too brief period of intellectual challenge in the English-speaking Caribbean (hereafter Caribbean), and perhaps one case of national experimentation with alternatives, the notion of democratic governance has suffered a mechanistic reversal. The litmus test for democracy has, once more, come to be the existence of party-political organizations whose leaders compete for national power in "free elections." This notion of democracy stems from a combination of historical legacy and ideology. The legacy of British colonialism has caused even the most critical and challenging minds of the region to accept a Westminster parliamentary model, suitably modified, as the sine qua non of democratic governance. The ideological element is more complex and indirect. It has to do with judgments, made in bilateral and multilateral relationships by the Western industrialized countries, as to the legitimacy of governments. Such judgments are made on the basis of the West's own models of democracy, rooted in the bourgeois liberalism that is at the heart of its system of industrial capitalism.

DEMOCRACY: ITS APPLICATION TO LESS DEVELOPED COUNTRIES

Ideologically, democracy is pitted against dictatorship, with the latter divided into fascism (dictatorship of the right) and communism (Marxist-Leninist dictatorship). However, the recognition by the Western political and intellectual establishments that dictators in the Less Developed Countries (LDCs) can be pro-Western (most are) has led to some accommodating reformulations. Many scholars gave up the notion of the desirability of democracy in favor of the more paramount goal of modernization. Such a goal, according to many, should not be jeopardized by sociopolitical disorder. The maintenance of political order thus came to be seen as a prerequisite for the successful transition to modernization. In the eyes of these scholars of "modernization," there was the danger that the process of transformation to modernity would produce the conditions for the emergence of dictatorship, either of the left or right, when it was allowed to degenerate into sociopolitical disorder.

The argument above has been most comprehensively stated by Samuel Huntington. For Huntington, "the problem is not to hold elections but to create organizations" (1968: 7) to "provide an assurance of political order" (ibid.: 9) in the face of the "mobilization of new social forces into politics" (ibid.: vii). There is a "gap" created between modernizing economic and social institutions and political development. This gap has to be filled by organization which is rooted in authority (ibid.: 7–8).

The vacuum of authority and power will invariably be filled, according to Huntington. In what he terms the "organizational imperative," the choice as to who will fill it is between "established elites [who] compete among themselves to organize the masses . . . or dissident elites [who] organize them to overthrow that system" (ibid.: 461).

In the interim, political order can be managed by elites ranging from the traditional to the modern. At one end there are the "modernizing monarchs" willing to transform their systems into "modern constitutional monarchies." In the middle are the "radical praetorians" coming to power in "middle-class breakthrough coups" against traditional monarchs or oligarchical military rulers. At the other end, there are the modern leaders of the one-party system.

The ideal for political development, according to Huntington, is the establishment of

strong, adaptable, coherent political institutions: effective bureaucracies, well organized political parties, a high degree of popular participation in public affairs, working systems of civilian control over the military, extensive activity by the government in the economy, and reasonably effective procedures for regulating succession and controlling political conflict. (ibid.: 1)

The point of quoting the above so extensively is that it is precisely such an ideal type that informs the organization of political democracies in the English-speaking Caribbean. The problem, however, is that the organization which ensues from it is not accompanied by the consensual precondition placed by modernization theorists upon its effective functioning.[1]

It is the central thesis of this chapter that in the absence of such consensus such a model serves merely to legitimize a system of domination and control.

There are two related reasons for this. The first is the explicitly bureaucratic nature of this "organizational imperative." In the absence of genuine representative government, this translates in LDCs into de facto control by a Westernized, educated elite with the prerequisite skills to staff and run these bureaucratic organizations. These organizations constitute the formal instruments of democratic practice.

If one moves from the merely ideological and propagandistic, the meaning of representative government shifts from a mere existence of the formal mechanisms of democracy such as political parties, periodic elections, and representative bodies. All of these can prove anathema to genuine representation because of the ease with which they can be transformed into an instrument of regimentation. This, in turn, creates the conditions for domination by those in control of these formal "democratic" organizations.

DEMOCRACY AND BUREAUCRATIC REGIMENTATION

The myth, of course, is that there is a symbiosis between these democratic institutions and mobilization. It is through the latter that interests are articulated and choices made. It is here where modernization theorists part company with democratic governance, at least temporarily. Mobilization in LDCs has been consistently viewed by them as problematic. In fact, the exposure of the problematic nature of mobilization and propositions for containing it are at the core of the agenda of modernization theory. In response, its advocates have extolled the virtues of regimentation in the name of "order." The function of regimentation has been stressed even for institutions integrally associated with democratic practice. In this vein, Huntington advocates that the role of the political party in LDCs should be "to expand participation through the system and thus to preempt or to divert anomic or revolutionary political activity and, second, to moderate and channel the participation of newly mobilized groups in such a manner as not to disrupt the system" (1968: 412). This is clearly not a representative function.

The reason mobilization is viewed as problematic is that it is driven by ideology. This leads to a condition where:

> Rhetoric is confused with reality, tactics with values, meaning with motives. The leaders are erratic, aggressive, and given to creating their own rules of conduct. By claiming the future, they disclaim responsibility for the present. And by manipulating political religion, they endow such conduct with morality. (Apter, 1965: 388)

The problem of mobilization is that it can "move toward greater totalitarianism" (ibid.). This is contrasted with what David Apter calls "reconciliation systems" which are "close to the Western notion of democracy only to the extent that they accept the normative implications of the secular-liberal model" (ibid.: 400). Such a system "works to reconcile diverse interests; it mediates, integrates, and above all, coordinates, rather than organizes and mobilizes" (ibid.: 398–399). The function of political organization in LDCs therefore boils down to the promotion of "secular-liberalism" and the prevention of mobilization.

What we are left with are political institutions which serve the function of bureaucratic regimentation. According to these modernization theorists, these institutions cannot serve the same functions as they do in the liberal industrialized countries because of the threat that mobilization poses to modernization.

It is interesting to examine why modernization theorists consider mobilization to be such a threat. It is because of the disorder that it brings under conditions where "the gains of rapid economic growth . . . are often concentrated in a few groups while the losses are diffused among many; as a result, the number of people getting poorer in the society may actually increase" (Huntington, 1968: 57). In other words, it is because of mass dissatisfaction with growing inequality and impoverishment. Surprisingly, these theorists have no problem with the bourgeois revolutions that initiate these conditions. They are celebrated as the catalysts for "freedom" with all the weight of the evidence of the inequity and repression of the feudal orders that they displaced. The propagandistic (and unquestionably racist) argument is that while capitalist progress brought equality and freedom to civilized Europe, it produces inequality in LDCs. While it freed Europe for the application of rationality and reason to human affairs, it creates the conditions for the flourishing of irrationality in LDCs. While order came to be consistent with justice in Europe, it demands injustice in LDCs. Thus, while mobilization was a prerequisite for progress in Europe, the two become contradictory in LDCs, at least in the short run.

Whatever else is said of modernization theorists, they did recognize the relationship between their brand of development and the growing inequality in LDCs. However, the notion of disorder in their analysis serves merely to legitimize domination as necessary for developmental transition. It is quite clear, from their own theoretical tradition, that the application of bureaucratic authority under conditions of inequality is bound to create the conditions for domination. This was clearly recognized by Max Weber, the godfather of their own epistemological tradition. In Weber's own words:

> Once it is established, bureaucracy is among the social structures which are the hardest to destroy. Bureaucracy is *the* means of carrying "community action" over into rationally ordered "societal action." Therefore, as an instrument for "societalizing" relations of power, bureaucracy has been and is a power instrument of the first order—for the one who controls the bureaucratic apparatus. (Weber, 1958: 228)

In other words, what bureaucracy does is to transform mobilization into rationally organized activity by those whose power is derived from their control of the bureaucratic apparatus. Of course, Weber did not see this as necessarily problematic. Whether or not it becomes so (and this is the crux of the matter) depends

> upon the distribution of economic and social power, and especially upon the sphere that is occupied by the emerging mechanism. The consequences of bureaucracy depend therefore upon the direction which the powers using the apparatus give to it. And very frequently a crypto-plutocratic distribution of power has been the result. (ibid.: 230)

BUREAUCRATIC STATISM AND ELITE DOMINATION

The argument of this chapter is that in LDCs, and specifically in the Anglophone Caribbean, the principal "sphere" occupied by the bureaucratic mechanism is that of statist organization. Such organization is designed to serve the power and accumulative interests of a particular segment of the middle class. The result has been oligarchic control by the representatives of this middle class. A combination of regimentation (disguised as democratic participation) and expertise (touted as the prerequisite for modernization) has served to legitimize this system of domination and to hide its true nature.

Once established in any sphere of activity, bureaucratic structures are almost impossible to destroy. Thus, the bureaucratic organization of colonial government in the Caribbean, as in all of the colonies of Europe, was transferred wholesale into postcolonial statist organization and expanded upon to include functions that were not part of colonial governance. This is particularly the case for economic functions, with states in the Caribbean acquiring wholly owned or jointly owned productive assets, and becoming involved in services and utilities. State expansion into economic activities became particularly important for clientelistic recruitment, which was at the core of the developing system of regimentation. The populist character of the independence movements also produced tremendous expansion in many areas of state activity. This was particularly true for health, education, and welfare functions which, by and large, became expanded after independence.

Somewhat more importantly, however, was that the new state-controlling elite in the postindependence era became responsible for organizing new bureaucracies to take over functions that were performed by the colonizing power. There was a constitutionally dictated requirement that colonies become responsible for their own defense and foreign affairs upon gaining independence. Indeed, it was the performance of these functions that distinguished governments under self-rule from constitutionally independent ones. So, typically, independence led to the expansion of the state bureaucracies concerned with security as defense forces and militias were added to police forces and volunteer battalions. There was also the establishment of bureaucracies for managing the international relations of the newly independent states, particularly Ministries of External Affairs. Additionally, there was the expansion of existing state bureaucracies (such as Ministries of Trade and Commerce, Ministries of Development, Finance Ministries, and the like) for undertaking the country's international activities.

The adoption of new bureaucratic functions and the expansion of old ones to include new activities, as it turned out, came to constitute the strategic pillars of power and accumulation for the middle class. The addition of defense forces and militias to a country's security forces provided the state-controlling elite with the means for violent coercive retaliation against those challenging their authority and legitimacy, or posing a threat to their power. Direct responsibility for international affairs provided this elite with direct access to international resources necessary for regime survival (see Hintzen, 1989a: passim). All of these activities, bureaucratically organized, dramatically increased the capacity of those controlling the state bureaucratic apparatus for clientelistic cooptation, retaliation, and control of behavior in expanding spheres of activities.

STATISM AND ELITE DOMINATION IN THE CARIBBEAN

In the Caribbean, there was a particular segment of the middle class that inherited oligarchic control of the postcolonial state through its political representatives. The manner and timing varied from country to country. For the most part, the representatives of this middle class were already ensconced way before independence was granted. There was some variation to the main theme. In Guyana, for example, it came to control the state just prior to the granting of independence, only after a period of protracted civil strife. In Grenada, this middle class gained exclusive control of the state only in 1979, five years after the country gained its independence.

Nonetheless, the segment of the middle class that inherited control of the state is uniform in its composition. Its distinguishing features are its education and white collar occupations. Its members neither own capital nor do they constitute a proletarian labor force. They work as clerical or bureaucratic employees in either the public or the private sector, holding jobs as civil servants, teachers, managers, foremen, supervisors, clerks, officers in the security forces, and the like. They constitute an intermediate stratum of salaried urban workers. They are identical to the intermediate stratum that has emerged in most ex-colonial countries with varying degrees of political success (see Harris, 1976: 171–179). In the West Indies, they are usually led by a group of politically active intellectuals and professionals who are at the helm of political parties and trade unions. These bureaucratized organizations serve as the basis of their own mobilization. The organizations also function for the regimentation of the lower class, usually through a combination of racial, ideological, and nationalist appeal cemented through a clientelistic structure.

Ironically, the political activities of this segment of the middle class began, typically, with mobilization for inclusion in the colonial structures of power. There were also demands for social inclusion in the circle of privilege and prestige enjoyed by the colonizing class. Trinidad was more or less typical of most Anglophone Caribbean territories. There, the Afro-Creole middle class became mobilized as early as 1823, even before the abolition of slavery, to fight legal restrictions placed on their civil and political rights. Once these restrictions were removed, their concern shifted to "financial security and class standing." Their political activity came to be directed at gaining equal standing with whites, and against the consequences for them of the operation of the system of white supremacy (see MacDonald, 1986: 36–41).

In the Anglophone Caribbean as a whole, during the first half of the twentieth century, more of the members of this middle class came to be represented in colonial legislatures and local councils through nomination or in elections with franchises limited by property and income qualifications. With this, they seemed quite content with their status as functionaries of the colonial state or of the colonized private sector.

The initial concern of middle-class leaders for the lower class emerged, with some exception, during the 1930s. The concern was more imitative than real. It came from middle-class elites caught up in the excitement of the success of the Labour Party in Great Britain, and from experiencing colonial rejection of their claims for a restructured representative government in which they were the major players.

The examples abound. The influence of the Labour Party was quite profound upon Clennel Wickham of Barbados. He returned from World War I service in the British West Indies Regiment in 1919 to a position of journalist on, and eventually editor of, a left-of-center journal. He was joined by Charles O'Neale, who had returned from Britain as a physician after an association with the Fabian Society as well as the Independent Labour Party. O'Neale had contested and won a county council seat in Newcastle in Great Britain. Upon his initial return to the Caribbean, he set up practice in neighboring Trinidad where he proselytized his socialism before eventually returning home in 1924. O'Neale was principally responsible for the formation of the Democratic League and the Workingmen's Association, both precursors to the Barbadian nationalist movement (see Hoyos, 1973). These Barbadians were associated with and influenced by the Grenadian journalist Albert Marryshow, who founded the Representative Government Association of Grenada, which he eventually built into a federalist movement with the help of fellow countryman and barrister C. F. Renwick. They touted the proposed West Indian Federation as the basis for independence. It was Marryshow who founded what was perhaps the most influential of the West Indian bodies in the first half of the century: the Caribbean Labour

Congress (formerly the West Indian Labour Congress). The Congress was patterned after and supported by the British Labour Party and launched and supported the careers of most Caribbean nationalist leaders. Eventually, its efforts paid off in the formation of a short-lived West Indian Federation in 1958 (see Emmanuel, 1978 and Singham, 1968).

The pattern of trade union mobilization by members of the domestic middle class under the influence of the British Labour Party and its Caribbean admirers was typical throughout the region during the 1920s and 1930s. In Dominica it was attorney Cecil Rawle (through a middle-class Representative Government Association). In Trinidad it was white Trinidadian Arthur Cipriani who returned from commanding the West Indian Regiment in World War I to form the Trinidad Workingmen's Association (TWA), which, in 1934, changed its name to the Trinidad Labour Party. In Jamaica it was former overseer and business-man Alexander Bustamante, who moved the Jamaica Workers' and Tradesmen Union to a position of militancy. He was founder member of the Bustamante Industrial Workers Union and the Jamaica Labour Party. He was also respon-sible for the emergence of attorney Norman Manley. The latter, more in the mold of the British labor politician, was founder member of the Peoples National Party. In Antigua it was the clerk Vere Bird, who was a founder member of the Antiguan Trade and Labour Party in the 1940s.[2]

Interestingly, all the lower-class leaders who took the same route during the 1930s never succeeded in gaining power in the representative governments of the post–World War II era. These included Hubert Critchlow of Guyana, who founded the British Guiana Labour Union as early as 1919, and who was quite instrumental in the Caribbean Labour Congress (CLC). Critchlow became quite an advocate for socialist restructuring of the colonial order in the 1930s (see Chase, 1964). They also included Uriah Butler in Trinidad, who rose to prominence in the TWA under Cipriani and who eventually went on to form the British Empire Workers and Home Rule Party in 1936. He eventually formed the Oilfield Workers Trade Union (OWTU), which has gone on to become one of the most powerful unions in the country. Both were eventually replaced in their political leadership roles by black middle-class professionals who even-tually came to power.

The point of the foregoing recapitualization of what, in the Caribbean, is well-known history, is to demonstrate the initial basis of middle-class power in bureaucratically organized unions and nascent political organizations. Impor-tant in all this was the role of intellectual journalists propagating the ideology of nationalism and socialism (such as Marryshow, Wickham, and O'Neale) and the middle-class organizations (such as the CLC and the various Representative Government Associations) out of which emerged the institutions for regiment-ing the lower class.

Most important, the ideological influence of this early group of middle-class leaders was the Fabianism of the British Labour Party. Fabianism emerged in

England within the context of the development of a "social democratic alliance" between capitalists and workers (see Amin, 1976: passim). Out of this alliance came the welfare state, which catapulted the intellectual and professional middle class to political power and gave their leaders control of the state bureaucracies and their distributive functions. This was the precise outcome in the Caribbean, as it was in all the LDCs that experienced decolonization in the postwar era.

It was bureaucratization that transformed lower-class mobilization into regimentation. Weber saw in this the transformation of community action into rationally ordered societal action. Such rationality in the Caribbean, as elsewhere, was directed at middle-class power, domination, prestige, and accumulation.

The "community action" phase was particularly evident in the labor riots of the late 1930s which rocked the entire Caribbean. The riots forced the British to constitute a commission of inquiry comprising social liberals highly influenced by the welfarist current of Fabianism in Britain (see Lewis, 1968: 90–93). Interestingly, the recommendations of the commission (see West India Royal Commission, 1945) were almost identical to the demands of the politicians discussed previously. The commissioners urged the development of a welfare scheme, labor legislation, and the active encouragement of trade unions and "the multifarious institutions, official and unofficial which characterize British public life" (ibid.: 94, 108). Indeed, the report gave birth to the Colonial Development and Welfare Organization, the precursor to the West Indian welfare state which became the basis for middle-class ascendancy (Lewis, 1968: 91). Ultimately, efforts to implement the recommendations of the commission led to the development and expansion of representative governments elected by universal adult suffrage.

By the time adult suffrage was introduced in the colonies, the lower class was firmly organized into political and labor bureaucracies dominated by middle-class leadership. Where they were not, Britain showed extreme reluctance to move the constitutional process along to full independence. In Trinidad, for example, universal suffrage, introduced in 1946, found the middle class weakly organized in a West Indian National Party. The latter was overshadowed by the lower-class Butler Party, which managed to win six of eighteen electoral seats in 1950, the largest of any single party. It was also overshadowed by the conservative Political Progress Group (PPG) representing the interests of the local white business class. Great Britain delayed the granting of self-government until the electoral victory in 1956 of a newly formed Peoples National Movement (PNM) under the leadership of a group of black and colored professionals and intellectuals headed by Cambridge-educated historian Sir Eric Williams. The PNM's formation was in response to a similar mobilization of the East Indian middle-class politicians from the business and professional sectors in a Peoples Democratic Party (PDP). The problem with the PDP, as far as the British Colonial Office was concerned, was that it opposed the colony's participation in a West Indian Federation which Britain supported and which was the centerpiece of the region's middle-class politicians' quest for independence (see Hintzen, 1989a: 42–45).

In Guyana, self-government and adult suffrage came with a radicalized group of professionals at the head of the trade union movement and mass political party. The Marxist-Leninism of the key leadership of the Peoples Progressive Party (PPP) alienated the domestic middle class, which failed to support it in its electoral victory of 1953. This very middle class supported Great Britain's disavowal of the party. It participated in the latter's decision, 133 days later, to suspend the constitution by which the PPP came to power by petitioning Britain to intervene. Eventually, the strategic power of the middle class imposed its will upon the PPP. The nationalist movement subsequently split into two factions supported by the country's East Indian middle class, on the one hand, and its black and colored middle class on the other. The interests of both these groups came to dominate the policies of the two factions. Race became the idiom of lower-class regimentation in the two political parties and their several trade union affiliates (see Hintzen, 1989a: 46–51; 1990).

Perhaps the political history of Grenada is most instructive on the issue of middle-class politics and Britain's support for it. Eric Gairy, a refinery worker, returned to Grenada from Aruba in 1949 to mobilize the rural peasantry and sugar workers against the white colonial estate owners. In 1950, he formed the Grenada Manual and Mental Workers Union (GMMWU) and, one year later, the Grenada United Labour Party (GULP). These two organizations persisted in exhibiting a personalistic and charismatic structure rather than evolving into a formal bureaucratic one, the typical pattern in the region (see Singham, 1968: passim). The domestic middle class, forever hostile to Gairy, became organized in the Grenada National Party (GNP) under the leadership of John Watts, a dentist. Great Britain was openly supportive of the GNP and hostile to Gairy and his GULP, frequently charging the latter with corruption, financial mismanagement, and unparliamentary conduct. The intervention of the colonial government, justified by such charges, produced GNP-led governments from 1956–1961. The party's leader, Herbert Blaize, became chief minister in 1960 under a constitutional change to ministerial government. The victory of Gairy's GULP in 1961 was again followed by charges of financial impropriety leading to its ouster from power in 1962 and another GNP government. It was Blaize who became the colony's first premier in 1967 under a new constitution of associated statehood with Great Britain. Gairy eventually captured unquestioned power in elections held that very year and led the country to independence. Nonetheless, he was always considered an outcast and embarrassment by the middle-class politicians who led governments in the region. These leaders joined with the conservative GNP in supporting the efforts of a number of radical middle-class professionals to oust him from power through mobilization campaigns undertaken during the entire period of the 1970s. In fact, the leadership of the GNP joined with a coalition of these groups, calling itself the New Jewel Movement (NJM), to form a united opposition to Gairy's government. The eventual ousting of the GULP from power by the NJM in the first coercive overthrow of an elected government in the English-speaking Caribbean was greeted with overwhelming support by the middle-class political leaders of the region.

The NJM proceeded to rely upon a highly bureaucratized Peoples Revolutionary Government (PRG) and strict regimentation to stay in power. Attempts by some members of the PRG to revert to the movement's mobilization structure for mass mobilization to restore sagging support led, ultimately, to the downfall of the party and to a U.S. invasion in 1983.

Thus, in Grenada, middle-class domination became firmly established only with the coming to power of a radical PRG government. The interim government which was put in place after the invasion, and the New National Party elected to power subsequently, were both able to rely upon the established bureaucratic apparatus developed and formalized by the PRG. On the other hand, the system of mobilization which characterized the government of Eric Gairy did not lend itself to this formalized structure. As a result, its structure of authority remained personalistic and centered around the charismatic appeal of its leader. Ironically, notwithstanding its election to power, GULP had very little legitimacy among Caribbean leaders. This was decidedly not the case with the PRG until quite late in its tenure. The fact that it came to power by force and persistently refused to hold elections seemed not to matter much, particularly in the initial phase of its rule. Of course, its highly bureaucratized system of government and its reliance on technocratic authority were quite consistent with the statist organization typical of the governments of the region. This tends to suggest that legitimacy derives more from the structure of organization of government rather than from its means of coming to power, despite the claims to democratic governance.

Ultimately, it was the conflict between the reality of bureaucratic and technocratic authority, on the one hand, and the charismatic authority that was reliant on mobilization, on the other, that led to the fracturing of the PRG. When this conflict came to a head the result was the violent self-destruction of the government.[3]

Bureaucratic statism, technocratic authority, and regimentation of the population in bureaucratized political parties and trade unions all combine in the Caribbean to serve the accumulative and power interests of the region's middle class. The representatives of this skilled and educated elite employ their "control of the governing apparatus" as their "source of power" (Trimberger, 1978: 7). Unlike the revolutionizing leadership that Ellen Kay Trimberger saw in Japan, Turkey, and Egypt, however, this middle class has acted to retain the structures of domination and exploitation characteristic of the colonial order. This is the primary explanation for the extreme crisis being experienced in the region today with such devastating consequences for the poor and powerless.

ANTIBUREAUCRATIC POPULISM

Grenada has seen the only attempts in the region to employ nonbureaucratized forms of governing. The first, in the personalistic form of Eric Gairy, was uninformed by a revolutionary ideology and remained mired in racial nationalism. It soon descended into the cult of personality and coercive repression which became indicators of its loss of legitimacy. The ideological vacuum was filled by the NJM. Ironically, the government that the latter produced became the basis for the establishment of middle-class power.

The second example of efforts to establish a nonbureaucratic form of governmental authority was with the NJM itself. Its ascendance to power was rooted in mobilization (as opposed to regimentation). With its transformation into the PRG, elements of the mobilization system were retained and efforts were made to incorporate them into its system of governance. A national adult literacy campaign was immediately launched through a Center for Popular Education (CPE). This served as one of the bases for generating active participation in the revolution. Under the auspices of a Ministry of Mobilization, mass organizations were set up to sustain the structure of mobilization. These included the National Youth Organization, National Women's Organization, and The People's Militia as well as the CPE (Noguera, 1989: 116–126). There was also the suspension of the 1973 (independence) constitution and efforts at public participation in policy making through zonal and village councils (Carew, 1985).

All of these efforts at government by mobilization served as thinly veiled attempts to camouflage the reality of middle-class power in the PRG, exercised by a rapidly expanding bureaucratic state structure highly dependent upon the transfer of resources from abroad (including human resources in the form of skilled personnel) for its survival.[4] It is significant that the factional conflict within the PRG occurred during a period of economic crisis stemming from declines in the flows of international economic support. The conflict, as it manifested itself, involved the faction in the party dependent upon mobilization pitted against those whose authority rested in their control of the state bureaucracies, including the military. Efforts at mobilization were quickly overcome by state retaliation. However, the severing of international ties that came as a result of such retaliation exposed the vulnerability of statist authority to outside intervention. The United States quickly took the opportunity to oust the remnants of the PRG from power through an invasion.

THE TRIUMPH OF HEGEMONY

In the Caribbean, middle-class domination is exercised through hegemony in the specific sense of the term as employed by Antonio Gramsci (1971). Middle-class leaders and intellectuals legitimize their domination through the development of ideology. The latter creates the conditions for the acceptance of their vision by the lower class; a vision rooted in their own middle-class culture but couched in terms of the appropriated culture of the lower class (see Hintzen, 1989a). Nationalism and developmentalism are at the core of this ideology. The former legitimizes an idiom of mobilization rooted in anticolonialism and sometimes anti-Westernism. This creates the conditions for middle-class control of the postcolonial state. Developmentalism justifies technocratic authority, particularly for the type of development planning typical of the region. Nationalism and developmentalism combine to create the façade of consensus that is touted as democracy.

The reality, however, is that the ties between middle-class political leaders and the lower class are exercised through clientelistic structures. It is the dependence of the lower class upon resources controlled by the state, and the control by middle-class politicians and bureaucrats over allocation of such resources, that guarantee support by members of the former for the latter. This is the central pillar of the system of regimentation that is at the root of Caribbean democratic practice.[5]

The second factor is that of coercion. Despite its touted consensual character, there is a tremendous reliance by every Caribbean government upon the coercive resources of the state. This is quite obvious in Guyana where coercion has become almost the sole basis of regime power, particularly since 1977 (Hintzen, 1989a). It has also been true, off and on, for Grenada, particularly under the Gairy regime during the 1970s and increasingly under the PRG during the later period of its rule. The PNM government of Trinidad and Tobago relied almost entirely upon coercive deployment between 1970–1973. Subsequent to 1973, coercion became a critical element in its efforts to ensure political order (see Hintzen, 1989a). This pattern is present throughout the region. The increasing reliance on the military and police for "national security" throughout the region has been too well chronicled to be disputed.[6]

The role of coercion is to protect middle-class regime power against dissidents and against the efforts of other sectors of society to mobilize against it. Increasingly, in the Caribbean, coercive deployment is used against lower-class dissent in the face of economic crisis and erosion of system legitimacy.

CONCLUSION

It is the structure of democratic practice, inherited as a legacy of Britain, that has catapulted the skilled, professional, and intellectual middle class to power. This power has been realized through their inheritance of control of the postcolonial state. The political leaders of this segment of the middle class have managed to consolidate such power through regimentation and coercive deployment. They have legitimized their authority by employing nationalist and developmentalist ideology. These, in combination, have freed them to pursue policies that are exclusively in their own interests. Increasingly, such interests have become tied to the intensified penetration of international capital in the region. This new form of penetration differs from the old reliance upon the export of primary agricultural and mineral commodities. It began in earnest during the 1960s with packaging and assembly-type import-substitution strategy particularly in Jamaica and later in Trinidad. It followed with the development of a massive complex of energy-intensive heavy industry in Trinidad during the 1970s. In its current phase, it has become characterized by the development of Export Processing Zones (EPZs) and the expansion of tourism (see Thomas, 1988: passim).

All of this has been accompanied by a dramatic expansion of the state in the typically mixed economies of the region for the development of infrastructure, in the ownership of utilities, for welfare and education, and in a growing security sector. The beneficiaries of all this have been "lawyers, accountants, engineers, and economists" (ibid.: 278) in addition to the class of domestic businessmen, civil servants, and clerks. Meanwhile, the lot of the lower class of rural and urban workers and peasants continues to experience dramatic declines. Such declines are quite precipitous in countries such as Jamaica and Guyana under the regimen of IMF-imposed programs of structural adjustment. However, the decade of the 1980s has seen the intensification of the "purely technocratic, pragmatic, and rational" approach to policy (ibid.: 269) in the entire region as a reaction to economic crisis. If anything, such a reaction caters even more to the interests of the middle class. In effect, it is a reaction which constrains even further the meager opportunities for betterment available to the lower class. The rational application of coercive force and the mechanisms of regimentation and control assure the survival of those middle-class regimes pursuing such strategies.

NOTES

1. The idea of consensus became a central tenet of modernization theory, particularly among scholars focusing on the problem of national integration and nation building. It is the underlying normative ideal in Huntington (1968), whose work is part of a genre that includes the contributions in Pye and Verba (1965), those in Deutsch (1963), and those in Almond and Coleman (1960), and the works of Hass (1958), Coleman and Rosberg (1964), and Kornhauser (1959) among numerous others.

2. Reviews of the careers and contributions of all of these leaders can be found in Hintzen and Will (1988).

3. For an excellent discussion of the different bases of authority among the post–World War II leadership in Grenada, see Noguera (1990).

4. This has led Pryor (1986: 219–247) to characterize Grenada under the PRG as a case of "foreign aid socialism" devoid of any socialist restructuring of the economy domestically. Typical of this form of socialism is the establishment of socialist bona fides through the mouthing of Marxist-Leninist rhetoric and support of the East Bloc in international fora. In return, these "socialist" countries expect substantial economic support from the radical bloc.

5. The clientelistic structure of West Indian "democratic" practice was fully explored by Stone (1980) and later by Edie (1991) for Jamaica. It is explored in Hintzen (1990) for Guyana and Trinidad, and by Noguera (1990) for Grenada.

6. See, in particular, all the contributions to Young and Phillips (1986).

2

Jamaica: Clientelism, Dependency, and Democratic Stability

Carlene J. Edie

Jamaica has succeeded in building and consolidating democratic institutions for over four and a half decades. Since the Universal Adult Suffrage Act of 1944, the Peoples National Party (PNP) and the Jamaica Labour Party (JLP) each have earned at least 40 percent of the aggregate vote in ten of eleven parliamentary elections held (see Appendix, Tables 9, 10, and 20). Over the past two decades, socioeconomic challenges to the democratic system have been severe. Of the island's two and a half million people, nearly 300,000 are permanently unemployed. The society remains highly stratified along racial and class lines stemming from plantation slavery. Africans (76.3%), coloreds or browns (15.9%), East Indians (3.1%), Chinese (1.2%), Europeans (0.8%), and Lebanese, Syrian, and other racial stocks (2.4%) make for a very diverse population. There are very high levels of relative deprivation among the black population at the base of the society, faced with comparably limited educational, income, and occupational opportunities. Since independence in 1962, Jamaican democracy has functioned in a procedural sense. The challenge it now faces is whether it can continue in its present institutional form, and whether it can cope with the deep-seated economic problems facing the country.

This chapter examines the origins, nature, and stability of Jamaican democracy. The basic thesis is that Jamaican democracy is anchored on patron-client relations that are reinforced by external relationships of international dependence. In the presence of acutely scarce resources, the political leaders in control of the state receive resources from overseas and can then distribute those proceeds to its clients, thus reproducing domestic political support for the regime in power. In this viewpoint, this explains the persistence of democratic government in that peculiarly pluralistic society. These propositions are developed and demonstrated below.

DECOLONIZATION, PARTY POLITICS, AND THE EMERGENCE OF CLIENTELISM

The 1930s were marked by working-class uprisings throughout the British West Indies, in protest against low wages, poor working conditions, and oppressive social conditions. Labor riots broke out in Jamaica in 1938, when an alliance of dispossessed black workers and peasants initiated militant political action against the colonial state. The British government immediately dispatched the Moyne Commission of Inquiry to investigate the riots which spread throughout the region. The commission's report led to the 1940 Colonial Development and Welfare Act (CDWA). Ultimately, the CDWA led to the creation of many bureaucracies for managing social welfare, such as the Jamaica Welfare Limited, the Land Settlement Department, the Central Housing Authority, the Cooperative Council, and the Agricultural Society. The middle-class-controlled state assumed a new role as an agency for promoting the welfare and safeguarding the standards of living of the majority of the population. The state was no longer limited to the functions of law and order, collecting revenues, and minimal welfare. Its scope was broadened to take an active part in extensive development programs. Bureaucratic expansion became the basis for middle-class ascendancy.

Ultimately, the commission's recommendations led to the development and expansion of representative governments elected by universal adult suffrage. The leadership of the labor and party organizations that subsequently emerged was quickly passed into the hands of the colored (brown) middle class. Alexander Bustamante (a former overseer and businessman) and Norman Manley (an attorney and cousin of Bustamante) stepped into the uprising, formed the Bustamante Industrial Trade Union (BITU) and the PNP, respectively, and became self-proclaimed leaders of the dispossessed workers and peasants.

The BITU and the PNP represented two distinct constituencies. The BITU represented the rural lower classes, as well as a small element of the propertied classes (traders). The PNP represented the new transforming middle class—the intelligentsia, teachers, civil servants, and all salaried state bureaucrats. The BITU and the PNP worked together for a brief period, although often in a stormy alliance. In 1942, ideological and personality differences led Bustamante to denounce the PNP and set up the JLP. The JLP articulated the same goals as its BITU-affiliate. It maintained its populist mass base among the lower classes, and won the support of the conservative rural middle classes and significant support from the upper classes of capitalists and large farmers. It held a firm commitment to an orthodox capitalist system with a dominant private sector.

Like the JLP, the PNP was not representative of a particular social stratum or of persons committed to a single socioeconomic theory. The PNP was established as an alliance of disparate elements united by their common commitment to the achievement of political self-determination. There was a genuine basis of support for the PNP's nationalist ideas, and the party worked on all these dissatisfactions with the aim of attracting support from those classes that were most affected by imperial political and economic arrangements—professional and clerical workers, and business and commercial interests, as well as the urban semiskilled workers and small farmers in the rural areas.

Labor and party organizations dominated by the middle class continued to monopolize electoral loyalties more than four and a half decades after their formation. During the postindependence period, third parties such as the Jamaica Democratic Party (JDP), the United Party (UP), and the Worker's Party of Jamaica (WPJ) existed for very short periods and then disappeared.[1] Middle-class elites have taken control of a competitive two-party system characterized by periodic changes of government between the JLP and PNP. Middle-class domination of labor and party organizations provided the framework for the subsequent development of clientelism.

INDUCED INDUSTRIALIZATION AND MIDDLE-CLASS DOMINATION

Monies allocated to the Jamaican state from the 1940 CDWA provided the infrastructure for subsequent inflows of foreign capital. Jamaica attracted an abundance of North American capital through the government's "industrialization by invitation" program, which offered a wide range of tax concessions and other incentives to foreign capitalists. Foreign investment led the Jamaican economy to grow throughout the 1960s by an average of nearly 6 percent annually (Jefferson, 1972; Girvan, 1971). Bauxite, tourism, and manufacturing became the largest sectors in terms of GDP in the Jamaican economy in 1968. Economist Owen Jefferson noted that "foreign ownership ranged from 100 percent in bauxite-alumina, to 40 percent in sugar and its by-products, 40 percent of transport, communications and public utilities combined and 55 percent of hotel capacity in the tourist industry" (1972: 8). The emerging local capitalist class benefited from the new investments, which provided profitable opportunities for merchants selling consumer goods and textiles; entrepreneurs selling services such as entertainment, restaurants, and transport; and real estate speculators.

External economic penetration of the postwar economy simply reinforced class and racial divisions within the society. In the foreign establishments, the high-level management positions were held by white expatriates, Jews, Lebanese, Syrians, or "Jamaican whites." Middle-management positions went to the browns, Chinese, and East Indian professionals. At the bottom were the black workers.

Significant class differentiation occurred in the middle and lower classes as a result of foreign investments. The state bureaucracy expanded, leading to the creation of new jobs for the brown and black educated middle class. This bureaucratic expansion has been the basis for middle-class ascendancy. Carl Stone noted that middle-class-led public sector expansion began in the post–World War II years but accelerated significantly after independence in 1962. Stone wrote that as a result of the inflows of capital and social pressures from the poor and lower middle classes, the public sector has grown significantly over the past three decades. This expansion has been reflected in the growth of public spending as a percentage of national income, the enlarged share of the public sector within the labor force and as a percentage of the total economy's wage bill, and in the public sector's increased contribution to GDP for public and administrative service (Stone, 1986: 42). Public sector employees in local and central government increased from 4,500 in 1943 to 57,000 in 1968; by 1980, the numbers had increased to 110,000. Public expenditure as a share of GDP went from 13 percent in 1950 to 17 percent in 1962, 21 percent in 1967, and 42 percent by 1977 (ibid.). By the late 1980s, more than 30 percent of total public expenditure was consumed by salaries and wages and clientelist patronage to party supporters, while another 32 percent was spent on purchasing goods from the private sector, which had become dependent on the government as its main market for selling goods and services (ibid.).

Skilled workers (brown and black) employed in the bauxite industry earned high salaries relative to their counterparts in other sectors. The unskilled and low-skilled had access to jobs in factories, hotels, gas stations, and transportation, and as domestics in middle- and upper-class homes. At the bottom were the (black and East Indian) agricultural laborers and the peasantry, who were displaced as large acreages of land were alienated from them and sold to the bauxite and tourist industries. The displaced peasantry migrated to the urban areas of Kingston and St. Andrew, and to England. Migration became an escape from the dispossession generated by these forms of foreign capitalist penetration of the economy. The majority of the black lower classes did not share in the new prosperity of the postwar era. As they were largely unskilled and uneducated, they were not able to benefit from the new jobs created within the private sector and the state bureaucracy. By the late 1960s, the unemployed numbered some 150,000, approximately one-third of the population of the capital city, Kingston. The unemployed survived through organized crime, petty crime, gambling, prostitution, and trade in illegal drugs (Lacey, 1977; Payne, 1991: 3–4).

These conditions were conducive to clientelistic recruitment of the lower classes into the middle-class-led party machines. A small percentage of the lower classes were later accommodated through clientelistic arrangements of the JLP and PNP electoral machines. This gave the middle-class state controllers the autonomy to pursue policies that were exclusively in the combined interests of external investors, local providers of capital, and the middle class itself.

EXPLAINING STATE-SOCIETY RELATIONS: THE CLIENTELIST FACTOR

Party politics works in the Jamaican milieu primarily through the mechanism of clientelism. The party system has been consolidated in the postindependence period as a network of patronage-based factions of the JLP and PNP. Party officials, labor leaders, state bureaucrats, government ministers, members of the private sector, intellectuals, and others are consistently engaged in patron-client relationships with high-ranking party and state officials. Clientelistic networks are also extended downward into the local electoral constituencies in both the urban and rural areas.

Both parties (JLP and PNP) emerged with and continue to maintain multiple class constituencies. They organize and recruit party supporters of differing social class origins. Once recruited as party supporters, participation by the masses has been restricted mainly to electoral activity (Stone, 1989a). Both parties are narrowly controlled by a closed elite at the top of the party hierarchy (Beckford and Witter, 1980). The structure of power in party organization in Jamaica reinforces patron-client relationships within the larger society. The party leadership of both the PNP and JLP controls the power apparatus in the party. Power is concentrated within a select group of members of parliament (MPs) and party office holders drawn disproportionately from the middle-class professions.

The MP and councillor are elected representatives of a constituency, and are the only links with the political directorate in the capital. The MP's clout has become almost supreme in getting assistance for the poor. For the poor, the necessities of day-to-day life—documents required for admission to school or a hospital, for a passport, for application for a job, and so on—are not so easily achieved. It is often only by personal intervention of an influential intermediary that a poor person can obtain any immediate result. The poor person then becomes dependent on bureaucratic intermediation performed by the party politicians and their clients working in the state bureaucracy. The MP's intervention secures the political support of the constituent.

National elections are often characterized by intense participation and violence.[2] The most deprived strata in the population become most involved in rank-and-file party activism and fight among themselves for spoils from the party system. The politicians of both the JLP and PNP and urban youth gangs have entered into symbiotic relationships despite public condemnation of violence and accusations against each other. The poor continue to be used to provide defense and protection for contending political groups in exchange for certain patronage benefits. The effect is to divide the poor into warring factions of antagonists who contend for control over the territory.

The cycle of patronage is perpetuated, as patron-client relationships exist between the state-controlling middle class and other elites. These relationships can be explained as a result of the dependence of all social groups in Jamaican society upon national and international agencies with resources. The capitalist class has been dependent on state assistance in the form of direct public investment, government programs of incentives and subsidies, and legislation that provided opportunities for enlarging its wealth. Because of its monopoly in certain key sectors of the economy (agriculture, manufacturing, communications, distributive trade, real estate, construction, etc.), it has been able to influence public policies in its own favor, as it posed a significant threat to governments who feared that private sector retaliation could lead to a withdrawal of capital and destabilization of the political system. Ultimately, the political leaders controll access to all forms of public resources and thereby have the power to determine the success or failure of the individual economic actor. As a result, a clientelistic relationship has been formed between the local capitalists and state-controlling party leaders, whereby the latter have been given support in exchange for access to the channels of capital accumulation.

Trade union elites also constitute an essential element in the clientelistic system because they control institutions geared toward mobilization. In 1974, the BITU, National Worker's Union (NWU), and Trade Union Congress (TUC) membership included 66 percent of the employed labor force. Other smaller unions had approximately 10,000 members (Gonsalves, 1977: 104). Given the union leaders' control over such large numbers of the laboring population, they have some leverage vis-à-vis the state leaders, whose survival depends on the maintenance of order in the society. In this context, union leaders are given access to government cabinet members, and to crucial policy-making processes. They cannot make policy, but they are given an input into the policy process. There is a reciprocal bond between political and union leaders whereby both interests are served through the instrument of clientelism. Clientelism serves to control the working classes, satisfy the individual interests of union leaders, and maintain support for the middle-class political order.

Bureaucratic elites represent the interests of the ascendant middle class, who benefit from state expansion. They derive benefits from direct access to state resources and through expansion of the state. They have considerable power derived from staffing and controlling state institutions and agencies. When their class interests are threatened, they have the power to sabotage the state-controlling political leaders. At the same time, some bureaucratic elites gain access to middle-class status through clientelistic ties to powerful political elites.

International resources have been a significant part of the patronage arsenal of the state-controlling political elites. The quantity of resources required to maintain an extensive state-centered patronage system has not always been available to the local economy. It became available during the postwar years when the economy was significantly modernized as a result of North American investments in the bauxite, tourist, and manufacturing sectors. In addition, foreign loans were available from numerous sources between 1965 and 1974. The World Bank made loans of J$6.3 million; the Canadian International Development Agency (CIDA) gave J$12.5 million; CIDA government-guaranteed loans were J$18.3 million; between 1963 and 1973, the United States Agency for International Development (USAID) gave J$11.6 million; and the InterAmerican Development Bank (IADB) gave J$24.3 million between 1970 and 1974 (Kirton, 1977: 86-87). Foreign loans were central to the development strategies of successive postindependence regimes, irrespective of the ideology of the party in power. Without access to international resources, a broad-based patronage system may not have been maintained. State expansion became the thrust of middle-class policies, as it has been an excellent way to gain resources required to maintain clientelism. Those contending for state power have been concerned with choosing ideologies that best allow access to external resources. Often, the transfer of external resources has been determined by the willingness of the political elite to maintain existing international relations that favor capitalist ideology.

THE MANLEY PERIOD: 1972–1980

The Michael Manley PNP government enjoyed considerable popularity when it was swept to power in 1972 after a two-term rule by the JLP, winning forty-seven seats in Parliament to the JLP's thirteen. The PNP had support from a broad sector of the population, consisting of the traditional middle classes employed in the state sector; critical sectors of the capitalist classes, which favored state protection of the local economy from external capital; and a broad segment of the urban working classes, as well as the militant and unemployed youth.

After its landslide victory, the Manley administration pursued expansionary policies and announced substantial reforms. The ideology of democratic socialism was introduced as a strategy to protect the poor and to correct the inequities of the Jamaican political economy. Because Jamaica's economy is characterized by international dependence, democratic socialism also called for a restructuring of the existing international economic order, which favored the wealthy industrial nations and locked the developing nations into a dependency syndrome.

The working classes were a key target for the PNP administration. The PNP government subsequently passed several laws which improved conditions for workers. First, a new Minimum Wage Law, introduced in October 1975, established a national minimum wage of J$20.00 for a forty-hour week; in 1978, that figure was increased to J$26.00 per forty-hour week. Prior to 1975, domestic workers sometimes earned as little as J$8.00 per week and the average weekly income paid by the state was J$20.00. Approximately 76 percent of the employed labor force received an income below the latter (Harris, 1977: 114).

Second, under the Employment Act of 1974, employers had to provide workers with advance notice of dismissal. The act also established equal pay for men and women. These measures were opposed by the business community, which felt that the government was "stirring up" the workers and "raising expectations" that could not be met. The third PNP initiative which targeted the working classes was "workers' participation." Worker participation was to be broadened to include participative management, share ownership, and worker representation at high levels of business policy formulation. According to surveys conducted by Jamaican pollster Stone (1977a: 182–202) an overwhelming majority of workers in all sectors supported in principle the concept of workers' participation.

Fourth, Project Land Lease, a major land reform program, was introduced to reduce social pressures in rural areas and to increase the amount of land under cultivation. Project Land Lease had three phases. Land Lease I involved leasing small plots of land for five to ten years from the government, which also provided the new farmers with credit for all major soil conservation, seed, harvesting, and transportation costs. Land Lease II was similar to Land Lease I but the government provided the new farmer with leases up to forty-nine years. Land Lease III was a cooperative farming program in the sugar industry in which community-structured organizations were to be set up to satisfy the basic needs of the community (Stone, 1977b).

Despite the government's good intentions, Project Land Lease served primarily as a service to the middle class via state expansion. The consequence of the government's land reform was not only to provide Jamaica's landless people with land but also to preserve middle-class dominance by placing the potentially disruptive rural poor under the administrative control of the government. The rapid developmental efforts were carried out under the direction of the government and the party. While the government tried to initiate an expansion of the class of small farmers, it simultaneously subjected them to close administrative control. Recognizing that these new landowners, with their newly acquired property, would have the incentive to support the political system, the government sought to guarantee this support. It saddled them with heavy debts from government loans, thus forcing them to comply with the wishes of the state or lose their property. This fear served to neutralize the small farmers.

The PNP made considerable efforts to strengthen public education. Public investment in education under the PNP rose from J$47,750,000 in the 1972/73 year to J$209,000,000, as education became free from the elementary level through to the bachelor's degree at the University of the West Indies. In 1972, over one-fourth of the adult population could not read or write, but as a result of the PNP's Adult Literacy Campaign, the government estimated that, by the end of its term, functional illiteracy had been cut in half (Manley, 1982: 77). The education program was well received by all social classes within Jamaica. It lost its momentum at the end when the island was in the grips of its economic crisis.

The PNP systematically used state resources to mobilize mass support through a strategy of clientelism. The PNP introduced the largest Special Employment Program in the history of Jamaica, using public sector resources to hold down unemployment levels. As was the practice in Jamaica, the greater part of the Special Employment Program was incorporated into the patronage system. Many of the crash programs (e.g., digging gullies, cleaning parks, building highways, etc.) were wasteful and brought loud objections from the middle classes. The poor had come to depend on the government for relief. They were seriously affected when these crash programs were suspended during the 1978–1980 economic crisis. The government's domestic programs helped to perpetuate the poor's psychological dependence on the government. Patronage mechanisms which linked the party to the poor at the base of the society remained in place rather than being reevaluated in the context of a democratic socialist society. Dependence on the state was reinforced by the massive welfare programs carried out by the government. The expectation that the state would continue to act as a patron became further entrenched in the minds of the people during the PNP's eight-year tenure in office.

While the PNP government actively pursued policies it believed would lead to a more egalitarian society, it advocated changes in the relationship between the wealthy industrial nations and the poor developing nations. Recognizing the detrimental effects of dependency on Third World economies (Manley, 1982), the PNP articulated the need to break those relations, but instead pursued policies which increased the dependence of the Jamaican state on foreign capital (Stone, 1982; Stephens and Stephens, 1987; Edie, 1986). Foreign capital was always targeted as a solution and became central to the maintenance of the Manley government. Pressured by dislocations in the Jamaican economy precipitated by the global oil crisis, the government was forced to seek capital resources from multilateral lending agencies, banks, and foreign governments to finance its development programs. The government continuously faced a balance-of-payments crisis and experienced six consecutive years (1974–1980) of negative growth. Local and foreign capital sources reacted with panic to the expansion of the state sector and the government's increasing involvement with Cuba. They protested against the government by withdrawing their capital from

Jamaican banks and withdrawing or decreasing investment in Jamaica. This reinforced the economic crisis which began in 1973 and which came to a climax in 1979 with the suspension of the IMF loans.

The PNP had made two IMF agreements in less than a period of three years, both of which ended in failure. Harsh austerity was imposed upon the people, unemployment continued to escalate, foreign exchange was virtually nonexistent, and the shortages of basic food goods continued. The government was faced with a crisis it could not handle. It faced a hostile private sector and a hostile international capitalist system. It faced the poor who withdrew support since the patronage-granting capacity of the government was restrained. The PNP was defeated in the 1980 elections, as the electorate opted for a new political elite in the JLP. The JLP won fifty-one seats versus the PNP's nine seats. The margin of victory in popular votes was eighteen percentage points, which reflects relatively even support given to both parties.

THE SEAGA PERIOD: 1980–1989

Foreign loans flowed into Jamaica in large quantities from 1981 to 1983, and the country's foreign debt went from US$2,237 million in 1981 to US$3,275 million in 1983 (Davies, 1986: 101). Edward Seaga's economic policy was dominated by a commitment to liberalization and market-oriented reform, and included the privatization of public enterprises, and movement of the free flow of goods and capital across borders. This policy aimed at strengthening the private sector so that it could no longer be manipulated by anticapitalist state controllers. Like Manley's, Seaga's economic strategy emphasized foreign borrowing to stabilize the economy and promote economic growth. Foreign lenders were interested in a favorable climate for investment, but the United States, in particular, had an interest in supporting Seaga's market-oriented policies to prevent the resurgence of socialist governments or interest groups committed to socialist policies.

Immediately after taking office, Seaga secured IMF loans of US$698 million over three years, with a 10 percent allowance provided for the application of the quarterly tests that the economy had to pass (Girvan et al., 1980: 113–155). The IMF's "seal of approval" enabled the government to obtain more than US$350 million from a consortium of Canadian, Japanese, West German, and Venezuelan banks, as well as the World Bank. In the first three years of the JLP government, Jamaica received an amount equal to 65 percent of all U.S. assistance to the country for the last thirty years (Thomas, 1988: 232). Total U.S. government aid to Jamaica during the first year of the Seaga administration climbed from slightly more than US$20 million in 1980 to over US$200 million by the end of 1981 (Payne, 1981: 436). In addition, momentum was generated in Washington to support a Seaga-led Caribbean Basin Initiative (CBI) to provide financial assistance for a new anticommunist alliance in the region.

These high aid levels directly reflected the perception of the nation's position as a stable pluralist democracy with a pro-Western foreign policy and a deep commitment to "Reaganomics." However, external financing came with tight policy strings attached, including IMF-imposed short-run macroeconomic management and medium- to long-term structural reforms encouraged by the World Bank. Prices were immediately increased on all imported items including oil, a liberal import policy was instituted, subsidies for basic foods were reduced, interest rates were increased, credit was restricted, and public sector spending was decreased as some public sector resources were reallocated to the export sector.

The inflow of foreign capital was expected to offset any political damage caused by increasing prices, reducing food subsidies, and decreasing public sector spending, and to set the stage for the economic miracle that was expected under the Seaga administration. Both the government and the IMF officials were so encouraged by the financial support that Jamaica received between November 1980 and December 1982, and by the investments promised, that they made unrealistic projections of economic growth in the economy. The government announced in June 1981 that bauxite production would be increased from the 1980 figure of 12.1 million tonnes to at least 26 million tonnes in 1983 to 1984 (*Jamaica Daily Gleaner*, June 1, 1981).

Far from expanding as anticipated, decline in the international demand for bauxite, coupled with changing production techniques, led to a fall in bauxite production to only 7.7 million tonnes in 1983 (Davies, 1986: 93). Government revenue from the industry fell accordingly, from US$206 million in 1980 to US$137 million in 1982 (*Economic and Social Survey*, 1983: 9.3–9.5). U.S. President Ronald Reagan assisted Seaga by ordering 1.6 million tonnes of Jamaican bauxite for defense stockpiling, sidestepping regulations for competitive purchases. Reagan's action softened the impact on the industry, but only made a limited contribution to the balance of payments because the United States insisted on paying for the bauxite, in part, by the barter provision of agricultural products (Payne, 1988: 116). The poor performance of the sugar and banana sectors aggravated the balance-of-payments problems caused by the fall in bauxite production. Sugar production declined by 46,000 tons between 1980 and 1982, and banana production by 11,000 tons over the same period.

Despite the JLP's efforts to dismantle all vestiges of "democratic socialism," the government was unable to move away from public sector dominance of the economy. The public debt held by the Bank of Jamaica increased by J$100 million in 1982, indicating that the distribution of bank credits continued to facilitate public sector access to resources (Looney, 1987: 222). Jamaican political leaders have always used clientelist and populist policies oriented to their political objectives. Seaga realized that he must meet some of the public sector service demands of the voters. In spite of his commitment to supply-side economics and the principles of the free market, Seaga was forced to increase taxation on the business sector to offset the budget deficits created by a high level of public spending. The business sector, caught in the grips of a depressed domestic market, high interest rates, high monetary policies, and scarce foreign exchange since 1984, was burdened with over J$100 million in new taxes in 1985. It reacted negatively, viewing these tax policies as a major disincentive to business investment. Seaga's credibility as a promoter of private investment was damaged, as he was constrained by clientelism which prevented him from shifting substantial resources from the public to the private sector, as was necessary for efficiency and economic growth (according to the supply-side economics to which he was ideologically committed).

The JLP dismantled the Worker Participation Schemes, the Sugar Cooperatives Program, the Food Farms, Project Land Lease, the Community Enterprise Organizations, the Home Guards, and Community Councils. However, it did maintain some of the existing policies and attempted to implement some welfare programs of its own. The State Trading Corporation was maintained, but its name was changed to the Jamaica Commodity Trading Corporation (JCTC). Employment opportunities continued to be created for government supporters in the JCTC. In 1985, the government launched social welfare services such as the Food Aid Program, providing food stamps to 200,000 indigent persons, 200,000 expectant mothers, and mothers with preschool children. In addition, 600,000 school children were scheduled to receive school lunches.[3] There was some attempt at job creation in the form of the Human Employment and Resource Training (HEART)[4] and Solidarity programs, funded by J$10 million of state monies and US$10 million from USAID. Solidarity was intended to accommodate the projected 13,000 youths each year who were unable to participate in training at the level of the HEART program. By mid-1986 the HEART program reportedly had 8,023 students in training with an additional 14,850 to be enrolled at the end of 1986. The Solidarity project reportedly had 10,000 participants in its first year ending November 1986 (Jamaica Parliament, 1986: 49).

By early 1983, the government was in a dilemma. Although the stabilization and adjustment policies were drastically applied, the government was facing balance-of-payments problems. Maintaining IMF policies dictated a series of policies with disastrous economic and political consequences. The need for foreign resources to meet its debt service payments (and thus to maintain its creditworthiness) forced a government committed to state and party clientelism to cut public spending, tighten fiscal policies, and devalue the dollar. These policies conflicted with the interests of the majority classes who had come to rely on the public sector for patronage resources for employment. Simultaneously, the government sought to squeeze whatever resources it could from the domestic economy by rapidly raising taxes on the business classes. Major cuts in domestic current spending in the public sector, along with devaluation of the dollar and raising private sector taxes, exacerbated the financial crisis in the economy.

By the end of 1985, the Jamaican economy had begun a downward spiral that alienated the upper, middle, and lower classes, and resulted in the election of a new government in February 1989. An economy that had come to rely heavily on foreign finance and its bauxite earnings was hit by an international recession, stagnation in the global bauxite/alumina industry, and marked deterioration in its terms of trade. Despite substantial foreign aid, economic growth had not been achieved. Wages fell, prices increased, and by 1987, there was mass apathy as the lower classes buckled under the burdens of the faltering economy.

Pollster Stone predicted a PNP victory of forty-eight seats with 57 percent of the popular vote in the 1989 elections. The results were almost identical: PNP, forty-four seats and 57 percent of the vote; JLP, sixteen seats and 43 percent of the vote (*Jamaica Weekly Gleaner*, February 13, 1989, 3). The JLP lost about 15 percent of the vote with respect to 1980, but its share of the vote remained high, reflecting the fairly even support given to both parties. Despite its substantial loss of seats, from fifty-one seats in 1980 to sixteen in 1989, the JLP continues to represent more than 40 percent of the electorate and thus remains a critical force in the political process.

THE MANLEY/PATTERSON PERIOD: 1989–PRESENT

The PNP government was returned to power in 1989, and Manley began an unprecedented third term as Jamaica's prime minister. Due to poor health, he retired from politics on March 28, 1992, leading to the succession of P. J. Patterson (deputy prime minister since 1989). This transition has strengthened Jamaica's democratic credentials. Democratic political succession has occurred at both the inter-party and intra-party levels since independence in 1962.[5]

In contrast to its democratic socialist policies of the 1970s, the 1989 PNP administration affirmed its faith in the free market philosophy advocated by its JLP predecessor, and has embarked on a crusade determined to create an environment conducive to market-led economic growth. The centerpiece of this development strategy is a compression of the state away from production or intervention in the economy. The present strategy accords a privileged position to business as the latter is given the task of generating economic growth.

The private sector has not yet been able to generate economic growth while the shrinking of the state has occurred rapidly. In its attempt to move away from statism, the PNP government is facing a host of political problems. Social and political tensions have increased as austerity measures have weakened support for the government. Inflation, high levels of unemployment, rising commodity prices, and high crime rates, among other problems, continue to plague the society. The PNP government is unable to offer populist initiatives that would be of benefit to the majority classes, as it is forced to operate within the narrow limits of the tight restrictions imposed by the World Bank and the IMF.

There has been a decline in the proportion of loyal party voters (both JLP and PNP), as it is more difficult to retain voter allegiance if there is less patronage to distribute. The central question facing Jamaican leaders is whether the two-party system and the political institutions of liberal democracy can be preserved if statism is abandoned and replaced by market democratization. The country is currently rife with distrust of both businessmen and politicians, as the lower and middle classes believe they have been abandoned at the expense of local and foreign capital.

A new pressure group emerged in January 1992, known as New Beginnings. The founding members consist of former JLP, PNP, and WPJ members, talk show hosts, university professors, journalists, and other middle-class professionals. An October 1991 poll by Carl Stone showed that some 25 percent of the people said they might support a third party and 20 percent said they would vote for either the JLP or the PNP or a third party (*Jamaica Weekly Gleaner*, May 9, 1992, 14). New Beginnings was formed, as one of the founding members put it, "because there is a social force developing outside both political parties which needs an avenue of expression" (ibid.: 4). To date, New Beginnings has not organized itself as a political party ready to challenge the JLP and the PNP.

There have been charges from both the left and the right of the political spectrum that the two-party system has failed, as apathy and leadership distrust prevail. There is great concern about the danger posed by the "drug dons" who have access to large amounts of money for distribution to poor communities. If the government is no longer able to supply the poor with patronage, it can be replaced by the "drug dons" who spread money in the economically depressed urban areas.

Disillusionment has created a political vacuum not seen since independence. In February 1992, 32 percent of the people favored the JLP, 30 percent favored the PNP, and 38 percent were uncommitted. This represents a significant decline in support of the PNP, which had 44 percent support in January 1989. The JLP did not gain the support of the disgruntled PNP supporters; the latter defected to the rank of the uncommitted (ibid.: 22). This is unusual for Jamaican electoral politics. The JLP has been weakened as a result of a leadership crisis within the party, as well as lower- and middle-class disillusionment with its free market policies.

The two-party system has been undermined by the JLP and PNP's inability to make significant changes in the lives of the majority of the population. The external resource base of party politics is shrinking as the state is finding it increasingly more difficult to secure the vast resources necessary to support its patronage system. With the end of the Cold War and the rebuilding of the Soviet Union and Eastern Europe, the Caribbean has not been given priority for U.S. aid funds by either the Bush administration or the current Clinton administration. The Patterson government remains committed to IMF structural adjustment policies, which demand first and foremost a decrease in public sector spending. The state has begun to lose its legitimacy in the eyes of the population as the government is no longer able to obtain the vast resources necessary for an extensive system of patronage. National elections were held on March 30, 1993. It appeared as if the PNP would have been susceptible to the economic crisis. However, the PNP scored a resounding victory at the polls, winning 53 seats (52% of the popular vote) to the JLP's 7 seats (48% of the popular vote).

PROSPECTS FOR JAMAICAN DEMOCRACY

Jamaica's public policy, clientelist party organization, and external economic relationships have created stable liberal democratic institutions. Despite continuous economic crises since the 1970s, national elections have taken place normally and power passed from the PNP to the JLP and back again to the PNP. Jamaica's democracy emerged within the context of abundant resources and an expanding economy, where the state enjoyed increasing revenues. However, genuine scarcity has been the norm for over the past two decades. Jamaica's thirty-year-old democracy has become fragile and vulnerable. The prospects for stability are dimmer now than they have ever been, even during the stormy decade of the 1970s.

Economic difficulties have made it imperative that both the JLP and the current PNP government accept IMF structural adjustment policies. As a result, the state's role in the economy has been weakened, and populist, welfarist policies have diminished. The state has therefore become weaker and is even more vulnerable to external capitalist actors than before. State controllers are now unable to pursue policies which may be beneficial to the majority classes, as such policies are always rooted in state expansion. A criterion for continued aid from the IMF is state shrinking.

Public support for the parties has diminished, although support for the political system has remained high. This is perhaps a reflection of the strength of Jamaica's democracy. Instead of rejecting the system as a whole, voters have consistently ousted the administration in power and replaced it with the opposition. The professional classes are now engaged in public debates about reform of the state and the economy, with the intended objective of extending democracy and not replacing it. Both the JLP and the PNP have lost support but democratic processes retain deep and wide support. But, in the long run, system support could diminish if the living standards of the black majority classes continue to decline, while wealth remains concentrated in a tiny white elite.

External actors, particularly the United States and Canada, appear to be committed to the stability of the Jamaican political system. Both the United States and Canada have recently canceled some of Jamaica's huge foreign debt, thus enabling the government to reschedule other loans and borrow new monies.

Such aid is intended to cushion the fragile regime and to prevent collapse. However, the foreign debt has to be greatly reduced in order to enhance the long-term stability of the political system.

"Drug dons" have become disruptive new players in the political game. Jamaica has become an important transfer point for drug trafficking between the United States and South America. Lower-class and unemployed Jamaicans have gained employment opportunities from international narcotics trafficking. Drug dons are effectively competing with the politicians for the urban and lower-class constituency. The state no longer has the resources to generate sufficient temporary employment for the poor. Thus, the foreign exchange and employment generated by the drug dons become very significant. Drug trafficking has brought violence, corruption, and confrontation with the United States, as well as a cocaine/crack drug problem among the Jamaican youth. The Jamaican government does not have the resources to effectively combat the problem. In 1989 U.S. President George Bush diverted aid earmarked for Jamaica's drug program to Poland, to help restore democracy in that Eastern European nation. Drug trafficking would not have become such an attractive alternative to the poor if unemployment levels were not so high.

Overall, Jamaica has a working form of parliamentary democracy that lacks the substance of Western democracies, but it functions nonetheless. The Jamaican people are committed to the practice of democracy, despite their limited participation in the political process. Since independence, both the rulers and the ruled have had a stake in the system and this guaranteed its stability. If clientelism can no longer be used effectively, the lower classes will not have a stake in the system, and the prospects for the survival of Jamaican democracy will then be dim.

NOTES

1. The WPJ dissolved itself in March 1992 after fourteen years. It replaced the Workers Liberation League (WLL) in 1978. The WPJ had been the strongest third party on the political scene since independence, although it never managed to gain more than 1 percent of the public's support during national elections.

2. See T. Lacey, *Violence and Politics in Jamaica* (Manchester: Manchester University Press, 1977).

3. See 1985/1986 Budget Speech by the Honourable Edward Seaga, Gordon House, May 24, 1985, Kingston, Jamaica.

4. In order to subsidize the HEART program, a system of payroll taxation was imposed whereby private sector employees whose monthly payroll exceeded J$7,222 were required to pay a 3 percent tax on the total wage bill, and the tax collections were used to assist with financing training programs in the areas of continuing education, cosmetology, business, agriculture, construction, crafts, and garments. The government reported HEART tax collections of J$5.5 million in fiscal 1982–1983, increasing to J$21.9 million in 1984–1985 (Alm, 1988: 477–496).

5. Since independence, there have been four inter-party transfers of government. The JLP served in 1962, 1967, 1980, and 1983, while the PNP served in 1972, 1976, and 1989. The JLP has had four leaders since independence: Alexander Bustamante, Donald Sangster, Hugh Shearer, and Edward Seaga. The PNP has had three leaders: Norman Manley, Michael Manley, and P. J. Patterson.

3

Guyana: Ethnic Politics and the Erosion of Human Rights and Democratic Governance

Ralph R. Premdas

For many decades, problems of human rights violations in the Caribbean pertained mainly to the non-English-speaking countries. Toward the last quarter of the twentieth century, these issues have now come to bedevil the former English colonies. For nearly two decades, the self-proclaimed Marxist state of Guyana under President Forbes L. S. Burnham became a notable example. The democratic parliamentary framework acquired in 1965 at independence was practically abandoned as the state became dictatorial, violent, undemocratic, and racist. Political and civil liberties were extinguished. The judiciary was also politicized and transformed into an integral instrument of regime tyranny. The public bureaucracy was corrupted and converted into a principal pillar of oppressive rule. The army, police, and security forces were overindulged and recruited to ensure loyalty to the paramount party. The press, free at independence, was denied newsprint and practically muzzled. Few crevices existed where one could hide from the purview of official enforcers.

This chapter examines the role of the self-proclaimed Marxist state in the repression of its opponents. It looks at some of the contradictions between ideology and the requirements of maintaining power. In particular, it focuses on the problem of human rights violations. It begins by looking at the colonial state, then proceeds into examination of ethnic and class politics.

THE COLONIAL HERITAGE: RIGHTS DENIED

For almost three hundred years, Guyana was a colony of Britain. Guyana had a relatively brief period of democratic practices lasting less than ten years

(1957–1965) when it was granted full independence under an artificial constitution modeled on British traditions and practices. Not only was the heritage of
democratic practices different from Britain in regard to the incubation period,
but when Guyana became independent, the new nation inherited an unintegrated multiethnic state lacking a common consensus of values and a society
riven by communal distrust and fear (Despres, 1967; Glasgow, 1970; Premdas,
1972).

Labor shortages that followed African emancipation in 1838 explain the recruitment of Chinese, Portuguese, and East Indians (from the Indian subcontinent) to
Guyana. Between 1840 and 1917, approximately 238,960 indentured East Indian
laborers arrived to work on the plantations (Nath, 1950). The indenture system,
however, was most oppressive and different only from the conditions of the slaves
by the fact that slavery was generally a permanent condition while an indenture
was fixed for seven years. Like the African slaves, the East Indians were practically
without any civil or political rights. Each plantation conducted itself as a separate
state with its own apparatus of law and order built around arbitrary rule. For the
most part, the plantation owners were an absentee group whose main interest was
"making a rapid fortune to enable them to return to Europe to spend it there leaving
only servants on the estate" (Ragatz, 1972: 118).

The end of the apprenticeship period in 1838 witnessed an African exodus
from the plantations, mainly to villages. By the end of the nineteenth century,
more than half of the African villagers would gravitate to urban centers where
they availed themselves of educational opportunities and acquired skills and
training (Farley, 1954: 95). Thus, by 1950, the Africans dominated every
department of the civil service, while their portion of the plantation population
was reduced to 6.8 percent by 1960 (Report of the British Guyana Commission
of Inquiry, 1965: 164).

Because of the appalling conditions of the indentured laborers, various
commissions of inquiry, including the Des Veoux Commission of 1871, inves-
tigated the plantations and eventually India decided to terminate the indenture-
ship system altogether in 1917. Indians who remained in Guyana continued in
various sorts of association with the plantations. Many were allotted land
contiguous to the sugar estates in exchange for giving up their contractual right
to return to India. By 1946, the Indian outflow from the sugar estates left only
a third as plantation residents; their urban presence was only 10 percent (ibid.:
95). In the 1960s, 25.5 percent of the Indian population was on sugar estates,
13.4 percent in urban areas, with the remaining 61.1 percent in villages. East
Indians in Guyana became predominantly rural dwellers serving either as sugar
cane plantation workers or independent farmers. The other ethnic elements in
the population were relatively small, but they too established their own peculiar
residential and occupational niches. Amerindians, the original peoples of
Guyana, were consigned to "reservations" in the country's sparsely populated
jungle interior areas (Sanders, 1969), while the Chinese and Portuguese gravi-

tated to urban centers where the former engaged in service industries such as restaurants and the latter in the professions and businesses (Fried, 1956).

By the beginning of the twentieth century, certain features were clearly embedded in the social and political system which would bear directly on the distribution of human rights. A communally oriented, multiethnic society was fashioned (see Appendix, Table 1, for the recent population distribution of ethnic groups). It was dominated by Europeans and an accompanying system of colonial laws and practices which institutionalized racial inequality along a color-class continuum. The wealth produced from the sugar plantations was repatriated to the imperial metropolitan center (London), leaving very little for the nonwhite population. In an interdependent and unintegrated communal order, the political balance was held by a colonial government originating in conquest, maintained by coercion, and perpetuated by a color-class stratified order.

HUMAN RIGHTS AND THE POLITICS OF DECOLONIZATION

Between the Great Depression and the early 1950s, dramatic transformations took place in British Guiana. The politics of decolonization was characterized by persistent pressure, agitation, and threats of violence. The depression brought to the surface the inequities of the plantation society. It greatly emphasized the precariousness of dependence upon the world market for survival and consequently underlined the need for workers to organize to protect their economic interests. Several trade unions were formed and there was a dramatic increase in strike action as the worldwide depression took its disastrous toll on the sugar industry. The price of sugar fell, unemployment soared, and wages plummeted. In one typical depression year, over 20,000 working days were lost to strikes and disturbances on thirty-eight sugar estates (Ayearst, 1960).

The strikes and other forms of agitation culminated in the appointment of the Moyne Commission, which was very critical of living conditions in the British Caribbean. The commission's recommendations for remedying the social and economic conditions in British Guiana were gradualist. It rejected demands for universal adult suffrage, and recommended instead a literacy test and an income requirement of G$120. As far as the unions were concerned, the colonial office did not intend to support the wide-ranging changes for which they agitated during the depression years.

Frustration of workers' demands, especially for representation in the decision-making bodies of the colony, persisted after World War II. Many Guyanese who fought with the Allies against fascism returned to live in an unfree and oppressive colony. The denial of adequate reforms invited the emergence of an anticolonial movement with radical demands. In 1946, a Political Affairs Committee (PAC) was formed, led by Cheddi Jagan and others; it espoused the theory of Scientific Socialism.[1] The salient feature of the PAC's ideological orientation was its nonracial analysis of the colony's living conditions, which appealed to workers and farmers of all ethnic groups. The activities of the PAC were agitational and it recruited many of the outstanding intellectuals in the country.

In January 1950, the PAC launched the People's Progressive Party (PPP). Its ideological aim was to build "a just socialist society in which the industries of the country shall be socially and democratically owned for the common good."[2] Essential to the party's electoral success was unity of at least a substantial number of Indians and Africans, who together constituted nearly 82 percent of the total population. The PPP's program called for cooperation of all racial groups. To ensure this end, Jagan and Burnham, an Indian and an African respectively, were installed as leaders of the party.

A commission of inquiry was appointed in October 1950 to review the franchise. The PPP lodged a strong petition for universal adult suffrage and self-government. The upshot was the granting to Guyana of the most liberal constitutional arrangement extended at that time to any British Caribbean territory. Two crucial aspects of the constitution were: (1) universal adult suffrage; and (2) a limited cabinet system that conceded to an elected majority the powers to govern most internal affairs of the colony.

When the first general elections under universal adult suffrage were concluded on April 27, 1953, the PPP won overwhelmingly, gaining eighteen out of twenty-four seats in the unicameral legislature (Premdas, 1973). The PPP assumed office with Jagan as leader and Burnham president of the party. The "dual charisma" of these two sectional leaders legitimized control of the government in the eyes of most members of Guyana's multiethnic society. Within five months of PPP rule, however, the British government would arbitrarily suspend the constitution and evict the party from power.[3] The suspension of the constitution and the eviction of Guyana's nationalist leaders from office signaled the eclipse of political rights. The franchise was withdrawn and the colonial government appointed persons from the plantocracy, the business community, and others sympathetic to it (including several who were defeated in the 1953 elections) to govern Guyana. British troops and local police entered homes of citizens, conducting arbitrary searches for "communists."

In 1957, the British colonial office planned new general elections under universal adult suffrage under a constitution substantially less liberal than the 1953 model. However, between 1953 and 1957, Jagan and Burnham disagreed over tactics of the PPP, parted company, and formed their own parties. The main difference then between contestants in the 1953 and 1957 elections was an ethnically divided independence movement around two different parties in 1957. The unified African-Indian leadership of the PPP in 1953 substantially suppressed communal voting proclivities between the two major communal groups. In 1957, a divided African-Indian leadership, each at the helm of a separate party, would elicit and exploit sectional fears and prejudices to obtain votes.

A new dimension was introduced in the quest for human rights in Guyana after Jagan's PPP won the 1957 elections. Independence from Britain became secondary to the fear of internal racial domination. It seemed that each ethnic group felt that its basic rights could not be protected by a government formed by another ethnic group. Although it recruited a strong group of Afro-Guyanese as cabinet ministers, Jagan's government was accused by Burnham's party of being an Indian "coolie" regime that tilted budgetary allocations in favor of Indian constituencies.[4] Every act of the government was interpreted through the medium of communal interests by the opposition. When the Peoples National Congress (PNC) government would assume sole control of the government a decade later, the PPP opposition would interpret government policies in the same vein. Nevertheless, both Jagan and Burnham continued to regard themselves as socialists, although the latter cast his beliefs in a mold of "mixed economy" while the former advocated nationalization of "the commanding heights of the economy." Burnham, therefore, projected an image as a moderate social democrat, while Jagan appeared as an extremist socialist ideologue (Premdas, 1973).

In the 1961 elections, both race and ideology would feature as factors in the campaign for votes, but the former would operate mainly as a powerful domestic mobilizer and the latter as an external force. The racial factor would align ethnic groups to political parties; the ideological factor would become salient in relation to Fidel Castro's accession to power in Cuba. Jagan won the 1961 general elections in an ethnically inflamed contest. As premier of Guyana, he rejected U.S. requests for a boycott of Cuba. He instead proclaimed Castro as one of the world's greatest liberators and expanded trade between Guyana and Cuba (Premdas, 1972; Hintzen and Premdas, 1983).

The 1961–1964 period was marked by demonstrations, strikes, civil war, and external interference. Burnham refused to support independence under a Jagan government. The issue turned on the proposition that it was better to be subservient to European colonialism than an Indian-dominated regime, even one run by a socialist. Hence, much of the agitation against the Jagan government was carried out by the Afro-Guyanese section of the population, along with mixed races and Portuguese elements (Report of the British Guyana Commission of Inquiry, 1965). The British government used the disturbances to postpone independence and alter the country's electoral system from the first-past-the-post simple plurality type to one of proportional representation.

When the new electoral system was announced, Jagan called out his sugar workers (mainly Indians) on a protracted strike, practically crippling the economy. The conflict inevitably assumed the form of ethnic confrontation and violence. Countrywide demonstrations deteriorated into civil war, mainly between Africans and Indians. Entire communities were uprooted, and mixed

Indian-African villages were "purified," rendered into ethnically homogeneous clusters.

New elections were called in 1964. Jagan lost to a coalition headed by Burnham and supported by the United Force (UF), a small capitalist-oriented party (representing mainly the non-Indian and non-African sections of the population). Jagan's supporters boycotted the granting of independence under the African-led Burnham coalition regime. Instead of independence being viewed as liberation from colonial oppression, it was regarded as the triumph of one ethnic group over the other. Ethnic domination meant colonialism of a different kind with the loss of civil rights and liberties.

During the 1964–1968 period, Guyana witnessed the development of state violence against the political opposition. The new premier was Burnham; his main interest was to consolidate his power as well as to prevent the ethnic domination of his communal group by the Indians. Burnham's coalition partner's main interest was to maintain the material and social privileges of the color-class system of stratification and a capitalist economic order. The external sponsor of the new regime was the United States, whose paramount concern was to destroy all semblances of socialist and communist influences in Guyana. Together, these three interests would formulate policies that strengthened the coercive apparatus of the state, repress Jagan's Marxist PPP, and institute a foreign policy consonant with U.S. interests.

The first item on the new government's agenda was to restore domestic tranquility. First, it identified Jagan's PPP as the sole agent of disorder in Guyana, absolving the coalition partners of any blame as instigators or participants. Second, a better-equipped and larger police force was required as well as the formation of a national defense force. Foreign aid from the United States provided resources to build these bodies. A state of emergency, which authorized arrests without trial, was part of the repressive package. The Jaganite leadership cadres at all levels were ruthlessly suppressed. The communal factor inevitably pervaded the entire law enforcement exercise.

The Guyana Defence Force was formed in 1965. Like the police force, it was recruited mainly from the African sector of the population. One of the effects of the PNC-led government was the dominance of Africans in the coercive apparatus of state.[5] This recruitment pattern provided a powerful basis not only for the protection of the African community from ethnic domination, but also for the maintenance in power of a communal government. The latter event might not have been originally intended but the predominant uniethnic membership of the coercive forces was bound to be exploited by politicians in an environment fraught with intercommunal fears and suspicions.

The overt destruction of the PPP apparatus was speedy. A vibrant PPP organization that pervaded all parts of Guyana was soon reduced to a skeleton body operating mainly at headquarters. Jagan retaliated. PPP supporters were instructed to boycott rice production and participate in numerous strikes in the sugar industry. Burnham pleaded for cooperation, noting that the task of reconstruction was a multiethnic endeavor. But like his predecessor, Jagan, who made similar appeals when he was in office, Burnham would learn that the de facto appeals to race during elections were not easily forgotten. They would create a monster which would haunt whoever had invoked its destructive powers previously. The party in power would be held captive to its preelection appeals. Followers demanded patronage at the expense of the vanquished ethnic enemy. To deny them would be to lose political support; to cater to their demands would be to further alienate the opposition. A bargaining middle ground to resolve and accommodate communal differences seemed nonexistent. To Jagan, the PNC coalition government was illegitimate; negotiating with it would be tantamount to conferring legitimacy on it. To Burnham, Jagan was the threat to his leadership. The two pillars of their respectively ethnic communities remained intransigent. The only means of managing conflict were state repression by one and demonstrations and strikes by the other. The political institutions lacked cross-communal legitimacy, however effectively they performed or however evenhandedly they formulated policies and administered the government. The quest for civil rights by then had become completely subordinate to if not eclipsed by ethnic rivalry.

BURNHAM SEIZES POWER: THE PROGRESSIVE LOSS OF RIGHTS IN A "SOCIALIST REGIME"

The year 1968 was a momentous watershed in Guyanese history, for it witnessed the enthronement of an illegal and illegitimate regime, which in subsequent years repeatedly rigged other elections thereby perpetuating its power. Jagan's PPP, even under the new system of proportional representation, with the rapid increase of the Indian population, stood a good chance of winning. Faced with this threat, the PNC embarked on a series of steps which would secure for it continued control over the government by illegal means. The Burnham regime, like its antecedent colonial power, would deprive the Guyanese people of the sacred political right to determine their destiny by participating via elections in decisions affecting their lives. But the rigging of the elections in 1968 was only the start of the erosion of human rights. Once it seized power, the illegitimate regime would face a gauntlet of persistent opposition resistance, boycotts, and strikes which added to its insecurity and forced it to abridge other rights such as freedom of expression, the right to a fair trial, and freedom from racial discrimination. A vicious cycle of self-reinforcing events would cast the Burnham regime in the role of a bigoted dictatorship which wrapped itself in the self-righteous rhetoric of socialism.

This section focuses on four main areas of human rights loss: (1) the franchise; (2) racial discrimination in the public service; (3) freedom of expression; and (4) arbitrary arrests. In all of these, repression was present in varying degrees, but as the regime's hold became more narrowly based and poverty grew rampant, the repression would cross ethnic lines and extend to the regime's own communal supporters.

Loss of the Franchise: The Right to Fair and Free Elections

The PNC discovered a way to eliminate the UF from the government a few months before the 1968 elections. The PNC required only three additional seats to command an absolute majority in Parliament; this it procured by inducing parliamentary defections. It gained a majority and sole control of the government. It then proceeded to reconstitute the independent electoral commission with its own sympathizers and to tamper with the electoral machinery. In what were established incontrovertibly as rigged elections, involving tens of thousands of fictitious overseas votes, the PNC would win an absolute majority of seats.

I refer to the 1968 elections as "a seizure of power." The electoral fraud was committed under the tight supervision of a politicized, communally lopsided police and military force. The central election office in Georgetown was barricaded like an impregnable fortress with high security fences, barbed wire, floodlights, and armed guards protecting its activities under utmost secrecy. The "overseas vote" was a new creation, literally extending the domestic electorate to England and the United States. It was wholly administered by the PNC's politically appointed ambassadors to the United Kingdom and the United States. It supplemented padded domestic voter lists. The PNC won nearly all the overseas votes and in a number of local constituencies it alone won more ballots than eligible votes on the roll.[6] Both the PPP and the UF were shocked by the results, but could do nothing against a government that now controlled both "the ballots and bullets."

To prevent disruption and to consolidate its power, the PNC embarked on a discriminatory policy of purging the army, police, and public service of practically all non-African elements, especially at the senior administrative levels. In the army and police force, the "cleansing" was more thoroughgoing, applying to all echelons, for the coercive apparatus of state had become critical in preserving the regime's power.

The rigging was repeated in the 1973 elections with the army openly seizing the ballot boxes. The PNC increased its parliamentary strength to two-thirds of the seats.[7] Elections scheduled for 1978 were postponed because the regime wanted to hold a national referendum to alter the country's constitution and introduce a presidential form of government. Like the elections, the referendum was also rigged but its fraudulence was widely publicized and exposed.[8] Elections in 1980 were again rigged but exposed by an international team of observers. Headed by Lord Avebury, chairman of the United Kingdom Parliamentary Human Rights Group, and invited by the Guyanese Human Rights

Association, the international team of observers concluded its report on the 1980 elections as follows:

We came to Guyana aware of the serious doubts expressed about the conduct of the previous elections there, but determined to judge these elections on their own merit and hoping that we should be able to say that the result was fair. We deeply regret that, on the contrary, we were obliged to conclude, on the basis of abundant and clear evidence, that the election was rigged massively and flagrantly. Fortunately, however, the scale of the fraud made it impossible to conceal either from the Guyanese public or the outside world. Far from legitimizing President Burnham's assumption of his office, the events we witnessed confirm all the fears of Guyanese and foreign observers about the state of democracy in that country.[9]

The fear of ethnic domination by others of his communal group and the desire to be prime minister impelled Burnham to commit electoral fraud. A PPP-PNC coalition could have averted this act but neither Burnham nor Jagan could work with or under each other. For Burnham, if ethnic domination was inevitably written in the script of Guyana's political future, then it would be preferable for him and his ethnic group to be dominant. The seizure of power was tantamount to an act of self-protection as well as an assertion of ethnic dominance of one communal group over others. Coercive power would be required to contain and quell opposition challenges to the government.

Abridgement of the Freedom of Expression: The Mass Media

The Guyana constitution guaranteed freedom of expression as a basic right of citizens. Under the Burnham regime, however, freedom of expression by the mass media was practically extinguished. Professor John A. Lent, a specialist on communications issues, observed:

in the 1970s, the government of Forbes Burnham virtually took over the Guyanese mass media, purchasing newspapers, nationalizing broadcasting, and harassing the opposition with legislative, economic, and physical sanctions. By the end of the decade, the government, by then socialist, owned both dailies—*Guyana Chronicle* and the *Citizen*—both radio stations, and a new television service. (1982: 376)

This was paradoxical since it was Burnham, along with Jagan, who, as leaders of the independence movement after World War II, became victims of the "Undesirable Publications Ordinance" (1947) aimed at curbing the propaganda efforts of the nationalists. When the jointly led PPP came to power in 1953, one of its first acts was to strike down the "Undesirable Publications Ordinance" in the name of socialist justice. Twenty years later, Burnham's self-styled socialist regime brought colonial repression full circle, this time with a vengeance, making the "Undesirable Publications Ordinance" seem innocuous by comparison to contemporary practices.

As a lawyer, Burnham attempted to institute controls over his political opponents by using state legalism. Hence, control over the mass media was never committed by flagrant violation of the law. Rather, by controlling the Parliament (via fraudulent elections), the law-making powers of the state were rewritten to suppress political opposition. Much of this opposition consisted of its communal enemy as represented by Jagan's PPP and its mass media arms, but was not confined to it. Nevertheless, in the context of a communally divided state, the racist implications of mass media suppression were inescapable.

The attack on the mass media began initially by government purchase of the *Guyana Chronicle* and *The Graphic* (two of the four daily newspapers) between 1971 and 1973. The third of the dailies, *The Evening Post*, disappeared for financial reasons.

The remaining opposition mass media newspapers included one daily, *The Mirror* (the organ of Jagan's PPP); a weekly, *The Catholic Standard*; and several periodic sheets, such as *Dayclean*. The government feared censure by the international mass media and therefore embarked on a set of policies intended to squeeze the activities of the opposition papers so that they might seem to choke to death on their own accord. The main device to achieve this end was a new law requiring a license to import newsprint and printing equipment. The impact of this legislation was devastating. *The Mirror* was reduced to a weekly and *The Catholic Standard* to a short irregular stencil sheet. Both papers found that their applications for the required license for importing newsprint were neglected and delayed by the government bureaucracy. *The Mirror* has been forced to close periodically and even equipment sent to it by the Soviet Union was refused entry into Guyana. On one occasion, during the 1972–1973 election campaign, *The Mirror* could not operate at all because no newsprint was made available to it. By the end of the 1970s, "the *Mirror* which at one time had published 17,000 copies on weekdays and 32,000 on Sundays, was down to only 12,000 copies of a four-page Sunday edition printed on expensive bond paper" (Nascimento, 1974: 7). *The Catholic Standard*, a paper very critical of the government's human rights violations, was reduced to a ghost of its former self. Even gifts of newsprint to *The Mirror* and *The Catholic Standard* were denied entry into Guyana (Thomas, 1983: 44; Baber and Jeffrey, 1986: 122–123).

Apart from the licensing of newsprint and printing equipment importation, the government resorted to two additional measures to suppress the mass media. In 1972, a Publications and Newspaper Act required newspapers to deposit G$5,000 with the Government Registrar and to provide two sureties to guarantee similar amounts. This was justified on the basis that, in the event of a successful libel suit, fines would be paid. The first victim of this legislation was *Dayclean*, which continued publishing but refused to comply with the law. Throughout the 1970s to the present, the government would persistently sue the opposition newspapers, dragging them before the politicized courts where they would be fined exorbitant sums repeatedly. On October 4, 1974, the second measure that the government enacted to stifle opposition dissent banned any literature that was deemed "prejudicial to the defence of Guyana, public safety, or to public order" (Nascimento, 1974). To complete its control of the mass media, in 1979 the government nationalized the only radio stations, Radio Demerara and the Guyana Broadcasting Service. Justifications of the stringent controls and ownership of the mass media were twofold: national development and scarce foreign exchange. The PNC argued that national development in a socialist state required that the mass media be directed so as to mobilize the people for development purposes. The excuse of scarce foreign exchange, which was available to the government's own media outlets, was used to suffocate the opposition papers into impotence (Thomas, 1983: 44; Baber and Jeffrey, 1986: 122–123).

Thuggery, Terror, and Violence

The use of formal and informal state-sponsored thuggery, harassment, inhuman treatment, assassination, terror, and violence has become part of the repertoire of repression liberally applied to maintain the power of the PNC. PNC tactics included rigging of elections, purging of the public service of communal and ideological enemies; purification of the armed forces and police of potentially disloyal personnel; politicization of the courts; the breakdown of the legal system as a constraint on arbitrary state action; public corruption; and rape of public treasure. The consequences of these actions were the breakdown of the economy and the impoverishment of the society, with malnutrition and hunger widespread, and finally, the mass migration of a third of the population overseas (Thomas, 1983). To catalogue all that happened from the day in 1968 when the PNC seized power through electoral fraud to the present would require an enormous effort filling many tomes of human rights violation.

In the 1970s, the PNC was faced with a paradox of power. As it consolidated its control of the Parliament, the courts, the coercive forces, the public service, and the mass media, it became more insecure and became vulnerable to opposition attack. In the mid-1970s, a new organization called the Working People's Alliance (WPA), headed by historian Walter Rodney, appeared on the political scene. The WPA organized and mobilized the entire spectrum of opposition forces, including Jagan's PPP, and unleashed a fierce assault on the government. The WPA was a cross-communal organization, unlike the PPP, which, although its leader Cheddi Jagan was socialist, was based on communal support of Guyana's Indians. In confronting Burnham's PNC, the PPP merely achieved a standoff. However, Jagan did succeed in periodically bringing the PNC government to a standstill through strikes and boycotts. But the WPA was different, with a multiracial body, and above all it was led, like the PNC, by an Afro-Guyanese.

If Burnham was able to maintain the loyalty of his communal segment and to cope with Cheddi Jagan by invoking the fear of Indian domination, he had no answer for Walter Rodney. Apart from being an African like Burnham, Rodney was also a socialist with a growing reputation among Third World intellectuals for his anticapitalist radicalism. Moreover, Rodney was a dedicated activist. He was successful in organizing antigovernment strikes and demonstrations in government strongholds such as Linden, throwing the ruling regime into panic (Kwayana, 1991).

At the time of Rodney's entry into Guyana's politics in 1974, the PNC had used open physical violence against its opposition sparingly, depending on manipulating the law and the courts. But as Rodney's WPA gained strength after 1976, the PNC employed a variety of informal and violent methods against the opposition, including the assassination of Rodney and several of his colleagues.

To harass and intimidate the opposition, the government employed the "muscular" sections of the PNC as well as the police, militia, state security, and army personnel, especially where the WPA and its supporters held meetings. This would be complemented by the House of Israel, a new organization headed by Rabbi Washington, an Afro-American refugee from U.S. justice. The House of Israel gained the reputation as the thuggery and assassination arm of the government, for its open activities of intimidation and violence had never been questioned by the police. After Burnham died and Desmond Hoyte became president, the latter dismantled the House of Israel. The leader, Rabbi Washington, was sentenced to prison for manslaughter in 1986. By the time the PPP came to power in 1993, this group had been eliminated.

In using state violence against its opponents, the government appropriated the term "terrorist" to describe the opposition. Father Mike James, writing in *The Catholic Standard*, noted that arbitrary arrest and intimidation had become a norm: "In recent years, security forces have felt free to arrest persons without explanation because they happened to sympathize with an opposition party, criticize the regime or merely attend an opposition public meeting."[10] The *Bar Association Review* of Guyana had called for an investigation of the brutality and terror that persons who were arrested experienced in custody. A statement issued in 1981 by the Guyana Bar Association alleged that over 800 people had been arrested since August 20, 1981 for unspecified reasons and detained without being given adequate food or without any right to receive meals from their relatives and friends.[11]

State terror had become entrenched and pervasive as a mode of maintaining the PNC in power. In the urban areas, especially in Georgetown, the repression became cross-communal, but in the rural areas where Indians predominate, it assumed a communal form. Rape, burglary, and arbitrary arrests by the security forces had become so prevalent that most villages became places of terror. The police were viewed not as a solution but as the source of the problem. Isolated homes became a target of official search and seizure exercises, because as the economy deteriorated and inflation reduced the real salaries of the police and security forces, the need for public plunder as a source of revenue became compelling.

By the diverting of scarce resources to pay for an inordinately expanded coercive apparatus, the country became increasingly impoverished. Malnutrition; lack of elementary medical care; deterioration of public roads, schools, and other facilities; and the frequent interruption of water and electricity supplies cast the tenor of society as one in deep crisis. Along with personal security, the basic rights to employment and material necessities also became a casualty of the PNC regime. The government passed legislation restricting the right to strike and, without notice or compensation, retrenched civil servants in response to IMF behests. In these areas, the government made its own communal section the primary victim of its arbitrary actions. Not only were basic necessities expensive and beyond the reach of most Guyanese, but those who held government jobs did so without security.

NEW ELECTIONS IN 1992: PPP VICTORY

The repressive and impoverished order in Guyana was seen as essentially a creation of President Forbes Burnham, so that when he died in August 1985, many optimistically saw in the successor Hoyte regime a change for the better. Under Desmond Hoyte, there were high expectations that free and fair elections would once again be returned to the Guyanese people. This expectation was rudely frustrated when Hoyte oversaw yet another rigged election in December 1985. For a while, Hoyte was protected by the persistence of the Cold War, but when the Soviet Union under Mikhail Gorbachev moved in the direction of political liberation which eventually saw the dissolution of the Soviet empire, Hoyte's hold on his undemocratically acquired power quickly faced challenges from the United States, his external sponsor.

In a series of small concessions which accumulated a momentum of their own, the democratic process was grudgingly restored in Guyana. This culminated in the October 5, 1992 general elections, when the free franchise first won by the Guyanese in 1953 was restored.

Central to the October 5, 1992 elections was the electoral machine itself, the procedure by which political power is legitimated in democratic settings. The words "free," "fair," and "transparent" became the defining terms and the substantive feature of the elections.[12] Hoyte had argued that previous elections, in which the PNC had claimed sizeable majorities, were authentic and honest, and he had no fear of another election returning the PNC to power. It was this assertion that stood at the center of the elections: the PNC's claim that its power was always legitimately acquired. This claim was, however, to be tested in 1992 through the intervention of external observers.

PNC opponents eagerly welcomed the challenge that would place power again in the marketplace of public opinion adjudicated by an electoral process that was to be free, fair, and transparent. The opposition forces equated honest elections with the defeat of the PNC. The Hoyte-led PNC put up a brave front, arguing that the electoral process was not the issue and that allowing external observers would not alter its tenure in office. What became clear, however, as the electoral machinery was being sanitized for free elections was that the PNC did not anticipate that the sanitizing process was going to be as thorough as it turned out. Secretly, it seemed, the PNC directorate felt that it was still going to be able to fix the elections even with the presence of external observers. In this calculation it was proved wrong.

The PNC progressively lost control of the Electoral Commission, almost in its entirety, to an independent electoral machinery and the Emory University-based Carter Center, something it did not expect to happen. President Hoyte was literally cornered by his own boastful promises that the PNC had nothing to lose from free and fair elections. When this bluff was called in one rigorous challenge after another (after nearly two years of delay), when the election machinery was thoroughly sanitized, it became clear that the PNC was headed for electoral defeat and disaster. By then, it was too late.

Hoyte gambled that the PNC could still fix the elections and had underestimated the persistency of the opposition forces and the Carter Center in fastidiously insisting on such things as an acceptable voters list, externally printed ballots and externally manufactured ballot boxes, and so on. In the support for procedures to ensure free elections, the issue had become prominently internationalized and Hoyte could not easily back out of his promises for fair electoral procedures. In the end, having lost control of the electoral process, and then the elections, the PNC simultaneously convinced observers that the elections of 1968, 1973, 1980, and 1985 were all fraudulent.

The October 5, 1992 elections attracted eleven contesting parties, among which were the three most prominent ones, the PPP, the PNC, and the WPA. Both the PPP and PNC were tested at the polls before in the 1957, 1961, 1964, and 1968 elections. The WPA was never tested for its popular support in free elections. It had, however, emerged as a major visible force on the Guyanese political scene with an articulate leadership. In the 1992 elections, the PPP, PNC, and WPA sought to define the partisan contest in peculiar ways. The WPA argued that the PNC was so unpopular that the contest was really between itself and the PPP. The PNC and the PPP acted in ways that suggested that the major contestants were the PPP and PNC, and others were of little consequence. As the election campaign got under way, it became evident that in a shrinking, race-replete arena, the greatest political space was taken up by the PPP and the PNC, with the WPA charging that it was being marginalized because of the ethnic appeals of the two traditional parties. The WPA was hoping for a three-way split in the votes so that it could be strategically placed to determine the winner. Instead, it was thoroughly thrashed and reduced to an insignificant electoral force.

In 1992, the Guyanese electorate consisted of 385,000 voters. Most had never voted, since Guyanese, for the most part, had ceased to pay much attention to the ballot because of the open rigging. In 1992, however, with a close contest in the making, citizens actively cooperated in registering for the polls. The campaign for voters was remarkably peaceful. Unlike previous elections, where the campaign for votes relied almost exclusively on party organization and mobilization, in 1992 the major parties relied heavily on mass media advertisements to communicate their message. The two major parties, the PPP and the PNC, hired professional advertisement firms from overseas to craft their appeals to the electorate. Whether this made any difference in the outcome, given the role of race in determining voter preference, is very doubtful. Despite the relatively low-keyed tenor of the elections, which were punctuated by only sporadic acts of violence, the momentous nature of the elections was appreciated by all citizens and observers. It was clear that should a change of government eventuate, a major watershed would be witnessed in Guyana and the Caribbean. The PNC was finally evicted from office and it seemed that a new era of change was at hand in Guyana.

CONCLUSION

Under the Burnham regime, an atmosphere of repression pervaded Guyana. Basic human rights, ranging from political dimensions (the vote, fair trial, etc.) to economic rights (employment, basic material needs) and social rights (racial discrimination), were extensively denied, especially to political opponents. As the main opposition came from a communal enemy, the repression assumed the predominant form of racism in a fascistic regime. In the end, political adversaries of all races faced the brunt of the regime's ire.

More general insights can be adduced from the Guyana case in relation to human rights and the state. The evidence suggests that the postcolonial state, claiming the mantle of socialist inspiration, can become an instrument of domination by an autocrat. The rhetoric of socialist deliverance from oppression and poverty can be resiliently manipulated to support the narrow needs of personal and party ambition. In multiethnic states, it is clear that political compromise over contending communal interests is vital for the very survival of the state. In Sri Lanka, Lebanon, Guyana, and elsewhere in the Third World, the tension, between the conflicting claims of communal identity on one hand and cross-communal economic equity on the other, must be reconciled by the state lest the very fabric of the society be torn asunder in perpetual civil war. The state can either adjudicate and survive, or oppress and perish.

NOTES

1. "The Cooperative Way in British Guiana," *PAC Bulletin* (November 6, 1940): 2.

2. "Aims and Programmes of the People's Progressive Party," *Thunder*, vol. 1, no. 4 (April 1950): 6–7.

3. *Suspension of the Constitution* (London: HMSO, Cmdn. 8980, 1953); see also Cheddi Jagan, *Forbidden Freedom* (New York: International Publishers, 1953).

4. See "Money Being Spent in Majority Party's Stronghold," *New Nation* (January 24, 1959): 1; see also Ralph R. Premdas, "Competitive Party Organizations and Political Integration in a Racially Fragmented State: The Case of Guyana," *Caribbean Studies*, vol. 12, no. 4 (January 1973): 5–35.

5. See Cynthia Enloe, "Civilian Control of the Military: Implications in the Plural Societies of Guyana and Malaysia," in *Civilian Control of the Military*, ed. C. Welch (Albany, NY: SUNY Press, 1976): 65–96.

6. See *Sunday Times* (London) (November 5, 1968): 20; Adrian Mitchell, "Jagan and Burnham: It's Polling Day Tomorrow: Has Guyana's Election Been Already Decided in Britain," *Sunday Times* (December 15, 1968): 25.

7. Janet Jagan, *Army Intervention in the 1973 Elections in Guyana* (Georgetown: New Guiana Co., 1973).

8. See *Guyana: Fraudulent Revolution* (London: Latin American Bureau, 1984): 75–76.

9. See *Something to Remember*, Report of the International Team of Observers at the Elections of Guyana (London, 1980).

10. *The Catholic Standard* (October 24, 1982): 1.

11. "Lawyers Call for an Investigation into Police Brutality," *Guyana Update* (London) (September–October, 1984): 3.

12. For a full account of the 1992 elections, see R. Premdas, "Guyana: The Critical Elections of 1992 and a Regime Change," *Caribbean Affairs* vol.6, no. 2 (January–March 1993): 111–140.

4

Trinidad and Tobago: Democracy, Nationalism, and the Construction of Racial Identity

Percy C. Hintzen

The Republic of Trinidad and Tobago (hereafter Trinidad) is a multiracial society. Slightly over 56 percent of its population is either of black or mixed racial origin. East Indians comprise slightly more than 40 percent of the country's population and there are small groups of whites and Chinese (less than 2% for each group).[1] Trinidad gained its political independence from Britain in 1962. Racial mobilization came to characterize political organization in the period immediately leading up to the departure of the British. The result was the coming to power of a black-dominated political party relying upon racial support from the black and colored populations. During the late 1970s and the entire 1980s, political and economic events produced conditions that acted, eventually, to destroy the solid racial support that the ruling party enjoyed, resulting in its eventual loss of power (see Hintzen, 1989a: passim).

This chapter examines the activation of racial and social identities in the organization of democratic practice in Trinidadian politics. It also shows how the strategy employed for ensuring political domination contributed, in a profound way, to the shaping and reformulation of relations among contingent racially defined groupings in terms of their "social affinities and antipathies" (Segal, 1992). Finally, it analyzes how "racial identity," however constructed, becomes politically salient. The point to be emphasized is that social identity and collective membership in idiomatically identified social categories do not automatically determine behavior. Their relevance in this regard is contextual and must be determined and explained.

CONCEPTUAL FRAMEWORK

Racial and ethnic categories and identities occupy center stage in analyses of almost all aspects of Trinidadian society, particularly its political organization. Historically, contingent social groupings, defined, perceived, and identified idiomatically in racial terms, have been at the root of social organization and regulation of Trinidadian society. This has led to the identification of the twin-island republic as multiracial.

Most analysts of Trinidadian society treat the boundaries separating its racially defined social groupings as historically unchanging. From this perspective, collective membership in these social groupings is seen to be transhistorical and unchanging. Accordingly, the particular circumstances of the introduction of members of these ethnic or racial "groups" to this ex-colony of Britain (and before that Spain), the history of their collective participation in Trinidadian society, and the nature and type of their resources and interests to be protected and enhanced, are considered to have placed racial groups in competition with each other. Such competition, it is argued, has been for the acquisition and protection of values, among which are included political power and economic resources.

The conceptual framework employed by Daniel Segal (1992) in the analysis of race and color in Trinidad is highly relevant to the understanding of democratic practice in that twin-island republic. This chapter relies heavily on this framework, employing as it does the social constructionist approach. The organization of social behavior is viewed in terms of the historical production of social groupings and their reproduction and reformulation over time. These historically contingent groupings appear as systems of representation and are identified idiomatically. Thus, the "meanings" of these groupings and the identities associated with them are contained and transmitted in "semiotic systems which presuppose and affirm regulating typifications and stereotypes" (Segal, 1992: 82). It is not merely the social groupings themselves that are products of historical construction, but the relations among them which "shape social affinities and antipathies" (ibid.: 81).

In the historical process of transition, contingent groupings, idiomatically identified in racial terms, came to be differentially organized for mobilization. In the process, boundaries and idiomatic identities were changed and the latter became the most salient determinant of political support. The salience of these reformulated social groupings and of the ability to regulate relations among them had to do with their significance in the competition for political power and for the preservation and enhancement of economic interests (accumulation).

Segal's approach focuses upon racial lexicons as a basis of understanding the "social pragmatics of racial idioms." In this case, social pragmatics pertain to the strategic ascendance of a reconstituted elite to a position of political domination. The focus of my approach is on the organization of democratic practice rather than on the construction of racial categories and identities, as is Segal's. In its political context, the construction of social phenomena is seen to be directly related to competition for power, resources, and privilege, and for control of the definition of prestige. At the same time, it is also directly related to the struggle against exclusion from or against limited access to desired values (political, social, economic, or otherwise). The two are opposite sides of the same coin in a relationship that is dialectical.

Political competition, as defined above, occurs among historically contingent groupings socially constructed in the same manner outlined for racial categories. However, an analytic distinction must be made between these groupings, whose relationships pertain to political competition, and those employing the lexicon of race. Even though, in some instances, the two may appear to be coincident, the relationship between them is extremely complex. Organization for political competition is, in the final analysis, instrumental: that is, directed toward the achievement of objectively identifiable ends. Competing political groupings may exploit and influence social categories and identities that have not, previously, figured in political organization. How this is done relates to the strategic demands of a particular historical moment. Racially constructed categories and identities, and the relations among these categories, can become part of this strategic equation. In the process, boundaries and relationships may become reconstructed. It is in this manner that racial groupings can become the basis for the organization of political relations.

The approach outlined above is fundamentally different from the more conventional notion of racial competition for political power. Such competition is implied in the concepts "ethnic politics," "political ethnicity," and the like. The approach taken in this chapter implies that relations between and among racially defined contingent groupings are regulated, as are the idiomatic definitions of the groupings themselves. Since there is "no inherent affinity between people sharing a common racial identity" (Segal, 1992: 81), it is unlikely that persons who share such an identity can have common objective political interests. Hence, organization for political competition with other racial groupings becomes highly unlikely, if not impossible.

Political organization in Trinidad cannot, therefore, be understood in terms of ethnic political competition. Rather, the reconstruction of racial identity and racial categories became strategically activated to serve the political interests of a newly emergent elite during the period of transition from colonialism to independence. This strategic activation was integrally linked to the phenomenon of nationalist mobilization. Hence, the "social pragmatics of racial idioms" (ibid.: 82), as they pertained to the political context, must be explained with reference to the formation of the nationalist movement.

DECOLONIZATION AND THE ACTIVATION OF RACIAL IDENTITY

The nationalist movement was born and nurtured in a twentieth-century tide of rising expectations among urban wage laborers frustrated by the structure of organization of the colonial political economy. It was directed at efforts aimed at the retention of more of the social surplus within the class grouping of wage laborers. In the second decade of the century, these frustrations, becoming manifest in sporadic episodes of labor unrest, led to the formation of a unified labor movement demanding better wages, improved conditions of work, and the establishment of formal collective bargaining procedures (see Ryan, 1972: 28–45; Oxaal, 1968: 80–95).

Quickly, labor organization came to be reformulated as educated and professional members of the colonized population took over positions of leadership. In the process, the new leaders formalized union organization and changed its political demands to reflect their own interests in political reform. By the 1930s, these leaders were using labor mobilization to back demands for more representative government, for the sharing of political power between colonial and local leaders, and for a shift of political control away from the British Colonial Office and its colonial representatives to "representative" institutions. In other words, with the incorporation of the educated and professional elites into labor organizations, the latter became transformed into protonationalist political movements (Ryan, 1972: 28–45; Oxaal, 1968: 80–95).

Widespread labor riots during the latter part of the 1930s forced Britain to agree to the shift to more "representative" government. By 1946, Britain had begun the introduction of universal adult suffrage in Trinidad and the full participation of elected locals in the political affairs of the colony (Hintzen, 1989a: 30–31).

The British Colonial Office made it clear (as it did in most British colonies) that the postwar constitutional changes were preludes to the granting of full independence. This was to come after a tutelary period, during which the terms of the transition were to be worked out. Britain's commitment to independence had a profound effect upon the reproduction of racial identity and the reformulation of social relations among racially defined social groupings. They gave political salience to both as political mobilization shifted to appeals to reformulated racial identities.

Highly organized political parties emerged in the 1950s led by black and colored intellectual and professional elites, and by East Indian and white businessmen and professional elites. These parties organized major segments of the population by appealing to reformulated racial identities. The shift away from labor organization became evident immediately with the introduction of adult suffrage in 1946. In response, the Peoples Democratic Party (PDP) was formed in the early 1950s by a group of East Indian businessmen. These businessmen, in control of the largest, predominantly East Indian sugar workers union and of Hindu religious organizations, used such control to develop relations of affinity between East Indian workers and agricultural peasants, on the one hand, and East Indian business and professional elites, on the other. In the process, East Indian identity, and more purposefully, "Hindu" identity, became politically salient.

A much more profound reformulation of black identity was occurring. Black and colored intellectuals and professionals began to fashion an ideology of creole nationalism in a manner that identified this form of nationalism with Afro-Trinidadian culture (see Yelvington, 1992: 13). The organization of the colored and mixed population within the nationalist movement and the latter's "Afro-Trinidadian" racial designation created the conditions for reformulation of "black" identity. Now, coloreds (descendants of black-white unions) and dooglas (descendants of black-East Indian unions) were included in the black social grouping, if only for political purposes.

There was a certain ambiguity in the reformulated "nationalist" movement. The black and colored intellectual and professional leaders of the movement, now politically organized in the Peoples National Movement (PNM) political party, insisted that it was "multiracial." They included a few East Indians in leadership positions of the party to support their contention. At the same time, cultural symbols identified with the black population became the basis of their political strategy. They attacked "white" domination of the economy, and alluded to East Indians as "a recalcitrant and hostile minority" (cf. Yelvington, 1992: 13, citing Ryan, 1972). As a result, the PNM came to be perceived, almost universally, as a "black" party (see among others Ryan, 1972; Yelvington, 1992; Oxaal, 1968).

Indeed, the nationalist movement was neither "nationalist" (i.e., all-encompassing) nor "black." Rather, it constituted the strategic organization of social relations, reformulated as they were, for the political ends of a noncapitalist and nonfarming, educated, bureaucratic, and professional elite reconstituted into a single aggregated interest group. Its instrumental aim was the capturing of control of the executive, legislative, and bureaucratic arms of the postcolonial state. That the Peoples National Movement, formed in 1956, appealed to a reconstructed "black" identity is merely coincidental and related to the historical pattern of the construction, reproduction, and reformulation of racial identity, coupled with the preponderance of blacks and coloreds within the social grouping of the ascendant elites whose interests it served.

Whites and "near whites" (light-complexioned coloreds) had seen their own opportunity for political power dashed in the throes of majoritarian politics, of the reformulation of racial identities, and of the growing political salience of the latter. By 1950, the relationship between an all-inclusive creole white population and the colonizers had become quite strong. A new constitution, making five ministerial portfolios available to elected local politicians, was interpreted and implemented by the governor in such a manner as to support the interests of this newly reconstituted "white" racial grouping. With an extension of representative government, white creole politicians, representing the interests of the business and planter elite, and mobilizing the white creole population, saw their chances for control of a postcolonial state disappearing rapidly (Hintzen, 1989a: 39–41; Ryan, 1972: 86–96). These business elites organized around a newly formed Political Progress Group (PPG) making appeals to the white creole racial grouping.

By the 1950s, the social grouping of white creoles had, certainly, become much more solid in the face of racial reconstruction of contingent social groupings, and the salience of the latter for the organization of political relations. Included among the white creoles, for political purposes, was the "near white" social grouping of fair-complexioned coloreds. It was not too long for this "near white" grouping to be incorporated with creole whites into the reformulated category of "Trinidad white" (see Segal, 1992: 87–89).

Thus, the political interests being served by the political parties that were making racial appeals to the reconstituted "black," "Hindu," and "white creole" parties became pellucidly obvious. The PPG in Trinidad initially opposed independence, clearly fearing that the interests of the business and planter sectors of the economy would be jeopardized if the racially based PNM came to power. So did the PDP for much the same reason. Ostensibly, the reason proffered for the development of enmity with the political organizations of blacks and coloreds was the support of the latter for independence in a federation with the rest of the overwhelmingly black British West Indies. Such a federation, it was argued, had the potential of making "East Indians" quite an insignificant minority.

The issue of federation was critical in the reformulation of political relations among racial groupings. The Butler Party, founded and led by Uriah Butler, had become by 1950 the single largest political organization in the country. It did so through its reliance on the vote of black and East Indian wage laborers and small-scale cultivators. The party, influenced somewhat by Garveyism, employed an antiwhite, anticolonial rhetoric. By the 1950s, the party had lost most of its East Indian support over the issue of federation (see Gomes, 1954: 690, cited in Ryan, 1972: 100).

The PNM won general elections held in 1956 by capturing thirteen out of twenty-four elective seats. The PDP managed to capture only five seats, all in rural electoral constituencies where East Indians enjoyed the overwhelming majority (Ryan, 1972: 100). In the face of this defeat, the PDP merged with the political representatives of the white business and planter elite to form a Democratic Labor Party (DLP). This was a strategic reorganization aimed at ousting the PNM from power. The conjoining of the two parties was quite natural given the rooting of their political interests in a common socioeconomic base. As businessmen, professionals, and planters, the East Indians and white leaders of the new party were opposed to any form of statist expansion. This placed them in strict political opposition to the predominantly black and colored, educated, noncapitalist, and nonplanter elite. The interests of the latter were best served by just such an expansion, concentrated as they were in the public sector.

The strategy of the PNM for regulating social relations among contingent groupings proceeded along two tracks. It continued its efforts to reconstitute black political identity. Increasingly, however, the focus of antipathetic relations came to be the Hindus. So successful was this strategy that, by the 1961 elections, the last before independence, the party was able to capture the votes of black oilfield workers and rural cultivators, most of whom had voted for the Butler Party and a Trinidad Labor Party in 1956. At the same time, the party began to accommodate and to make compromises with the country's business interests. It got rid of its radical wing, compromised with the United States over the presence of a military base on Trinidadian shores, repudiated communism, declared itself procapitalist and pro-West, and positioned white businessmen in advisory positions in government. In exchange, Britain agreed to a constitution that fixed electoral boundaries in a manner that was extremely favorable to the party. In 1961, helped by this favorable drawing of these electoral boundaries, the party was able to win in twenty of the twenty-nine constituencies despite capturing a mere 48 percent of the popular vote (see Hintzen, 1989a: 58–63; Ryan, 1972: 197–203; and *Report on the General Election*, 1961).

THE POSTINDEPENDENCE PERIOD: RACIAL POLITICS, PATRONAGE, AND DEMOCRATIC PRACTICE

With independence, the PNM's strategy of accommodation with business and planters continued. At the same time, it continued to ensure that the interests of workers in the public sector (professionals, managers, and skilled and technical labor) were protected and expanded. The two goals were accomplished through the development of "mixed-economy" capitalism which allowed for growth in the public sector as well as for state-generated and -supported private sector expansion. This approach had consequences for the organization of the elite social grouping. The group of businessmen and large cultivators came to be included within the boundaries of these elite groupings, now reconstituted into a solid interest-based political grouping.

Reformulation of Ethnic Identities

During the 1960s there was significant reformulation of ethnic identities as these pertained to political behavior. These reformulations were accompanied by significant changes in the political relations among the racially defined social groupings. The solid "East Indian" social grouping became reproduced in the form of a rural Hindu category. The "urban bias" of the PNM, and its neglect

of small-scale agriculture and of the East Indian sugar constituencies, contributed significantly to this reformulation. The strategic actions of a Hindu
leadership who employed increasingly anticreole rhetoric further consolidated
this change, as ethnic identity gained increasing sway in the politics of this
reconstituted social grouping.

Much the same process of reformulation was going on among black wage
laborers, even though much less perceptibly. Economic crisis became the
trigger for the reformulation of racial identity, as it pertained to politics. In 1965,
black workers joined with East Indian sugar workers in a campaign of strikes
and violence against the PNM government. The party retaliated coercively and
by passing an Industrialization Stabilization Act that was aimed at preventing
worker mobilization (see the Industrialization Stabilization Act, 1965). In the
late 1960s, the effects of an economic downturn were being felt, particularly in
the oil industry with its predominance of black oilworkers. There was a resultant
escalation of black worker unemployment and underemployment. All of these
had implications for the former affinity between black workers and the PNM.
The result was a transformation of political organization. Such a transformation
was heralded by a reformulation of black identity, especially as it related to
political behavior. This reformulated identity became the basis of organization
for mass revolt among the country's urban black workers and students, and for
a rebellion in the predominantly black army. The rallying cry of the revolt and
rebellion was "Black Power." Up to 1973, the government had to engage in a
coercive campaign to combat serious challenges from a black guerilla movement which seemed to enjoy much sympathy within the black lower-class
population. The PNM barely managed to survive these challenges to its power.

During the 1960s, the organization of social groupings employing racial
idioms came to be confined, increasingly, to the urban and rural working class,
and small farmers. This stemmed from a combination of the reality of divergent
socioeconomic interests, the effects of the political strategies of competing
elites in shaping social antipathies, and cultural differences that had become
emphasized in the nationalist discourse. Since Trinidadian nationalism was
identified with Afro-Creole culture, Hindus found themselves outside of the
boundaries of Trinidadian identity.

The idiom of nationalism had an opposite effect upon the planters, businessmen, state bureaucrats, professionals, managers, clerical workers, and skilled
and technical workers. The ideology of creole nationalism reflected the collective histories of these economic groupings and their dependents.

The signifying distinction of "creole white" does convey, semiotically, the
notion of an existing relationship between the white population and Afro-Trinidadian cultural forms. Thus, creole nationalism was not anathema to white
identity. The history of East Indian creolization was much more recent. The
adoption of Christianity is one indicator of such creolization, urbanization is
another, and education a third. Higher education and urbanization are very much

characteristic of East Indians in occupational categories that place them in the social grouping of the ascendant elite. Moreover, there is an association between Christian conversion, urbanization, and postprimary education. In other words, urbanized, Christianized, educated East Indians were most likely to be creolized and, as a result, more predisposed to identify with Trinidadian nationalism. The political relations of the Muslim grouping were conditioned more by religious differences with Hindus and the historical emergence of Hindu identity. The salience of this emergence for political behavior, and the fact of this emergence, left the Muslims alienated from the "East Indian" party. This was reinforced by the greater propensity of Muslims to become urbanized and by the endogamous nature of Hindu social relations, particularly marriage (see Clarke, 1992). Members of the Muslim social grouping were, as a result, much more likely to develop affinity and supportive relations with the PNM. Hence, despite the "black" identity of the PNM, the party was able to secure the participation, support, and affinity of white creoles, Muslim and Christian East Indians, and creolized Hindus. In turn, members of these racial groupings came to be highly involved in party and government affairs, and to secure a share of government appointments.

In sum, during the 1960s, the various segments of what is conventionally considered to be the middle and upper classes had become reconstituted into a solid social grouping of elites, at least for political purposes. Politically salient groupings within the lower classes continued to be racially signified. Given the majoritarian demands of democratic organization, the continued power of the PNM required strategic incorporation of either one or the other of the major racially designated sociopolitical groupings.

By the end of the 1960s, there was a growing antipathy developing between the government and the social grouping of the black working class (see Hintzen, 1981: 265–266). Antigovernment mobilization and rebellion in the early 1970s forced the government to accommodate the interests of the black working class in its policies. It did so through the development of a system of racial patronage financed by a levy on the incomes of the ascendant elite (see Hintzen, 1989a: 73–74). The program of patronage was expanded significantly when state revenues experienced a windfall bonanza after dramatic increases in the prices of petroleum exports following the 1973 Middle East war. Subsequently, the PNM government embarked on an orgy of spending directed at the accumulative interests of the elites as well as the social grouping of the black working class (see Hintzen, 1989a: 73–77). Government policy continued to have a regulating effect upon the political relationship between the two racially defined sociopolitical groupings of blacks and Hindus, and this continued to reinforce the relations of affinity and support between the PNM and the former. The persistence of enmity was also sustained, partially, by continued use of the racial idiom in political appeals for support.

By the mid-1970s, radical intellectuals and union leaders were beginning to see the possibilities offered by developing relations of affinity and support with the Hindu sociopolitical grouping. These elites were buoyed by the exhibited weakness of the PNM during the disturbances of the early 1970s. Many had participated in anti-PNM mobilization. Accordingly, a United Labour Front (ULF) was formed in 1976 by an alliance of the radical elite with the Hindu Maha Saba. In 1977, a more moderate ULF, purged of its more radical members, entered into a loose arrangement with two opposition parties. One, the Democratic Action Congress (DAC), had its support organized within the black population of Tobago. The island was purposely neglected in PNM policy after its political representative had pulled out of the party in support of demonstrators in the 1970 rebellion. The second party, Tapia, was headed by a black moderate intellectual who had begun to articulate concerns about the policies of the ruling party. This alliance presaged the beginnings of a new reformulation of the relations among racially defined contingent social groupings, if not of the contingent social groupings themselves.

Government Loss of Elite Support

Support from the Hindus was slowly beginning to figure in development of the strategic realignments of the political relations of the ascendant elite. This had to do with a growing perception that the ascendant elite's interests were no longer represented by the PNM. Enormous budgetary and foreign exchange surpluses derived from escalating oil prices after 1973 allowed the government to continue to underwrite the accumulative interests of the elite, while supporting the black lower class through an enormous patronage largesse. Things began to change as early as 1978, when the economy began to experience a significant decline in export earnings from petroleum production. Between that year and 1981 the real value added of the petroleum sector dropped precipitously amid fears that fiscal and foreign exchange surpluses accumulated since 1973 were in danger of disappearing. In 1982, government revenues went into deficit for the first time since 1973. There was considerable concern for the economic future as public debt began to escalate (see Hintzen, 1989a: 179–181; Bobb, 1983: 94; *Trinidad Guardian*, June 30, 1983: 3). The elite grouping began to place blame squarely on state distribution of patronage and upon the government policy of energy-intensive industrialization. Patronage, of course, was related to the government's efforts to cater to the interests of the black working class. The beneficiary of the industrialization policy was popularly perceived to be foreign business. Thus, the government was coming to be viewed, increasingly, as acting against the interests of the very elite social grouping out of which it emerged.

There was some effort on the part of the government to counter the effects of the erosion of strategic elite support. By the end of the 1970s it had begun to extend the patronage largesse to rural Hindus. This attempt at the reformulation of strategic political relations paid some initial dividends. In 1981, for the first time, the party was able to make inroads in rural East Indian constituencies. It also managed to retain enough support from those social groupings that formed its original support base to win twenty-six seats in a thirty-six-member Parliament. In the 1981 elections, the party was challenged by a ULF/DAC/Tapia "National Alliance" and by a new party, the Organization for National Reconstruction (ONR). The formation of the latter was the first clear and unambiguous demonstration that the professional and business elite no longer saw its interests represented by the PNM. The inroads that the ONR and the National Alliance made in "middle" and "upper" class urban constituencies was significant in absolute terms, but not enough, separately, to produce a PNM defeat. Nonetheless, the indications were clear. The reformulation of political relations was quite threatening to the party's continued ability to hold on to power. Its support base was becoming confined, increasingly, to the social grouping of the black Trinidadian (as opposed to Tobagonian) working class. It was to the latter's interest which it now catered through an elaborate system of patronage.

The reformulation of political relations by the elite social grouping was strategically organized to accomplish precisely what the PNM had in the 1960s. The goal of such reformulation was to ensure that the political interests of this elite continued to be served by the state. In the new reformulation, however, the black working class was to be left out of the strategic equation. Political affinities were to be developed with the rural Hindu social grouping and the blacks in Tobago. By 1983, this strategic formula was realized in the formation of a loose coalition that called itself The Accommodation. Its effectiveness was tested in local government elections held that same year. The result was a resounding defeat for the PNM, with The Accommodation capturing 54.07 percent of the popular vote to the PNM's 39.11 percent (Ryan, 1989: 43–45). The ruling party lost control of all but three urban municipalities and one county council, winning fifty-four local government seats to the opposition's sixty-six.

The success of The Accommodation led to formalization of the coalition in the formation of a National Alliance for Reconstruction (NAR). This new party contested general elections in 1986. In its campaign, not only was the appeal to race deemphasized, but there was a frontal assault on "racial politics." This strategy exemplified the new party's efforts to distance itself from the PNM by reformulating the relations of enmity between the creolized elite social grouping and the rural Hindus to those of affinity. At the same time, the party retained its affinity with the black social grouping in Tobago.

The NAR won a landslide victory, capturing thirty-three of the thirty-six parliamentary seats and 67 percent of the popular vote, thus ending the thirty-year rule of the PNM. The defeat was a clear demonstration of the isolation of the PNM from its original elite base. The latter's victories came in the three black working class constituencies (see Ryan, 1989: 85).

The PNM fell victim to its very successes in creating conditions for upward mobility of the black working class into the occupational groupings of the reconstituted elite. Massive earnings from oil-generated wealth between 1973–1981 were pumped into the economy in ways that decidedly benefited the black lower class (at the expense of the East Indian rural lower class). Opportunities in government services, business, and the professions, and from an enormous, racially rooted system of patronage, catapulted many blacks into the higher socioeconomic grouping. When the economic boom collapsed, these blacks responded in defense of their newly acquired interests by supporting the NAR opposition.

In effect, the NAR was nothing more than a reconstituted PNM, in terms of the political interests which it represented. It employed a different strategic formula in its relations with politically salient racial groupings. Affinity with the black working class was jettisoned and replaced by affinity with rural Hindus.

Once the NAR came to power, the fragility of this formula became evident. Unlike the PNM, in its relationship with the black working class, its leaders refused to accommodate the Hindu leadership, nor did they make any effort to cater to the interests of the rural Hindu population. The political leaders of the former ULF became increasingly marginalized in government. This produced a split in the ruling party. In 1988, five members of Parliament, all former members of the ULF, were suspended from the ruling party. Included among them were four ministers, one of whom was Basdeo Panday, deputy prime minister and former ULF leader. The five proceeded to form a political caucus group known by its acronym, CLUB 88. Three of the five, including Panday, were subsequently expelled from the NAR. The expulsion left the NAR without its majoritarian base of support.

All this occurred during a period of rapid economic decline that had precipitated intervention in the economy by international financial institutions. In 1988, the NAR government was forced to approach the IMF for assistance. Economic policy came to be dictated by an IMF-imposed regimen of structural adjustment. This was a prerequisite for the fund's blessing of and support for a program of debt rescheduling by its international creditors.

In the 1980s, the ruling party was forced, among other things, to embark on two rounds of devaluation, to cut back significantly on public spending, to divest itself of public assets, to abandon state-funded projects (particularly those in the energy-intensive sector), to cut public sector salaries, to retrench public sector workers, to curtail financial support for the private sector, to cut back significantly on patronage, to eliminate subsidies, and to increase utility rates. As a result, real incomes plummeted, unemployment increased phenomenally, and the level of poverty increased. The economy had moved into severe recession (see Ryan, 1989: 318–342).

With the intervention of the IMF, the government had lost much of its control of the economy to international financial institutions. It was in no position to serve the political interests of the elite group which it represented. This compounded the problem caused by the departure of its rural Hindu supporters.

A Crisis of Legitimacy

By 1990, the government was facing an absolute crisis of legitimacy. On July 27, 1990, a group of Afro-Muslims (known as the Muslimeen), whose numbers were less than 300, exploded a bomb in the national police headquarters, invaded Parliament, and took the prime minister, seven cabinet ministers, and a number of parliamentarians hostage. This precipitated a total breakdown of law and order in the capital city and its environs, and a near demobilization of the police force. The weakened regime was forced into negotiations with the rebels. The general attitude of most segments of the population was to support neither the rebels nor the ruling party. Once the police force was remobilized, some of its actions tended to indicate efforts to use the occasion to get rid of both. In this climate, the government agreed to the granting of amnesty, which it attempted to ignore, once the rebels surrendered when expected support from the population failed to materialize. The legality of the agreement was eventually upheld by the courts and the rebels were eventually freed unpunished (see Ryan, 1991: passim).

The black Muslimeen, without any discernable support from any segment of the population, was nonetheless able to exploit disenchantment and the crisis of legitimacy in the country to organize a bid to oust the government from power. Its efforts almost succeeded, helped by a seeming initial reluctance on the part of the military and police to intervene in support of the government. The police had, at the time of the attempted coup, been engaged in acrimonious labor negotiations with the ruling party. Its membership had suffered significant cutbacks in wages while work conditions were deteriorating badly. The force had lost much of its prestige and esteem. Its desire to see the regime out of office was matched only by its unwillingness to allow the Muslimeen to take power.

What the events of the attempted takeover indicated was that the NAR had lost its ability to control politically salient social relations. The consequence, when combined with the desertion of the elite over its failure to represent and protect the latter's interests, was political isolation. The NAR had become the instrument of international financial institutions. Many of its efforts were confined to creating the conditions for debt servicing through a program of structural adjustment.

The social grouping that state policy consistently and persistently favored during the entire period of the NAR government was the strategically unimportant blacks in Tobago, the sister island, which had been allocated only two of the thirty-six parliamentary seats. The NAR had reversed a PNM policy of neglect. It committed state expenditure to the development of infrastructure for the expansion of the tourist industry on the island. This policy did not come without costs. Perceptions by "Trinidadians" of a policy bias toward "Tobagonians" reinforced animosities that had begun to emerge during the rule of the PNM.

Elections were held in 1992 and the NAR was defeated in every constituency but the two in Tobago. The elections signaled a reversion to the pattern of the 1960s in the organization of political relations among social groupings. The elite social grouping returned to the fold of the PNM, which continued to use the idiom of race to appeal to the black working class. The political organization of the rural Hindus returned to its former exclusivity. Hindu elite interests came to be represented by a new party, the United National Congress (UNC), that had developed out of CLUB 88. That party won all the rural East Indian constituencies.

BROADER IMPLICATIONS

The conceptual debate over race and its distinctiveness from other categorizations of human beings has served to divert attention away from the perceptive foresight of W. E. B. Du Bois that "the problem of the twentieth century (will be) the problem of the color line" (Du Bois, 1949). The fact that he was referring to the racial division between whites and nonwhites does not detract from his amazing prescience. For the twentieth century, race has, indeed, become "the major preoccupation of mankind" (Segal, 1967: 1) prompting one author to proffer that "today, transcending everything (including even the nuclear threat) there is the confrontation between the races" (Tinker, 1977: 134–135). My only contribution to this debate will be to adhere to the advice of Paul G. Lauren (1988: 3) and consider a "racial factor" to be present "when one group of people, united by their own perception of inherited and distinctive racial qualities, are set apart from another group with (supposedly) separate inherited and distinctive racial qualities." In other words, the differences between or among the groups have to be perceived and defined in racial terms. The concern of this chapter, however, has been with much more than racial perceptions. Rather, it is with how social groupings, organized according to such perceptions, become organized in political behavior.

An almost universal feature of the post–World War II era in underdeveloped countries is the historical emergence of an ascendant grouping of white collar clerical, bureaucratic, professional, and intellectual elites who own neither capital nor land, and who do not constitute a peasantry. This elite is distinguished by its Western education, the basis for the upward mobility and ascending social status of its members.[2] Political leaders coming from and representing this social grouping have managed to erect and institutionalize systems of organization that serve its exclusive accumulative and power (political) interests. They have done so by regulating the relations of politically strategic social groupings. Regulation is achieved by reformulating the boundaries of such social groupings and by making politically salient the signifying idiom of identity.

Those included in these social categories also contribute to their construction and reformulation. They do so by being perpetually engaged in a struggle against the limitations imposed by the boundaries of their own social grouping and by the regulation of their social relations with other groupings. It is strategic regulation on the one hand, and struggle against its limitations and impediments on the other, that result in the ongoing process of historical emergence, reproduction, and reformulation. The process is, invariably, political.

In Trinidad, such strategic regulation and struggle were conducted within the context of the majoritarian demands of democratic political organization. Elites were not the only beneficiaries. Lower-class Afro-Trinidadians, for example, were able to reformulate themselves in opposition to a newly emergent elite. This reformulation forced the regime to create conditions for the upward mobility of its members. Black Tobagonians were able to exploit alliances with the regime to secure resources for economic growth.

CONCLUSION

What this chapter demonstrates is how democratic organization can be manipulated in the service of the interest of a dominant social grouping. In Trinidad, strategic manipulation came to be related to reconstruction and reformulation of racial and socioeconomic groupings over time. The regulation of relations among social groupings is one basis of domination. In Trinidad, the idiom of class proved quite important in the challenges of the ascendant elite to colonial rule. With the transition to independence, politically salient social constructions changed from class to racial groupings.

The conclusion to be drawn from this chapter is that the assumptions that inform notions of racial competition in political relations are incorrect. The construction of social groupings employing the idiom of race is, invariably, related to strategies of regulation for domination and control. Trinidad has been characterized by the construction, reproduction, and reformulation of racially defined groupings. The introduction of these groupings in the political context has been associated with the historical emergence and political ascendance of an elite social grouping of bureaucrats, professionals, managers, and intellectuals. Eventually the grouping came to include businessmen and large-scale farmers. Its political ascendance had to do with its ability to strategically regulate affinities and antipathies among racial groupings whose boundaries were constantly changing. The importance of racially defined social groupings for political organization was the role these groupings played in creating and sustaining the conditions for political domination. This was irrespective of the democratic nature of political organization.

NOTES

1. These figures are taken from the 1980 population census reported in the *Population Census of the Commonwealth Caribbean* (Mona, Jamaica: Census Research Programme, University of the West Indies, 1980).

2. See Harris (1986: 171–179) for a discussion of the characteristics of this reconstructed social grouping.

5

Barbados: Democracy at the Crossroads

Neville Duncan

Barbados is, today, a relatively peaceful society. There is a fairly decent level of general education.[1] There is a reasonably good network of social welfare services.[2] The housing stock, which is respectable, is constantly being upgraded. The income distribution gap between rich and poor, though considerable, is less than is the case for most Anglophone Caribbean states. There are fairly modern facilities and structures and little overt evidence of abject poverty.[3] This has been achieved on the basis of a low-skilled commercial economy supported by tourism (Watson, 1986b).

Full internal self-government, and then formal independence, created a situation in which the new political managers of the state provided tremendous new opportunities for the old planter-mercantile classes, which were best placed to take disproportionate economic advantage of state-supported and state-sponsored activities. New space was created for well-placed members of the majority population in the burgeoning public and private bureaucracies, in the "preferred professions," and in tourism and manufacturing. At no time did any of this challenge the hegemonic economic rule/dominance of the old planter-mercantile elite which still controls the bulk of wealth in Barbados.[4] Such space has contracted considerably and, in addition, the number of persons knocking on the door of opportunity has increased geometrically. The 1991–1993 IMF and subsequent World Bank programs will, predictably, ensure further reduced opportunities for the mass of the population.

The basic thesis of this chapter is that Barbados is presently a society in crisis and is at a major decision point along its political development trajectory. This thesis is fully assessed in order to establish the options and identify the best model to pursue in order to strengthen and widen democracy. The process of party consolidation in Barbados is examined to demonstrate that, in terms of a liberal democratic framework, the country had a most creditable performance. The economic performance of Barbados is briefly reviewed in order to identify political consequences of fiscal and financial decisions. Contemporary political-economic developments are examined in order to reflect on the major political developments and transitions which have occurred. Current issues about economic enfranchisement are also placed in the context of the argument being developed.

PARTY CONSOLIDATION IN BARBADOS

Barbados was one of the few territories in the Anglophone Caribbean which retained the Old Representative System (ORS) of government until it was replaced by the independence constitution of 1966. Even under the limited franchise system of the ORS in the post-1937 period, it became possible for "popular-oriented" parties to compete for the elected seats available in the House of Assembly (Cheltenham, 1970; Duncan et al., 1978; Emmanuel, 1979; Beckles, 1990). For example, the Barbados Progressive League (BPL), officially launched in October 1938, won five seats in the 1940 elections to the House, and Governor Sir Grattan Bushe appointed G. H. Adams (later Sir Grantley), its leader, to the Executive Committee. In this regard, the 1944 general elections were very important.

By a 1943 law, women acquired the right to vote and to be members of the House, and the voting qualification was reduced from fifty pounds sterling to twenty pounds sterling. This led to a drastic change in the composition of the Assembly. Sixteen of the twenty-four seats were won by the two labor- and socialist-oriented parties, the BPL and the newly formed West Indian National Party (known as the Congress Party [CP]) of W. A. Crawford. The BPL then reverted to its original name, the Barbados Labour Party (BLP).

It was not until the 1946 general elections, contested under "the Bushe experiment," which offered a semiministerial system, that there was sufficient authority for the coalition government of the BLP and the CP to influence policy making and policy implementation in their own name. Nonetheless, the Legislative Council, comprised of the representatives of the white planter-mercantile classes, with powers at least coordinate to those of the Assembly, made decision making difficult for the government. Coalition dissension complicated the situation. However, full universal adult suffrage was implemented for the 1951 general elections.

With the commencement of the full ministerial system of government in 1954, the basis for the modern party system and party-based government was truly laid. At that point there was full access to the Assembly by mass-based parties, and by 1954, as a result of the Bushe experiment, there was full internal self-government with the executive accountable to the Assembly.

With remarkably stable periodicity, general elections have been held nine times under adult suffrage—in 1951, 1956, 1961, 1966, 1971, 1976, 1981, 1986, and 1991. In itself, this attests to the uncontroversial and even-tempered pace of political evolution in Barbados. At no time were the election results seriously questioned, and the transitions from one party administration to another, when they occurred in 1961, 1976, 1986, and 1991, were smooth and uncomplicated, and indicated a measured change from one party to another (see Appendix, Table 9, column 3).

In that time, too, there were changes in the leadership of the BLP from Sir Grantley Adams (1938–1971) to Bernard St. John (1971) to J. M. G. M. "Tom" Adams (1971–1985), then again to St. John, as prime minister (1985–1986), to Henry Forde (1986–1993), and now to Owen Arthur (1993–). All these changes came after the usual competition, with the exception of the second accession of St. John to party leadership, and all leadership positions were quickly consolidated.

The Democratic Labour Party (DLP), formed in 1955, first controlled the government in 1961 and retained it until 1976. It was under the single dominant leadership of Errol Barrow until he died in office as prime minister in 1987. Prime Minister Erskine Sandiford is now the effective leader of the party, although he experienced some initial difficulty in consolidating his position and is currently weathering the storm of requests for his resignation over his handling of the economy. This may not, however, be a long-lasting situation. Thus far, no internal revolt in his party seems imminent, though much debated by the public. Up to this point in time, both the BLP and the DLP are well entrenched as competing parties in a two-party system, drawing their support evenly from all social, racial, and ethnic strata in what is a strongly homogeneous society.

The DLP emerged as a dissident offshoot of the BLP. Increasingly, after 1951, the radical wing of the BLP, led by Barrow, found its lack of access to formal positions of power intolerable. The split between the BLP and the Barbados Workers Union (BWU), led by Sir Frank Walcott, over Barrow's nonappointment to a ministerial post, provided the latter and the other dissidents the golden opportunity to establish a new party. The DLP took advantage of that split. Attracted to its ranks were some former members of the defunct CP, and the timely involvement of some independent members of the House added to the strength of the new party.

In spite of Sir Grattan Bushe obviously favoring Tom Adams in appointments to the Executive Committee, the CP won seven seats to the BLP's nine in the 1946 general elections. The BLP won twelve seats in 1948 but three of these were due to the crossing of the floor to the BLP by members of the CP. In addition, the conservative party still managed to capture a significant number of seats. When the DLP was formed there was the hope that it could make inroads into the conservative support and bring out more of the working and lower-class vote in its favor.

From the 1956 general election result, it was not at all clear that the DLP would be the all-conquering party of 1961 through 1976. Barrow, the party leader, failed to win a seat in St. George, and the party only secured four of the twenty-four seats in the Assembly and 19.9 percent of the votes cast in that election. The BLP, with fifteen seats and 49.3 percent of the popular vote, seemed well established. The Progressive Conservative Party (PCP), formerly the Barbados Electors Association, maintained a presence in the Assembly for the old elite with three seats and 12.5 percent of the votes.

Undoubtedly, the peculiar voting system of double-member constituencies, with each being able to cast two votes, either as a plump vote for one candidate, or one for each candidate of the same party, or as a split vote—one each to two parties—enabled the "old guard" of planter-mercantile interests and their "brown" and black middle-class conservatives and liberals to persevere, with some electoral relevance.

This peculiar system was abandoned for the 1971 general elections, when it was replaced by the simple majoritarian system of one man, one vote and single-member constituencies. The DLP secured eighteen of twenty-four seats with 57.4 percent of the popular vote. There was the total demise of other parties and independents as the DLP/BLP rivalry became established. Since then, the two-party system has become institutionalized in the form of BLP/DLP rivalry along a tolerable ideological dimension (see Appendix, Table 2).

The demise of the CP, presaged in 1951, was completed in 1956 with the entry of the DLP in the contest. In the 1961 general elections, the new Barbados National Party (BNP) marginally improved upon the conservatives' share of the votes obtained in 1956. The DLP secured 36.3 percent of the votes and a majority of the seats, at the expense of the BLP, whose share of the votes declined from 49.3 percent in 1956 to 36.8 percent in 1961. The BLP, with the larger percentage of the popular vote, secured only five seats, while the DLP obtained fourteen seats, and, at the same time, the percentage turnout was only one point up on the percentage share obtained in the previous elections. This outcome did not stir deep and lasting resentments.

The BNP held on until the 1966 general elections, at which it obtained 10.1 percent of the votes cast. Thereafter, there was no question that Barbados had become a two-party state. Table 2 reveals a combined BLP/DLP share of the popular vote in excess of 92 percent in subsequent elections. Since that time, neither of the two major parties has fallen below a 40 percent share of the popular vote, and in the last five general elections, the margin between the two parties never exceeded 10 percent. Nevertheless, each party always won a sufficient number of seats to govern effectively. Alternation in power, from election to election, always remained a credible expectation.

The general elections held on May 28, 1986 produced, even by Barbadian standards, a stunning victory for the DLP (Duncan, 1986; Watson, 1986). The party swept to victory with twenty-four of the twenty-seven seats in the House of Assembly. With nearly 60 percent voter turnout, the DLP obtained 89 percent of the seats. The groundswell of support toward the DLP was enormous. Its share of the votes represented an increase of 42.5 percent over its 1981 popular support. The swing to the DLP, at the national level, was 7.3 percent. It gave the impression that the liberal democratic system was working perfectly.

The 1991 general elections indicated that a watershed had been reached. The turnout was uncharacteristically low, although the issues were of extreme importance. Preelection surveys indicated that a large percentage of those who did not vote were persons in the age group 18–28. The victorious party failed to secure as much as 50 percent of the votes cast and accounted for only 31.4 percent of the total electorate. The DLP appeared to have been chosen as the least undesirable of the partisan offerings to the electorate. Within eight months of the elections, crowds of 10,000 to 15,000 were marching in two separate marches (led by the Trade Union Coalition) against measures introduced by the government. The prime minister paid scant regard to this outpouring and declared that he was the duly elected leader and could only be removed from office by another general election whenever he chooses to call it. The prime minister is hoping that through effective and successful policies his government will recover its lost legitimacy and calls for his resignation from critical sectors in the political economy will subside.

CURRENT ECONOMIC ISSUES

The massive electoral victory of the DLP in 1986 was secured on the basis of extravagant promises made to the people of Barbados. These unfulfilled promises have now come to haunt the government. The 1991 general elections saw the return of the DLP for a second term, largely on the basis of not conceding that the economy was in desperate trouble.

Since 1946, the Barbadian economy had not experienced a sustained period of very high growth in GDP. Nevertheless, in spite of the two oil price shocks and the accompanying stagflation in the world economy, it never descended into disaster until now. Indeed, by 1976, the economy was in an upward phase based upon good tourism performance, its growing capacity to reduce its oil import bill, and a modest improvement in the manufacturing sector during this 1973–1980 period. In this same period, the balance of payments was negative only in 1977 (Worrell, 1981).

The picture changed somewhat in the 1981–1985 period. The government was confronted with serious economic problems as sugar, agriculture, manufacturing, and tourism, the key sectors of the economy, recorded, in general, very low rates of real output growth. Although the rate of inflation declined substantially, unemployment increased significantly and the fiscal deficit of Bds$181 million in 1981 and Bds$94.7 million in 1985 caused serious concern (Downes, 1986).

In 1981, the overall balance of payments was in deficit. The government obtained a twenty-month standby loan from the IMF, for US$35 million, and a compensatory financing loan of US$28 million to counter the effect of a decline in earnings in tourism and sugar (Duncan, 1982). The collapse of the Caribbean Multilateral Clearing Facility had left Barbados being owed US$60 million by Guyana, now reportedly, with interest added, at Bds$150 million. This was largely responsible for the reliance of Barbados on IMF financing at that time. Since then, the overall balance has been positive but precarious. Indeed, many of the foreign loans contracted in the 1981–1985 period served the function of keeping the overall account in a positive balance, although artificially.

As the government moved on an expansive capital works program with only small surpluses on the current account, heavier reliance was placed on external capital. The national external debt moved from Bds$44.1 million in 1975 to Bds$444.0 million in 1985 (a tenfold increase). Along with that movement, GDP at factor cost moved from Bds$701.0 million in 1975 to Bds$1.706 million in 1981, and Bds$2.181 million in 1985 (*Barbados Economic Report*, 1987). Its debt service ratio remained fairly low until it jumped to 26.4 percent of export and tourism earnings in 1990 from 3.8 percent in 1981 (*Barbados Economic Report*, 1990).

Between 1983 and 1989, Barbados experienced seven consecutive years of growth in its GDP. The change in GDP growth at constant prices moved from 5.6 percent at the end of 1986 to *minus* 3.1 percent in 1990 (Harker, 1991: 7). The merchandise trade balance, which was *minus* Bds$623.8 million in 1986, declined further to *minus* Bds$1,112 million in 1990 (*Barbados Economic Report*, 1990: 1). GDP, which had surpassed Bds$1,000 million in 1979, was Bds$1,706 million in 1981; at the end of 1987 it stood at Bds$2,499 million and was Bds$2,965 million in 1990. Per capita income moved from Bds$6,811 in 1981 to Bds$9,850 in 1987 and to Bds$11,500 in 1990 (ibid.: 44, 46). This rapid growth in GDP could be partly attributable to the sizeable growth in the foreign debt. The Adams administration (1976–1985), through its activist foreign policy directed toward securing international funds for its capital works programs, presided over the initial rapid increase in the size of that debt. Substantial sums of money poured into the economy from multilateral lending agencies, friendly governments, and private bank consortia.

The present government had expressed serious concern about the rapid growth of foreign debt since 1976, but it has fallen into the same mode of thinking and acting as the previous government. Central government debt moved from Bds$863.7 million in 1983 to Bds$1,856.6 million in 1990. The previous administration had found some comfort in the fact that the debt service ratio was relatively low and manageable. The ratio moved from 2.6 percent in 1981 to 6.3 percent in 1986 to 15.4 percent in 1990 (ibid.: 30).

The difficulty with this argument lies in a number of factors. With weak or declining performance being exhibited by important sectors of the economy, especially the foreign exchange earning sectors, great care was needed in using foreign loans. Much of the foreign borrowing has increasingly come to be dominated by the government rather than the private sector, and has been put largely into capital works projects which, while they do wonders for the GDP, the infrastructure, and temporary job production, have hardly led to sustained income generation for the economy, especially in foreign currency earnings. Indeed, central government foreign debt as a percentage of GDP rose from 18.3 percent in 1983 to 28.2 percent in 1990 (ibid.).

The taxation reform program, begun in earnest in 1977 with the introduction of a tax credit system, was designed to reduce or completely remove the incidence of income taxation to taxpayers with the lowest incomes. In 1981, the government sought to address budgetary deficit problems and began to shift the incidence of direct taxation. In that year 1,800 taxpayers were cut from the tax roll and personal allowances were increased. The government was subsequently forced later in the year to tighten bank credit, raise interest rates, increase bus fares, impose a transport levy, and introduce higher charges for various licenses.

By 1983, the government was in an expansive mood and its National Development Plan (1983–1984 to 1987–1988) revealed the intention to inject at least Bds$750 million into capital works programs. This did not put a stop to the tax reform effort of the government. Wide-ranging tax reforms dominated the budgetary proposals in 1986 and in 1987. The major emphases were on income tax reforms and on large discretionary changes in the indirect taxation system (which appeared to be in need of rationalization).

A radical shift in income taxation occurred in 1986, a general election year. The BLP government introduced a budget in which it offered substantial tax credits to taxpayers. The first Bds$10,000 of all incomes was to be free from income taxation. The opposition DLP presented its alternative budget, which promised the first Bds$15,000 of income to be free of income taxation and promised an allowance package which could exceed that sum in total, among other features.

This "back raise," in poker terms, of the BLP proposals was a dominant factor in the electoral victory of the DLP. It was little wonder since, as Michael Howard (1988) has shown, the 1986 measures considerably reduced the tax liability of the middle- and upper-income groups. Howard (1987) showed that the ratio of indirect taxes and levies to total tax revenue rose from 46.3 percent in 1977 to 58.6 percent in 1985, and that personal income taxation as a ratio of total tax revenue fell from 30.1 percent in 1977 to 23.3 percent in 1985.

In a more general way, the 1986 DLP budget was predicated upon the assumption that it was desirable to increase the level of effective demand in the economy to stimulate economic activity, and that by giving tax relief to the private sector the latter would quickly be able to take advantage of the favorable circumstances and produce the urgently needed new jobs. It is difficult to assess whether the latter situation would have eventuated, for in the next five fiscal year budgets (1987, 1988, 1989, 1990, and 1991 [twice]) severe tax impositions were placed on taxpayers through increases in indirect taxation, new levies on income, and a surcharge on incomes. The main objectives were to cut back on the alarming growth of the current and overall fiscal deficit, and to meet the sharply growing increases in government expenditure, although it was the stated intention to sharply curtail expenditure. For those purposes, record levels of new taxation revenues were sought from taxpayers. This change represented a fundamental divergence from the populist philosophy and purposes of the 1986 budget. The one could have led to faster growth in the economy while the latter led in the end to slowed economic growth and reversal.

For a long time the debate in Barbados centered on the best approach for the Barbadian economy. This was a debate not merely between government and the official opposition but within the ruling party as well. Party political developments since March 1985 were probably among the reasons that the political directorate retreated from the usual caution and gradualism which characterized fiscal and monetary policies in Barbados.

With the death of Errol Barrow and the subsequent reorganization of his cabinet, new prime minister Sandiford took the opportunity to assume the portfolio of minister of finance, which now gave him full directive control over the economy. His first budget, in 1988, delivered the coup de grace to the 1986 budget, and restored Barbados to a heavier taxation regime, commitment to a balance on current accounts, and a greater concern for prudence in economic affairs. Needless to say, he had to deal with strident cries of betrayal of manifesto promises, and although the prime minister persistently argues that he has not touched any of those promises, his budgetary philosophy and his fiscal measures add up to a sharp departure from the spirit of the 1986 policies of his party.

ECONOMIC CRISIS AND PARTY FACTIONALISM

The year 1989 was very important for the ruling Democratic Labour Party and its leader, Prime Minister Sandiford. Having had the top leadership thrust upon him in June 1987, with Barrow's untimely death, he and his administration had, first of all, to withstand a difficult period in the management of the economy. Second, Sandiford had to manage a major rift in his party which eventually led to the formation of a new political party, the National Democratic Party (NDP). Third, he had to face an intense barrage of open opposition criticism of his leadership style and management of the economy. Finally, the DLP had to use this year to begin to prepare for general elections constitutionally due by May 1990.

Dr. Richard Haynes, who had resigned his portfolio as finance minister, resigned from the DLP in September 1987. He formed the NDP, along with three other defecting DLP members of Parliament. This reduced the DLP number of seats in the House of Assembly from twenty-four to twenty. In addition, the NDP now had more seats in opposition than the BLP, which had won the support of 40.4 percent of the electorate but only three seats (Duncan, 1989).

The NDP was officially launched on February 1, 1989 and the governor general appointed Haynes as the official leader of the opposition in the House, unseating Henry Forde, leader of the BLP. This gave the NDP a more central public position from which to launch its attack on the government. The NDP was also able to appoint two senators to the Upper House, unseating the two appointed by the BLP.

There was considerable public discussion on the appointment, given that the NDP had not faced the electorate as a party, and, more importantly, that the BLP had the support of over 40 percent of the voting population. Proposals were made for the introduction of a proportional system of elections and for an elected Senate, as fears were expressed for the future of democracy in Barbados. Nonetheless, the majority of Barbadians believe that the present simple majoritarian system has served the country very well and, although a third relevant party will probably produce some close outcomes in the next general elections, the electoral system is unlikely to be changed by any of these parties.

The NDP has since established itself as a genuine political force in the country, oftentimes taking the lead in raising critical public issues, in the rapid establishment of a viable political organization, and in attracting to its ranks interesting supporters and good potential candidates. It promised, somewhat unrealistically, to achieve full employment within five years of attaining power and affordable housing for all by the year 2000.

The ruling DLP entered the 1991 general election with a record of a careful, if sometimes overly cautious, approach to financial and fiscal management of the economy. The economy had produced a solid real growth rate of 3.5 percent in 1989, the same rate as in 1988. Both the *Institutional Investor* and *Euromoney* magazines listed Barbados as the most creditworthy nation in the Western Hemisphere after the United States and Canada, ranking forty-seventh and fifty-second respectively on the world listing. Nevertheless, the opposition parties had vigorously pursued a line of attack charging the government with gross mismanagement of the economy, overtaxation, and "squandermania." They failed to unseat the government. The NDP did not survive the 1991 elections as a parliamentary-based party. It lost all the seats it previously held and all but one candidate lost their deposits.[5] The party continues now as a pressure movement.

On October 8, 1992, Prime Minister Sandiford revealed a "Supplementary budget" designed to meet most of the demands/suggestions made by the IMF and World Bank. The supplementary budget sought a new additional tax take, higher than any previous budget save the last, of Bds$62.6 million in less than six months. Extended over a fiscal year it will become the heaviest tax extraction ever. The wages of public employees were cut by 8 percent, those earning more than Bds$15,000 a year are paying a stabilization tax of 4 percent on gross income, employment levies and national insurance contributions were increased, consumption tax was increased by 3 percent, petrol tax was increased by 11 percent, and there was a 20 percent tax increase on "luxury" imports. Duty-free concessions to industry were removed and a tax credit system put in place for firms which re-exported. There was to be a cut of Bds$22.9 million in subsidies to public sector enterprises, included in the overall cut in government expenditures of Bds$114 million.

The overall aims of the budget were to reduce the effective level of demand for consumer items and thus save on the foreign exchange component, and to reduce the projected fiscal deficit of Bds$328 million to 1 percent of GDP. The urgent intention was to secure a US$58.1 million loan from the IMF ($28.4 million as standby; $29.7 as compensatory and contingency financing). US$41.1 million was promised immediately once an agreement with the IMF was approved, US$32 million of which would pay off a Japanese bullet loan[6] due on October 4, 1991. At the very last moment, the Japanese deferred the payment date by six months. In addition, the local private sector raised US$12 million for a loan to the government and Venezuela was to provide a loan of US$20 million.

The political fallout from these measures was a growing loss of confidence in the ability of the prime minister to get Barbados out of the financial disaster. He himself exacerbated the political crisis in many ways. He found it more important to attend meetings which kept him out of the country, such as the IMF/World Bank meeting in Bangkok and the Commonwealth Conference in Harare, for nearly three weeks after he brought his budget to the Assembly. He left without even holding a press conference. He broke off, unilaterally, discussions with trade unions bargaining on behalf of public servants, on alternatives to the 8 percent cut in salaries, which was imposed after a most unsatisfactorily conducted poll of public servants. He then announced a layoff of at least 2,000 of 5,600 casual and part-time public employees, denying them, through administrative changes to the National Insurance Scheme and government procedures, the full severance payments and unemployment benefits normally due to workers in the public sector.

He also actively began seeking sale of the highly desirable government shares in the Barbados External Telecommunications (BET) and the Barbados Telephone Company, much to the annoyance of prospective local purchasers, to raise about US$50 million. The BET shares were actually snapped up by the parent company, Cable and Wireless, which also secured a remarkable twenty-year extension on their exclusive license to provide such services in Barbados.

In addition, the prime minister announced a 50 percent increase in bus fares, which went up to 75 percent a few months later. Rents for government houses were increased by 50 percent. Before his supplementary budget, he had increased interest rates and raised the deposit percentage of commercial banks with the Central Bank. All of this seemed to be extraction without relief or compromise.

On November 23, 1992 in a televised statement, Sandiford publicly defended his policies. He claimed that, first, the assaults on his management capabilities were unwarranted since, up to the end of 1989, there was growth in the GDP, and 1989 was indeed a record year for growth. Second, he had taken timely measures to meet the emerging problems which he outlined. Third, he was being humane in seeking to make adjustment without devaluation.

Sandiford is quite correct in saying that any government in power faced with similar policy choices would hardly have done any better. He anticipates that the measures he took will achieve stabilization of the economy, check loss of foreign reserves, and restore Barbados to international financial health. He anticipates that with the help of a World Bank program and IADB loans, growth will resume after the end of the 1992–1993 fiscal year. The Barbados Central Bank reported on July 20, 1993 that the Barbadian economy held steady between January and June 1993 and that the level of economic activity for 1993 would be "no lower" than in 1992. The Central Bank pointed to continued improvement in the external sector, evident in the net international reserves being Bds\$34.5 million (Bds\$1 = US\$1) higher than the January–June 1992 level (*Jamaica Weekly Gleaner*, July 30, 1993, 11). Meanwhile, the thousands of persons laid off and those dependent upon them, and the thousands of personal adjustments which the rest of the population will have to make, will ensure that there will be no early recovery of jobs or the ability to sustain oneself and one's family.

THE CRISIS IN POLITICAL AUTHORITY AND PROSPECTS FOR THE FUTURE

Barbados, as with all developing countries, often makes the assumption that foreign aid-led development is the correct way to proceed to achieve maximum and equitable welfare for its people. Economic growth is perceived as the main vehicle for increasing human happiness. Thus, GNP growth becomes a collective goal and valued in itself, not just for the owners of capital but for all because everyone benefits from a rising GNP. They are anxiously watching over the balance-of-payment figures, the growth rate, the relative unit of labor cost (RULC), and the savings ratio so as to "pass" the IMF's quarterly assessment tests.

Many governments now see the externally oriented industrializing process as capable of success, so they liberalize, deregulate, and privatize their economies, destroying indigenous manufacturing and agriculture for the domestic market in the process. They correctly try to reduce the size of governments but do so inappropriately. Much of what the IMF and the World Bank require Barbados to do should be done according to the needs and capabilities of the Barbadian people and economy and in a time frame which does not harshly dislocate the economy (McAfee, 1991).

The main charges by the welling opposition forces in Barbados are that the prime minister deceived the country as to the true state of the economy during the January 1991 general election campaign, that he acted too late to stabilize the economy, and that he has still not kept the country fully informed on all aspects of the negotiations with the IMF and his plans to bring about economic recovery, even with the belated publication of the Letter of Intent to the IMF.[7] In addition, there is the charge that the government has persistently broken the law in its excessive borrowing from the Central Bank, above the statutorily set limit, and in so borrowing has been largely responsible for the foreign reserves crisis now being experienced. The government, in other words, failed to contain its expenditures and has brought Barbados an "unnatural disaster" (McAfee, 1991), caused by gross mismanagement, notwithstanding the continued decline in the productive sectors (agriculture, tourism, and manufacturing).

The crisis in political authority has been manifested in several ways. Political leaders are depreciated, especially if they inherit their top leadership position from erstwhile dominant leaders who emerged from the battles of the colonial era. The courts have been put under pressure from the economically powerful, drug barons, and politicians themselves. Religion, especially the established denominations, has begun to lose its controlling sway over attitudes and behavior, especially when archaic notions come in conflict with current science. New religious movements enjoy a field day in the open marketplace for the minds of men, women, and children, especially those with doctrines of physical, social, and political withdrawal from society. The social fabric appears to be disintegrating into an alarming and persistent outbreak of crime, child abuse, spouse beatings, suicides, increase in pathogenic disorders in people, drug abuse (of both legal and illegal drugs), poor service and interpersonal relations, absence of restraining standards, and rampant consumerism.

Economically, there has been a growing disjuncture between trained capacity and the types of jobs created by both governments and the private sector. The emphasis upon managing the foreign exchange accounts, balancing budgets, and increased and redirected taxation, often following guidelines set out by international lending agencies, has led to the ignoring of alternative development strategies.

These approaches have led to disillusionment and cynicism. People have voted with their feet and migrated, or some have retreated into drugs, religion, popular music, and general disorderliness. Generally, the politicoeconomic order has failed to deliver the goods and honor the promises and expectations generated in the attempt to win political support and establish authority on a stable footing. Yet, underlying all these negative features are aspects, certainly in Barbados, which hold out the promise of a new agenda having a chance of being successfully implemented. That new political agenda, and that new political economy of change, must be processes which are based on successful efforts to create a stronger democracy. These positive aspects are:

1. A wiser and better-educated citizenry at present than at any time in the past;
2. A citizenry which no longer regards traditional political participation through political parties and periodic elections as overridingly important;
3. A citizenry which is demanding partial or full participation in previously sacrosanct areas of economic, political, and social life;
4. A citizenry which is alive to the structure of power and privilege in the society and wants to be "included in";
5. A citizenry which is slowly awakening culturally, in spite of overwhelming North American and European cultural penetration, and is developing, thereby, a more dynamic self-image more willing to authenticate its own;
6. A citizenry which is slowly awakening to the economic opportunity provided by credit unions and other forms of cooperative organizations; and
7. An awareness by the citizenry that because each person now exercises more choice over the direction of his or her life, there is more personal responsibility, and this, in turn, offers more scope for experimentation in the way in which we live, work, and play with each other.

The pace of these developments will not slacken as we approach the twenty-first century. Indeed, the pace is quickening. The public response to the prime minister's handling of the economic crisis is not bloody self-destruction and self-immolation. It strongly indicates the need for more, not less, democracy in all spheres of existence.

Much of what we call democracy is really liberalism. In liberalism there is emphasis on private property, competition, initiative, individualism, and the marketplace. Modern liberals, however, accept that government is obliged to intervene in economic and social life in an attempt to dampen some of the sharp inequalities that are a natural by-product of the free market. This is what is mistakenly referred to as liberal democracy today. This led us in Barbados to emphasize welfarism as the basis of our democracy. All available evidence suggests that the types of programs based on the theory that the poor are poor because of educational and training deficiencies have not been successful. The rich and middle strata in Barbados have benefited at a rate far exceeding the poor from welfare strategies. What government leaders have not seriously considered as a solution to poverty is a program of wealth redistribution and a full-employment economy.

One of the best ways of conceiving of democracy is as a social, economic, political, and cultural system enjoyed by those who are politically relevant. In this way they also enjoy, in Abraham Lincoln's words, "government of the people, by the people, and for the people." For those who are not (fully) politically relevant (usually the vast majority) to the extent that some of them really think about it, it really means, instead, government on behalf of the people, representative government, and by persons of "high" principles. It has become a form of government in which some of the people, chosen by all, govern in all public matters all of the time (Barber, 1984: xiv).

There are many ways in which it could be shown, specifically in Barbados, how a political agenda to strengthen democracy could be made. The most formal would be to examine the constitution and make recommendations that would enlarge the opportunities for wider and more intense participation. This is a necessary task. It could be suggested that organizing politically to bring about some rapid and forceful changes would prepare the way most effectively for a revamping of the political order. Yet, although it is almost true to say that every important event in Caribbean political history has been caused or determined by violence, it is similarly true to say that these have often been "settled" in the wrong way and with the worst possible outcomes.[8]

None but the most perverse would agree that the "democratic" constitution and "democratic" practice of local political party organizations work. Perhaps they do, in the sense that they were never meant to operate as stated and organized but, instead, when a party is in power, all should defer to the parliamentary party, its cabinet members, and especially the prime minister. All that actually happens is that members of Parliament should hold constituency branch meetings periodically, should find it advisable to hold regular consultations with constituents about their personal matters, see to it that delegates are chosen to annual general meetings of the party executive council meetings, and for these to operate as popularity gauges and trumpet-blaring occasions for the prime minister and his or her parliamentary colleagues.

In theory, the resolutions of branches and of the national party council meetings should have strong persuasive or even binding force upon MPs and ministers, but this is known to be an unreal belief in practice. Theoretically, too, the branches have power to nominate candidates and have the credible expectation that, except on extraordinary grounds, their choices would hold. In practice, the party leader dominates the process.

In theory, too, the creation of the party manifesto should be the work of hundreds of party organizers based on concrete work of many more persons, resolutions of branches, and advice from consultants and well-wishers, and be manifestly an open process. In practice it is the work of a handful of people, kept secret even from candidates, until the official announcement of the document and its distribution. None of this adds up to democratic functioning. However, it is indeed true that opportunities for meaningful participation abound within the party organization. Members' apathy is blamed for the failure of involvement. This is really not a good enough response. Those who have tried to participate and have failed will say that the structure of the organization and the nature of leadership personalities erect an iron curtain to involvement with dignity.

The absence of a properly headed and quality staffed secretariat is the major cause of the weakness of political parties in Barbados, which instead rely upon inadequately researched information; shockingly poor intra-party communication; extremely weak and obnoxiously dependent financial bases; untrained organizers, campaigners, and candidates (prospective or actual); and the effective shutting out of rising young stars from political participation in party activities. This ad hocism and dilettantism suits the overweening personal ambitions of wheeler dealers and aloof leaders very well, but leaders would be stronger, more prepared, and more knowledgeable about happenings in the party and country than ever before if these problems were overcome.

A political party should have effective mechanisms for the recall of nonperforming elected representatives. This is not a mechanism for anarchy in a party but for strengthening the organization. Procedures can readily be established which rule out frivolous charges, provide adequate opportunities for justification, involve the wider constituency at some stage, and still allow for the real possibility of removal for unjustified nonperformance at constituency and national levels. These will also have the effect of building public confidence in the party and shield the leader from making on his or her own difficult decisions of this nature. It also implies that the constituency's wishes concerning an appropriate candidate must be regarded more seriously by the party executive.

The natural training of future leaders, the sense of salience which it induces in party members, the recognition which will come from effective and creative suggestions and participation by individuals, will immeasurably strengthen the party organization. It will also, paradoxically, significantly reduce both the apathy and anarchy which alternately characterize party meetings and deliberations.

Apart from a national integrity legislation and procedures, a political party should have its own integrity rules and procedures, which if breached by members of Parliament, candidates, party officials, party-appointed board members, and critical other persons will end up in recall, dismissal, or severe reprimand.

Corruption is rampant in political, social, religious, and economic life. As an indication of how seriously opposed a party is to this issue, it must set in motion its own mechanisms, including a watchdog committee, to monitor and punish offenders. A country is as ethical and as righteous as its party organization.

A party must have an effective two-way communication system at all levels of party functioning. This means also the frequent availability of policy papers, a newspaper, video, and audio tapes of speeches of party members at home and abroad, an accounting of stewardship, and the like, recorded for posterity in a properly run party library.

One could continue to multiply the recommendations. The point is that there must be a conscious shift from dilettantism and personality cultism to expertise, wide-scale participation and involvement, deliberate training and recruitment, and accountability of all officials. As the party is, so will the society become. Is it any wonder therefore that the party is dull and unenterprising and offers so little beyond tokenism to the youth? The party organization must be transformed despite the entrenched persons who would deny meaning and purpose to its membership, which wishes to become more and meaningfully active. Knock the structure of weakness and authoritarianism with force, determination, and belief that it will fall, and it will.

The party is the essential building block of democracy in Barbados. By creating within itself an image of what it wants the wider society to be, it can become a more effective instrument for peaceful change. When the party, however, comes to reflect the wider society in need of change, in its class biases, racism, and ethnicity, its political corruption and patronage, its elitism and other forms of particularism, it is of no use to the transforming and democratizing process. If the party in structure, organization, and values remains locked in the 1940s, 1950s, and 1960s, as indeed it appears to be in Barbados, and does not adopt current and future management forms and styles, then it renders itself a useless instrument in bringing the country into the global political economy.

NOTES

1. Barbadians typically claim a 90 percent literacy rate. What is in dispute is the degree of functionality of that formal literacy rating.

2. The range and quality are really quite good and include piped water and electricity in 90-plus percent of the homes; free primary, secondary, and tertiary education along with free school books and meals; medical care and free pharmaceuticals, among others.

3. While there are one or two notorious areas, there is the marked absence of the shanty towns which characterize areas in western Kingston, Jamaica, and on the outskirts of Caracas, Venezuela.

4. The state has provided services, some of which the private sector ought to provide for their employees. Many who can pay for services nevertheless receive them free of cost. Corporate ownership and control, the vast portion of land, and the distributive and services sectors remain largely in the hands of a few, primarily white, families.

5. All candidates pay a token amount to be a candidate. The deposit is forfeited if a candidate fails to receive a certain proportion of votes. In this case, all except one candidate received fewer votes than the proportion allowed to have their deposits refunded.

6. A bullet loan is a type of demand note or short-term loan similar to a balloon payment. Barbados would pay the interest on the balance over the period of the loan and the principal must be paid at the end of the loan period.

7. This letter has since been revised given subsequent negotiation with the Trade Union Coalition. Its contents have not been made public and an IMF agreement was reached on February 7, 1992.

8. Guyana under Forbes Burnham (1964–1985), Jamaica under Michael Manley (1974–1980), and Grenada under the Peoples Revolutionary Government (1979–1983) should have encouraged the search for a less revolutionary and violent route.

6

Grenada: From Parliamentary Rule to People's Power

Dessima Williams

G renada has had five postindependence regimes. The most ideologically different ones have been the Grenada United Labour Party (GULP) government of Eric Matthew Gairy, 1974–1979, and the Peoples Revolutionary Government (PRG) of Maurice Bishop and his New Jewel Movement (NJM), 1979–1983. The other regimes are: a postinvasion Interim Council administered by Nicholas Brathwaite, October 1983 to December 1984; a pro–United States, elected New National Party (NNP) government of Herbert Blaize; and, since March 1990, the National Democratic Congress (NDC), led by Prime Minister Nicholas Brathwaite. From these regimes, two major postcolonial models of democratic institutions and practices have emerged. This chapter examines these models, exploring their essential differences in philosophy and institutions, and in the practice of democracy.

The chapter begins by reviewing the development of democracy in colonial Grenada. This is followed by an examination of democracy in the Gairy years, 1951–1979, and of the participatory democracy and revolution of the PRG, 1979–1983. The chapter concludes with a comparison of the two.

Government of Grenada, 1951 to 1991

September 1951–1962	Grenada United Labour Party (GULP)—Eric Matthew Gairy administration
October 1962–March 1967	Grenada National Party (GNP)—Herbert Blaize administration
April 1967–March 13, 1979	GULP—Gairy (second term)

March 1979–October 1983	People's Revolutionary Government (NJM/PRG)—Maurice Bishop administration
October 19–25, 1983	Revolutionary Military Council (RMC)—Hudson Austin–Bernard Coard administration
October 25, 1983–December 30, 1984	Interim Council—Chair, Nicholas Brathwaite
January 1, 1985–March 13, 1990	New National Party (NNP)—Herbert Blaize administration; died in office, replaced by Benjamin Jones
March 15, 1990–present	National Democratic Congress (NDC)—Nicholas Brathwaite administration.

THE SETTING: DEMOCRACY IN CONQUERED COLONIAL GRENADA

Grenada was originally inhabited by Caribs, Arawaks, and Siboynes who left little by way of democratic institutions which Columbian Grenada incorporated.[1] After the extermination of the indigenous peoples by 1650, the French controlled the island from 1674 to 1762. The island came under British rule in 1762, then the French regained control in 1769 only to lose it again to the British in September 1783, with the Treaty of Versailles. The British controlled it consistently from 1783 to 1974.

European colonial administration in Grenada, as elsewhere, was uneven: rights, freedoms, and privileges for the select (few) whom the system legitimized; conditional inclusion for those who could be certified; and brutal dictatorial rule for those delegitimized and thus deprived of any basic human rights, however constructed. All material, social, political, cultural, and security rights accrued to the slave-holding class by virtue of its "right," first of domination and later of hegemony in the colony. The principal institutions for control were the plantation as a socioeconomic system and the source of material wealth; and the colony, a state-society complex, reservoir and dispenser of acceptable norms, values, and ideas. Neither provided democracy for the slave. France, Grenada's first colonial authority, pursued a political system at home and in its colonies with the explicit goal of developing itself, and as such, "Grenada had to fit into this imperial matrix": civil government administration, Roman Catholic religion ("the church was a pillar of the colonial process"), military garrisons, land, slaves, and the cultivation of export crops (Brizan, 1983: 23–24).

British colonialism developed, extended, and institutionalized this "democratic" trajectory. On becoming the successor power in 1762, local British authorities established an executive council and a general assembly made up of the victorious British colonists and a now-displaced French elite, whose presence in the assembly would be tolerated "provided they had sworn allegiance to the King of England" (ibid.: 32). Thus, one of the earliest representative institutions, starting in 1764, was an assembly of twenty-four members of the "landed and monied class," which governed 35,000 slaves and a handful of planters, resident in six parishes, home to a burgeoning plantation production (ibid.: 35).

An Election Act of 1792 delineated stringent rules against French and free coloreds in Anglo-French rule in Grenada: to qualify as a candidate a person had to be a "white-skinned male" adult, with land and income, born on the island, and a Protestant (ibid.: 51). Voter eligibility carried similar race, gender, wealth, and religious qualifications. The overwhelming majority of the population, Africans held in slavery, were not factored into the representative democracy, even as they were the foundation of the production of wealth. For this political constituency, democratic expressions took the form of running away, revolts, uprisings, and rebellions against plantation bondage, and in pursuit of individual and collective freedom. Some cultural festivals, such as the carnival, were permitted.

By the early 1800s, with the abolition of the slave trade and rising production costs, the plantation system began its decline. With it came limited political liberalization. A class of colored and freed blacks (15% of the population), as well as a merchant class, appeared. In the 1820s and 1830s, the legislature bestowed upon this group "some of the rights enjoyed by white men . . . including in some cases . . . the right to elect their own representatives to the Assembly and to be members of the Grand Jury" (ibid.: 107–108). Thus, colonial democracy had expanded from the 5 percent of white male subjects and their families to include the 15 percent of coloreds and free blacks and their families. Still, this expansion did not include over 80 percent of the population, the African agriculture-producing class. They remained objects (legally slaves, morally dismissed from having human needs) in the infant democratic process emerging. A definition of democracy which speaks of participation of the majority would not therefore be applied to this period of political rule in Grenada.

In 1838 slavery was abolished. From the African majority a large peasantry was born with the legal status of apprentices. Their presence was augmented by a small mulatto or colored class emerging alongside the African mass: the East Indian, Scottish, and English imported indentured labor. Land ownership reflected the class hierarchical and oligarchic nature of society: 95.8 percent of landowners owned approximately 28 percent of the cultivable land (less than 10 acres each), while 4.5 percent of landowners owned close to 72 percent of the land (between 100 to 1,000 acres apiece). In 1935, 100 years after emancipation, a Land Settlement Scheme sought not land reform, but "land transfer, that is, the redistribution of land per se with total disregard of the redistribution of economic power" (ibid.: 230).

In 1876, the Grenada Legislature removed representative government in Grenada when it voted to return the island to Crown Colony status. All political offices held were appointments of the queen of the colony, the queen of England: a governor, lieutenant-governor, an executive council, and a legislative council. Representation was afforded through district boards which allowed the small emerging business class (more male than female) to have a say in regional affairs of the parish. According to George Brizan, despite these concessions, "political power (under Crown Colony government) remained firmly in the hands of the Governor until the early 1950's . . . [and] the mass of the population remain detached and politically unaware" (1983: 214–215).

In 1877, Grenada became part of a collective regional administrative arrangement, with a regional governor. Internally, there was an executive council selected by a local lieutenant-governor, and an assembly of elected members. In this postemancipation period, "political elitism" continued, as Table 3 (see Appendix) demonstrates.

Between emancipation and the beginning of the twentieth century, social conditions and political status remained virtually unchanged for the mass of the population. Poor, ill-housed, and paid meager wages, former slaves still did not have the vote. A small group enjoyed economic monopoly, and for the rest of the population there was no economic democracy. Monopoly capitalist economics and social inequalities were in place. The social bondage was replicated between citizen and colonial authority. Socially acceptable and legitimate behavior belonged to colonial authority and those who mimicked them, who were not the majority. This created an identity crisis for the Grenadian of African descent, since it marginalized the majority of the people and allowed for the development of a low self-esteem of Africans who did not look or feel like Europeans. "Good English" or the "Queen's English" was associated with English governors, schoolteachers, and the urban elite, while what was spoken by ex-slaves was considered "Bad English." English ways and language, as well as European religions,[2] ideas, and lifestyles, dominated the cultural forums of Grenada. The African religion of Shango, widely practiced, was frowned upon. The queen's birthday and coronation were national holidays, yet there were no national heroes like Carib chief Kaierouanne, French-African rebel Fedon, and, especially, not Gamay, the African woman who coorganized the eighteenth-century uprising Fedon's Rebellion.[3] British hegemony, it seems, succeeded, grounded in the psychological traits, cultural practices, belief systems, and sociopolitical structures of the colonial classes (and their admirers) who governed/ruled Grenada.[4]

The 1925 constitution ushered in a significant forward movement. It removed Crown Colony status, provided for an elected legislative council, and offered political participation to the small colored class, and for the first time (elite) women could vote. From these groups new political forces emerged. One such politician, Theophilus Albert "T. A." Marryshow, descendant of freed blacks, became an agitator for representative government and for a West Indies Federation.[5]

By the 1950s, Grenada's agro-proletariat unleashed a national democratic uprising against colonial polity and authority. The immediate causes for protest were poor wages and deplorable living conditions; but at the heart of the protests were also deep resentments against denial of social, cultural, and political rights. Marryshow, then the leading political opposition figure, was as unprepared as the upper-class urban leaders to oppose the exploitative plantation system which was at the root of the problem. Leadership would not come from Marryshow or his class, but from a different socioeconomic stratum. A leader who came to be seen as the "reincarnation of Fedon" (Brizan, 1983: 249) came from among the class of the most exploited and discontented, and as such his rise and his mobilization of the discontented were signs that a new political reality had dawned in Grenada: mass peasant participation, leadership, and followership, in national politics.

NATIONAL DEMOCRATIC UPRISINGS, AND POLITICAL AND CONSTITUTIONAL DEVELOPMENTS OF THE 1950s

The national democratic uprising of the agro-proletariat in the early 1950s dramatically shifted politics in Grenada. It began when a British owner tried to evict agricultural workers on La Fillette Estate in an attempt to institute a less obligatory contract between himself as owner-planter and the estate workers in the long-standing system of *metayer*.[6] Angered, they demanded compensation under the Worker Compensation Ordinance, and began strikes and other protests.

The issues raised were as much those of representation as they were of poverty: daily wages in 1935 were about one shilling, the same as they had been nearly one hundred years earlier, immediately after emancipation. Wages in 1935 were a mere 15 percent of earnings of Grenada's four major export crops—cocoa, nutmeg, bananas, and sugar (see wage table, Table 4, Appendix). In the late 1940s "86 percent of the houses in Grenada were still wood, wattle and mud, 80 percent were either one or two-room dwellings" with anything from six to fifteen people in these houses (ibid.: 240).

The assault of 1950 heralded an attack on what had passed for a just and democratic social order and led to a change in the way in which the ruling class and government had done business in Grenada. Two forces were simultaneously unleashed: a mass (largely peasant, with sympathizers from other classes) demanding economic and political rights, and a Grenadian leadership grounded in rural values, but whose vision of democracy, leadership, and politics were shaped by sexism, authoritarianism, and colonialism. This watershed period unfortunately did not, nor could, erase all undemocratic cultures and practices; the authoritarianism and gender inequalities which remained in the political culture have contributed to the character of democracy developed on the island to date, dogging every regime since. Nevertheless, what was accomplished then was a severe crack in the colonial order, as "bitter class hatreds, the haves against the have-nots," erupted publicly.[7] The voice, if not all the interests, of the masses could no longer be ignored.

They chose to represent them Eric Matthew Gairy, a young national with trade union experience returning from neighboring Aruba. Gairy immediately formed the Grenada Manual and Mental Workers Union (GMMWU). The GMMWU, which had now won the loyalty of estate workers, called the first island-wide strike. The nation exploded in 1951 as strikers demanded higher wages and better living conditions. The GMMWU seized upon the socioeconomic frustrations to push for democratic expansions, particularly concerning wage increases. In September 1951, a new constitution gave full adult suffrage, an elected legislature, and very liberal terms for candidates to political office. Gairy formed the Grenada United Labour Party (GULP). The newly formed GULP, with the large mass base of GMMWU, excited at their labor victories, contested national elections in October. Winning five of eight parliamentary seats, and with 37 percent of the electorate or 60 percent of the votes cast, it entered Parliament on a populist and pro-agricultural worker platform with a strong union base. Gairy, himself unschooled, was now the declared national hero of the people, and unchallenged by Marryshow or the British colonial authorities, became leader of the Executive Council. Gairy, his political machinery, and the system of Gairyism remained dominant and sometimes hegemonic in Grenadian political development until 1979.[8]

DEVELOPMENT AND DEMISE OF REPRESENTATIVE DEMOCRACY AND GAIRYISM, 1951–1979

Gairy's relation to the development of political participation and representative democracy in Grenada can be divided into three areas: inheriting and administering the British colonial model (notwithstanding the social revolt of which he had been a part); moving away from it and establishing his own system, Gairyism; and, in an attempt to remain at the political helm, destroying representative democracy and democratic participation in Grenada. All these three phases are important in understanding the nuanced history of democracy in Grenada, if for no other reason than the fact that "Gairyism" remained an enduring political philosophy throughout the 1979–1983 revolution, and aspects of the colonial political culture and Gairyism (masculinity and authoritarianism) appeared in the revolution. Finally, Gairyism experienced an upsurge from 1984–1987, and although diminished now, is at least ideologically alive.

"Inheriting and Presiding Over" the Colonial System

In this first phase, which began when opposition agitator Gairy was first appointed Chief Minister the Honorable Eric Matthew Gairy, a potential democratic change of revolutionary proportions was stunted. This was because the colonial administration's goal of "restoring order" on the rebelling masses coincided with Gairy's ambition to inherit the helm of power at any cost. As the masses protested, looted, and burned, sometimes at Gairy's instigation, and sometimes on their own volition and initiative, the British authorities succeeded in getting the very same "Uncle Gairy," "The Leader," to get the protestors to call off their strike. Social historian Merle Collins recalls it this way in her fictitious autobiography:

> My dear people, . . . You should go back to work. Victory is ours. They had to give in. Wages will be wages whatever the price of cocoa. Victory is ours. You will get a fifty percent increase in wages. Not as much as we wanted but one step at a time. (Collins, 1987: 32)

This signaled Gairy's willingness to work with and within the British system, a fact confirmed over the years as he swiftly moved up through the ranks via appointments and elections.[9]

Grenada was maintained as a colonial polity (whose political economy was based on labor's exploitation), principally for export agriculture and an infant export-import trade and domestic commerce. Because of the island's disadvantageous participation in the global economy, it was the recipient of foreign aid, which basically meant British grant-in-aid of several million pounds annually. The state was presided over by an elected government headed by the monarchy (the queen of England), with her representative the governor, a bicameral legislature, and a judiciary branch of the British Privy Council. Representative democracy continued.

On coming to office, GULP inherited the administrative apparatus of the colonial democracy. Gairy maintained the civil service as it was, dominated by expatriates and non-Grenadian Caribbean nationals. The GULP administration protected private property with its skewed land, resource, and wealth distribution. European religion and the church as a defining pillar of civilized society received their support, and traditional liberal freedoms (e.g., habeas corpus) were honored.

It is fair to say, however, that there were several defining characteristics of the early Gairy rule. First, Gairy brought in to office a philosophy of the social, political, and economic right of "the little person"—generally rural, poor, African in all essential ways, and with little high school education. Stories of dark-skinned rural people getting across the color bar in schools, banks, and tennis courts after 1951 abound, and are attributed to Gairy's political philosophy of "Grenada for all Grenadians," which meant extension of social legitimacy beyond mulattoes and whites. Second, trade unionism made a debut in the politics of the state and of governance. The GMMWU, largely made up of estate workers, was the organized voice behind the GULP, and the two worked in near-absolute tandem.

Finally, though he abided by the traditions, codes, and structures of British colonialism, both in political and cultural ways (proportional representation, elections, "Good English," bureaucracies), Gairy's leadership always seemed headed in a different direction, fed by a different set of sensibilities and preferences than those of his political predecessors; of course, this influenced both his understanding and practice of democracy and politics. Political representation and symbolisms were very different for Gairy. His profound sense of African spirituality, and his large Afro-Caribbean constituency, led him to bring into public gaze as well as into his political style, Grenada's large non-Anglo culture and tradition. This was best represented by the Shango prayer-meeting-turned-political-rally, and the Shango priestess as a revered and sacred do-gooder and political kingmaker. To this must be added his overwhelming sense of his own importance, power, and destiny. He spoke of himself as "the man from the East who God sent to rule Grenada."

By 1954, the political-psychological impact he had on the population could often coopt, or defuse, the threat of strikes and mass uprisings. In 1955, the Grenada National Party (GNP) was formed. Its task was to bring in to electoral life a more indigenous plantocracy and the burgeoning commercial elite. Brown-skinned middle-class professionals, uncomfortable with the peasant and working-class culture and social dominance of GULP, also joined the GNP.

Gairyism

Democratic politics, electoral and otherwise, was controlled by Gairyism after 1951. After a political sabbatical from 1962 to 1967 brought on by an electoral defeat (as well as a period of suspension from 1957–1961 for political misconduct), the Gairy political machinery was returned to office and remained there by fair and foul means until 1979. Gairyism became popular political culture, ideology, and state management. Gairyism can be understood as the crafting and exercise of a system of intensive and highly personalized patron-clientelism, relying on ridicule and on force, and driven by aggressive nationalism. The trajectory of a matter-of-fact, routine liberal parliamentary democracy which brings in the masses as voters, producers of wealth, and consumers of colonial hegemony while leaving real political, social, and cultural power in the hands, pockets, and institutions of a minority elite—the Gairy Revolution and administration derailed that. Gairyism was its replacement—that synthetic, contradictory mix of part popular empowerment and part open dictatorship, with the personal and political figure of Gairy—not English rule—as the icon of ideology and politics (see Singham, 1968). Democracy suffered setbacks as personal aggrandizement and victimization took over from earlier principles regarding the prosperity and inclusion of the masses. Gairy was more interested in maintaining power through his charisma and populist fervor, as well as through an increasing authoritarian and repressive manner in dealing with opposition forces. However, his appeal as a powerful symbol of cultural representation and father-like savior never lost its attraction.

From 1950 to 1970, agriculture accounted for 31 percent of the labor force, and contributed 30 percent of the GDP. In 1969, 82 percent of the island's sales came from the export of agro-products, that is, nutmeg, bananas, and cocoa. This led to a large planter class with vast power. Neither Gairy and GULP nor John Watts, Herbert Blaize, and the GNP challenged this power. Gairy, historically, insulted the upper class and their interests, but by the late 1960s he had become owner of many businesses through property confiscation and corruption. The GNP had always aligned itself with the middle-class and export-oriented sectors of the Grenadian electorate. Thus, the contest between GULP and GNP was over the propriety of rule and land to redistribute wealth into the hands of their respective select few. The Grenadian people, once again, had become objects of the agenda of political parties.

From 1946 to 1972, the plantocracy increased control over the productive apparatus of the island, as land ownership became drastically concentrated. The populace realized that increasing profits of agro-exports[10] reached fewer hands due to monopoly control and government corruption, and they demanded change.

By the 1970s, there was 44.6 percent unemployment, while unemployment and underemployment reached 74.6 percent. Wages did not keep up with rising prices. (The opposition media monitored the populace's declining wages, standard of living, and health and education facilities.) This proved dramatically damaging to a regime whose claim to legitimacy in the 1950s was based on the improvement of workers' living conditions.

In 1967, Grenada, along with several other British colonies, attained statehood (full internal self-rule), one step away from independence. During the 1970s, the state underwent a crisis in production, organization, legitimacy, and governance. Gairy's moral grip was loosening, especially among the elites with whom he had a reciprocal relationship based on an exchange of their skills and knowledge for his support. They soon discovered he considered them dispensable. Dismissals, property confiscations, public humiliations, affairs with their wives, removing them from GULP: these were all ways that Gairy dealt with his inner advisors and loyalists, and with the opposition, in his bid for supreme authority. He came to rely more and more on brutality and coercion to protect his rule. Opposition and counter-hegemonic forces ascended to the position of agitator once held by the mass movement Gairy led.

Gairy now chose to respond to the widespread dissatisfaction (along with his own very deep distrust of the opposition) through a variety of legal and extralegal measures. He set aside the advancement of representative rule, legalities, and the civil norms of governance. He formed the Green Beasts, a paramilitary outfit trained and inspired by Chile's Augusto Pinochet. A long series of violations occurred: violation of human rights, the effective closure of

Parliament because the prime minister refused to hold regular sessions (convening only to railroad select bills through), prohibition of eleven categories of workers from strike action, illegal arrests and detention, and illegal seizure of property.[11]

The regime's use of force was insufficient for rule. Gairy turned to the cultural appeal once more to major visible and influential institutions in civil society. He placed himself in the company of Shango priestesses, to create a mythical persona. In 1978, he said in Parliament, "He who opposes me, opposes God," and ordered priests to recite pro-GULP speeches in Sunday mass. In 1979 during his Throne Speech he referred to himself in the third person, "The Prime Minister, Dr. the Right Honorable Sir Eric M. Gairy." His aura helped maintain the ideological aspects of his rule at a time when his desire and ability to meet the needs of the people had collapsed. Gairy's brutality, corruption, and eccentric behavior furthered his reputation as not being interested in any genuine attempt to maintain representative democracy. He virtually closed Parliament, which, as was true in the rest of the Anglophone Caribbean, had become accepted by a large majority of the population as the site and symbol of democratic rule.

THE NEW JEWEL MOVEMENT'S DEMOCRACY

The sustained radical opposition against Gairyism which came to the fore in the early 1970s had its genesis, interestingly enough, in the same antislavery and postemancipation rebellions which propelled Eric Gairy in the early 1950s. This time, as the public rose up against economic, social, and political decay, and paramilitary terror, there was a leadership not just willing to adjudicate grievance within the system, but to do what Gairy had failed to do—change the system of politics in Grenada.

Popular protest as a cultural form of struggle for internal self-determination took shape in the nurses' strike against intolerable hospital conditions in the 1970s, mass strikes to force Gairy's resignation in 1973–1974, and public discussions and agitation through a People's Convention, the People's Trial of Lord Bronlow, and the People's Congress, all in the late 1970s. These mass mobilizations and deliberations, and people's assemblies, were institutionalized as an expression of popular will, of protest *and* decision making. It is these people's democratic institutions which enabled the Grenadian people to fashion an alternative to the hegemonic ideology of Westminster parliamentary rule.

The events of the 1970s contributed to what Robert Cox sees as the prerequisites for the creation of a counter-hegemony: an articulate and coherent display of an alternative worldview; a sufficient concentration and command of power; and new institutions to sustain the counter-hegemonic view. The "worldview," anti-Gairy people's power, was reasonably coherent even though it was still an ideologically amorphous middle-class concept, expressive of the mass anti-Gairy coalition of social and political dissenters whose leadership was provided by a basically middle-class cadre of young men. However, there was no denying that this movement, in the main, was of the masses themselves, that it represented a rejection of the failure to attain greater and more meaningful liberal democracy under Gairy, and that the citizenry believed it held a vision for something new and "better." Even those bothered by NJM's use of force in coming to office held out the hope that this was an unfortunate means to a better future.

New NJM institutions also emerged in that period. There were cells of people's power. Village groups, and NJM party support groups as they came to be known, were developed (and sprung up on their own) to discuss collectively the events of the day and to give support to the NJM. After 1979, these groups emerged "officially" as village, zonal, and parish councils, which provided the base of people's power, and a source of fresh, uncensored ideas from the people.

Simultaneously, with the crisis in Gairyism and mounting public protest, a revolutionary party was formed which could take advantage of the objective conditions in Grenada to overthrow the existing systems of plantocracy, neo-colonialism, and Gairyism. Community organizations, student organizations, and study groups were formed, printing protest booklets and papers, speaking out, and holding public fora. Attorney Maurice Bishop founded the Movement for the Assemblies of the People (MAP) in 1973, as an alternative parliament; Unison Whiteman, Diant Trump and Teddy Victor led the Joint Endeavour for Welfare, Education and Liberation (JEWEL), and published a newspaper bearing the same name. On March 11, 1973, JEWEL and MAP joined to form the New Jewel Movement (NJM) and immediately called for a people's convention on Gairyism and independence, to be held in May 1973.

In its 1973 party manifesto, the NJM adopted the view that a new and different type of democracy could be adopted in Grenada. The NJM's party manifesto stressed the need for dramatic improvements in the living conditions of the people before putting forward its solution: "People's Assemblies For Power to the People." Changes were proposed in virtually every area of political life, thus setting the NJM apart from its predecessors GULP and GNP in the scope and detail of its reviews and its recommendations. The manifesto called for a centrifugal place for governance by ordinary people, a direct and stark inversion of the 1792 and 1925 constitutions and colonial eras as a whole. It said: "NJM stands solidly behind *People's Assemblies* as the new form of government that will involve all the people all the time. . . . To us, People's Assemblies will bring in true democracy." At its very minimum, this was an attempt by the NJM to transform the very written and unwritten definitions of political citizenship for ordinary people.

The populace was terrorized by a paramilitary force roaming the streets, inflicting punitive measures. Prisoners were held without bail, severely beaten, and robbed by the police. This sort of violence led the NJM to charge that there was no law and order in society, and that the present regime could not be counted on to restore moral integrity to public office and institutions. A phase of mass strikes commenced against the Gairy regime to protest widespread violence and abuse of human rights. The NJM convened a People's Congress in Seamoon on November 4, 1973 attended by over 20,000 people. The key result of this congress was the People's Indictment—a resolution which charged the Gairy regime with crimes against the people. This indictment was a stunning achievement in terms of attacking the Westminster basis of legitimacy for Gairy's rule.

The importance of the congress for understanding the breakdown of colonial order and hegemony in Grenada cannot be overstated. Despite harassment, fear tactics, and repression, one-sixth of the population of the island attended a congress which directly accused the Gairy leadership of criminal actions and asserted the people's right to establish a government responsive to their needs. It is this grounding principle—that the people have an exclusive and inalienable right to bequeath or withdraw legitimacy from their government—which played an important part in Grenada's democratic struggle for the next decade, 1973–1983.

Two weeks after the People's Congress, Gairy responded to the people's call for his resignation by ordering his secret police to ambush and severely beat six NJM leaders. This symbolized Gairy's fear and self-perceived vulnerability. He lost his remaining legitimacy. Gairy's public brutality against the NJM leadership mobilized the masses even as it brought mainly middle- and upper-class fence-sitters onto the side of the NJM. From this point onward, the NJM leaders knew that they had public political support to break Gairy's hold on power. The NJM formed an alliance in 1976 and entered Parliament as the leading opposition. But at the level of civil society, they aimed to break not just Gairy's hold but strategized to break the hegemonic grip of "liberal" representative democracy, by the intensified discussions of "participatory" democracy. The NJM organized a three-pronged strategy: campaigning for (all) and winning (three) seats in Parliament; mobilizing popular support for its party even as it pushed an alternative politics; and condemning Gairy/Gairyism to Grenadians abroad, and to Caribbean and international audiences. In March 1979, with its own military force, the NJM overthrew what was left of the Gairy regime and came to office as the People's Revolutionary Government (PRG).

The NJM/PRG's Model: "Participatory" Democracy

There were ten major expressions of the NJM/PRG's political system and policy initiatives that, taken together, signal a departure from what was prevailing in pre-PRG Grenada as well as in the rest of the Anglophone Caribbean. Indeed, the debate continues as to what kind of departure. They can be listed as follows.

First, the revolutionary seizure of state power set the PRG at variance with the norm where the transfer of political power had always taken place exclusively through the ballot box, by fair or foul means. The NJM stormed police and military barracks, seized ministers, and called out an ecstatic, admiring public.

Second, through the Grenada Declaration, the constitution was suspended, save for habeas corpus and other basic instruments for the legal safety of the citizen. The PRG declared itself into office, merging both executive and legislative power, and issued "people's laws."

Third, the rejection of "liberal" democracy, the Westminster model of Parliament and the reformulation of how to conceive and practice "true" democracy. The replacement was people's power expressed through participatory democracy. Parish and regional zonal councils and political interest groups (unions, women, farmers), all tied to the New Jewel Movement, formed the structure of political life and from them a National People's Assembly would be elected and approve a new constitution. (The assembly, the national elections, and the new constitution never materialized.)

Fourth, the development of mass organizations as interest groups in lieu of political parties. The PRG did not want any more parties, but built a structure for more participation by the masses within the same ideology.

Fifth, a new understanding of and the state's commitment to the social contract which redefined and made explicit rights and obligations and instituted enforcement mechanisms in some cases. One area was taxes. The PRG eliminated income tax for the lowest paid income earners (below $12,000 yearly) and taxed corporations 55 percent of their profits, which financed social development.

Sixth, in the PRG's framework, *people* made politics and not institutions. People were considered political subjects (decide, act, enact, create), and were more than constituents of political elites. People were at the center of the model.

Seventh, culture, language, race, and ideology had a greater and more explicit role in breaking the old models. The PRG developed language and culture as empowering categories. It rewrote primary schoolbooks and curricula and retrained all the nation's primary teachers. It brought artisans, steel drummers, African dancers, and patois to the school, while it collected the poetry of ordinary voices, which was used as a tool for communication and validation of the ordinary citizen and his or her world. Given legitimacy within the national cultural character and fabric, ordinary and local cultural icons helped shape and transform the old character and personality of state and society (Henry, 1990: 79–80).

Eighth, the NJM/PRG fostered a new state-society complex as a system of governance. It achieved this with NJM/PRG members holding leadership in the mass organizations and assemblies, and by joint literacy, health, and cultural campaigns between government and civil organizations. The liaison between the PRG and the pro–PRG Airport Development Committee is one good example of this.[12]

Ninth, a noncapitalist economic development policy was adopted. The PRG pursued a mixed economy—the state, private industry, and cooperatives making a triumvirate for production. The state set the political direction of economic democracy with its policy of profit sharing, retaining 51 percent in all joint ventures, and putting workers on its corporate boards so as to close the gulf between workers and management.

Finally, the idea of repositioning Grenada in the regional and international arena was very path-breaking. Grenada marketed itself as a member of an oppressed but struggling humanity, becoming a member of the nonaligned movement with sympathies for the socialist world, and strong anti-imperialist sentiment.

PARTICIPATORY DEMOCRACY, PEOPLE'S POWER: MYTH IN THE FACE OF REALITY?

Controversy has raged in the postinvasion literature regarding the political attainment of the PRG, which itself claimed that it was constructing "a new civilization" in Grenada (see Heine, 1990). Others have claimed that political life in Grenada under the PRG was nothing short of repression (Ryan, 1990), and that when the Gairy period is also examined, Grenada has never experienced the liberal democracy assumed to be the case for its neighbors in the Anglophone Caribbean.

PRG's Democracy versus (Parliamentary) Liberal Democracy: Making the Old Explicit? Or Something New?

The PRG had enunciated five principles of its new democracy. First, a democracy must provide material benefits commensurate with the needs of the people. Grenada was impoverished, with a very high illiteracy rate, so the PRG spent an average of thirty-two to thirty-seven cents per dollar on social, cultural, and educational services.

The PRG believed that "liberal" democracy was inadequate for Grenada, mainly because its structure of wealth, power, and opportunity systematically excluded the masses of the people. They believed the near-exclusive reliance on periodic national elections placed inadequate emphasis on decision making and overall participation, particularly for the working people. Their vision was for something more inclusive, more explicit, even more emotional, and surely more pro-working people. Rhetorically and organizationally, the PRG shifted away from "liberal" democracy, calling the new model "participatory" democracy. In large measure, what emerged was a grassroots, community-based democracy as the nucleus and model for national politics. This was similar to

Jesse Jackson's Rainbow Coalition in the United States. Was the PRG's participatory democracy more of the same, or was there anything new?

In evaluating the record of the PRG and making some comparisons with that of the colonial and Gairy eras, some of the most helpful assessment has come from a survey taken in 1984 by Eudine Barriteau and Roberta Clarke, when the majority of Grenadians were still in the emotional, political, and organizational wake of the overthrow of the PRG in October 1983 and the U.S.-led invasion which followed six days later.

The Barriteau-Clarke poll found that "50.9 percent felt that conditions of living had improved . . . 26.1 percent [said] conditions had remained the same and 17.8 percent felt that conditions of living had deteriorated." This was attributed to a decline in unemployment and an improvement in education and other social amenities (see Table 5, Appendix). The pollsters concluded that their finding pointed out that the majority of Grenadians were satisfied with the economic and social policies the PRG had initiated (Barriteau and Clarke, 1989: 69). But was this improvement due to the PRG's system of participatory democracy?

A second PRG criterion for democracy was political participation. Prior to the advent of the NJM in the early 1970s, the two major parties, the GULP and the GNP, dominated organized national politics. The NJM itself mobilized political participation, this time through interest groups. There were three forms of participation: the mass organizations (i.e., National Youth Organization, National Women's Organization, Progressive Farmer's Union, etc.), public rallies (i.e., African Liberation Day, Festival of the Revolution, Heroes Day, National Women's Day, Rally to Receive Heads of State, Rally to Protest U.S. Military Movement in the Region), and local and communal levels of participation. Schools and communities encouraged emulation of outstanding performances carrying revolutionary messages. Many were rewarded with the National Science Award, the National Poetry Award, and the National Militia Award. The National Women's Organization organized as much as one-fourth of the female population over the age of eighteen. The PRG believed that mobilization and participation worked hand in hand. Mobilization raised the likelihood of participation, and in 1981 the PRG created a Ministry of Mass Mobilization to coordinate civil-political support for the revolutionary government.

Barriteau and Clarke found that Grenadians were willing and eager to discuss and confront matters relating to the PRG (ibid.: 1). They also found that "47.1 percent of the people believed that the PRG's attempt . . . was successful to bring about participatory democracy; 19.5 percent disagreed and 22 percent were unable to assess." It was the mass organizations to which Barriteau and Clarke's respondents turned, for they made decisions in the zonal council. And, shedding light on their view of their experience with democracy in the country, many added, "It was the first time it happened" (ibid.: 71).

One important source of discontent was identified: that the party's control superseded every level of involvement and decision making, and this is revealed in that if people were truly involved, "when the crises [of October] came, people would have known" (ibid.). Support was highest among the more educated (some relevance to the fact that Gairy's base was among uneducated and agricultural workers).

Institutions created by the PRG were "singled out" for mention: the mass organizations and the parish and zonal councils, and the national budget process. Of note is the fact that some 60.2 percent of youth aged eighteen to twenty-five, who had experienced the last years of Gairy, gave the highest support (60.2%), and the lowest came from those who would have been around for the Gairy-led 1950s revolution (38.1%).

Since what happens to women is a key indicator of democratic advances, Barriteau and Clarke's finding that "the PRG appears to have had a substantial impact on the social conditions affecting women is instructive. Some 75.5 percent of the sample stated that conditions for women improved," compared to 8.2 percent who saw no change and 5 percent who believed women's lot had worsened (ibid.: 67). It is not known whether the 5 percent who felt conditions had worsened believed this was due to the failure to undo gender inequalities. By the time of the collapse of the revolution, Grenadian women had become conscious of their oppression based on gender inequalities, but this never gained organized voice within the party, state, or revolution.[13]

The third democratic principle was the right to elections. The PRG vacillated and stumbled on how it would allow for this. In the end, three things seemed clear: that elections should proceed from lower to higher organs, that a new constitution should be the basis for national elections, and that the NJM and the leadership it sanctioned should be the victor of this process. Before the PRG's demise, only one of these three goals was achieved: near-universal elections of all lower bodies: the National Women's Organization (NWO), Trade Union Council, National Youth Organization (NYO), and the Progressive Farmer's Union (PFU).

An important debate has been waged over elections. Whereas Gairy was accused of rigging elections, the PRG never held any direct national elections, save those it approved of in the mass organizations and the trade unions. Elections are "arguably the only concrete form of wide involvement in public affairs . . . and [are] equated with people's control over and participation in the governing of their affairs." A majority (62.6%) said they favored the PRG policy of not holding elections (ibid.: 74).

The fourth principle of accountability was also a major part of the PRG's vision of democracy, and was directed at eliminating the gap created between public officer and social responsibility, as well as the very specific systematic corruption and arrogance which marked the rule of the previous administration. Accountability was achieved within the context of huge salary cuts for ministers, outlawing corruption in the state, and frequent public appearances of government ministers, and party and state bureaucrats, in front of mass public gatherings to present and discuss their services. A highlight of this was two national conferences on the budget in 1981 and 1982. One thousand national delegates, including business groups, met to study and edit the nation's budgets.

The fifth and final principle was the right of the nation to defend itself. Educated, mobilized, and conscious, people in the revolution were to know what they were fighting for and what revolution means. A People's Militia was a way for the whole society to be held responsive and responsible in case of any threat. However, prior to the Coard-led Central Committee coup in October 1983, the ammunition and arms, which were stored in depots, were emptied. There was a professional army, the Peoples Revolutionary Army, and a fervent reliance on international solidarity and diplomacy.[14] It was the political divisions of October 1983 which weakened the national defense. The assassination of the commander-in-chief, Maurice Bishop, divided and demoralized the People's Militia and the army. The U.S. invasion found a vulnerable nation, only partially defended.

CONCLUSION

Representative democracy in colonial Grenada (1600–1950s) was representative of elite political power, sometimes French-Catholic, sometimes English-Protestant, as they traded places at the top of the governing totem poles. It was not until 1925 that coloreds gained voting rights and a quarter century later that over 80 percent of the people did so. Stringent rules of wealth, acceptable language, and citizenship debarred the nation from political rights, economic well-being, and social and cultural legitimacy.

At first the Gairy administration presided over a watershed transfer of political rights to ordinary citizens (the vote, trade unionism) and some increases in wages. For a time immediately after the 1951 elections, the country seemed poised for true democratic representation within the liberal framework. Parliamentarians elected after the 1950s represented broader political interests than before, and in civil society, while a transfer of economic power did not take place, a cultural pluralism of sorts existed. Nevertheless, it must be borne in mind that women and the poor never had equal representation. That period was swiftly curtailed as the hero who brought the crowds off plantations and their democratic interests into streets, government, schools, and churches crushed all when he used dictatorial methods to attain personal ambition. The Gairy administration, partly in service to the landed and commercial elites, partly in service to autocratic aggrandizement, subverted the full emergence of liberalism in Grenada, and in so doing, helped a reconsideration of its very efficacy in that polity.

To deny the expansion of democracy in Grenada in the years of PRG rule would be to falsify the record of the revolution and to be irreverent of the efforts of the tens of thousands who undertook democratic expansion and believed they attained it—parts of it, moments of it.[15] Indeed, at the level of mass politics, under the PRG, there was first a renewal and expansion of the promised liberal democracy never attained under either the colonial or Gairy eras. But the PRG promised people's power for a new civilization. Much was attained but democracy was being built on masculinist, commandist, and authoritarian notions of power as ideological segmentation and cultural norms inherited from the distant (colonial) and immediate (Gairy era) past. Relentless and terrifying pressures from the United States aggravated these legacies, and militarism increased in a model designed by citizens to end violence. The implosion and comradecide of October 1983 culminated this trajectory.

Speaking in 1984 at a rally to commemorate the fallen Grenada Revolution, Kenrick Radix, former PRG and NJM leader, called on the population to prepare for the second revolution. One, it is hoped, not just of people's *power*, but of people's *democracy*, for which much of the foundation has already been laid by the democratic history of the Grenadian people.

NOTES

1. Very little is known of the democratic legacy of Grenada's indigenous peoples. George Brizan suggests that for the Caribs, decision making resided with a hierarchical council of elders, led by a *cacique*, or priest-leader; from this council, women were excluded, suggesting a leadership model based on gender separation/exclusion. Further, only men could be *caciques*.

2. Grenada today is 50 percent Catholic, 40 percent Church of England (Anglican) Protestant. As late as the 1960s, young Catholic women were sent to find sinners and converts in rural Grenada.

3. Fedon's Rebellion was one of the largest claims for a more just and democratic society put forward by the African (slave) mass in Grenada at the time. It succeeded by putting power in the hands of the rebels for eighteen months between 1795 and 1796. Jan Carew's *Grenada: The Hour Will Strike Again* suggests that the goal was universal freedom and this involved a democratic structure of decision making. In terms of its acceptance and popularity among the "slave-citizenry," records indicated there was overwhelming support. Eventually Grenada's first majority-rule government was overthrown by the intervention of the British.

4. See Dessima Williams, "Achieving Hegemony Under Hegemony: Grenada–U.S. Relations, 1979–1983." See Chapters 5 and 6 (Unpublished) Ph.D. dissertation, George Washington University, 1992.

5. Coloreds like Marryshow, Donovan, and others took up the issue of representative democracy in the formation of the Grenada Representative Association (1917), and in new publications such as the *Torchlight* (1915).

6. This is a system where landless peasants till the land of large estates in exchange for the right to keep a portion of crop grown. For a fuller understanding, see Brizan, pp. 233–234.

7. The words of an urban merchant, W. E. Julien, as reported in Brizan, p. 248.

8. This period of union populism would represent the demands of the workers, all over the British West Indies, but it would be short-lived, with leaders like Bustamante and Gairy quickly becoming authoritarian Anglophone Caribbean equivalents of Latin American *caudillos*.

9. Gairy may have been no different a politician than others like Robert Bradshaw of St. Kitts and Norman Manley of Jamaica, who could wrestle control of the state only in alliance with the British colonial power. The landed and commercial elites as well as the governor and colonial office in London truly held power.

10. The 1960s were boom years for Grenada's agricultural exports.

11. See the Duffus Commission of Inquiry into the Breakdown of Law and Order in Grenada (Government of Grenada, 1974).

12. This committee was formed, with PRG encouragement, to publicize the airport project, sell bonds to raise funds, and generally educate the public on the needs and potential benefits of the project.

13. This is the author's own experience and is substantiated by discussions with several (leading) women in the party and revolution.

14. For instance, Grenada proposed to the OAS that the Caribbean should be a zone of peace, independence, and development. The government should enact that, and trade unions and peace movements should fight for that.

15. See, for example, *Is Freedom We Making: The New Democracy in Grenada* (St. George's: Peoples Revolutionary Government, 1982) or the film by John Douglas and Samori Marksman, *Grenada: The Future Coming Toward Us* (New York, 1983).

7

Belize: Challenges to Democracy

Alma H. Young

This chapter is devoted to a discussion of democracy in Belize, a relatively new nation, but with a 300-year history of British colonialism. On one level "democracy" seems to be functioning well: there are two established parties, there has been electoral turnover in office, legislation is crafted by an elected body, and there is popular interest and participation in the political arena (most visibly in the more limited electoral arena). Yet, on another more fundamental level, there are several security issues which threaten the further strengthening of democracy in Belize. These issues include: the lack of a strong national identity, aggravated recently by the large influx of refugees from the neighboring republics; the increased use of security forces for social control, due in large part to the penetration of drugs (in terms of both drug money and the drug culture) into the society; and the lack of secure borders due to neighboring Guatemala's claim to the country. If these issues are left unresolved, they threaten to further curtail opposition within the political arena, a hallmark of democracy.

MODERN POLITICAL HISTORY OF BELIZE

Belize, a former British colony known until 1973 as British Honduras, obtained its independence in 1981. Like most of the English-speaking Caribbean, to which it has been drawn historically, Belize retained the Westminster form of government. Belize experienced an inordinately long period of decolonization, slightly more than thirty years. During that period, Belizeans were schooled in the trappings of democracy: a governing party and an opposition;

functions of government undertaken by distinct bodies, including an impartial judiciary; a well-trained civil service; a functioning media; and periodic elections with the possibility of turnover in electoral office.

The decolonization process in Belize began in 1950, shortly after the governor used his reserve powers to devalue the local currency. Opposition to that act was swift and intense, and became the basis for political organizing around a nationalist movement (see Grant, 1976; Shoman, 1987). In September 1950, the Peoples United Party (PUP) became the country's first effective political party. In 1954 the PUP was victorious in the first election held under universal adult suffrage, and George C. Price became the acknowledged leader of the nationalist movement.

While the PUP controlled the government and politics in preindependence Belize, other parties and political factions did exist (see Young, 1992). Most of these political groupings opposed independence, fearing that independence would only increase the country's economic and territorial insecurity. Opposition to independence stemmed from the fears aroused by Guatemala's claim to the territory of Belize. The opposition has gone through various party labels, but by the early 1970s the opposition had coalesced into the United Democratic Party (UDP). Other than the issue of independence, there is little in terms of policy or ideology to distinguish the UDP from the PUP. Until the late 1970s, all electoral contests resulted in major victories for the PUP.

In January 1964, Belize received full internal self-government, with the governor responsible for defense, foreign affairs, internal security, and the civil service. After more than seventeen years as a self-governing territory, Belize gained its independence on September 21, 1981, with George C. Price becoming the country's first prime minister.

The 1980s witnessed the full development of the two-party system in Belize. Voters changed governments twice, in 1984 and again in 1989, and did so peacefully. On December 14, 1984, in the first general elections since independence, the PUP was swept from office by the UDP, winning twenty-one seats to the PUP's seven. Even George Price lost his seat. Dissatisfactions with the PUP's foreign and economic programs led to its defeat.

While in opposition, the PUP worked hard to reorganize itself as a party. In the September 1989 general elections, the PUP again became the governing party. The PUP won fifteen seats to the UDP's thirteen seats, and George C. Price was once again prime minister of Belize. While the UDP lost the 1989 elections, Manuel Esquivel, the former prime minister, kept his seat in the House. For the first time in its history, Belize had a former head of government on the opposition side of the House.

The 1980s also saw another major development that had a significant impact on the strengthening of democracy in Belize: the growth in the media. The number of newspapers proliferated, with each political party or faction having its own newspaper, usually published weekly. *Amandala*, the only "independent" newspaper in Belize, became a national newspaper and garnered the largest circulation. Radio Belize, the government-owned radio station, finally got some competition in 1990 when the owners of *Amandala* received a license to open an alternative radio station. Later that year, Radio Belize was freed from direct government control when the Belize Broadcasting Network became a statutory corporation, the Broadcasting Corporation of Belize (*Amandala*, July 13, 1990, 1).

Local television finally came to Belize in the late 1980s. First, government opened a station in 1988; now there are two additional stations doing local programming. In the last general election there were televised debates among the major candidates. There are now televised press conferences and radio carries some of the proceedings in the House of Representatives. Gone are the days when news was tightly controlled and every radio in Belize was listening to the news as broadcast by Radio Belize.

Just as there were events in the 1980s which seemed to hold the promise of greater democratization in Belize, so there were events which threatened that promise. The first of these was the influx of large numbers of Central Americans fleeing the civil conflicts engulfing the region. Their presence in Belize not only sharpened the divisions within the country between the two major ethnic groups, but made a national identity more difficult to define.

ETHNICITY, NATIONAL INTEGRATION, AND THE REFUGEE CRISIS

Belize holds a unique position on the Central American mainland as a predominantly English-speaking, former British colony. For most of its history, Belize has seen itself, and has been seen by others, as a social, cultural, and political island on the Central American mainland. Belize is a nation of exceptional ethnic heterogeneity, with the two largest groups being Afro-Creoles of West Indian heritage and Mestizos, traditionally from Mexico and Guatemala. Other ethnic groups include Garifuna (black Caribs), Mayan and Ketchi Indians, Chinese, East Indians, Lebanese, and even settlements of Mennonites. According to the 1980 census, Creoles make up approximately 40 percent of the population, while Mestizos make up approximately 33 percent and are fast gaining in number. Creoles are heavily represented in Belize City, the former capital of the country and still its financial, cultural, and population center. (Belize City, which is 75 percent Creole, accounts for approximately 30 percent of the country's population.) Mestizos live mainly in the northern districts of Corozal and Orange Walk, areas that are geared toward export agriculture.

For the past one hundred years Central Americans have been immigrating to Belize in search of land and jobs. The country's extremely low person-to-land ratio, coupled with the need for agricultural laborers (agriculture accounts for more than 70 percent of the country's exports), has historically made Belize an ideal resettlement site for people from surrounding republics. However, the flow of Central Americans into Belize was accelerated in the 1970s when armed conflict in Guatemala, El Salvador, and Nicaragua escalated and continued throughout the 1980s. Because of the Central American crisis large numbers of refugees have been entering Belize, both legally and illegally. The latest figures put the number at 40,000 (*Amandala*, January 17, 1991, 5). While most Central American nations have a significant number of refugees, for Belize, with its population today of only about 190,000, the numbers are seen as alarming (see Everitt, 1984). There is a feeling among many Belizeans that they are being "swamped by outsiders."

In an attempt to manage the steady flow of refugees into Belize, the government in early 1984 announced that it would extend an amnesty to all "undocumented aliens" within a period from June to September. During that period more than 12,000 aliens registered their presence in Belize. Around the time of the amnesty, officials from the Ministry of Home Affairs spoke of 16,000 "illegal squatters," mainly from Guatemala, El Salvador, and Honduras. These were in addition to the 4,600 persons in the country recognized as refugees by the United Nations High Commission for Refugees (UNHCR). In a 1984 broadcast, then Home Affairs Minister Vernon Courtenay said the refugee situation "is unsatisfactory and poses a threat to our Belizean heritage" (*Central American Report*, June 15, 1984, 180).

This perceived threat to the Belizean heritage has less to do with the official allegation that the Central American refugees are responsible for an escalating crime rate (which will be discussed later), and more to do with changes to the ethnic composition of the country. With the influx of Central American refugees, the population becomes more Mestizo. The changing ethnic makeup is compounded by the fact that large numbers of Afro-Creole Belizeans have been emigrating for years to the United States, England, and Canada in search of work. It is estimated that over the past four decades 60,000 Creoles have left Belize for work in the United States.

In the late 1960s and early 1970s, the role of ethnicity in creating a national identity was prominent in Belizean politics. Through a process of cooptation and isolation, ethnic politics at the time did not reach a level of violence, although fears of loss of jobs, housing, and status ran high among Creoles. Out of that fear grew the country's Black Power movement in 1968 (Young, 1970). The local impetus for the Black Power movement was the Price government's attempt at the time to emphasize Belize's links to Central America. Throughout his political career George Price has felt that identifying more strongly with the Central American republics would hasten Belize's independence and forestall Guatemala's claim to the country. For Creoles, the government's attempt to link Belize more closely to Central America was seen most starkly in the late 1960s with the government's decision to move the capital away from the Creole stronghold of Belize City inland fifty miles, to use pseudo-Mayan architecture for the government buildings in the new capital, and to give the capital a pseudo-Mayan name, Belmopan (see Hyde, 1969).

Many Creoles argued then, and the argument has begun to resurface lately, that blacks are being robbed of their political power in Belize, just as they have been in other black enclaves along the Atlantic coast. In a number of coastal cities, from Colon in Panama, Limon in Costa Rica, Bluefields in Nicaragua, Puerto Cortes and Ceiba in Honduras, to Livingston and Puerto Barrios in Guatemala, blacks are the predominant group, but they are generally cut off from the political and economic mainstream of their countries. Historically, in Belize it was different, for blacks were integrated into the political and social fabric of the country. However, a greater emphasis on the Central American heritage of the country makes many Afro-Creoles fear that they are put at a disadvantage and will lose political power in their own country.

In order to forestall any political movement among the Creoles, and in order to be seen as managing the steady flow of refugees into Belize, the government instituted the amnesty program in 1984. The amnesty program was a prelude to the establishment of a system of documenting all non-Belizeans and creating legal/administrative guidelines for those already in the country. The task of working out the details of which individuals would be accepted into the country and under what conditions was left to the UDP government that came into power in December 1984.

The new government indicated that it would take a more restrictive position toward the continued illegal immigration. By June 1985 the government had passed measures against the employment of undocumented persons, increasing the fees on firearm permits to non-Belizeans, and adding to the penalties for any infringement of the immigration laws. Later that year it increased the fees for permits for foreigners to work in the country and to apply for permanent residence. In August 1985 the government also appointed an Immigration Advisory Committee, consisting mainly of senior civil servants.

According to Joseph Palacio (1990), the most significant work of the committee has been establishing a more streamlined procedure for the screening of persons applying for refugee status. The government still has not developed policies and directed resources so that the new Central American immigrants, along with Belizeans of different ethnic backgrounds, can feel that there is a place for them in the Belizean society and economy. Rather, the government finds it easier to fall back on old stereotypes about Central Americans and thus attempt to assuage the fears of Afro-Creoles and others.

In the process, the serious work of developing a national identity for the country that reflects the reality of its ethnic diversity is removed from the national agenda. The refusal to grapple with that reality makes the functioning of democracy more difficult in Belize. Furthermore, to have within Belize growing numbers of persons from the neighboring republics who have no real experience with democratic institutions and values creates the possibility of the weakening of the political culture. Defining the Belizean identity becomes a more difficult task, but a more necessary one.

DRUGS: THE WITHERING OF SOCIETY

When Turkey entered into an agreement with the United States in 1973 to shut down its poppy fields, much of the international narcotics trade transferred from Southeast Asia to Latin America. Like its neighbors, Belize began to see the effects of drug activity and drug money within its society. These effects include government's greater willingness to use security forces for social control, and a rising crime rate.

The crime rate escalated just as the influx of refugees from the neighboring republics increased. Central American immigrants have largely been blamed for the rising crime rate. The government has charged that the upswing in the number of murders and armed robberies is due to "strangers to Belize": most of the incidents occur in the sugar belt in the north where there is the largest concentration of Central American immigrants. Many of the aliens come originally as cane cutters with valid work permits. When their permits expire, they disappear into the jungles and are joined by relatives and friends who settle illegally. Many are believed to become involved in the lucrative business of marijuana cultivation in the dense jungle interior. The government alleges that these marijuana fields are often guarded by men heavily armed with automatic rifles and submachine guns.

Because it is estimated to be one of the largest marijuana suppliers to the United States, Belize has been under great pressure from the U.S. government to pursue more aggressive programs against marijuana cultivation. During the UDP years, the United States became an extremely influential and highly visible force in Belizean affairs.[1] In return for U.S. aid, the UDP government cooperated with Washington's efforts to curb the escalating transshipment of drugs through Belize. Not only have Belizean security forces been going through the dense jungle on search-and-destroy missions, the government has also used chemical sprays on the drug fields. As a result of the spraying more than three thousand plantations covering an area of 14,400 acres were destroyed in the late 1980s (*Amandala*, August 15, 1989, 3).

The war against drugs has come with an internal price, a price which negatively impacts the functioning of democracy in Belize. There have been an increasing number of arrests and convictions for cultivating and selling drugs. Roadblocks have been set up along the Northern Highway, with automobiles searched at random. Drug laws have been stiffened, including, for the first time in Belizean history, the provision for trials without juries (*The New Belize*, October 1983, 86). A law passed in July 1990 introduced a new offense of "drug trafficking" and established mandatory minimum sentences for drug traffickers (*Amandala*, July 13, 1990, 1). The law also extended the jurisdiction of the courts and strengthened the powers of arrest in order to combat the international drug trade.

The crackdown on drug activity has been so massive that in some quarters it is feared that the Belize government may use the enforcement of drug laws to become more repressive toward its citizens. These fears came to the fore in November 1987 when the UDP government presented a bill in the House of Representatives to establish an independent Security and Intelligence Service (SIS). The identities of the members of the service as well as the work of the service were to be kept secret. The director of the service was to have the same status as the commissioner of police, under direct ministerial control.

Officially, the SIS was to be established to deal primarily with espionage, sabotage, subversion, and terrorism, both from internal and external sources. There was immediate speculation, however, that the SIS was established mainly as a mechanism to stem drug trafficking in and throughout Belize. As such, it would be used for internal social control rather than for threats from outside.

The PUP's stance against the proposed Security and Intelligence Service was very strong. During the public debate on the bill the opposition focused on the potential for the SIS to be used to infringe civil liberties, possibly leading to a police state (*Amandala*, December 10, 1987, 1). Throughout the Caribbean, there is concern that under the rubric of fighting drugs, government leaders are repressing their own people (see Duncan, 1991). In the name of the war on drugs, enemies of the government "can be repressed with impunity, protests can be foiled and dissent weakened" (Young, 1991: 14).

The SIS bill was passed in the House of Representatives in December 1987 over vehement objections from the opposition. Major protests reached a dramatic point when a fire was set in the home of the minister of home affairs, the major architect of the SIS bill. The government blamed the fire on the PUP. One of those charged with arson and arrested was Thomas Greenwood, a former high-ranking officer in the Belize Defence Force (BDF) during the PUP administration. The case against Greenwood and two others was dismissed by the Supreme Court in November 1988 after the judge ruled that the statements taken by the police from two of the defendants were not admissible as evidence. Later, Greenwood was an unsuccessful PUP candidate during the national elections of 1989.

Shortly after winning the 1989 general elections, the PUP government kept one of its campaign promises and eliminated the SIS. The government ordered SIS agents to report for patrol duty with the police force, and the agency to distribute its resources among other ministries. The duties previously assigned to SIS were taken over by the police department, in its Special Branches Division (*Central America Report*, November 3, 1989, 345). The Special Branches Division has the major responsibility for countering drug trafficking in Belize.

For a number of years the Belize government has conducted joint police and military drug searches. Invariably these searches result in violence. Lately these searches have uncovered stashes of cocaine, and have pointed to the fact that Belize is fast becoming a transshipment point for drugs destined for the United States from South America. For example, on October 4, 1990, a joint police/military operation along the Northern Highway resulted in the discovery of 470 pounds of cocaine with a street value of $20 million. Four men were arrested: a Colombian living in Miami, a Honduran living in Belize, a Belizean living in Miami, and a Belizean living in Belize City (*Amandala*, October 12, 1990, 1).

Fearing that the police could not handle the increase in drug activity, in late 1990 the PUP government began deputizing military officers as special constables to work on drug cases. The Belize Chamber of Commerce and Industry and the Belize tourism industry supported the government's use of BDF soldiers as special constables to assist the Belize police force in dealing with the recent crime wave in the country. The Human Rights Commission and some elements of the press criticized the government for deputizing soldiers as police. The opponents feared that expanding the role of the military into the civilian life of the country could result in a curtailing of civil liberties (see Huggins, 1978: 149–171).

The government's response addressed only the legal issues: that the Defense Act provides for the deployment of the Belize Defence Force in support of the civil authorities in the maintenance of law and order, and the Police Act provides for the commissioner of police to appoint special constables. The public was assured that the special constables would be under the control of the commissioner of police and would follow the same regulations that regular police follow. The issue of civil liberties and the role of the military in maintaining social control were left unaddressed by the government.

Drug activity in Belize has increased to such a point that plans are reportedly under way by the U.S. Drug Enforcement Agency (DEA) to open an office in Belize (*New York Times*, December 18, 1991). The DEA's eradication efforts against local marijuana growers in the mid-1980s were not popular among Belizeans, but its war against cocaine traffickers is viewed with approval by many. The local police are not thought to be equipped to handle major drug traffickers. More to the point, perhaps, is the fact that many Belizeans consider drug activity to be carried out by foreigners (including aliens resident in Belize) and therefore they think enforcement measures will not affect them.

In wanting to rid their society of drug-related crime, many Belizeans are prepared to enlarge the role of security forces (both internal and external ones) within the country. There appears to be little realization that in the process the government arms itself with measures that might lead to greater repression of various elements within society. While in opposition, the PUP leadership saw this possibility and thus reacted strongly against the SIS legislation. Integrating security forces into the fabric of society is not conducive to a well-functioning democracy.

TERRITORIAL DISPUTE

Guatemala's claim to the territory of Belize has been the central issue in Belizean politics since the 1950s, when the nationalist movement began. Yet neither the government nor the opposition has sought to adequately mobilize the people on the basis of the issue. Nor has the local elite reached a consensus of opinion on how the issue should be resolved. Historically, this lack of consensus has been due to the fact that competing groups within the political leadership differ on Belize's national orientation and its foreign alliances (Young and Young, 1988).

What has come to be known as the Anglo-Guatemala dispute stems from a poorly worded treaty between Britain and Guatemala in 1859. In return for recognizing the boundaries of Belize (at the time British Honduras), Britain agreed in Article Seven of the treaty to construct a road from Guatemala City to the Atlantic coast. For a number of reasons the road was never built. The dispute lagged until the 1930s, when diplomatic efforts to resolve the dispute resumed, but to no avail. In 1940, the Guatemala government adopted a hard line on the issue. It stated that in lieu of Article Seven not being fulfilled, Guatemala now had the right to recover territory "ceded" in 1859. In 1945, Guatemala adopted a new constitution which declared in Article One that "any efforts taken towards obtaining Belize reinstatement to the Republic are of national interest" (Bloomfield, 1953: 67). The slogan "Belice es nuestra" became a popular rallying cry, especially of the more conservative groups in Guatemala.

It was in this environment that the nationalist movement in Belize began. Until the 1970s, the PUP, under the leadership of George C. Price, directed much of its efforts at trying to bolster its claim that Belize's economic and political future lay with Central America and, therefore, by extension, that some accommodation had to be reached with Guatemala. On the other hand, the main plank of the opposition has been that the country's constitutional advance should be within the British Commonwealth, in effect denying Belize's connection with Central America. "No Guatemala" became the rallying cry of the opposition. They also demanded that Britain retain control over the country until a resolution of the dispute with Guatemala was found. Eventually their demand became no independence without a suitable defense guarantee from Britain. This issue held up independence for seventeen years as Britain sought to grant independence without any defense obligations, and the PUP government sought a resolution to the crisis that would respond not only to the demands of Guatemala but to its own opposition (see Young and Young, 1988).

In the mid-1970s, Belize, wary of waiting for a diplomatic resolution of the Guatemalan claim, took its case directly to the international community, and won support for its right to self-determination and territorial integrity. In 1981, after winning a unanimous vote in the United Nations on a resolution calling for its independence with territorial integrity, Belize opted to go forward with independence. The territorial dispute, however, still was not settled. International support for Belize forced Britain to agree to defend the country for "an appropriate period"; after independence a 1,600-man contingent of British troops was to be stationed in Belize. Britain also agreed to provide more intensive training for the BDF, formed in 1978. Britain's defense guarantee effectively foreclosed the opposition's position against independence. However, the opposition refused to be a party to independence negotiations with Britain. Constitutional independence still found the country divided on the Guatemalan issue.

Starting in the mid-1980s, a number of events occurred which signaled a greater possibility of resolving the territorial dispute. In 1984 the opposition UDP became the governing party and, under prodding from the United States, became more amenable to discussions with Guatemala. In 1986, Guatemala elected its first civilian administration after almost thirty years of military rule. The constitution that was written in 1985 to make way for civilian government in Guatemala deleted the clause "Belice es nuestra." The administration of Vinicio Cerezo proved more accommodating and more conciliatory toward Belize. During Cerezo's first year in office, Guatemala lifted trade restrictions against Belize and resumed diplomatic relations with Britain. Diplomatic relations between the two countries had been interrupted since 1963 because of the territorial dispute.

In May 1988 the Guatemalan government initialed a joint accord with Belize to create a Belize-Guatemala permanent commission, with Britain as observer, to work out a compromise to the dispute. The commission began to meet regularly, often in Miami. Guatemalan officials became more conciliatory in their demands; instead of demanding land rights, what they sought was an adequate outlet to the Caribbean Sea. Guatemalans also want to be able to penetrate the Caribbean market, a goal that is impeded in part by the Caribbean countries' wariness of Guatemala's intentions toward Belize. In the meantime Guatemala appears to accept the fact that Belize is becoming more integrated into Central America. At the twentieth session of the Organization of American States (OAS) in December 1990, Belize was unanimously granted membership into the body.

By late 1991 the work of the Belize-Guatemala Commission appeared to be reaping benefits. First, on August 14, 1991, Guatemala recognized "the right of Belize to self-determination," the first time such a recognition had been made. In that same statement, President Jorge Serrano reiterated his government's pledge to continue negotiations and "exhaust all civil legal means that may lead to the final resolution of territorial differences" (quoted in *Labour Beacon*, September 7, 1991, 9).

Then, on August 16, 1991, the foreign minister of Belize, Said Musa, introduced a bill in the House of Representatives which would define and delimit Belize's territorial waters in such a way as to allow Guatemala access to the Caribbean Sea through its own territorial waters. The bill would limit Belize's territorial waters to three miles in its southern area (rather than the twelve miles provided for by international law). In introducing the Maritime Areas Act (MAA),[2] Musa said the provision granting Guatemala access to the Caribbean Sea should be seen by Guatemala as a sign of good faith on the part of Belize to negotiate. He reminded the members of the House that this had been a long-standing Guatemalan demand and one that both Belizean parties had considered reasonable in the past (*Spearhead*, September 1991, 1, 2).

Finally, in September 1991 the president of Guatemala issued a statement that said in part: "In view of Belize's actions [in limiting its territorial sea] Guatemala expresses its willingness to continue direct discussions with *the independent state of Belize* in order to arrive at a definitive solution to the dispute" (*Amandala*, September 13, 1991, 10; italics added). The Belize government immediately issued a statement saying that it welcomed the declaration that Guatemala recognizes Belize as an independent state. It went on to state that it would continue to negotiate directly with Guatemala to bring an honorable conclusion to the problem.

The British government also issued a statement that said it welcomed the Guatemalan president's recognition of Belize as a "sovereign, independent state." The British government committed £22.5 million (about BZE$75 million) as an initial contribution to launching joint projects to renew and extend the road network between Belize and Guatemala (ibid.: 10–11).

The UDP said that it welcomed the declaration by the Guatemalan president, but that the party would have preferred a more explicit statement of recognition. (i.e., the Guatemalan statement did not say "we recognize Belize as an independent state"; rather it spoke of "the independent state of Belize" within the sentence about its willingness to continue negotiations). The UDP also warned the Belize government that it considered negotiations with Guatemala to be ongoing and that any proposals that emerged must be submitted to the Belizean people for ratification by way of a referendum.

In an attempt to forestall any public outcry over the proposed Maritime Areas Act, the government's strategy was to show bipartisan support for the MAA and to demonstrate the goodwill of the Guatemalan government. Musa, the PUP government's foreign minister, and the former foreign minister in the UDP government, Dean Barrow, both publicly supported the MAA as a bipartisan effort and said that their support demonstrated that the issue of the territorial dispute was being moved out of party politics (*Amandala*, September 20, 1991, 1). To show his government's support, the Guatemalan president accepted an official invitation to visit Belize on September 21 to participate in Independence Day celebrations. However, a few days before he was to visit Belize, the Guatemalan president was forced to cancel his visit at the insistence of right-wing elements in his country, including the military (*Central America Report*, September 27, 1991, 283).

On September 16, 1991, Musa and Barrow paid an official visit to Guatemala. Upon their return to Belize, they said it was agreed "to integrate a bilateral commission" (i.e., including Belizean and Guatemalan negotiators) to seek agreements in the economic, social, and cultural areas. These included joint exploitation of defined areas of the exclusive economic zone of Belize for mutual benefit; permanent access of Guatemala to the Caribbean Sea with reciprocal use and development of port facilities; and cultural and educational exchanges. They agreed that such actions would facilitate Belize being more fully integrated into the Central American development process (National Bi-Partisan Commission, 1991).

AN EXPERIMENT IN "PARTICIPATORY DEMOCRACY"

Shortly after the return of Musa and Barrow from Guatemala it was decided that Musa, Prime Minister George Price, and former prime minister Manuel Esquivel, representing a bipartisan effort at the highest levels, would begin a tour of the country to explain firsthand the substance of the present discussions with Guatemala and the nature of the proposed agreements which would end the territorial dispute, if accepted by the people of Belize and Guatemala.

At the second stop on their national tour, Price, Musa, and Esquivel met with more than 800 Belizeans from the southern port town of Punta Gorda in the Toledo District who said they rejected the Maritime Areas Act because it would give to Guatemala traditional Belizean fishing grounds which are important to local fishermen. The residents also voiced concerns that Guatemalan gunboats and coast guard launches were already "enforcing" the three-mile limit, shooting at and chasing Belizean fishermen who crossed over the limit.

After the meeting in Punta Gorda, the merits of the proposed MAA began to be publicly debated. Major groups in Belize started taking positions on whether they were for or against the MAA. For the first time in the country's history there appeared to be a serious discussion of the territorial dispute and of a way to resolve it.

Supporters of the MAA included the Belize Chamber of Commerce and Industry, the Bar Association of Belize, the City Council of Belize, the Human Rights Commission of Belize, and the Society for the Promotion of Education and Research (SPEAR). SPEAR, a nonprofit organization, is led by a former foreign minister in the PUP government who spearheaded the effort in the late 1970s to win international support for the independence of Belize. SPEAR's support of the act was based on recognition of the fact that a treaty, formalizing the sea boundary between the two countries, must be put to a referendum of the people. In its published statement, SPEAR stated: "We commend the leadership of both parties for uniting on this issue and together consulting the people, since we are convinced that a solution to the dispute can only be achieved with a unified national understanding" (*Amandala*, October 18, 1991, 5).

In the first couple of months of the debate, opposition to the MAA came mainly from individuals, led by the UDP-appointed senator from Toledo. Other groups opposing the MAA included the National Garifuna Council and Los Angeles Belizeans (i.e., a group representing Belizeans living in Los Angeles; the other major concentration of expatriate Belizeans, living in New York, remained silent on the issue). Then in mid-November 1991, Phillip Goldson resigned as deputy secretary general of the UDP over disagreement with the position of his party's leadership on the MAA, and this changed the nature and intensity of the opposition. Since the nationalist era began, Goldson's main political agenda has been no territorial concessions to Guatemala. He has always been able to block initiatives endorsed by Price which tried to resolve the territorial dispute.

The current PUP government had assumed that the MAA would not suffer this same fate since the leadership of the opposition and that of the government were in favor of the proposal. The MAA had been negotiated by the UDP while it was in power. However, it had not been discussed with the public nor the UDP rank and file. When the PUP came back into power in 1989, they accepted the proposal on the table and the leadership of both parties agreed to take the proposal to the public. The meetings around the country began shortly after the maritime bill had been introduced in the House. The public was assured that any treaty between Belize and Guatemala would be presented to them for ratification. They were told that the Maritime Areas Act was preliminary to a treaty and therefore was not subject to a public vote.

In early December 1991, Goldson, along with Derek Aikman, a UDP member of the House, and Hubert Elrington, a former UDP attorney general, formed the Patriotic Alliance for Territorial Integrity, an organization set up for opposing the passage of the MAA currently before the House of Representatives. At a press conference held on December 10, Goldson said that the Patriotic Alliance was founded as a national body "to provide the Belizean people with a listening ear and to give a voice to the Belizean people to speak to the world." Goldson told the press that the message he heard in 1948, when he first became involved with the Guatemala dispute, is the same that he hears today: the territorial integrity of Belize is not negotiable (*Amandala*, December 13, 1991, 6).

The goals and objectives of the Patriotic Alliance for Territorial Integrity, announced at the press conference, include:

1. To support the demand of the Belizean people that the territorial seas of Belize shall extend to the median line in the south;

2. To assist in organizing the strong opposition of the Belizean people to the passing of the Maritime Areas Act, either in its original or amended form, unless it is first submitted to a referendum of the Belizean people;

3. To take all action, including constitutional, legal, and political, to defend the territorial integrity of Belize;

4. To champion the demand of the Belizean people for the actualization of their full political, legal, social, economic, and human rights as guaranteed by the Belizean constitution;

5. To champion the demand of the Belizean people that the present immigration policy, which has had the effect of flooding the country with Central American aliens, be ended; that a more responsible and balanced policy be put in its place with the object of ensuring the preservation of the Belizean way of life (*Amandala*, December 13, 1991, 6).

The fifth demand is reminiscent of Goldson's historic concern with the preservation of the Belizean way of life, which, to him, centers around Afro-Creoles and their connection to Britain and, by extension, to the English-speaking Caribbean. After all, the impetus for the original split within the PUP in 1958 was the dispute between Goldson, who wished to have Belize become a member of the West Indies Federation of the 1950s, and Price, who preferred a Central American orientation for the country. The MAA controversy is a reminder that among the political leadership the question of a national orientation for the country remains unsettled. The refugee issue and the Guatemala question continue to be caught up in the battle to define the national identity of Belize.

The Patriotic Alliance began holding public meetings in Belize City and, during the week that the vote on the MAA was expected in the House, the Patriotic Alliance began a twenty-four-hour vigil in the heart of Belize City. The biggest boost to the Patriotic Alliance campaign came on January 15, 1992, when the Council of Management of the Public Service Union (PSU), the country's largest union, voted to institute a full-fledged strike on January 17, in an attempt to force the government to suspend its scheduled vote on the MAA.

The government responded immediately to the strike threat by seeking and winning a temporary injunction against any form of "industrial action" by the PSU (*Amandala*, January 17, 1992, 1). Following on the heels of the government's response to the PSU, the Belize branch of the National Teachers Union voted to oppose the MAA.

Throughout the controversy the PUP leadership held solid in its support of the MAA. Within the UDP, however, the debate over the MAA exacerbated the factional divisions. Factional fighting seemed to reflect the fact that the UDP is a merger of three former political parties that joined together in 1973: the probusiness Liberal Party; the National Independence Party, the historic party of opposition; and the People's Democratic Movement, the latter two of which had championed the resolution of the Guatemalan issue before the granting/acceptance of independence. With Manuel Esquivel at the party's helm, the liberal faction of the UDP gained ascendancy. However, when the Guatemalan issue came once again to the fore, Goldson became an active voice within the party, a voice with great legitimacy since he had for so many years been the lone figure of opposition in the legislature. With the creation of the Patriotic Alliance by three of their leaders, the UDP support for the MAA began to weaken.

The factionalism within the UDP came to a head on January 12, 1992, when, at a meeting of the National Executive Committee, Esquivel and Barrow, party leader and deputy leader respectively, forced the expulsion from the party of Derek Aikman, Hubert Elrington, and lawyer B. Q. Pitts. Goldson resigned in protest and was joined by Samuel Rhaburn, the member of the House from Belize Rural North (ibid.). The ouster reflected the probusiness faction of the party trying to retain its ascendancy, and the party's support of the MAA. Esquivel was also trying to isolate Goldson within the party. Ousting Goldson was unthinkable, given his stature within the UDP.

When Goldson and Rhaburn joined the ousted trio, the party began to question the wisdom of its position on the MAA issue. The party leadership was mindful of the strength of Goldson's support against the MAA in Belize City, the UDP's electoral stronghold. Thus the ouster had the unexpected result of forcing Esquivel and Barrow to announce at a news conference later that week that the party officially withdrew its support of the MAA. As members of the National Bi-Partisan Commission, Esquivel and Barrow said they still supported the bill's passage, but they would accede to the wishes of their party's members and vote against it in the House (ibid.).

On January 17, 1992, the Maritime Areas Act was passed by the House of Representatives, sixteen to twelve. All PUP members voted for the bill; all opposition members voted against it (*Amandala*, January 24, 1992, 1, 5). By holding firm as a party, the PUP members were able to carry out their historic goal: rapprochement with the Guatemalans. Whether that rapprochement brings the country the desired economic and political benefits, including integration within Central America, remains to be seen.

CONCLUSION

The controversy surrounding the MAA succeeded in generating the greatest discussion on the Guatemalan issue that the country had ever experienced. For the first time, the government was proactive in explaining the issue (at least in terms of the proposed legislation) to the public. Amendments were made to the legislation as a result of concerns expressed by the public. The bipartisan nature of the political support for the legislation, at least until the week before the vote, was historic and gave promise that the political elite might learn how to form a consensus around an issue that has been of major importance since the nationalist era.

At the moment when Barrow and Esquivel gave their active support to the MAA, the Guatemalan issue was taken out of party politics and elevated to an issue of importance to the nation as a whole. Likewise, when Barrow and Esquivel later announced that they would follow the dictates of their party membership and not vote for the bill, it showed that the parliamentary system worked well. They knew that if they voted against the wishes of their constituents, most of whom lived in Belize City, they were unlikely to be reelected. Thus, in the electoral arena, the power of the populace was felt. Beyond that arena, the power of the populace could be expected only in extraconstitutional areas such as strikes, protests, and riots. What we have not seen in Belize is a way for the populace to have a sustained impact on policy making. The kinds of institutions that would make that possible are not yet in place in Belize. Thus, for most purposes, political decision making is largely done by elites.

The bipartisan commission served a useful purpose in helping leaders from both parties learn to work together. However, when Goldson resigned his leadership post in the UDP in order to form the Patriotic Alliance, it was a reminder of how difficult it is to fashion a consensus on the Guatemala issue. The formation of the Patriotic Alliance was a strong signal that the Guatemala issue is intertwined with a number of other issues (such as national identity) which generate intense feelings within large segments of the population. Unless properly defused, such intensity can wreak havoc on democratic aspirations.

When opposition to the MAA began to reach a groundswell, the government decided to cut off national debate and put the issue to a vote in the House. Wishing to ensure that the proceedings would go smoothly (i.e., as planned by the governing party), the government used its security forces to keep opponents at bay. Limiting debate in such a fashion and resorting to the use of force within the parliamentary setting does not bode well for democracy.

The government has assured the public that the final resolution of the dispute with Guatemala will be put into treaty form and that the treaty will be put to a referendum. Whether there will be a referendum on a treaty will be a good test of the relationship between "the ruler and the ruled." What some fear is that resolution of the issue will come in bits and pieces, passed by the legislature or enacted by ministerial authority, without ever having a full public debate or a vote of the people. If that should happen, then an important opportunity for popular political participation will have been lost. Only with effective participation by individuals in the decisions that affect their lives can democracy be said to truly exist. On that measure Belize has a long way to travel before it can be called a true democracy.

NOTES

I am indebted to Dennis H. Young for his helpful comments during the writing of this chapter.

1. The United States had a major influence on the UDP government. In 1985 the United States's $14.5 million balance-of-payments support loan to the new Esquivel government, which complemented a US$7 million IMF standby credit, was the predominant factor in pulling Belize out of foreign debt arrears and improving the country's short-term financial situation. For the remainder of the 1980s U.S. aid continued to pour into Belize, as the United States sought to create a stable ally in a country with one foot in Central America and one foot in the Caribbean.

2. Clause 3 of the Maritime Areas Act defines Belize's territorial sea as being twelve nautical miles wide, with two exceptions. One exception has to do with the situation where the territorial seas of two adjacent states meet; in such cases, the median line will form the boundary between the two. The other exception, and the one that caused the ensuing controversy, was that in the southern waters Belize would retain the existing three miles territorial sea. Therefore, from the south entrance of the Sarstoon River and up to Ranguana Caye, Belize's territorial sea was to extend for three miles only, not the twelve miles allowed by international law. The bill also declared a 200-mile exclusive economic zone (EEZ) for Belize.

8

Suriname: The Politics of Transition from Authoritarianism to Democracy, 1988–1992

Betty Sedoc-Dahlberg

Following eight years of a leftist-oriented military regime in Suriname, the 1987 general elections resulted in a civilian government that lasted until December 24, 1990 when the military seized power for the second time. The civilian government consisted of a grand coalition of the three largest ethnic parties—the Creole's National Party of Suriname (NPS), the Hindustani's Unified Reform Party (VHP), and the Javanese's Party of Indonesian Peasants (KTPI). The coalition was named The Front for Democracy and Development (hereafter The Front).

After the December 1990 coup d'état, the military installed an interim cabinet dominated by members of the tiny National Democratic Party (NDP), its political arm. On May 25, 1991, the Surinamese people voted for the second time in four years for return to civilian rule. However, compared with the 1987 elections the setting was significantly different. The elections resulted in a victory for the New Front (NF), a new coalition consisting of The Front coalition partners plus the Surinamese Labor Party (SLP)—despite a substantial number of seats for the NDP and the Democratic Alternative 1991 (DA '91). Ronald Venetiaan, the presidential candidate of the NF, was elected on September 6, 1991 by 80 percent of the United Peoples Congress (VVV) and was inaugurated ten days later.

This chapter deals with the following questions: how can the performance of the civilian government of 1988–1990 be assessed in terms of regime survival and (re)democratization? What can be expected from the new civilian government with regard to the implementation of its expressed policy goals? To what extent can the external environment contribute substantially to the process of democratization in Suriname? Can the case of Suriname be helpful in identifying critical areas regarding the transformation from authoritarian to democratic-pluralist systems?

THE CIVILIAN GOVERNMENT: 1988–1990

Domestic Politics

As a result of successful cross-communal mobilization caused by strong antimilitary sentiment in the populace, The Front received 86 percent of the votes in the elections of November 1987. The government was confronted with a civil war, drug problems, a black market, poor functioning of weak democratic institutions, and conflicting ethnic interests.

Several attempts were made to end the civil war, starting with peace negotiations in St. Jean (French Guiana). Despite intimidation of the military, the Kourou Peace Treaty was signed by all members of the cabinet on August 19, 1988. However, it could not be implemented. The virtual nonexistence of civilian ruling power became manifest when the leader of the army, Ltd. Col. Desi Bouterse, stated in an interview at the Memre Boekoe Kazerne (military barracks, headquarters) that peace could not come into force as long as he himself was not willing to settle an agreement with the Jungle Commando (JC).

The government observed the increasing dissatisfaction of the populace but was not able to act. The regime had to cater to the interests of the powerful military since neutralization or accommodation of the National Army (NL) had not been successful. Suriname was regularly involved in drug trafficking. Instead of carrying out a full investigation, both the police and the army accused each other of involvement of elements of their forces in drugs.[1] External assistance was requested but not effectuated.

The Front cabinet struggled against the black market in foreign exchange but was not able to terminate its existence. The main constraint was the availability of foreign funds. Negotiations with the Dutch to reopen the suspended development aid were not successful. The indirect impact of the external environment on domestic politics is most evident in this area.[2]

Weak democratic institutions also contributed to the poor performance of the government. The Front government lacked an institutionalized form of communication with its supporters. Consequently, involvement in decision making was missing. Representatives of ruling political parties in district councils complained about a lack of communication and information. Efficient functioning of the traditional parties was still missing and more efficient institutionalized channels of participation in which civilian support groups could operate were not implemented. This author takes the view that the lack of democratic principles and relationships on a micro level in the broader society as well as in political parties is a fundamental constraint for democratizing the Surinamese society. Only in the Creole NPS did signs of a shift from authoritarian to more democratic structures emerge. Here, emancipatory processes in the different ethnic groups are relevant for understanding structural imbalances in the country's political system.

Conflicting ethnic interests were caused by the widening gap between the financially better situated upper strata of the VHP and the process of marginalization of an increasing number of poor Creoles. The purchase of land by Hindustani became an important issue as well as their control of the black market, business, and trade.[3] The government was not able to work out more balanced policies with regard to this problem.

Under The Front administration some progress was made with regard to termination of international isolation, restoration of social and civil rights, increase of financial reserves (see Appendix, Table 6), and substantial reduction of violation of human rights.

Foreign Policies

In contrast with the military, the civilian government did not need to use foreign policy to obtain internal as well as external legitimacy for its regime. Under civilian rule (1988–1990), the country's foreign policy focused on diversification of international relations, exploration of bilateral and multilateral donors, and integration in the hemisphere. Friendly relations with members of the nonaligned movement and democratic-pluralist regimes were (re)established. This policy was an integral part of the policy of diversification of international relations. To further integration in the hemisphere, support was expressed for regimes transforming from authoritarian to democratic-pluralist systems. Membership in the Caribbean Common Market (CARICOM) and participation in the Caribbean Basin Initiative (CBI) would serve the cause of hemispheric integration and would allow for the exploration of donors for financial aid to restore the economy. Problems with the reinstatement of Dutch aid reinforced the Surinamese government to explore these opportunities in the hemisphere and in the wider international environment. As a result of policies of diversification of international relations, Brazil and Venezuela became, next to the Dutch, the main suppliers of financial assistance.

THE FRONT GOVERNMENT AND STRATEGIES FOR REGIME SURVIVAL

Underestimation of the complexity and nature of domestic sociopolitical issues, as well as patronizing Dutch policies, has contributed to the rise and fall of regimes in Suriname. Apanjaht (ethnic party identification and voting) politics and lack of financial resources led to a political climate in which foreign capital became vital for the regime. Strategies for regime survival have been worked out and applied successfully in a number of cases in the past in Suriname as well as other countries in the Caribbean. The Front government took formal power from the military after the 1987 election. Because of the coup of December 24, 1990, it did not complete the constitutionally established five years of rule. Why did strategies of regime survival not work as well as had been expected? How valid are these strategies for Caribbean societies in transition from military, authoritarian rule to democratic systems?

To evaluate strategies for regime survival in Suriname during the period from 1988 to 1990, I have adopted Percy Hintzen's (1989a) analytical framework, presented in his comparative study on Guyana and Trinidad. According to Hintzen, practical ideology, patronage, state control, coercion, and international realignment are five strategies for gaining or retaining control of the state. Given the analytical as well as politico-historical relevance of Hintzen's framework for Suriname, the regime survival strategies are each introduced briefly and followed by an analytical description of the Suriname case.

Practical ideology is expressed in sociopolitical programs for the organization of the state. It is presented by leaders as a means of communication to politically strategic actors (local and international). With the implementation of their policies, regimes further and protect their interest. By its nature, practical ideology can be constantly changed over time to suit changing circumstances. Shifts in the content or definition of their ideological position have become quite typical of many political leaders as they struggle to respond to changes in the international and national arenas that affect their own chances of gaining or maintaining political power and influence. Such shifts can be seen as attempts to appease actual or potential strategic opponents. When political decisions are dependent on the availability of resources and priorities of external donors, these shifts in ideological position and policy goals of the regime contribute to an image of inconsistency.

The rationale of the sociopolitical program of The Front regime was formulated and presented in the Government Declaration of May 1988. Two main policy goals, to change the constitution with regard to the position and the status of the NL, and the reopening of the Dutch development aid for the recovery of the economy, were not accomplished. Intimidation of the NL on the one hand, and Dutch pressure on The Front government to control the military as a precondition to reopen development aid on the other hand, resulted in the inability of the regime to work out balanced policies to maintain support of powerful domestic and international actors which possess strategic resources. Attempts to appease actual or potential strategic opponents failed. Domestically, channels of communication were poorly developed and the mass media (public television and radio broadcasting service) did not function with full autonomy or were still controlled by antigovernment forces. Consequently, the regime lost a substantial part of its supporters who criticized its disregard of essential issues, such as the position of the NL and its relationship to the society and the democratic state.

Political patronage is a pillar for regime survival. Economic and sociopolitical conditions contribute to this phenomenon in society. Resources of the state are used for distribution of patronage in exchange for support. With these resources clientelistic ties can be developed with strategic elites and other supporters of lower social strata. Through allocation, successful patronage can generate support of the masses and strategic groups (including the military and high-ranked civil servants). Patronage may even demobilize opponents and critical supporters.

The Front regime has focused on the recovery of the economy. The budget deficit was substantially reduced and the amount of foreign currency reserves increased as indicated in Appendix, Table 6. Because of the unsuccessful negotiations with the Dutch to reopen the development aid, The Front missed financial resources that could have been used for patronage politics. It was, nonetheless, not willing to use the limited state resources for the distribution of patronage in exchange for support. Consequently, traditional clientelistic ties, a vertical dependency relationship with strategic elites, did not develop further and an increasing dissatisfaction occurred among supporters of the social and economically weaker strata, mainly the Creoles. Political patronage was, however, not banned. Public land for sale was secured by the government and purchased by the wealthy. The retention of NDP supporters at positions in the administration may have resulted in less open antiregime actions but not to the extent of demobilizing them as NDP supporters or opponents.

State control is strengthened when activities under the domain of the state bureaucratic apparatus are expanded. This strategy for regime survival was supported by the foreign-educated, left-oriented intellectuals in the 1960s. The rationale of this strategy is to remove resources from the control of opponents. These resources are then made available to the regime and can no longer be used for antigovernment mobilization. Consequently, the private sector becomes politically weakened while deactivation of trade unions is part of strategic state expansion. The one-party system and party paramountcy can be employed to reconstruct the ruling party for the service of statism. The state bureaucratic apparatus becomes an instrument of control. The regime can accomplish the demobilization and regimentation of every organization. Through actions the state can manage to penetrate and control vital resources. In cases of state control of resources, the economic performance in the 1970s and 1980s in the Caribbean (including Suriname under leftist military rule) was poor. The collapse of Marxist-Leninist systems in Europe further stimulated The Front to carry out policies directed toward privatization.

During Front rule, strategies to weaken international business, to miniaturize the private sector, or to effectively deactivate the trade union movement were absent. To the contrary, The Front government emphasized its preference for further commercialization of the productive sector. The trade unions received the freedom to act according to their social rights prior to the coup. In this respect, demobilization to end antiregime activities and regimentation to organize activities in support of the regime were hardly implemented as strategies.

In order to survive, political leaders in developing nations have often used the coercive apparatus of the state against political opposition, dissident groups, and elite opponents. Coercion is most effective as a temporary measure but can also be used by the regime to ensure survival. The process of militarization in young nations, a government's unfamiliarity with newly adopted institutions, and poor functioning of democracy contribute to the use of this strategy to survive. In the political history of Suriname, civilian governments have not used coercion as a survival strategy. The Front government was confronted with labor strikes as well as other forms of protest. Like the conflict with illegal armed groups, The Front was not able to find appropriate solutions to end the civil war or to control the NL. This turned out to be the most important constraint.

In case of a threat of survival, a regime can seek alternative suppliers for those resources which it obtains in international exchanges and upon which its survival depends. This strategy of international realignment may be extended to a supply of arms as well as consumer goods or even to ensure assistance in case of a coup or civil war. Upon its installment in 1988, The Front government was confronted with the effect of disastrous economic policies carried out by the junta between 1980 and 1987. The lack of foreign currencies compelled the regime to explore opportunities for international exchanges. The Cooperation Treaty (for US$1.7 billion) signed with the Dutch in 1975 seemed to be the most appropriate resource. However, in its negotiations with the Netherlands to resume the suspended development aid, The Front was not able to respond to conditions of controlling the military formulated by the Dutch government. Furthermore, despite its delicate position vis-à-vis the powerful military, The Front did not attempt to secure its survival through an international or bilateral agreement for assistance in case of a coup. Moreover, the civilian government was not able to design a military policy to construct and maintain democratic relationships between civilians and the military. Given the conflicting political interests between the NL and the regime, and the government's lack of access to state power, the pivotal question is whether domestic survival strategies could ever be implemented without substantial support from the external environment.

Prior to 1980, political patronage, state control, international realignment, and practical ideology had been used for regime survival in Suriname. Coercion was not applied as a survival strategy. According to international standards regarding coercion, the minor role played by the police (1975 and after) in cases of labor strikes cannot be called state coercion. The army was never used as an instrument for regime survival of civilian governments. Changes with regard to the international political constellation, including shifts of ideological orientation in the Soviet Union and Eastern Europe, may make state control as a strategy for regime survival obsolete. Hintzen's analytical framework for regime survival appeared to be valid in Suriname under civilian rule in the period prior to the military coup. However, due to a lack of access to state power and financial resources, it lost its relevance in the period of transformation from authoritarianism to democratic-pluralism. From the analysis below, one can ascertain that survival strategies have been fully applied by the military-installed Interim Cabinet.

THE COUP OF DECEMBER 24, 1990

Instead of encouraging confrontation with the military, The Front tried to follow a strategy of appeasement: no budget cuts for defense; no implementation of the Kourou Peace Treaty;[4] no change of the constitution on army matters; no sanctions or in-depth investigation in cases of violation of human rights; no reaction on the public humiliation of the president (he was called a "joker" [figurehead] by Commander Bouterse), and so on.[5] The strategy of appeasement failed because the government did not understand that the military's objective was politically, but not militarily, motivated. It wanted control of the state. Consequently, accommodation or neutralization of the military could never be expected to be successful.

Between 1988 and 1990, three strategies for the removal of the civilian regime have been identified. First, crises initiation groups were created as an integral part of antigovernment mobilization. Tucayana, Anguila, and Mandela (illegally armed groups supported by the military) emerged. They were instrumental in this stage. However, since antigovernment mobilization had not automatically resulted in a promilitary attitude of the populace, this strategy was finally evaluated as unsatisfactory and insufficient, and was supplemented with the aim of direct participation in political decision making.

Second, the disappointing outcome of the elections for the military could be compensated by the formation of a "national cabinet" in which the NDP would be incorporated. In this period, labor federations were instrumental in promoting strikes. The slowly recovering economy was further damaged. This strategy finally failed because The Front leaders refused to install such an undemocratic cabinet.

Third, to accelerate the takeover of the country's political fabric, pressure was put on the government to call elections before they were scheduled. From the military's point of view, the government was not willing to call the elections. Consequently, the NL seized power on December 24, 1990 when a telephone call was made to the president to inform him of their coup. On December 29, the National Assembly unwillingly held a special meeting to "legalize" the coup and "approve" the installation of the presidential and vice-presidential candidates nominated by the military.

THE INTERIM CABINET

The NDP (the political arm of the army) was dominantly represented in the Interim Cabinet installed by the military in January 1991. The cabinet was widely identified as a political cabinet instead of an interim cabinet. Since it faced upcoming elections, its policies were focused on short-term effects as well as anticipated Creole dissatisfaction with the dominant position of the Hindustani party (the VHP) in The Front. The fourteen Interim Cabinet ministers' (all but one were Creole) main strategy was to encourage further outbidding in the Creole NPS. In most cases measures were targeted toward Creoles, who have been the main beneficiaries. For instance, to improve the standard of living of the Creoles, consumer goods such as Dutch herring were imported duty free and sold at low prices. Land was distributed among the poor. The infrastructure was improved and jobs were offered to the socioeconomically weaker strata in Creole neighborhoods.

The practice of patronage politics led to a complete plundering of the scarce financial resources. Given the oppressive nature of the regime, the Interim Cabinet profited from a relatively quiet climate because the mass media applied a self-imposed censorship and labor federations did not strike. The intention to shift to state economic management was evident. Implementation, however, was not feasible due to the country's financial situation.

All applicable strategies for the regime's survival (including coercion) were fully executed by the Interim Cabinet. Political patronage was paramount because of its extensive use of state resources. The NDP cabinet was, however, continually confronted with time constraints, the unpopularity of its policies, antimilitary sentiment, and the successful campaign of the multiethnic coalition blocs, as well as international isolation.

Previous experience of the 1980s taught the military that the foreign policies carried out to hide the political illegitimacy of its regime were not successful, nor did foreign policies result in improvement of the country's economy. Despite some financial profits (loans from the IADB and the European Community [EC]), no substantial economic assistance was received. Diversification of international relationships was not accompanied by sufficient resources needed for regime survival.

In January 1991 the military-installed cabinet sent goodwill missions to the Caribbean, the United States, Brazil, Venezuela, and Europe (the Netherlands and the EC) to "explain" the background of the coup and make events understandable. As in the 1980s, the military found out for the second time that the international environment can no longer be made instrumental for the survival of this type of regime. Furthermore, with the changing relationship between the superpowers, any possible substantial external support for the military in Suriname has vanished. Brazil supported the civilian government and the army (Colonel Bouterse) by supplying equipment to the military. Given the NL's vested interest in a good relationship with Brazil, it remains to be seen if the Surinamese army can afford to ignore Brazilian requests in the future. Like Venezuela, Brazil can play a significant role in supporting the regime in its struggle for democracy.

ELECTION OF MAY 25, 1991 AND THE NEW CIVILIAN GOVERNMENT

The Front coalition won the elections, although with a less overwhelming victory of thirty out of fifty-one seats in the National Assembly (DNA). The opposition was formed by DA '91 (a new coalition of split-offs of the big traditional ethnic parties) with nine seats and the NDP (the political arm of the army) with twelve seats, which represents an increase of ten seats compared to the 1987 elections.

Preparation for the elections in May 1991 started directly after the military coup in December 1990. Sixteen parties were registered at the ballot office by March 15, 1990. Two party coalitions participated in the elections: the New Front and the DA '91. None of the radical leftist parties, including the NDP, went in coalition.[6] Compared with the 1987 elections, significant differences are observed with regard to coalition partners, position of parties, actors, and campaign issues.

The Front changed its name to the New Front (NF), indicating the enlargement of the coalition with the tiny Surinamese Labor Party (SLP). The SLP's supporters are mainly (1) members of the labor federation's Centrale of 47 Unions (C 47) and Governmental Workers Organization (CLO); (2) a faction of the extinct Party of the National Republic (Fred Derby's Nationalist Socialist Party); (3) (ex)NDPers or associates; and (4) ex-Front members. In the 1987 elections the SLP was not able to win one seat in the DNA. All coalition partners believed that for regime survival, the incorporation of the SLP in the NF was of strategic importance.

As a result of outbidding of traditional parties, a new coalition emerged called the Democratic Alternative 1991 (DA '91), consisting of ethnic parties. The participation of the BEP (the Maroon Party) in this coalition is remarkable. Since its inception, the BEP has aligned with the NPS. The high expectation of its members (the main victims of the civil war) for a peace settlement, and their disappointment with the failures of The Front government to do so, were decisive factors for the incorporation of the BEP in DA '91. However, the government's low profile in terms of expressing its stand during conflicts between the NL and the Jungle Commando (JC), and the lack of an in-depth investigation on and/or compensation for victims and relatives of descendants of violations of human rights, have also contributed substantially to increasing dissatisfaction with The Front government. Many intellectuals and elements of the middle class, as well as members of business and trade circles, are members of DA '91. Its weakness is a lack of any government experience. The incorporation of anti-Front regime and antimilitary factions contributed to this weakness as well. With nine seats in Parliament, their numbers were not impressive but still represent a strong showing. During the campaign meetings, it became evident that DA '91 was not able to identify and communicate properly with the lower strata of all ethnic groups. Thus far, no connection has been made with grassroots organizations. It remains to be seen whether this party coalition can survive in the 1990s.

The NDP did not necessarily look for participation in a coalition. Through its Interim Cabinet, this party had backing from the army, and a grip on the total public administration system (including the election machinery and access to the state financial resources). Because of fear of repression, labor unions, NGOs such as the Organization for Justice and Peace (OGV), and the mass media, it kept a low profile. Prior to the elections of May 25, 1991, patronage was extended to all ethnic groups. Extensive misuse of state financial resources and open favoritism—profits for NDPers and collaborators—characterized the Interim Cabinet. The patronage politics of the NDP Interim Cabinet resulted finally in a nationwide critique and lack of trust in its presidential candidate, Jules Wijdenbosch.

A change of position of actors in the political arena was manifest in the NPS and SLP. The leader of the NPS, Henck Arron—a person of "political centrality"—decided to concentrate on the party. Consequently, he has not been available for any governmental position. Arron had been in politics for thirty years. He served as a member of Parliament, a member of several cabinets, prime minister, and vice-president. In the capacity of Front leader, Arron kept his finger on the most vital vein of the ruling coalition. His political power had not declined but converted from vice-president to a less vulnerable, but equally or even more crucial position.

Fred Derby, leader of the SLP, together with the party leaders of the NPS, VHP, and Javanese Farmer's Party (KTPI), became a Front leader and spokesman of the NF coalition. Derby had been a member in the House of Parliament when his extinct party, the Party of the National Republic (the PNR), participated in the National Combination of Parties (NPK) from 1973 until 1978.[7] He was a well-known politician and labor union leader. Since its origin, his labor union federation C 47 had been an ally of the PNR. In the 1980s period of civilian government, his unions often backed the military. He was a supporter of the "National Cabinet" and went in 1990 to Europe (the Netherlands and the EC) to promote isolation of The Front government. Derby's participation in the New Front was seen by some political observers as a move by the NPS to reduce social turbulence, to strengthen the Creole element, and to counterbalance the military. For the military it was seen as a loss of a "crisis-making instrument."

The structure did not encourage any civilian party leader to take physical risks through direct confrontation with the army. Consequently, issues on investigation of human rights violations, demobilization of the armed forces, or abolition of duty to serve defense forces were unheard. All competing parties claimed to change the constitution to focus on drug prevention, to work out an adjustment program for the recovery of the economy, and to investigate commonwealth membership with the Netherlands. Thus, ideologically significant differences in campaign programs were absent. The military-backed NDP showed strong support for the army while other parties did not reject the existence of an army but looked for its integration in society. Subordination of the armed forces to the government was formally accepted by all parties. In reality, however, the army's involvement in politics—anti-Front government mobilization—was evidenced continually during meetings and press briefings in the military headquarters.

The issue of membership in a Dutch Commonwealth was introduced by the Dutch. DA '91 favored membership and announced that it would work out a proposal. Reactions of other campaigning parties varied from "no comment" to moderately positive. The NDP's nonrejecting rhetoric was caused by the overwhelming positive popular response for commonwealth membership.

In comparing the 1987 and 1991 elections, a number of differences have been observed. The external environment (bilateral and multilateral OAS, CARICOM) rejected the second coup strongly and substantially supported and assisted elections to redemocratize the country. Venezuela, the United States, and the Netherlands regularly made supportive statements. Furthermore, developments in the Soviet Union and Eastern Europe, as well as the changed relationship between the superpowers, have confused the radical left's ideological orientation and belief in support from the international environment. During the election campaign, radical leftist rhetoric in NDP, Progressive Union of Workers and Peasants (PALU), and Peoples Party (VP) circles was absent: the repeatedly "have/have nots" dichotomy of previous campaigns was not heard!

A shift was observed from an optimal mobilized electorate in 1987 to a moderate interest in the ballot in 1991. (In 1987 the voting turnout was 86%; in 1991, 62%.) The Front's input in terms of propaganda through mass media or distribution of propaganda material was minimal because of financial constraints, as well as for strategic reasons. This is in sharp contrast to the NDP's expensive campaign and overuse of public and private mass media.

The combination of poor governmental performance, the stagnation of the economy, the unsuccessful policies with regard to the reopening of Dutch development aid, and regime subordination to the military contributed to The Front's loss of eleven seats in the DNA. The NDP increased its number from two to twelve seats. It is therefore disputable as to whether the NDP's electoral success was predominantly a result of its disastrous short-term, targeted patronage politics or basically related to the poor performance of The Front government. As far as DA '91 was concerned, it was evident that this coalition collected nine seats from ex-Front supporters. This was the result of a successful anti-Front government and antimilitary mobilization.

In the period after the general elections and prior to the presidential election in the VVV, the Interim Cabinet campaigned intensively. During this period, the irresponsible spending of scarce state resources became manifest in the broader society. Extensive discussion in Front campaigning meetings about this issue and the exposure of the negative effects on the country's economy contributed to a dismantling of the NDP's policies. One may therefore conclude that a "second" public "judgment" of the NDP policies took place in September 1991, when the VVV voted so overwhelmingly for The Front's presidential candidate. In contrast with the DNA, Ronald Venetiaan, the presidential candidate of the NF, was elected with 80 percent of the 811 VVV votes. The NDP candidate, Jules Wijdenbosch, received 12 percent, and Hans Prade, DA '91 candidate, received 8 percent.

CONCLUSION

In the process of transformation from authoritarianism to democracy, the civilian government was not able to control the state and to explain to the electorate the processes and mechanisms that led to democracy. Evidently, it could not implement a number of its policies, such as a peace settlement with the JC to end the civil war, termination of the black market, economic recovery, resumption of Dutch development aid, and control of illegal violence. In cases of violent conflict and illegal violence, the judicial system did not intervene.

The government's failure was basically due to the continuation of state control by the military. President Ramsewak Shankar's weak performance and a lack of internal cohesion of the ruling Front, coupled with external constraints, contributed to the culmination of public dissatisfaction and substantially enabled the military to realize the December 1990 coup.

Strategies for regime survival did not work because of The Front's lack of access to state power and unsuccessful communication (negotiations) with politically strategic local and international (Dutch) actors. Because of a lack of state financial resources, political patronage was limited to the sale of public land. The wealthy, mainly Hindustani, benefited most from these policies. The result, however, of these patronage politics has been the furthering of fragmentation and communalization of Suriname's politics.

To obtain popular support, the NDP Interim Cabinet carried out politics for short-term political profits: duty-free imported consumption goods (such as Dutch herring and salted meat) at relatively low prices. Local financial reserves were used for the infrastructure. Land was distributed and peace talks were held with the JC.

The appearance of two competing multiethnic coalitions and one multiethnic party (the NF, DA '91, and the NDP consisting of elements of the major ethnic groups) running for elections was a novelty in the country's political history. In the long term, the "voting" effect of these processes of outbidding remains to be seen. In order to survive, the new civilian administration must work out strategies to demobilize politically organized groups which have rallied behind its political opponents. These groups may otherwise continue to disrupt the sociopolitical order by mounting persistent challenges to its authority and by engaging in antiregime activities. At the same time, the regime should seek to strengthen its mass support by implementing continuous communication channels. The performance of the NF will be of crucial importance for the survival of DA '91 and the further growth of the NDP. In 1992 the Democratic Party (an offshoot of the NDP) emerged. Its two founders are assembly members who reject the NDP policies carried out during the Interim Cabinet.

Between December 24, 1990 and May 25, 1991, the majority of the Surinamese population was forced to submit to illegal rule since (de facto) a quasi-legal cabinet was installed. Through the constitution, the military created a way to legalize its coup, called "intervention." Ironically, it appears to this author that if the country's citizenry could effectively communicate with their leaders, the country might move more quickly and surely toward democracy than if their fractious elites remain in control of power.

Power relations are not only present in macropolitical institutions. In the social hierarchical systems built by the party elites, instruments of oppression and ideological control are developed resulting in a "socially rooted" authoritarianism. This socially rooted authoritarianism has sources more profound than the disputable legacy of the military regime of the 1980s. These asymmetrical power relations in society are not affected by a shift of regime or power at a macro level. I am thus obliged to analyze the transition through the micropractices of power, untouched by elections and shifts from authoritarianism to democracy.

Political transition toward democracy will be effective only when the process of dismantling the complex network of microsocially rooted authoritarian relationships to which the lower classes have historically submitted would change. It may be true that the struggle to defeat military authoritarianism during the 1980s may as well have generated support for democratic liberties and values.

Constitutional changes on the position of the military; a peace treaty with the illegal armed forces; the reduction of overliquidity of local currencies through a Forex auction system;[8] the approval of the structural adjustment program by the National Assembly; and the implicit, public condemnation and judgment of the violation of human rights through the commemoration of the tenth anniversary of the December 8, 1982 massacre[9] are essential achievements of the Venetiaan administration. They contributed to the weakening of the grip held by nondemocratic forces.

Like its predecessor, the new civilian government is confronted with similar constraints such as an empty treasury, and a power-seeking and -keeping military. One should bear in mind that military political repression is a part of an elite culture intolerant of effective opposition. Consequently, a strong unified government opposing the military may soon find itself confronted with repression and increasing violence in the society.

The potential for a civilian-military elite settlement exists. But these accords also have the considerable potential to vanish in a flurry of betrayal or in a string of "accidents" or fusillade of bullets. The strong antimilitary elements in the society,including grassroots organizations such as the OGV and other nongovernment organizations (NGOs), may continue to reject any pact with the army. They have the potential to undermine interelite cooperation and progress toward a political settlement. Moreover, the country's citizenry appears not to be ready to support a government that wants to carry out policies of interelite settlement with the army. The assembly members of the ruling coalition prefer a complete replacement of the military leadership after Ltd. Col. Bouterse announced his withdrawal in November 1992.

A solid integrated domestic and foreign policy and strong interaction between domestic politics and the external environment may be of crucial importance for survival of the existing civilian government. The danger of reversions is present, particularly if the external environment becomes more tolerant of governments where the civilian president is only a figurehead with little or no real power.

To minimize the risk of a coup, the civilian government should, with external assistance, implement military policies to reduce the political prerogatives of the military. These policies should be characterized by fewer inconsistencies and genuine democratic standards. But, if it is true that the army voluntarily accepts civilian control in political systems with institutionalized democratic control (conditional political subordination) because of internalized democratic norms, a vicious circle exists, because leaders of democratic parties in Suriname practice undemocratic politics at the micro level. The Surinamese case illustrates that electoralism and democratization of the society are not identical. With the election of local and regional representatives in the VVV, the first step has been made to a structural form of participation in political decision making. In the parties, an increasing number of members require the same developments.

Furthermore, a civilian government like the Surinamese, with fragmented party systems, often does not have the capacity or will to exert civilian leadership over the armed forces. Instability of the civilian regime during the 1988–1990 period was due to the regime's willingness to accommodate the military's policy preferences. At that time it seemed as if the military-civilian relationship had improved, but the legitimacy of the civilian government was undermined.

It remains to be seen if the new civilian government, if backed by strategic external actors, will be able to work out an appropriate policy to place the military in the proper framework of a democratic-pluralist system. However, developments and expectations beyond these lines may be possible.

NOTES

The majority of the acronyms in this chapter are from the Dutch names.

1. Interviews on Apinti, a local broadcasting station, August 25, 1990. Paramaribo/Suriname.

2. The Dutch signed a Development Cooperation Treaty with Suriname in 1975. For more information about the Dutch impact in Suriname, see Betty Sedoc-Dahlberg, "The Suriname-Dutch Relationship within the Framework of Policymaking and Planning," *Planning Bulletin,* no. 5–6, ILPES Santiago 1979; and Betty Sedoc-Dahlberg, ed., *The Dutch Caribbean: Prospects for Democracy* (New York: Gordon and Breach, 1990).

3. In the 1980s an increasing number of wealthy Hindustani families emerged. The accusation that they all made it through illegal business and collaboration with the army is not correct. Furthermore, under The Front regime public land became available for sale. Mainly wealthy Hindustani benefited from these patronage politics since few members of other ethnic groups could afford to purchase these lands. See also Chapter 8 in Sedoc-Dahlberg, ed., *The Dutch Caribbean*; and Edward Dew, *The Difficult Flowering of Suriname* (The Hague: Mouton,1976).

4. The Kourou Peace Treaty between the government and the Jungle Commandos (JC) was negotiated in Kourou, French Guiana and signed in Suriname on August 19, 1988.

5. Previous to the coup, Ltd. Col. Bouterse returning from his trip to Europe expressed his grievances about the Dutch refusal to authorize his visa and about his isolation at the airport in the Netherlands. He blamed the president, who was on the same flight, for an inappropriate attitude at that time and called him a "joker."

6. Marxist-Leninist-oriented Surinamese student movements in the 1960s in the Netherlands were transferred in the 1970s into political parties. They never have been able to obtain one seat in the House of Parliament. With the military coup two of these parties, the VP (Peoples Party) and the PALU (Progressive Union of Workers and Peasants), have been able to come to the core of political decision making. A part of the VP formed together with the military party, the National Democratic Party (NDP). See also Dew, *The Difficult Flowering of Suriname.*

7. The PNR (Party of the National Republic) was founded by Eddy Bruma. He studied in the Netherlands in the 1950s. His leftist political orientation and Afro-cultural orientation made it impossible in multiethnic Suriname to obtain supporters of all strata and ethnic groups. After the elections of 1987 the PNR has not manifested itself anymore.

8. A Forex auction system is a foreign exchange auction system organized by the Central Bank to control the black market.

9. This was an infamous execution of opponents of the military junta. Professional classes, labor union leaders, university intelligentsia, and workers were assassinated.

9

Dominican Republic: Electoralism, Pacts, and Clientelism in the Making of a Democratic Regime

Rosario Espinal

What makes democracy possible and sustains it remains a highly controversial theme in political theory. Are there functional requirements for a successful transition to and consolidation of democracy? Should democratization be viewed instead as the result of contingent events?

This chapter begins with a brief account of social requirement and contingency theories. The objective here is twofold: to highlight some of the problems with contemporary democratic theory for the study of democratization in less developed capitalist societies, and to suggest alternative conceptual formulations. The remainder of the chapter discusses democratic development in the Dominican Republic in the context of the suggested alternative theoretical approach.

FOUNDING DEMOCRACY: SOCIAL REQUIREMENTS, CONTINGENCY, OR SOMETHING ELSE?

In his seminal article, "Transitions to Democracy: Toward a Dynamic Model,"[1] Dankwart Rustow provides us with both a devastating critique of social requirement theories and an alternative model to study democracy that emphasizes choice over requirements. According to Rustow, a major problem with functionalist explanations is their inability to account for the origins of democracy; that is, how democracy comes into existence in the first place. Instead, functionalist explanations are more concerned with specifying the conditions needed to preserve or enhance democracy, such as the level of economic growth, industrialization, literacy, or civic values.[2]

Rustow's genetic theory of democracy rests on six propositions.[3] First, there is the need to distinguish correlate from cause: the tendency to fuse the two as functionalists do is troublesome because it remains unclear whether democracy is a cause or effect of such variables as literacy rate or civic culture. Second is the emphasis on "a two-way flow of causality," or "circular interaction," between politics and socioeconomic conditions. Third is the emphasis on the study of political mechanisms by which social and economic background conditions influence democracy as the natural sphere of political analysis. Fourth is the study of choice as central to the political process. Fifth is the reciprocal influence between beliefs and actions, which means that "circumstances may force, trick, lure, or cajole non-democrats into democratic behavior," while their democratic beliefs may ensue in due course by a "process of rationalization or adaptation."[4] The sixth assumption has to do with the genesis of democracy itself, and can be broken down into three connected arguments: (1) the transition to democracy is not a worldwide, uniform process, involving the same social classes, the same issues, or the same methods of solution—on the contrary, a variety of social issues, problems, and solutions may be compatible with democracy; (2) democratic evolution is not necessarily a homogeneous process over time, but different factors may become crucial during successive phases; and (3) democratization does not entail or require cultural uniformity throughout society concerning democratic values and behaviors.

Rustow's alternative model relies then on contingency, on the possibility of an occurrence. More importantly, it contemplates the possibility that nondemocratic actors, forced by some historical circumstances, may behave democratically. Once this happens (the decision phase), the consolidation of democracy relies then on habituation, a process whereby political actors rationalize their commitment to democracy through the successful resolution of issues by relying on democratic rules, and the establishment of effective links between government and the electorate.

Stressing choice over functional requirements became appealing to political analysts who studied recent transitions to democracy in less developed capitalist countries.[5] What remained uncertain, however, was the nature of the process that would follow the transition in societies historically characterized by severe socioeconomic inequality, and where the transition itself had coincided with a major economic downturn and a rapidly changing social structure. Here the issue of procedure versus substance gained importance.[6] Emphasizing procedures as the defining characteristics of democracy made it easier to reach a workable definition of democracy and ignore the mounting structural obstacles to democratic consolidation. Emphasizing structural impediments, on the other hand, made it practically impossible to suggest a high probability (if any at all) for democratic consolidation.

As newly installed democratic regimes remained fragile through the 1980s, the discussion over procedure versus substance in democracy building gained more importance. A central question dominating the debate was the following: Are structural impediments insurmountable, or are obstacles to democracy largely the result of ineffective political leadership? Addressing this issue, Terry Karl moved a step in the right direction when she argued in favor of discarding the search for democratic preconditions, while warning against falling into excessive voluntarism. She proposed that decisions made by social and political actors be viewed as responses highly conditioned by the types of socioeconomic structures and political institutions already present, for such conditions "may either restrict or enhance the options available to different political actors attempting to construct democracy."[7] This argument helped shape the thrust of this chapter.

In accordance with Rustow, I believe it is the task of the political analyst to specify the political mechanisms by which social and economic conditions influence democracy. The problem I find, though, with Rustow's model is that by emphasizing the genetic question he seemed to assume that once democracy was established (the decision phase), consolidating it was simply a matter of habituation. Instead, I wish to argue that given the unique problems of under-development, reaching and sustaining the habituation phase is highly problematic in less developed capitalist societies, increasing the likelihood of a fragile democracy in lieu of a consolidated one.

Consequently, a theory suited to the analysis of democracy in less developed capitalist societies should spell out the political mechanisms (both institutional and ideological) whereby the relationship between leaders and the electorate, and between social groups and institutions (state and civil society), is always being constructed and transformed. The advantage of emphasizing mechanisms over social requirements or contingency should be obvious. It moves research away from the search for socioeconomic preconditions such as economic growth, high rates of literacy, or a democratic culture, which might be lacking in the first place. Instead, democratization is viewed as an ongoing and open process, though not necessarily an incremental one, that could be sustained as Rustow argues on a variety of socioeconomic situations. Within this approach choices are certainly important, yet they must be examined in the context of the highly complex socioeconomic and political circumstances under which they are made.

What I seek to substantiate here is that to detach procedural from substantive issues in the study of democracy seems unwarranted, particularly in the case of less developed capitalist societies. This is not to say that democratic regimes in less developed countries are likely to collapse simply because of socioeconomic adversities. What I suggest is that by analyzing procedures (elections, for instance) in light of the substantive issues at stake (low wages, for instance), we may be in a better position to begin unraveling the mechanisms whereby social conflicts are politically processed, and the significance of these mechanisms to accomplish (or not to accomplish) three fundamental objectives if democracy is to be consolidated: freedom of the citizenry to participate politically, government responsiveness, and overall governability.

This chapter discusses three political mechanisms and their impact on democratic consolidation in the Dominican Republic: electoralism, pact making, and clientelism. I illustrate some of the problems that clientelism has posed for Dominican democracy: in particular, its detrimental effect on the newly established political elite, on whom the fate of democracy relied so much. On the other hand, sustainable pact making has been almost absent in the Dominican experience despite various attempts to reach social concertation. Overall, the government's efforts to remain isolated from social pressures curtailed its ability to respond effectively to major socioeconomic issues, damaging therefore its own capacity to rule. Torn by social antagonisms reflected in protests and electoral volatility, governing elites tried to manipulate the electoral process, hoping in so doing to secure an electoral advantage.

DEMOCRACY: THE REDEFINITION OF POLITICAL SPACES AND POSITIONS

Democratization implies the redefinition of political spaces and positions. Previously excluded social and political actors are likely to become more visible in society as they gain the right to participate and voice their concerns. Opening spaces for previously excluded social and political actors means, on the other hand, the articulation in the public sphere of different political views on a variety of issues.

For those who emphasize procedural aspects, the redefinition of political spaces and positions means primarily that new rules of political participation, which recognize the right of all (or at least most) constituted groups to voice their concerns within established political channels (voting, lobbying, striking, pact making, and the like), are established. Democracy here is about agreements over the "rules of the game," not about the resolution of unmet social needs.[8] For authors who emphasize the centrality of substantive issues, the redefinition of political spaces refers largely to the possibility of incorporating long-standing social demands. This view has been traditionally endorsed by Marxist scholars, although it is not their exclusive domain.

The decision to establish new rules or rely on old ones is an empirical and historical question. Specifically, the decision to establish new political rules is linked to the organizational strength of various social and political actors, their ideologies, and the overall assessment rulers make of their ability to govern under certain socioeconomic and political conditions. This does not mean that democracy cannot be narrowly defined in terms of political procedures; it certainly can. Yet in order to understand the complexity of the democratic process, one must look at the complex interaction between procedural and substantive issues, between political and socioeconomic ones. Put differently, politics is more than politics; it encompasses numerous themes that pertain to lifestyles, values, and standards of living, all of which are likely to become highly relevant (and affect each other) in the process of democratization.

In the Dominican Republic, as elsewhere in the Caribbean and Latin America, the democratic project embodied at the outset both political and socioeconomic ideals. For almost two decades the Dominican Revolutionary Party (PRD) had voiced the need for major political and socioeconomic reforms, and crafted its political platform around ideals of democratic participation and social justice. This led the PRD to a major electoral victory in 1962. Yet, with a country highly polarized, coupled with adverse international conditions, the PRD was soon overthrown. The coup of 1963 opened a chapter in Dominican political history highly charged with repression, and political and social exclusion,[9] a situation the PRD sought to undo once more in the late 1970s.

The victory of the PRD in the 1978 elections, following the twelve-year-long presidency of Joaquin Balaguer (1966–1978), boosted expectations that major political and socioeconomic changes were forthcoming. After all, the PRD had campaigned on issues of social redistribution and political participation, even if the revolutionary rhetoric of the past had been toned down by 1978. Yet eight years in office (1978–1986) made little difference toward the fulfillment of those goals. A variety of factors, having to do with adverse economic conditions, business opposition to the PRD, international pressures to impose austerity measures, and a highly ineffective political leadership, account for the disastrous performance of the PRD while in government.

The return of Joaquin Balaguer to the presidency in 1986 did not represent a brighter future for the consolidation of democracy. Balaguer had traditionally ruled in an authoritarian fashion, and there was little evidence in 1986 that he would change his leadership style dramatically, even though it was unlikely that he would reverse some basic democratic gains. Thus, by 1990, when Balaguer was reelected with 35 percent of the votes cast,[10] it was evident that Dominican democracy remained highly fragile, yet, paradoxically, highly consolidated in its own fragility.

In subsequent sections I discuss three mechanisms—electoralism, pact making, and clientelism—that allow us to highlight the interplay of political and socioeconomic issues in the democratic process. They also reveal the complexities of forging democracy under highly adverse political and socioeconomic conditions, and illustrate as well the weaknesses and strengths of Dominican democracy.

ELECTORALISM

That elections are central to modern democracy is beyond doubt. First, elections allow the citizenry to choose a government among political contenders. Second, elections provide for the shifting of governing elites whenever the electorate is dissatisfied with the performance of those who govern. Third, an electoral victory gives the winner a sense of political mandate, and legitimacy, to initiate a certain course of action.

In the Dominican Republic, elections have played the dual and contradictory role of sustaining and undermining democracy. The four elections held during the period of democratization (those of 1978, 1982, 1986, and 1990) have been competitive and allowed for changes in government leadership, yet three of them were highly disputed.

In 1978, followers of the incumbent Joaquin Balaguer attempted a coup when it became evident that the PRD was ahead in the electoral count. High-ranking military officers broke into the electoral office the morning after election day, stopping the counting of the ballots. The impasse generated by this action lasted about two months, a period during which it was unknown whether the PRD would take office. Finally, the Electoral Board shifted results around in four provinces in order to grant Balaguer's party a majority of representatives in the Senate. Short of being completely out of power, the PRD accepted the results announced by the Electoral Board, which granted the PRD the presidency and a majority in the House of Deputies. This way, the founding elections (i.e., the elections of the transition) were marked by irregularities, and the terms of the transition itself were ultimately decided by the Electoral Board.

The 1982 elections were somewhat smoother, yet the period preceding them was plagued by disputes between opposing tendencies within the PRD about whether or not the government would stage fair elections. Shortly after the inauguration of the Guzmán administration, opposing tendencies in the PRD led by Salvador Jorge Blanco and José F. Peña Gómez mounted a campaign accusing Antonio Guzmán of seeking reelection. Guzmán's reluctance to ban reelection was viewed by opposing tendencies within his own party as evidence of his intention to seek reelection. Indeed, this issue brought about some of the most heated debates within the PRD and helped define the cleavages that plagued the PRD in the years to come.

The 1986 elections were more controversial for two different reasons: the late appointment of Electoral Board members and the intensity of intra-party factionalism in the PRD. By mid-1983 appointments to the Electoral Board were still pending. With the PRD split in two factions and Balaguer's party in command of 37 percent of the senators, no group had a clear majority in the Senate to impose a nominee to chair the Electoral Board.[11] Such delay in appointments damaged the credibility of the Electoral Board itself and weakened its ability to conduct the electoral process efficiently. In an effort to provide legitimacy to the electoral process, the government appointed, on request of the opposition, a "Comité de Notables" (a committee of highly prestigious individuals), headed by the archbishop of Santo Domingo, to oversee the elections. While important in providing a legitimate framework for elections to take place, such an ad hoc arrangement undermined the power of the constitutionally established Electoral Board.

PRD factionalism reached its peak in November 1985 when the party convention headquarters was assaulted by armed men (allegedly linked to the Blanco faction), who sought to stop the counting of the ballots to prevent the nomination of Jacobo Majluta, Blanco's main opponent. The counting of the ballots was never completed. Instead, top PRD leaders signed a pact (Pacto La Unión) in January 1986, whereby they agreed to grant Majluta the presidential nomination, while the Blanco faction secured important congressional posts. Though the PRD was apparently united prior to the May elections, the disregard for the democratic vote of the party's rank and file, and the accord reached behind doors by the party leaders, had devastating electoral consequences for the PRD in 1986 and facilitated the return of Balaguer.

The 1990 elections were highly disputed. Balaguer, known in the past for staging fraudulent elections, did little to constitute a credible Electoral Board. The president of the board was a highly controversial figure with little capacity to mediate among contending political parties and factions. Thus, complaints of frauds were made public even before elections took place. Moreover, as early results were announced, the opposition Dominican Liberation Party (PLD) formalized complaints of fraud to the Electoral Board. Thereafter, the electoral process would only become more controversial. Accusations continued and the actions taken by the Electoral Board only contributed to generate more confusion (for instance, a recounting of the ballots began in some districts before the first count was over). About two months after election day, the Electoral Board declared Balaguer the winner, with Juan Bosch of the PLD a close second (35% and 34% of the votes respectively), while the PRD ranked third with only 23 percent of the votes.

As this account illustrates, mistrusted elections have been the rule rather than the exception in the Dominican Republic during the democratic period. Delays in the appointment of Electoral Board members, controversial appointees, and excessive party factionalism, among others, have prevented elections from becoming an important factor in democratic consolidation. Although there is no verifiable data to confirm the following statement, I would venture to say that it is likely that such highly contested and poorly managed elections have worked against the consolidation of democracy.

What these incidents reveal is that for political parties and politicians, elections are primarily the means to secure a victory, regardless of how dubious the mechanism might turn out to be. Hoping to rely on fraud to win an election, major political parties have failed, either while in government or in the opposition, to promote reforms of the electoral system that could secure fair and effective elections. Not only have they retained the old rules, but they have also misused them hoping to secure an electoral advantage.

These events may be explained in voluntaristic terms. It could be argued that politicians simply made decisions they thought would help their own cause. Yet they can also be explained on two other accounts: institutional legacy and structural adversity. The former refers to the long history of fraudulent elections in the Dominican Republic, a recourse used by authoritarian governments to remain in office with an apparent legitimacy. The latter refers to the limited capacity of government to meet social demands, and, therefore, remain popular. I would suggest that a combination of these three factors—narrowly defined personalistic interests, institutional legacy, and structural adversities—accounts for the tendency among Dominican politicians to manipulate elections, thereby preventing elections from becoming an important source of democratic consolidation.

PACT MAKING

The PRD was a party historically identified with reformist ideals and revolutionary rhetoric. Although the PRD (in the 1960s) never opposed capitalism, it favored agrarian reform and diplomatic relations with communist countries. Indeed, this explains much of the fear the PRD inspired then among dominant groups. Yet, in an effort to gather international support and sharpen its more centrist social democratic ideology, the PRD joined the Socialist International in 1976.

Its historical commitment to reformism and its newly adopted social democratic stance fostered expectation that the PRD would bring about major democratic reforms in the country. Indeed, the PRD had forged an image as a guarantor of social rights as well as individual rights. These expectations (and the transition itself) brought about the proliferation of social organizations of labor and other popular constituencies, who sought to define their own political spaces and positions under democratic terms. Business also experienced tremendous organizational growth. For one, some business groups mistrusted the PRD in its capacity to rule in favor of business; a reason why they quickly organized. On the other hand, newly formed business groups also sought to define their own political spaces and positions in the new democratic arena.

Defining new political spaces and positions in a newly established democratic regime did not always prove to be smooth and agreeable. Increasing mobilization of labor and other popular constituencies was viewed as a threat by business, who put tremendous pressure on the PRD government to curtail labor actions. Business feared most that increasing labor organization and mobilization, combined with a prolabor stance of the PRD, would turn organized labor into a powerful political actor, with the capacity to set the tone for the socioeconomic reforms still pending.

Indeed, the relationship among labor, business, government, and other popular constituencies proved to be highly complex throughout the 1980s. In examining the interaction of these four sectors, we can roughly identify three different periods and administrations. The first period lasted roughly from 1978 to 1982, with the first PRD administration headed by President Guzmán. It was one of increasing tensions between labor and business, with the government proving highly inefficient in its capacity to mediate. This was also a period of harsh confrontations between business and the government over issues of economic and social reform.

The second period lasted roughly from 1983 to 1986, with the second PRD administration headed by Blanco. It was one of relative peace between labor and business, and between business and the government. The harsher confrontations here took place between a variety of newly organized popular constituencies and the government. The third period corresponds to the presidency of Balaguer (1987–1991). It could be characterized as one of confrontation between a variety of popular constituencies and the government, of increasing disenchantment of business with the government, and much government disregard for agreements reached between business and labor in their attempts to avoid social and political clashes. What follows is a discussion of some of the economic issues, social upheavals, and political events that characterized these three periods.

During the Guzmán administration, the main source of tension between the government and organized labor was increases in gasoline and diesel prices (between 1979 and 1981 prices rose more than 100%). Although the taxi drivers' unions were the most active in organizing strikes and other forms of demonstrations, they gained the support of large segments of society who suffered directly from the negative impact of higher fares. Pressed by the second oil crisis and the mounting foreign debt, the Guzmán administration consistently asked for a truce, yet unions had little incentive to remain inactive. First, the standard of living was eroding rapidly. Second, organized labor had just come out of years of repression and suppression of demands and it was unwilling to give up its right to struggle that easily. Finally, unions were highly politicized, and any problem was likely to be used by the opposition to show strength through labor actions. The number of strikes, threats of strike, stoppages, and other forms of demonstrations increased from a total of eighty-eight in 1979 to 225 in 1981.[12] All this happened in a context of increasing labor organization in multiple unions, but at the same time labor became fragmented as the main political parties struggled to control a fraction of organized labor by colonizing a labor confederation. Thus, despite increased labor activism, the Guzmán administration, as well as business, managed to get by without engaging in serious collective bargaining.[13]

The first PRD administration was also the subject of harsh attacks carefully orchestrated by important segments of the business community. In addition to the fear that PRD's reformist rhetoric had traditionally inspired in business, the interventionist policies pursued at the outset by the Guzmán administration did not help promote business confidence. Hoping to revitalize the economy, the government pursued three highly controversial measures: a nationwide increase in the minimum wage, the creation of many new government jobs, and price controls. Politically and economically vulnerable, pro-Balaguer business groups sought leadership positions in various business organizations, which they used to mount a harsh campaign against the Guzmán government.

The second PRD administration headed by Blanco was more successful in fostering harmonious relations with business. Two factors contributed to this change: (1) by then, business felt less threatened by the PRD, and (2) by the early 1980s the government began adopting austerity and other adjustment measures with which business felt more at ease. Also, organized labor was weaker by then. Its inability to bargain effectively during the first PRD administration, coupled with increasing fragmentation of the labor movement, made it a less effective political actor.

The major challenges to the government came then from loosely organized popular sectors who rioted against the harsh adjustment measures that were introduced by the Blanco administration after signing an agreement with the IMF in 1983. These riots were harshly repressed by the government, contributing to damage the democratic reputation of the PRD and of the administration. Determined to impose unilaterally IMF-induced adjustment measures, the administration ended without any significant pact making. Instead, the government sought to isolate itself from social pressures in making economic decisions, while repression was used extensively to contain food riots.

The return of Balaguer to the presidency of the Dominican Republic in 1986 did not augur better times for negotiation and pact making. Historically, Balaguer had been an authoritarian president who made decisions on his own regardless of the opposition. Here we can identify two phases during his most recent presidencies: the first, which covered the period from 1986 to 1990, was characterized by a replay of measures adopted during his previous administrations in the 1960s and 1970s. They consisted of restraining current public expenditures (thus wages were kept low despite rampant inflation) and engaging in a massive public works program. The second phase started in 1990 when Balaguer gave in to the IMF after resisting the signing of an agreement for four years.

As Balaguer proceeded with his massive construction programs and his imposed low wages in the midst of rampant inflation, discontent with his policies became widespread. In early 1988, riots broke out in various parts of the country, and in March, the newly formed, nonlabor-based *Coordinadora de Luchas Populares* (Coordinator of Popular Struggles) organized a major general strike. Showing much popular backing during the strike, the Coordinadora was viewed with resentment by labor leaders, who sought rapidly to disassociate themselves from this more activist and lesser known popular organization. Thus, labor confederations refused to endorse a second general strike called for by the Coordinadora in April.

It was at this juncture that the Catholic Church called for a national dialogue and succeeded in bringing business, labor, and government to the negotiating table in what was known as the Tripartite Dialogue. Representatives from the lesser known Coordinadora were not invited to participate despite their increasing power in appealing to large segments of society, and their success in organizing riots and general strikes in previous months.

In late May 1988, the archbishop of Santo Domingo, José López Rodriguez, announced an agreement endorsed by all the parties involved in the Tripartite Dialogue. The accord contained eight points dealing with a variety of issues, including a health insurance plan for working-class families, an increase in the minimum wage, and changes in labor legislation. By June, however, labor confederations began to defect, arguing that after signing the accord, business increased prices without consultation, while the government did nothing to prevent it. Six of the seven labor confederations subsequently withdrew from the Tripartite Dialogue altogether.[14]

Tensions between business and the government continued to worsen in 1989. Important segments of the business community rejected Balaguer's state-led developmentalist program based on large public expenditures on public works. In an attempt to pursue his expansionist program, Balaguer imposed sacrifices on business that went beyond their expectations for compromise, such as government controls over exchange rates and compulsory exchange of foreign currency at the Central Bank. Moreover, as the electoral campaign began in early 1990, Balaguer became more confrontational with business, hoping to gather popular support for the May general elections. Thus, in February 1990, business representatives withdrew from a committee set up by Balaguer in November 1989 to make policy recommendations.

Although Balaguer succeeded in retaining the presidency, the 1990 elections were highly contested. It is important to highlight here that the combined effect of discontent, the state of the economy, and the dubious electoral results helped produce four general strikes against the Balaguer government during the last six months of 1990. These strikes were primarily organized by nonlabor popular organizations, which had gained tremendous ascendancy during the late 1980s as the power of organized labor dwindled. The first strike, held in June, received widespread support. Even business used this opportunity to show dissatisfaction with the government. The strike in August stopped most activities in the country but had clear political overtones: it was a "civic mourning" convened by the opposition Dominican Liberation Party to protest the inauguration of Balaguer as president. The strikes held in September and November, however, were failures. With labor and popular organizations highly divided, they could not even agree on a common goal for the strike (whether to concentrate on economic grievances or ask for the resignation of Balaguer), or on the duration of the strike. After the June strike, prior to his inauguration as president on August 16, 1990, Balaguer sought to bring business under his wing by proposing a Pact of Economic Solidarity, whereby the government met some business demands, such as the liberalization of the exchange market.

Plagued by economic troubles, including high inflation and shortage of foreign currency, in 1990 Balaguer's regime was forced to reduce its state-led economic program in favor of liberalization. In 1991, the government signed an awaited agreement with the IMF, which Balaguer had resisted for four years in an attempt to proceed with his massive public works program. Despite the recession that accompanied the slowdown in public construction, 1991 proceeded without major social clashes. Business was now on better terms with the government, while organized labor was highly divided. Tensions between organized labor and the rest of the popular movement also made the coordination of general strikes more difficult, while emerging factions within the nonlabor popular movement helped damage the public image of this belligerent movement.

This account illustrates that it was the combined effect of several factors that prevented the establishment of broadly based social pacts: in particular, the economic crisis, the unwillingness of the government to protect and enforce sectoral agreements, and disputes and divisions within organized labor, and between organized labor and popular organizations. Consequently, efforts at pact making such as the Tripartite Dialogue ended soon with defection. Unlike the Western European experience, where economic troubles and social democracy encouraged pact making,[15] in the Dominican Republic neither the economic crisis nor the social democratic stance of the PRD led in the same direction. Instead of promoting pact making, the PRD sought to colonize a segment of organized labor, helping thus to further divide a small and factionalized labor movement.

CLIENTELISM

Short of a strong commitment to address social needs, and burdened by economic adversities, elected governments of the Dominican Republic resorted to clientelism (the exchange of goods for political support), hoping to secure a social base of support. The clientelistic strategies of these various governments differed, however, as well as the outcomes.

The fact that the PRD, a party historically committed to democracy and social justice, also engaged in rampant clientelism while in office was quite troublesome for many voters. Aggravating the situation was the fact that the PRD allowed for government corruption precisely at a time when it adopted highly unpopular adjustment measures. Public corruption was first denounced by PRD leaders themselves who opposed the Guzmán administration. These accusations had the paradoxical effect of damaging the reputation of the PRD as it concerned the Guzmán faction, but bringing much support to the candidacy of Blanco, who portrayed himself as a truly democratic alternative in 1982. Blanco's campaign rhetoric was not only about implementing a social democratic platform, but also about ending corruption in government. As a result, despite much discontent with the Guzmán administration, PRD electoral support diminished little between 1978 and 1982, declining from 52 percent to 47 percent.

But while corruption charges against the Guzmán administration were viewed primarily in the context of severe rivalry within the PRD (e.g., a few high-ranking government officials were publicly denounced), charges of government corruption during the Blanco administration acquired new twists. In the latter case, corruption took more clientelistic overtones. As adjustment measures were introduced in 1983 and 1984 as part of the IMF package (measures which made imports more expensive), the Blanco administration began granting import-duty exemptions to active or potential supporters. These exemptions primarily concerned articles such as automobiles, whose prices had become excessive even for the upper middle class.

This highly selective clientelism,[16] although fostering a small clientele primarily of the middle-class background, proved highly detrimental to the Blanco administration. The government soon became highly unpopular, while failing to fulfill most campaign promises. Although the unpopularity of the administration is not the only factor that explains the poor showing of the PRD in the 1986 elections, when it only received 34 percent of the votes cast, it was certainly a major factor.

Upon returning to office in 1986, Balaguer sought to reinstate his clientelistic network based on public works, with many projects located in the city of Santo Domingo.[17] If nothing else, this proved to be important in the 1990 elections when Balaguer surprisingly carried the highly populated district of Santo Domingo. Yet, unlike previous Balaguer administrations, where corruption among high-level officials was common, this time Balaguer sought to control corruption-related scandals among high-ranking officers in an effort to preserve his diminishing electoral advantage.

CONCLUSION

Dominican democracy remains highly fragile: elections are frequently disputed, sectoral groups have failed to institute effective channels of conflict resolution, and clientelism remains central to the governing process. Yet in spite of several disputed elections, failures with pact making, and persistent clientelism, Dominican democracy is still standing in the midst of highly adverse economic conditions. This fact alone led me to suggest earlier the need to refine our instruments of analysis in order to grasp the complexities under which the democratic process unfolds in less developed capitalist countries. While socioeconomic conditions do not seem to entirely determine democratic possibilities, and indeed democratization may well proceed under highly adverse structural conditions, the existing socioeconomic conditions seem to facilitate a certain course of action over others. In the Dominican case, we witness, for instance, how, when facing economic adversities, various governments resorted to different forms of clientelism in an effort to secure political support while implementing highly unpopular economic measures.

Another point that the Dominican experience illustrates is that mechanisms that may prove useful under a certain political regime may not prove so useful under another; or mechanisms that may prove adequate under certain economic conditions may not prove so adequate under others. Electoral fraud and clientelism illustrate this point well. While they may work well under authoritarian regimes, by providing some apparent legitimacy to an otherwise illegitimate government, or by securing some political support to an otherwise distasteful regime, they are of dubious usefulness in a democracy, which relies on fairer political competition and the possibility of elite circulation in government.

Finally, I would say that the reliance on political mechanisms that are exclusive rather than inclusive has prevented the sustenance of a "consolidated democracy" in the Dominican Republic. Instead, what seems to have consolidated is a precarious democracy; one that I have called elsewhere "crisis-prone democracy,"[18] where uncertainty about the future of democracy seems greater than the uncertainty about electoral results or policy outcomes typical of democracy.

NOTES

1. Dankwart Rustow, "Transitions to Democracy: Toward a Dynamic Model," *Comparative Politics* vol. 2, no. 3 (1970): 337–364.

2. S. M. Lipset, "Some Social Requisites of Democracy: Economic Development and Political Legitimacy," *American Political Science Review* vol. 53, no. 1 (March 1959): 69–105.

3. Rustow, 344.

4. Ibid., 344–345.

5. See, for instance, G. O'Donnell, "Introduction to the Latin American Cases," in *Transitions from Authoritarian Rule: Latin America*, ed. G. O'Donnell, P. Schmitter, and L. Whitehead (Baltimore: Johns Hopkins University Press, 1986); and Larry Diamond and J. Linz, "Introduction," in *Democracy in Developing Countries: Latin America*, ed. L. Diamond, J. Linz, and S.M. Lipset (Boulder, CO: Lynne Rienner Publishers, 1989).

6. See, for interesting discussions of these issues, Samuel Valenzuela, "Democratic Consolidation in Post-Transitional Settings: Nation, Process, and Facilitating Conditions," Kellogg Working Paper No. 50, University of Notre Dame, 1990; and Terry Karl, "Dilemmas of Democratization in Latin America," *Comparative Politics* vol. 23, no. 1 (1990): 1–22.

7. Karl, "Dilemmas of Democratization," 6.

8. Some authors have even argued that democracy is not necessarily the most efficient system for solving long-standing social grievances. See P. Schmitter and T. Karl in "What Democracy Is . . . and Is Not," *Journal of Democracy* vol. 2, no. 3 (1991): 75–88.

9. This was the case both under de facto governments between 1963 and 1965, and under the twelve-year-long presidency of Joaquin Balaguer from 1966 to 1978.

10. Only a simple majority is needed to win the presidency.

11. The Dominican Constitution states that it is the responsibility of the Senate to appoint the members of the Electoral Board. The board consists of a president, two members, and three substitutes.

12. Department of Labor Economics, Labor Ministry of the Dominican Republic (unpublished records).

13. Indeed, business remained quite firm in its decision to restrain collective bargaining.

14. See, for more details, Rosario Espinal, "The Dominican Republic," in *Latin American and Caribbean Contemporary Record*, ed. J. Malloy and E. Gamarra, vol. VII (New York: Holmes & Meier, 1990): B–406.

15. For a discussion of conditions that can lead to class compromise, see A. Przeworski and M. Wallerstein, "The Structure of Class Conflict in Democratic Capitalist Societies," *The American Political Science Review* vol. 76, no. 2 (June 1982): 215–238; and A. Przeworski, *Capitalism and Social Democracy* (Cambridge: Cambridge University Press, 1985).

16. A more detailed analysis of this idea is found in Rosario Espinal, "The Defeat of the Dominican Revolutionary Party in the 1986 Elections: Causes and Implications," *Bulletin of Latin American Research* vol. 9, no. 1 (1990): 103–115.

17. Balaguer invested in construction projects on average RD$127.9 million a month in 1987, RD$221.2 million a month in 1988, and RD$295.2 million a month in 1989. *El Siglo*, August 15, 1989.

18. I first used the term in "Torn Between Authoritarianism and Crisis-Prone Democracy: The Dominican Labor Movement," Kellogg Working Paper No. 113, University of Notre Dame, 1988. See, for further elaborations, Rosario Espinal, "Between Authoritarianism and Crisis-Prone Democracy: The Dominican Republic After Trujillo," in *Society and Politics in the Caribbean*, pp. 145–165, ed. C. Clarke (Oxford: Macmillan, 1991).

10

Puerto Rico: Problems of Democracy and Decolonization in the Late Twentieth Century

Carmen Gautier-Mayoral

✳

Puerto Rico, an island with a population of 3.5 million, presents three outstanding characteristics in the late twentieth century. It is prosperous by Caribbean standards, but it has an extremely dependent economy. The limited democracy available (in a territory granted barely 15% of all powers of government) is enthusiastically embraced by over 85 percent of the voting-age population, who regularly go to the polls. Deferred decolonization, as well as increasing illegal immigration, is a characteristic it shares with the remaining subsidized colonies of the Caribbean, particularly Guadeloupe, Martinique, and the U.S. Virgin Islands but also—to some extent—Aruba and Curaçao.[1]

This chapter deals with the tensions between decolonization and democracy resulting from Puerto Rico's status as a "prosperous but dependent economy." The main argument is that elements of "benign colonialism," coupled with internal political and economic contradictions, produced a vanishing plebiscite, a "no" vote in an identity referendum, and a New Progressive Party (pro-statehood) 49.1 percent plurality in the 1992 elections. The chapter concludes with an analysis of the politics of immobility shared by some of the subsidized colonies of the Caribbean.

THE ECONOMY: "PROSPEROUS DEPENDENCE"

The Puerto Rican economic model of the 1950s was based on "industrialization by invitation" of U.S. capital. The economy grew at the rate of 7.6 percent

An earlier and briefer version of this chapter appeared in *Radical America* vol. 23, no. 1 (1990): 21–32.

in 1950, 6.8 percent in 1960, and 9.7 percent in 1970, but by 1973 real growth had slowed to 1.33 percent or less a year until 1986.[2] The Reagan expansion in the United States during the 1980s, however, positively affected the economy in the ensuing three years, including a 4.9 percent growth rate for fiscal 1988, a 3.6 percent growth for fiscal 1989, and only a 2.2 percent growth for 1990. In fiscal 1991, the island's economy again grew less than 1 percent, affecting the labor-intensive construction industry, which contributes about 10 percent of the gross national product.[3] The notable, but declining, improvement in the three pre-1991 years was due to four main factors: (1) the drop in the value of the dollar; (2) a moderate drop in interest rates in 1988; (3) the drop in the price of oil—which in the winter of 1989–1990 again rose steeply, only to fall after the war in the Persian Gulf; and (4) the strong defense of Section 936 of the U.S. Internal Revenue Code made by the governor in 1985 and 1986. Unemployment was officially 16.1 percent in late 1991,[4] up from 14.4 percent in 1989, down from a high of 24 percent in 1983, and higher than the 15.5 percent for 1988. Unofficially, it is over 30 percent with a net participation rate of only 41 percent in 1980, risen to 45 percent according to Planning Board figures in 1988, but possibly much lower nowadays with a demise in tourism.[5]

Why has Puerto Rico been confronted since the mid-1970s with many of the enormous problems of the 1930s, problems which, like ghosts out of the agricultural past, have returned to an "industrialized" island? Compared with the rest of the Caribbean, the island had undergone an early (1948) process of industrialization. It had exported 834,000 persons,[6] or 48.7 percent of its 1970 working-age population, between 1940 and 1970, while public health and per capita income had improved enormously. Yet many problems of the past returned in full force.

These include: (1) massive unemployment and underemployment of the dimensions mentioned above; (2) a colossal public debt; (3) unemployment of young university graduates (which in 1980 led to a definite government policy to "encourage those Puerto Rican professionals who cannot find jobs on the island to join the ranks of Hispanic professionals in the U.S."[7]); (4) a phenomenal growth of the bureaucracy in the 1970s, with government jobs accounting for 69 percent of the 121,000 jobs created between 1970 and 1979 (the bureaucracy again grew by 29.6% between 1985 and 1989);[8] (5) a very high eligibility for federal poor relief: 77 percent in 1936[9] and 65 percent in 1976, and 610,972 families in poverty in 1989, of which 55,000 are in extreme poverty;[10] and (6) both economic crises (during the 1930s following the Great Depression and the 1970s following the OPEC oil crises of 1973–1974) were considered structural, not cyclical;[11] (7) absentee U.S. corporations continue to take the money off the island;[12] and (8) in 1992 Puerto Rico was the fourth market for the United States in Latin America.[13]

Interestingly enough, these coincidental manifestations have not yet produced the level of revolutionary unrest prevalent in the 1930s, although social unrest has reached near crisis levels in the last ten years. The DuPont Plaza Fire on New Year's Eve 1986, brought about by labor unrest, caused over ninety deaths by asphyxiation. The large labor protest against the privatization of the telephone company, held in March 1990, showed part of the unhappiness with the present situation. An October 1991 poll showed that 56 percent of respondents considered crime the biggest problem in the country, 95 percent were especially interested in this problem, and 91 percent would also like to curtail drug abuse as an incentive to crime. Eighty-seven percent considered that things were going "very badly" here, and showed scant hope that the politicians will improve the situation (*El Nuevo Dia*, November 5, 1991, 4–5). In late November 1992, the island's per capita homicide rate (23.2 killings per 100,000 crime population) was the highest in the United States. At the end of 1991, only Washington, D.C., with 80.6 killings scored higher than San Juan, with 77.1 slayings per 100,000.[14]

Puerto Rico's economic boom of the 1950s and 1960s was built on a very shaky tripod: (1) an investment capital surplus in the United States after World War II, looking for profitable and secure locations abroad; (2) the federal transfer and other payments into this economy; and (3) the massive emigration of Puerto Rican *campesinos*. By 1974 each of the three legs of the tripod had suffered substantial modifications and a fourth one had been added to Puerto Rico's very vulnerable economy: public debt.

Leg Number 1: Foreign Investment

Foreign investment grew and bank deposits were heightened after 1976, due to Section 936, the new possessions corporations tax arrangements, of the U.S. Internal Revenue Code, which converted Puerto Rico into a financial export platform. Federal law requires that the profits of the 130 transnational U.S. companies located on the island be deposited in island banks for at least six months, in order to be available for new investment in industry in this high unemployment area. The Government Development Bank receives 10 percent of those profits, at no interest, under Puerto Rican law. The rest go to the commercial banks—mainly the four North American and two Canadian banks with branch offices on the island[15]—at 6 to 7 percent annual interest. In exchange for this, their deposits and interests are to be exempt from U.S. tax upon repatriation, and they pay a toll gate tax of 10 percent upon leaving Puerto Rico, reduced to 4 percent if they leave their deposits on the island for twelve to eighteen months.[16]

The innovative measures of the Caribbean Basin Initiative (CBI) were delegated to the government of Puerto Rico, which happily assumed it in the second Reagan administration as part of the restructuring of the Puerto Rican economy. Nevertheless, in 1986 Congress seriously questioned the benefits for Puerto Rico of keeping the 936 tax loophole. The governor's success in maintaining that section of the

Internal Revenue Code intact was based on linking the future of 936 with his twin-plant industrial promotion program in the Caribbean, as part of the U.S. Caribbean Basin Initiative. To ensure the survival of Section 936, the government of Puerto Rico must continue to show whether this program has in fact been aiding the Caribbean countries in improving their economies,[17] pledging US$100 million a year for commercially competitive loans. By the end of 1991, the Hernández Colón administration had overfulfilled its pledge, having approved loans to Caribbean and Central American states totaling about US$700 million, for a range of ventures, mainly in Trinidad and Tobago, Barbados, the Dominican Republic, Jamaica, and Costa Rica.[18]

Leg Number 2: Federal Funds

Federal funds grew almost geometrically after 1976, becoming the only real area of growth during the rest of that decade. As a percent of GNP, total federal expenses in Puerto Rico grew from 15.1 percent in 1965 to 38.5 percent in 1980, down to 34.3 percent in 1984, but never less than 30 percent for the rest of the 1980s. The outlays to the public sector for roads, electricity, water, sewers, ports, and other services, and public corporations, also improve the services available to the federal, civil, and military government in Puerto Rico.

Leg Number 3: Unemployment and Emigration

Unemployment and emigration have both shown a degree of growth. Although the population of Puerto Rico increased by 37 percent between 1970–1971 and 1982–1983, the total number of persons employed on the island in 1983 was lower by 4.1 percent than the amount of people working in 1972, and by 7.4 percent of those working in 1981. However, the upswing in the economy later in the decade offset—to some extent—that reduction. The official unemployment figures conceal that part of the labor force who have lost all hope of finding a job, the *desalentados* (hopeless). The high rate of unemployment growth, sustained for a long time, shows that it is structural. It is also technological. The working class—except for those employed in highly sophisticated jobs—has stagnated quantitatively and in absolute terms, and loses numerical force to other social groupings in Puerto Rican society. Construction jobs, however, as well as those in fast-food establishments, proliferated temporarily in the 1986–1989 period. But stagnation is evident in both the increasing ranks of the young unemployed (between the ages of sixteen to twenty-five, the future workers) as well as in the diminishing levels of unionization—9 percent of all workers in 1985, reduced to 6 percent in 1987, and less than 5 percent in 1990, including 2 percent in government.[19] The fact that the export platform industries, the *maquiladoras* (or factories "invited" to Puerto Rico by the program initiated in 1947), whether high technology or just plain manufacturing, pass *through* Puerto Rico but are never part of it does not bode well for the unionization of laborers.

With work so scarce in Puerto Rico, and U.S. citizenship to guarantee at least the right to enter and work in the United States, the figures show a slower flow of emigration in the 1970s than in the 1960s or in the early 1980s. However, all emigration figures must be taken very, very carefully. For example, the Planning Board 1985 *Data on Migration* shows that after 1980 and including 1984, 125,845 people migrated from Puerto Rico, whereas the U.S. census Hispanic study claimed in 1986 that almost one half million Puerto Ricans had left the island in the first five years of the 1980s, 70,000 of them professionals. About 2.3 million Puerto Ricans, or 40 percent of the total number of islanders here and in the United States, were said to reside in the states in 1989.[20]

Leg Number 4: Public Debt

Public debt grew astronomically after 1960. This growth was initiated due to the creation of infrastructure for capital-intensive companies which paid no taxes and produced very few jobs in an economy with large unemployment. It was expanded after the decision of the Puerto Rican government to counteract the 1973–1975 recession with countercyclical measures that multiplied the public investment program through borrowing. The gross public debt (GPD) of Puerto Rico as a percentage of GNP grew more than two and a half times, from 30 percent in 1962 to 73.9 percent in 1976, and has since been reduced to barely twice the original amount, 61.2 percent in 1988, as GNP rose and the absolute debt also rose, though not apace. As elsewhere, Puerto Ricans pay for debt through lower salaries, lower profits for "national" enterprises, and denationalization of wealth.

THE LIMITED DEMOCRACY

Although the 1952 Commonwealth Constitution gave a new veneer of respectability to the home rule provided for Puerto Rico under the Federal Organic Acts—including an Elective Governor Act approved in 1947—it did not in fact bring any fundamental change in the powers of government.[21] Even as home rule, the Commonwealth Constitution is rather poor, since it leaves not only the usual foreign relations and defense in the hands of the metropolitan power, but also customs, military draft, citizenship, regulation of immigration and aliens, post office, control of internal and external communications, presence of military bases in Puerto Rico, obligatory use of U.S. freighters for shipping, minimum wages, and so on, in the hands of Congress. The Puerto Rican elected government was left the control of purely local matters, administering the economy, but was never able to make the important decisions on the legs supporting it.

At the same time, the extension of federal aid to ever-greater proportions of the Puerto Rican population has contributed to a bipartisan political system with alternation and cogovernance of the two major parties and fewer opportunities for a political status change. The enjoyment of the perquisites of local (subordinated) power has entertained most leaders, and the drive for a change toward statehood or toward a more autonomous form of commonwealth or free associated statehood had been largely neutralized by the 1980s.

✗   The Puerto Rican privileged classes enjoy a social peace paradise financed not from their own profits, but from the pockets of the U.S. taxpayers. Under this situation, the Puerto Rican upper classes are unique in Latin America: they enjoy the benefits of partnership with U.S. capital without having to pay the costs in any significant way; they do not pay federal taxes and they make use of federal funds to make economic concessions to the working classes and the marginal sectors without having to affect their profit margins. This political paradise makes the Puerto Rican upper classes wholehearted supporters of U.S. colonial dominance. They pay the price of remaining a subordinate bourgeoisie, and of transnational capital dominance of the economy, but they are more than willing to do so in exchange for the tranquility of a democratic political system where labor is scarcely organized and where no coup d'états are needed to avert mass struggles or social revolution. Internal social decomposition, however, is every day more evident.

The United States has made several economic concessions, such as permitting certain free trade measures with other countries (mainly Japan), benefiting certain sectors such as automobile dealers and importers, and has made other concessions in terms of permitting Puerto Rican participation as a separate nationality in some international cultural and sports events. These symbolic concessions have contributed to the fragile equilibrium. They also help to maintain the illusion among many Puerto Ricans that the commonwealth status has already produced decolonization.

Nevertheless, Puerto Rican governments of both the Popular Democratic Party (procommonwealth, or status quo) and the New Progressive (pro-statehood) Party have made at least seven equally unsuccessful attempts at gaining more powers for the island since the 1952 constitution.[22] The most recent one started with outgoing Governor Colón's second inaugural announcement in January 1989 that he would seek a plebiscite in the U.S. Congress for a vote on the status of Puerto Rico, followed by a similar message in President George Bush's State of the Union speech in February, backing—as every president since Truman has done—self-determination for Puerto Rico. Colón would agree to any status voted upon by a majority on the island, but he preferred statehood.[23] A tie vote of ten to ten in early March 1991 ended two years of congressional hearings at the Senate Energy and Natural Resources Committee (in Washington, San Juan, Ponce, and Mayagüez) on a second (1991) bill for a status referendum. It became apparent that as the dependent

Puerto Ricans seemed nearer to asking for statehood, the U.S. Senate had serious misgivings about that possibility.

A result of this last event was the approval in San Juan of a law providing for a yes or no referendum vote on a series of democratic rights of Puerto Ricans. These included, among others, "the right to choose a status of full political dignity without colonial or territorial subordination to the plenary powers of Congress; the right to vote on three status alternatives—Commonwealth, Statehood, and Independence; the right that any referendum on status will guarantee, under any alternative, our culture, language and own identity, which includes our international sports representation; and the right to guarantee, under any alternative, the U.S. citizenship, safeguarded in the U.S. Constitution."[24] On December 8, 1991, 1.2 million of an electorate of 2 million went to the polls, and defeated the proposals 54 percent to 46 percent.

In January 1992, the prostatehood New Progressive Party (NPP) had included in its platform the holding of a three-way status plebiscite in Puerto Rico in 1993, which it now seems to be able to do after winning the November 1992 elections. The outgoing governor of the Popular Democratic Party (PDP) announced that he will not run again, and passed on the leadership of his party to Luis Muñoz Marín's daughter,[25] who is committed not to touch status in the next four years. Also, although the U.N. General Assembly decided in 1953 (at the request of the United States) that Puerto Rico was now a "Commonwealth" of the United States, and thus Washington was no longer obliged to send annual reports on its administration of the island to the world organization,[26] the case of Puerto Rico has been on the agenda of the U.N. Decolonization Committee continuously since 1972. Beginning in 1977, members of the political elite of all the political parties and currents on the island, as well as the Puerto Rico Bar Association, have been making annual pilgrimages to New York to protest the lack of decolonization.[27]

DEFERRED DECOLONIZATION

What is the meaning of these 1989–1992 events for the Puerto Rican polity? Why is the annual pilgrimage to the U.N. Decolonization Committee so enticing to Puerto Rican politicians of all hues?

The electoral behavior and the ideological leanings of the majority of the population were found during the 1980s to have no correlation with the astronomical growth of federal funds, until the announcement in early 1989 of the (now defunct) plebiscite for June 4, 1991. Increased dependence on federal funds did not mean consistent growth of the New Progressive Party at the expense of the Popular Democratic Party, nor a dramatic turn to the statehood status option. On the contrary, the majority of Puerto Ricans were still in favor of the continuation of commonwealth status or the status quo, in one form or another, during the 1980s. After all, as Richard Weiskoff (1985: 4) pointed out:

"An island with 60 percent of its people dependent on food stamps and the rest working in foreign-owned factories or in federally supported government offices can hardly be expected to elect a status that might jeopardize that arrangement."

Independent or split voting had also arisen due to the enormous amounts of federal funds going to the municipalities, amounts which varied from one and a half to twelve times the funds received from insular sources. These funds have made the mayors and local bosses independent of the party chief or candidate for governor. But the most notable political effects of massive federal funding have been the deflation of the labor movement in the 1970s and 1980s, and the stagnation of the proindependence parties in an ever more dependent society.

However, when holding a plebiscite in Puerto Rico became important to the United States in early 1989, and an erroneous staff report of the Senate Committee on Natural Resources mentioned loss of U.S. citizenship under any option other than statehood, the statehood preference grew to 41 percent of the electorate in October 1989, and to 43 percent in January 1990.[28] Two coexisting and contradictory, yet intertwined, situations, "the attempt to restructure and modernize the Puerto Rican economy," and the "permanent" wobbly supports on which that economy stands, have now crashed against the reality of political status. Restructuring, to succeed, will require greater autonomy or sovereignty of action on the part of the Puerto Rican polity, in order to be able to carry out some of the measures which ensure "selection" of beneficial foreign capital in the newly industrializing countries (NICs): South Korea, Taiwan, and Singapore.

Already, initiatives toward agreements with other developed nations have been stopped by the U.S. State Department, as in the case of Japan.[29] Others have not been able to be carried out, as in the cases of commercial treaties with Venezuela (November 1987) or certain agreements with Spain (May 1988). The October 1991 agreements with Spain may also be suspended against the growing relationship of that country with the EC toward the 1993 single market, now to include the seven countries of the European Free Trade Area. An upside is Spain's selling itself to the EC as the partner which will be able to bring the Latin American market to the community (and the Caribbean market, via Puerto Rico).

The "permanent" wobbly supports are an apparent drag in that the supply of funds does not depend on decisions made in Puerto Rico or on efforts exerted by anyone on the island, although the economy is very carefully and even inventively administered, as the CBI program shows. Nevertheless, by virtue of the U.S. military's need for Puerto Rico in its Caribbean defense strategy[30] as well as for naval and guerrilla war practice, and due to the pharmaceutical transnationals' need for their 936 privileges to maintain their competitiveness in the world legal drug market, the wobbly legs have acquired a certain "permanence." This helps to create an artificial equilibrium which sustains both

U.S. dominance and the growth of prostatehood sentiment in the island's electorate.

It seemed that the time had come when the restructuring of the economy needed some changes in the political relationship of the Commonwealth of Puerto Rico to the United States; hence, the push toward a plebiscite in 1989–1991 and the referendum of democratic rights to petition Congress on behalf of the Puerto Rican people. At the same time, the "necessity" for the wobbly legs to go on sustaining the economy and the limited electoral democracy seemed to counsel the voters to choose statehood, or at least not to question the "permanence" of the relationship with the United States.

Therefore, the contradiction will continue to exist between the need for more "sovereignty" to carry out some of the measures which ensure the "selection" of foreign capital as in the NICs, and the deep and continuous, but joyously assumed and creatively managed, dependence which supports electoral democracy at the base of the Puerto Rican economy. Only if restructuring were to achieve such a degree of success, that the limited democracy could survive without the sustaining wobbly legs, would the Puerto Rican electorate follow the government in its eventual search for greater sovereignty. The entire vacuous discussion around the so-called "Associated Republic"—which is neither associated nor a republic—from the time it was proposed in 1985 as "what had been decided on in Washington," until its eventual use as a "bogey man" by the prostatehood NPP to effectively take away votes from the Popular Democratic Party in 1988, has been nothing more than the staging of this contradiction (Gautier-Mayoral, 1988; Orellana, 1987).

Another reason for the U.S. urgency to hold a plebiscite in Puerto Rico in 1989 could have been the panic of the far right that the U.S. would "lose" Panama and Guantánamo in the year 2000, and its desire to make Puerto Rico a state so that the real estate where the bases are located would always remain part of the United States.[31] President Bush, trying to win over the electorate of his predecessor, may have been influenced by part of that far right in his February 1989 message announcing that he "preferred statehood" for the island. But the situation changed drastically by the end of 1989 after the invasion of Panama and the collapse of Communism in Eastern Europe, and then in the Soviet Union.

An additional reason for the United States to push the plebiscite in early 1989 might have been an agreement on the Caribbean since the 1986 Reagan-Gorbachev meeting to push disarmament and open the Soviet Union and Eastern Europe to *perestroika* and *glasnost*. Besides lowering the Soviet Union's support of Nicaragua and Cuba to make the Central American Esquipulas peace treaty possible, it may have included the holding of a plebiscite to take the case of Puerto Rico—one of the oldest cases presented every year before the U.N. Decolonization Committee—off the organization's agenda. General Assembly Resolution 43/47 of November 22, 1988, declaring the present decade the International Decade for the Eradication of

Colonialism in the world, would seem to support this explanation for the plebiscite.

Nevertheless, this plebiscite vanished because it made no sense for Puerto Rico at the time, given the aforementioned contradictions in its economy and the dream of enormous new markets in Eastern Europe and the Soviet Union for U.S. transnational companies in 1990.[32] The federal budget for fiscal 1991, as early as January 1990, when it was submitted, did not include any allotment of funds for the plebiscite requested by Bush in his 1989 State of the Union message.[33]

The evidence of ninety-four years of rhetorical support to self-determination, together with very little action in that direction, makes one suspect that at least as far as Puerto Rico is concerned, Congress has not shown any belief in self-determination, and the various U.S. presidents have made beautiful, but empty, declarations for the consumption of the United Nations and not directed either at Puerto Rico or at Congress. As was pointed out by Harvard-educated retired chief justice José Trías Monge:

> Among modern peoples, the Puerto Ricans have the longest colonial history in the world. . . . In spite of profuse expressions by the United States in favor of self determination [in the twentieth century], this right has never been recognized for Puerto Ricans outside of rhetorical manifestations. . . . The process has been degrading both for Puerto Rico and for the U.S. In a world where colonialism . . . is already a finished force, Puerto Rico is kept in a non-dignified situation, neither inside nor outside, governing itself in [a very small] part and [mostly] governed by others, in a situation without international respect.[34]

Also, this U.S. preoccupation with the island's political status, as the experience of the last twenty-eight years has shown, is superficial. Ever since the U.N. Decolonization Committee came into existence in 1962, the U.S. executive and legislative branches have been playing at the game of "studying Puerto Rico's status in order to grant the island more powers" in whatever direction. As soon as Puerto Rico seems to be going in one direction, a Washington pronouncement of some sort changes the direction, and it becomes a new game.

In February 1987, the National Security Council appeared to be no longer interested in its 1985 push toward an associated republic status for Puerto Rico. By January 1992, the 1989 presidential-congressional push for a plebiscite (to be held in Puerto Rico in June 1991) had disappeared altogether. The loss of interest by the transnational companies in the Caribbean, the Congressional Budget Report estimate of an immediate US$9 billion cost of statehood, and the right wing's fear of the "browning of America" all took priority as more pressing concerns on the agenda. But in the eternal status discussions, as in the heavily dependent Puerto Rican economy, there is always room for a new gimmick, such as a nonself-executing plebiscite or "beauty contest" which in no way fulfills the international requirements for decolonization, nor any other function than lip service to self-determination. Such was the December 8, 1991 referendum on our identification as Puerto Ricans "in order to petition Congress with those rights we all agreed upon," and such will be the November 1993 plebiscite among the three options to be held by the Puerto Rican legislature as promised by the program of the triumphant NPP government-elect.

If the transnationals are happy, the Pentagon is satisfied and the Puerto Rican electorate cannot be expected to jeopardize the artificial economy that keeps them afloat. We can call this the politics of great creativity in using the funds either transferred here or kept on the island until their tax-free repatriation to the United States, and of immobility in relation to status.

The politics of immobility are not, however, singular to Puerto Rico. This recurring model of "subsidized colonies," with no growing movement for independence, is by now well established in the Caribbean, and perhaps in some remaining Pacific colonies as well. Let us briefly examine the Caribbean examples.

THE POLITICS OF STATUS IMMOBILITY IN THE SUBSIDIZED COLONIES OF THE CARIBBEAN

At the onset of the 1990s, we find a substantial group of dependent Caribbean territories in various stages of "self-government" and of "apparent or postponed decolonization" which are generally not in the list of territories studied or decided upon by the U.N. Decolonization Committee. They pertain to a newly developed category of colony in the late twentieth century: welfare colonies, or colonies heavily subsidized by their respective metropoles (capitalist centers of Western Europe and North America that dominate over peripheral dependent Third World countries). Examples in the Caribbean include: (1) U.S.: Puerto Rico and the U.S. Virgin Islands; (2) France: Guadeloupe, Martinique, French St. Martin, and Guyane; and (3) the Netherlands: Aruba, Curaçao, Bonaire, Dutch St. Martin, St. Eustatius, and Sabá.

With the exception of the United Kingdom, which has never had any qualms about having colonies, the other metropoles of the industrial world withdrew most of their possessions from the official list of nonautonomous territories via different types of constitutional arrangements long before the "Magna Carta of Decolonization" (GA Resolution 1514 [XV] of December 1960) had been approved.[35]

Nevertheless, the continuous petitions for change in the constitutional arrangements, both to the Netherlands as well as to the United States, and in a lesser manner also to France and the United Kingdom—throughout the thirty-one years of deliberations of the U.N. Decolonization Committee—are clear proof that the constitutional situation in those territories has not been stabilized.

Since both the subsidized colonies and the countries of the periphery are inserted in the same global economy as the heavily industrialized countries of the center, their insertion neither neutralizes nor eliminates the political and economic arrangements which form colonial subordination, provided those arrangements are profitable or highly valued by the leaders of global production, particularly in the central countries.

This brief discussion does not study in juridical detail any of the negotiations, desires, trials, mythical or real plebiscites, and other mechanisms of constitutional discussion occurring between these subsidized colonies and their respective metropoles. Instead, I examine: (1) the present state of simulated decolonization in all of these Caribbean colonies; (2) the use of these colonial territories, particularly for the United States and France, in the metropoles' military strategy and global economic planning in the 1990s; and (3) the absence of strong independence movements in any of these territories.

Simulated Decolonization

Puerto Rico's ties to the cycle of aid and dependency are equally evident in all of the other client colonies of the Caribbean. When almost 29 percent of disposable income on the island comes from metropolitan transfers of funds, a total separation from the United States could mean an immediate shortfall of almost one-third of individual incomes. The same seems to occur in Aruba and the other Netherlands Antilles, where aid donated by The Hague is one of the highest per capita in the world.[36] Thus, the 1990 proposal for a new Commonwealth of the Netherlands ensures Dutch citizenship and continuation of economic aid from The Hague, two of the principal worries of the electorate.[37] In the Departements D'Outremer (DOM) of France, public transfers represent almost three-fourths of the resources of these territories, as opposed to one-fourth coming from exports of goods and services.[38] They are now asking the French government for the status of free associated states, due to their fear that the European unified market will not serve their interests as Caribbean peoples. Nevertheless, on November 25 and 26, 1992, the farmers of the French Antilles joined the French farmers' protest at the European decision to lower their subsidies in agreement with U.S. requirements for open trade. The airports in Point à Pitre and Fort de France were closed by bananas lying on the runways.

The per capita incomes and capital flows in the subsidized colonies of the region (very high for the Caribbean) attracted a substantial migration from impoverished neighboring islands. Thus, thousands of undocumented Dominicans come to Puerto Rico; eastern Caribbean peoples travel to Guadeloupe and Martinique; residents of the Leeward and Windward Islands and southern Caribbean to the U.S. Virgin Islands; and Antilleans from the Anglophone Caribbean to the British Virgin Islands, where they are considered foreigners and their work permits are annually renewed. They come to earn money in hard (metropole) currency, and send it home to their families.

Continuous migration of Puerto Ricans to the United States (one-half of our population lives there); Dutch Antilleans to the Netherlands (one-third of their population is in the metropole); and of Francophone Antilleans to France (one-half of Guadeloupeans live in France) shows that the economic situation of all of these dependent territories is extremely precarious.

These territories have had their economies turned into what Guadeloupean Felix Proto calls "a consumption economy and a leisure society, without the productive mechanisms to support it. It has very high costs of production and living standards, and equally high ratios of unemployment, [and out migration] accompanied by a limited production for trade with the metropole, and almost nonexistent trade with its Caribbean neighbors" (Proto, 1989: 5). This last factor is less true of Puerto Rico, which, as the largest of the subsidized colonies, has served as the centerpiece of the CBI.

Strategic Arrangements

For strategic reasons, both military and commercial, the U.S. and French metropoles keep these small colonial territories in a politically decolonized world. Although in a world that may be divided into trading and currency blocs, the commercial should be uppermost, the military reasons play a bigger part. The U.S. antidrug war, kept on the back burner until after the November 1992 elections, plays an important role. The French and Dutch governments jealously protect their territories from this plague, but the military relation with U.S. forces in the region goes through NATO, in the case of the Netherlands, and through bilateral agreements between Paris and Washington, in the case of France. Puerto Rico has been used as a base for AWACS flying warning flights over the Caribbean since February 15, 1990, and 29,000 additional acres in the green areas of Puerto Rico were requested by the U.S. Army in 1989 to train guerrillas for antidrug warfare.

France is also interested in both Guyane and New Caledonia (a Pacific territory) for military strategic reasons relating to nuclear exercises for the French Armed Forces.[39] It uses Guadeloupe as a way station for the transport of fissionable materials to its nuclear experimentation sites of Mururoa in Polynesia. Martinique belongs to the integrated network of the International Military Broadcasting Organization, and a geostationary satellite covering the North Atlantic may be stationed there soon.[40]

Absence of Strong Independence Movements

The scene of absolute impoverishment caused by the "lost decade for development" in Latin America and the Caribbean presents a regional scene of increasing poverty, every day more distant from First World standards.[41] The subsidized colonies, territories of extreme economic dependence, still keep considerably higher standards of living than the countries of absolute impoverishment. Their per capita incomes, inflated by the external funds they receive, make them extremely cautious when it comes time to select a political solution for their people. The popularity contests called plebiscites, to be held in 1993 in the Virgin Islands and perhaps in Puerto Rico (like the new constitution offered by the Netherlands, and the French denial of a change of status for their DOM while insisting on raising their social and economic standard of living from Strasbourg),[42] will be a form of apparent decolonization, which will be given much publicity to leave matters politically the same, and perhaps economically worse.

Nevertheless, the concerns of the powers in the region will tend to maintain the high subsidies in the territories, and the fear of retreating into bitter Caribbean poverty will keep the electorates faithful to the apparent decolonization. The politics of immobility in relation to status or political relationship is rampant in the Antilles. It is not an exclusive model in the region, but an adaptation of the electorates of islands with very fragile economies tied to the cycle of aid and dependency.

NOTES

1. See Carmen Gautier-Mayoral, "La descolonización aplazada de las colonias subsidiadas del Caribe en el contexto de la economía global de los años '90," presented at the third meeting of the Caribbean International Relations Study Group of the Latin American Council for the Social Sciences (CLACSO), held at Cancún, Mexico, January 28–February 1, 1991; published in *El Caribe Contemporáneo* no. 24 (1992): 61–76.

2. Rubén Berríos Martínez, *La independencia de Puerto Rico: razón y lucha* (San Juan: Partido Independentista Puertorriqueño, 1983): 326.

3. See L. Albanese, "Proposal tags 5 percent of 936 funds for construction," *San Juan Star* December 17, 1991, B-1. Per capita personal disposable income grew only by 1.2 percent (ibid., B-4).

4. Cf. Ivonne García, "Jobless rate up to 16.1% in November," *San Juan Star* December 26, 1991, B-1. The official unemployment rate for Puerto Rico, even in the big growth years of early industrialization (1950–1972), never dropped below 13 percent.

5. The rise was due to a boom in tourism and tourism-related facilities caused by the drop in the value of the dollar. Nevertheless, see Deborah Ramírez, "Jobless Rolls Omit Thousands Without Work," *San Juan Star* December 13, 1988, 1. Newly elected NPP governor Dr. Pedro Rosselló has promised a big rise in tourism, but this will depend more on the Caribbean tourist market than on his efforts.

6. José E. Vázquez Calzada, "Demographic Aspects of Migration," Center for Puerto Rican Studies, City University of New York, *Cuadernos, Taller de Migración*, Cuaderno 2 (1974): 4.

7. Miguel Rivera Ríos, president of the Puerto Rico Planning Board, in *El Mundo* April 11, 1980, 4. In this same newspaper Governor Romero announced he would receive all the Cubans then waiting at the Peruvian embassy in Havana. Currently it is estimated that about 20 percent of all emigrants are professionals (ibid., 11).

8. See Tomás Stella, "Desmedido el crecimiento en la burocracia," *El Mundo* January 29, 1990, 4, 5.

9. Federal Emergency Relief Administration, *Report* (Washington, DC: Government Printing Office, 1936).

10. A. Martínez, "Los niveles de pobreza . . . 1980–89" in *El Nuevo Día* January 30, 1990, 14; and "Estiman en mas de un millón los pobres en la Isla," *El Nuevo Día* January 19, 1990, 23; General Accounting Office, *Puerto Rico, Update of Selected Information Contained in a 1981 GAO Report* (GAO/HRD–89–104FS): 22 reports 43.5 percent eligible for Nutrition Assistance program in 1988.

11. Puerto Rico Reconstruction Administration, May 2, 1936, report to Dr. Gruening; *Report to the Governor of the Committee to Study Puerto Rico's Finances* (San Juan, 1975), also published in San Juan as the *Informe Tobin* (San Juan: University of Puerto Rico Press, 1976); and U.S. Department of Commerce, *Economic Study of Puerto Rico*, 2 vols. (Washington, DC: Government Printing Office, 1979).

12. In 1970 63.5 percent of net income in manufacturing on the island went to salaries and only 36.5 percent was profits; in 1984 the situation was reversed: only 31.6 percent of net income was used for salaries while 68.4 percent was apportioned to profits. Their share grew to 72.6 percent in 1987, and 73.3 percent in 1989, while the allotment to salaries waned to 27.4 percent and 26.7 percent respectively (Banco de Fomento, 1990). Please note that although 1987 and 1989 were years of growth or recuperation in the economy, the share of the income going to the workers was ever lower.

13. Puerto Rico was in 1935 the ninth market for the United States in the world, the first in Latin America. In 1974, it was the fifth market of the United States in the world, but by 1985 it had dropped to the tenth, with only 1.3 percent of the population of the United States or .08 percent of that of the world.

14. Statistics Division of Puerto Rico Police Department, November 27, 1992, as reported by Gino Ponti, "Puerto Rico Crime Wave Reaches Tidal Proportions," *San Juan Star* November 30, 1992, 3.

15. In 1983, the foreign banks held 84.7 percent of the 936 funds; in 1984, 83.7 percent. Citibank and Chase Manhattan alone held 49 percent of the deposits in 1983 and 57 percent in 1984. See Banco de Fomento, "Comparison of Market Shares as of December 31, 1984, 936 Deposits" (1985).

16. The banks generally use the 936 funds for what they previously used their regular deposits, and buy U.S. government bonds which yield 10 percent interest with their regular deposits. Since they only pay 6 to 7 percent to the 936 corporations, the arbitrage operations produced a minimum of $189 million to the commercial banks in Puerto Rico in 1984. The Government Development Bank earned some $40 million in the same manner. These figures have grown apace in the latter part of the last decade and the beginning of this one.

17. See Subcommittee on Oversight of the House Ways and Means Committee, *Report on the Committee Delegation Mission to the Caribbean Basin and Recommendations to Improve the Effectiveness of the Caribbean Basin Initiative* (May 6, 1987), and P.R. Economic Development Administration, Caribbean Development Office, *Puerto Rico's Caribbean Development Program*, a Progress Report to the Ways and Means Committee, U.S. House of Representatives, San Juan, September 15, 1988. As of 1989, the CBI II law requires the Puerto Rican government to loan $100 million a year to CBI countries.

18. See Canute James, "Puerto Ricans ponder future," *The Financial Times* January 7, 1992, 6.

19. Over one-third of all unionized workers work in public corporations.

20. See General Accounting Office, *Puerto Rico, Update*, 22.

21. See Luis Muñoz Marín, testimony before U.S. House of Representatives, July 12, 1949, quoted in Vicente Géigel Polanco, *La Farsa del Estado Libre Asociado*, Río Piedras, Edil, 1972, 30.

22. Fernós-Murray bill of 1959; Aspinall bill of 1963; Status Commission bill of 1964; proposal for Puerto Ricans to vote for the U.S. president (1970); "The New Pact of Association" (1974–1975); the proposal for a "Yes or No" Statehood referendum for 1981; and the equally ill-fated "Puerto Rican Plebiscite Bill," which ran its course in Congress at the Committee of Natural Resources, under Senator Johnston, from February 1989 until March 1991. The previous attempts by Puerto Ricans in Washington between 1899 and 1945 are too numerous, and equally unsuccessful, to mention.

23. Cf. February 9, 1989 State of the Union Message to Congress in U.S. Government, Office of the President, *Weekly Compilation of Presidential Papers of President George Bush* (February 6–12, 1989), Washington, DC.

24. Law No. 85 of September 17, 1991, Puerto Rican Legislature, as quoted in a Congressional Research Service December 4, 1991 Memorandum from Johnny H. Killian of the American Law Division to Representative Robert Lagomarsino, Republican, California.

25. Victoria Muñoz is the daughter of Luis Muñoz Marín, and the granddaughter of Luis Muñoz Rivera, our only prime minister under a Spanish autonomist government in 1898, and later president of the Unionist Party and resident commissioner for Puerto Rico in Washington (1909–1916). Former NPP governor Carlos Romero Barceló (1977–1984), resident commissioner-elect for Puerto Rico in Washington, is the grandson of Antonio Barceló, president of the Unionist and later of the Liberal Party, and also president of the Puerto Rican Senate. A Caribbean dynastic custom is about to occur again.

26. GAOR 748 (VIII) of November 27, 1953.

27. Cf. Carmen Gautier-Mayoral and Maria del Pilar Argüelles, *Puerto Rico y la ONU*, Río Piedras, Edil 1978; and C. Gautier-Mayoral, "33 años del caso de Puerto Rico en la ONU," in C. Gautier-Mayoral, A. I. Rivera Ortiz, and I. E. Alegría Ortega, *Puerto Rico en las relaciones internationales del Caribe*, Río Piedras, Huracán, 1990, 36–69.

28. Please see Yankelovich/Stanford/Klapper public opinion poll, *El Nuevo Día* October 2, 1989, 4: 37 percent for commonwealth, 12 percent undecided, and 4 percent for independence; and Kaagan Research Associates, Inc. public opinion poll, *El Nuevo Día* February 13, 1990, 4: 36 percent for commonwealth, 9 percent undecided, and 5 percent for independence.

29. This happened in December 1986, in the midst of a Japan-bashing orgy being carried out by the U.S. Senate.

30. Particularly in the 1990s with the war on drugs as a new national security policy. See Waltraud Queiser Morales, "The War on Drugs: A New U.S. National Security Doctrine?" *Third World Quarterly*, vol. 11, no. 3 (July 1989): 147–169.

31. Think tanks such as the American Security Council, author of the *Santa Fé* I (1980) and II (1988) reports, the American Enterprise Institute, the Heritage Foundation, and others—not to mention the Pentagon—have voiced the importance of keeping Puerto Rico for the defense of the Caribbean.

32. See Peter Gumbel, "U.S. Firms Flock to Moscow Despite New Impediments: Lure of Huge Untapped Markets Overrides the Complexities of Perestroika," *The Wall Street Journal* October 24, 1989, A20 on the negative effect of this dream on the Puerto Rican economy.

33. See *El Nuevo Día* January 30, 1990, 4.

34. *Historia constitucional de Puerto Rico*, Río Piedras, Editorial Universitaria, 4 vols. 1981–1984, vol. 4, ch. XLVI, pp. 249–250, my translation.

35. In 1946, the French Antilles and Guyane were put under the Assimilation Law of May 19, converting them into *Departements D'Outremer* (DOMs) or Overseas Departments. The following year marked the Elective Governor Act for Puerto Rico, 1952 the Commonwealth Constitution, and 1953 the General Assembly Resolution recognizing self-government. In 1954, the Charter of the Kingdom of the Netherlands was installed for the Netherlands Antilles and Suriname. The U.S. Virgin Islands still remain on the list, and Puerto Rico's case has been

presented annually since 1972 in the U.N. Decolonization Committee. Suriname is independent since 1975 and Aruba was granted separate status in 1986.

36. Rita Giacalone, Freddy Martínez, and Peter Verton, *Curaçao y Aruba entre la autonomía y la independencia*, Mérida, Venezuela, *Consejo de Desarrollo Científico y Humanístico de la Universidad de los Andes*, 1990, ch. 4. On the need of aid for Aruba, see also Robertico Croes and Lucita Moenir Alam, "Decolonization of Aruba within the Netherlands Antilles," in *The Dutch Caribbean, Prospects for Democracy*, ed. Betty Sedoc-Dahlberg (New York: Gordon and Breach, 1990): 94–100. On the whole Dutch Caribbean, see Gert Oostindie, "The Dutch Caribbean in the 1990s: Decolonization or Recolonization," *Caribbean Affairs* (Port of Spain) vol. 5, no. 1 (January–March 1992): 103–119.

37. *Cabinet for the Netherlands Antillean and Aruban Affairs, Sketch of a Commonwealth Constitution for the Kingdom of the Netherlands*, The Hague, March 1990. The worries dealt with a guarantee of democratic government, defense, and protection against exploitation by the international illicit drug traders, as well as fear of the road followed by Suriname, especially the denial of Dutch aid after coup d'états in that republic, as reported in "New constitution proposed for the Netherlands Antilles," *Caribbean Insight*, vol. 13, no. 5 (May 1990): 6–7.

38. Felix Proto, *The Guadeloupe Region as it Stands*, Basse Terre, Guadeloupe Region Regional Council, Republic of France, 1989, ch. 5.

39. Donna Winslow, "Economic, Social and Demographic Developments in New Caledonia under the Matigan Accords," p. 9, paper presented at the Pacific Regional Seminar of the Decolonization Committee held in Vanuatu, May 9–11, 1990, in celebration of the thirtieth anniversary of GA Resolution 1514 (XV).

40. Daniel van Euwen, "Caribe francés, temores anti una mayor 'cercanía' europea," *Nueva Sociedad*, no. 119 (November–December 1990): 48. For further study, see Robert Aldrich and John Connell, *France's Overseas Frontier, Départements et Territoires D'Outremer* (Melbourne: Cambridge University Press, 1992).

41. For example, the Dominican Republic has returned to a technological situation approaching the nineteenth century, with scant electricity; Haitians had to suffer for five years after the fall of Duvalier to install their first elected president ever, only to have him overthrown eight months later; a previously prosperous Jamaica, whose economy went to pieces in the 1980s; an eastern Caribbean population escaping in boats toward Guadeloupe and Martinique; and a gravely impoverished Cuba after it lost its Soviet aid and subsidized buyers of sugar.

42. See *Plan POSEIDOM* (Strasbourg: European Council, 1990) of the European government in Strasbourg.

11

Cuba: Unchanging Change— The Boundaries of Democracy

Carollee Bengelsdorf

Cuba stands out among Caribbean nations as the only Marxist-Leninist regime linked to the former Soviet Union. Its political economy was transformed after 1959 under the impact of the Cold War and Cuba's incorporation into the socialist economic bloc dominated by the Soviet Union. With the demise of the Soviet Union and the emergence of democratization movements in Eastern Europe, observers point to Cuba as the next domino to fall.

Democracy, or the absence of it, was a central issue in the collapse of actually existing socialism[1] in the Soviet Union and Eastern Europe. At the same time that Cuba faces the most dire economic pressures as a result of this collapse, the question of democracy, which so haunted twentieth-century socialism, is once more at the forefront. The central conundrum remains, as it has for the past thirty-three years: to what degree is the Revolution willing—or capable—of fulfilling the democratic promise which has always lain at the heart of its social project, and has been evoked over and over again in moments of severe crisis and transition. This chapter examines the political and social processes that have transpired in Cuba over the past decade that may shed light on the constraints on democracy in this Caribbean nation.

This chapter is adapted from *The Problem of Democracy in Cuba: Between Vision and Reality,* © 1993 by Oxford University Press, Inc.

PERESTROIKA: THE CUBAN RESPONSE

During the last half of the 1980s, the Cuban Revolution, in accounts by a spectrum of commentators from the right to the left, emerged as the negative or flip side of what was portrayed as a massively far-reaching movement in the direction of democracy, or radical reform, in the Soviet Union. In this comparison, Fidel Castro became the "fossil marxist"[2] or, alternatively, the "aging hippy"[3] "at the tail end of the communist movement . . . totally isolated from outside realities."[4] If Mikhail Gorbachev was pragmatic, then Fidel was intransigent. If Gorbachev was future-oriented, then Fidel was backward looking. If Gorbachev was credited with heralding, or at least facilitating, the end of the Cold War, then Fidel was seen as "acting more and more like a Cold Warrior."[5]

Indeed, in response to events in Eastern Europe, Fidel chose to label himself an "inflexible socialist."[6] It seems important, however, to unpack the web of factors which underlay his critique and to locate its roots within what was transpiring in Cuba itself. The world, looked at through Cuban eyes, is a much different place than the world observed with U.S., or for that matter Soviet, eyes. These differences involve historical as well as political, economic, strategic, and demographic considerations. They justified and explained, in the minds of the Cuban leadership, Cuba's refusal to step into line with what was transpiring in the rest of the actually existing socialist world.

First, the Cuban Revolution was a genuine mass uprising with widescale popular support: it was not imposed from above by occupying armies, as was the case in Eastern Europe. The Stalinist yoke which strangled the Soviet Union and Eastern Europe and contributed so directly to their disintegration had and has no real hold over Cuba. The history of the Revolution and of its various experiments and heresies, if nothing else, demonstrates this.

Second, if Poland's enemy has traditionally been Russia or the Soviet Union, this was not true of Cuba, even if relations with the Soviet Union were not always cordial. Cuba's enemy, at least from the end of the nineteenth century, has been the United States. The threat posed by the United States further underlines Cuba's understanding of the world and of its place in that world. Cuba is a Caribbean nation and it identifies itself with the Third World. If (as it could be argued) Eastern Europe as a whole, and the Soviet Union in the era of the Russian Revolution, shared many characteristics with Third World countries, nonetheless, there was no conscious (to say nothing of proud) articulation of this. As a Caribbean nation located on the American continent, Cuba necessarily sees the world quite differently than does Hungary, or Czechoslovakia. Given a historical interaction with the United States which has been marked and marred by an almost classical relationship of economic and political domination, revolutionary Cuba could never look to U.S. capital to "bail it out," as did Poland, or have any expectation of U.S. goodwill in doing so. Nor could it identify itself with those countries in the world—the industrialized, capitalist countries—which it understands as the basic source of human misery, impoverishment, and underdevelopment in the Third World.

Finally, Cuba is a 700-mile-long island of ten million people. If it does not have to deal with multiple nationalities living within the confines of a single nation, at the same time it does not enjoy the abundance of natural resources that might, in the end, enable it to go it alone if necessary.

But these differences alone cannot explain Fidel's overt hostility toward the democratization process under way in the late 1980s in the Soviet Union, and the transformations which were then taking place in Eastern Europe. Rather, Fidel's problems with *perestroika* must be traced to three fundamental factors.

The first of these is the very real commitment of the Cuban Revolution to a high degree of economic egalitarianism, and the understanding that any widespread introduction of market mechanisms and private property must inevitably undermine the possibility of such egalitarianism. Economic and social stratification on the scale envisioned by Soviet planners at the end of the 1980s would not be tolerable to the present Cuban revolutionary leadership. We hear this rejection echo through the decisions, in 1986, to end the five-year experiment in private farmers markets and to suspend the 1982 law which allowed for the purchase and sale of housing. Both were put in place in the early 1980s to introduce flexibility into the effort to solve the pressing problems of food availability, and distribution and shortage of adequate housing which, by the late 1970s, had come to dominate discussions of problems of daily life in Cuba. The bitterness of Fidel's denunciations of farmers who were making 50,000 to 60,000 pesos a year from a single hectare of land planted in garlic (*Granma Weekly Review*, December 14, 1986, 13), and of other 100,000-peso-a-year "hole in the wall operations" (*Granma Weekly Review*, April 19, 1987, 12), have particular resonance here.

Fidel's second major concern about *perestroika* centered around Gorbachev's willingness—for whatever reasons—to accommodate to Western, and particularly U.S., demands. The constant question for Cubans had to be, what if Cuba became the next demand? How would Gorbachev react if the West—and specifically the United States—began (as indeed it did by the summer of 1990) to make Cuba the next prerequisite to continuing arms reduction, or most favored nation status?

Where, the Cubans asked, in Gorbachev's vision of a "common European home," was the Third World? This query echoed through all of Fidel's comments on the new East-West spirit of détente. Thus, in his 1989 speech marking the thirtieth anniversary of the Revolution:

> There are two kinds of survival and two kinds of peace, the survival of the rich and the survival of the poor; the peace of the rich and the peace of the poor. That is why the news that there may be peace, that there may be détente between the United States and the Soviet Union does not neces-

sarily mean that there is going to be peace for us. (*Granma Weekly Review*, October 14, 1990, 5)

Or, again, in his comments at the burial of Cuban soldiers killed in African wars:

In many of those (Eastern European) countries no one speaks about the tragedy of the Third World. . . . What resources can the Third World—in which billions of people live in subhuman conditions—expect from such developments? (*Granma Weekly Review*, December 17, 1989, 3)

Fidel's assertions were a bitter response to what he understood as the likely consequences of these events for the Third World in general, and for Cuba more specifically. Fidel sees himself as living in a world which has changed drastically, in the shadow of a superpower which has not changed at all. From Fidel's point of view, *perestroika* did not trigger movement into the future; rather it meant a return to the past. It strengthened, rather than weakened, the sinews of the Cold War. It was, after all, the bipolar world which created the space for the Cuban Revolution to survive.

The U.S. invasion and occupation of Panama, and its economic and military stranglehold on Nicaragua, which effectively succeeded in forcing the Sandinistas to cede political power, foster in Cuba a sense of isolation and provide convincing proof for them of increasing U.S. militancy in its drive to dominate Latin America. U.S. intransigence about Television Martí and the measures passed by Congress which make the embargo more harsh are understood in this light; they serve, at a minimum, to justify the leadership's renewal of a state of siege mentality which, in its wake, leaves extremely unfertile grounds upon which to discuss or even consider alternate options. In such an atmosphere, socialism becomes synonymous with nationalism, and unity—a closing of ranks—which, as the Cubans have understood it since José Martí's efforts to forge a single Cuban movement to drive the Spaniards from the island, becomes the tried and proven strategy and requirement.

RECTIFICATION: A REEXAMINATION OF THE REVOLUTION?

The Cuban Rectification Campaign was formally introduced in 1986, almost at the same moment that *glasnost* and *perestroika* were becoming household words in the Soviet Union. Initially, some Cubans saw the Campaign as a series of readjustments of the economic mechanisms within the Economic Management and Planning System (the SDPE). Some saw it as a catch-all label for political and economic measures which would have to be taken in the aftermath of dramatic decreases in foreign exchange earnings. Some understood it to be the means by which Fidel could rid himself of those around him—the techno-crats—who were bothering him. Others, by contrast, at least in its early days, saw in it the initiation of a period in which "everything is once again up for grabs": that is, a critical point at which the basic structure and workings of the Revolution could be reexamined.

The question of whether the Rectification Campaign would address, either directly or indirectly, issues of popular empowerment and democracy remained vague and unanswered. Nowhere in its revival of late 1960s values and slogans was there any discussion of the very undemocratic nature of this period. It was evoked always with the qualifier that it was an era which suffered from certain problems of "idealism." What was meant by "idealism" in this context was never precisely defined, but it was nonetheless clear that the label did *not* encompass a critique concerning the absence of institutional channels and formal platforms by which people had any control over, or even say in, the decisions being made, or the policies being adopted by the leadership. Nor, on the other side of this, was there any discussion of the need or the means by which to revive the kind of effervescent, far-reaching informal discussion and debate which did characterize that first decade, and was terminated in the aftermath of the failed 1970 harvest.

Evolution of the Campaign

According to many Cuban social scientists, the original impetus to Rectifi-cation began with the 1983 invasion of Grenada.[7] Here, above all, the Soviet response, or rather lack thereof, made it crystal clear to the Cubans that they were on their own in facing a far more hostile and actively aggressive U.S. administration, and that this reality required of them a structural rethinking of military strategy. The new strategy was designed around a concept of *guerra popular*: the organization of massive numbers of people into territorial militias (involving something more than two million people—that is, roughly one-fifth of the island's population) rather than sole reliance upon a professional army.

The dramatic nature of this change was evident on a number of levels. First, given their experience with "people's war," Vietnamese military advisors were substituted for their Soviet counterparts. Second, the "people's war" strategy fell under the direct jurisdiction of the party, rather than the army. All this, Cuban analysts argue, tended to undermine the position of an elite of military officials and soldiers which had developed during the 1970s. It also provided the basis for Fidel's constant response to the queries concerning the absence of democ-racy in Cuba, most recently in Brazil, to a gathering of church people:

We don't just have the vote, we have the weapons in the hands of the people. Can a people who have weapons in their hands be enslaved? Can a people who have weapons in their hands be oppressed? Can a policy be imposed on a people who have weapons in their hands? And how can such a miracle be possible unless there's a total identification between the people and the nation, between the people and the Revolution? (*Granma Weekly Review*, April 8, 1990, 10)

The second moment identified by Cuban social scientists as a milestone in the evolution of the Rectification Campaign centered on the issue of ideology. Here again there was a structural outcome: in December 1985, the enormously powerful ideological apparatus of the party, which was widely seen within the party itself as a stronghold of conservatism, was literally dismantled. Tony Pérez, the Politburo member who had been secretary of ideology on the Central Committee, was dismissed from his post, and the ideology section, which within its jurisdiction had controlled the departments of science, culture, education, and revolutionary orientation, was broken up. The impetus for this dismantling seemed to come out of critiques of the manner in which those in charge of ideology had enforced the application of a kind of dogmatic Marxism-Leninism in various areas, beginning with the manner in which Cuban history itself was taught and learned in the school and university system. The application of schematic, preset formulas about "workers' states," through which Cuban history was strained and reshaped, meant that the actual dynamics of that history had been lost, and replaced by an artificial, superficial, and distorted assemblage. This same rigidity and dogmatism was also seen as the source of the closing of the faculty of sociology in the university during the 1970s, and of a general deterioration and devaluation of the social sciences, leading to further erosion in the way in which Cuban reality and the history of the Revolution itself were taught and studied. Fidel himself, in his lengthy 1984 interview with Frei Betto,[8] eliminated for Cubans, one key element of what had always been a rigidly held Marxist formula: scientific atheism. (The issue of religion, and the Revolution's changes of policy with relation to it, continues to reverberate, as will be discussed later.)

In 1986 the economic crisis hit full force, exacerbated by the rise in strength of the dollar in international markets and the decline in oil and sugar prices, with the resulting dramatic halving of Cuban foreign exchange earnings. This crisis, and Fidel's disagreements with the solutions proposed by key Central Planning Commission (JUCEPLAN) figures, led directly to the actual declaration of the Rectification process, and to its first stated targets, which involved the structure of the economy, and a process, at least in theory, of virtually dismantling the economic mechanisms which had been put into place during the 1970s to regulate that economy. Here in particular the focus was upon the organization of work, the determination of salaries, and the level of decentralization in the economy.

From this moment (marked by the 1985–1986 Third Party Congress), the leadership, and particularly Fidel, began to lay stress once more on key features of the 1960s (denounced as idealistic in the 1970s): voluntarism, the moral impetus to work, the capacity of the masses to accomplish the seemingly impossible, combined with an ever-increasing emphasis upon efficiency in production to make maximum use of scarce resources. It was at this point that the thinking of Che Guevara—and particularly his economic thought—was revived and used both as a critique of the 1970s, and as a justification for and occasional guide to the policies of the 1980s and beyond. Yet, noticeable once more for its absence, despite the claims to the contrary, was any full and open discussion of democracy and the lack of it, either in the workplace or in the society as a whole.

In their presentation of a logical progression to the Rectification Campaign, Cuban social scientists point next to the aftermath of the Ochoa and de la Guardia trials.[9] Here, they argue, it became clear that the party itself, and political institutions as a whole, needed to be reexamined. The upcoming 1991 Fourth Party Congress became, in this recital, an event of transcendental import, the expression of an ever-widening, ever-deepening reevaluation of the Revolution. In this context, the March 1990 "Call" or announcement of the beginnings of preparation for the congress was given its most radical reading. Statements in the "Call" about the "unreal quest for unanimity, which is often false, mechanical and formal," and the need for "democratic discussion in the Party and the Revolution, as part of the quest for solutions," have particular resonance here (*Granma* (Daily), March 16, 1990, 5). They point further to the fact that for the first time, the framework for the discussions within party cells which led up to the congress was set not in the form of declarations or conclusions to be essentially assimilated, but rather in terms of themes and questions.

Even if this trajectory has validity, it is apparent that at every turning point, it is Fidel who initiated the change. This simply reinforces the clear sense one gets that ordinary Cubans were waiting, as they always have, for Fidel to sketch out the direction, the lines, and the scope of the Campaign. Indeed, the Campaign was marked by the ever more tangible weight of Fidel's presence. As in the 1960s, he was constantly in the process of initiating new schemes to achieve seemingly impossible goals. The revival of the microbrigades is one example of this. The creation of the workbrigades in construction and agriculture—groups of workers who labor twelve to fifteen hours per day in Stahkonovite fashion, live in groups in facilities equipped and provisioned at a level far higher than the general population, and receive pay some 60 percent higher than the national mean salary—is another (Rodríguez, 1990: 69–70). So too his plan, in the face of dramatic declines in food imports, to organize the entire population into *mobilizaciones* (usually for two-week periods) to do voluntary work in the countryside in planting and bringing in harvest (*Granma Weekly Review*, October 14, 1990, 4).

The weight of Fidel's increased public presence was captured by his continual appearances on television: one felt again, as one did in the 1960s, the way in which he sought almost to convert himself into a material force in development. If some of those committed to the Revolution have begun, particularly in the wake of the Ochoa trial (an event which no one on the island appears to have accepted at face value), to question his leadership in private, it is certainly Fidel who remains in command, and it is Fidel who will determine, in the end, the definition and parameters of "democratic discussion in the Party and the Revolution."

Fidel and the Third Generation

In doing so, he faces a set of critical problems. Perhaps the most critical reality is a generational one: it revolves around the issue of young people, and how to engage youth in an ongoing commitment to the Revolution. Here is a population of young people, fully half of them born after the Revolution, with no personal memory of life before 1959 and no knowledge of a time when free education and health care and job security were not readily available to everyone. It is to this generation that an increasingly aging revolutionary leadership must appeal, and the shape this appeal should take is not at all clear. Cuban youth of this third postrevolutionary generation have concerns about personal freedom and individual expression. The fate of any democratic effort in Cuba will depend critically on the degree to which the young understand themselves to be enfranchised in a system which speaks, and permits them to speak, to their own concerns. The Cuban response, thus far, to the "youth problem" has been conservative and limited.

The Cubans have sought to deal with the "youth issue" by encouraging the incorporation of more young people into already existing governmental and party institutions, and by emphasizing the importance of their role in these institutions. Thus, for instance, within Popular Power, the official governing structure, there has been a conscious and concerted effort to increase the number of young (as well as black and/or female) delegates and deputies. In this same vein, the role of the Union of Young Communists (UJC) as the central pillar of the Revolution, and as its voice to young people in general, has been underscored, and the head of the UJC, Roberto Robaina, has been elevated to the status of Politburo member.

Indeed, Robaina's name comes up usually within the first five minutes of any discussion with party cadres of the issue of youth. He is seen as iconoclastic, charismatic, and respected as a leader by young people both within the UJC and outside it. If these adjectives sound strangely familiar, one might recall that such terms were, and still are, used to describe Fidel. One gets the sense that Robaina's rapidly enlarging political stature has everything to do with the belief that in Robaina, the Revolution has found, in the short run, the "Fidelista" link to the third generation, and, in the long run, a natural and direct substitute for Fidel in a post-Fidelista Cuba. And all this, without, therefore, having to reconsider the terms and the very *meaning* of the basic manner and form in which political power has been invested in these thirty-three years since the Revolution's accession to power.

And if the rhetoric of the appeal to sacrifice is the same, so too, and with specific reference to youth, there is clear continuity in the paternalism which has so characterized the Cuban Revolution. The 1989 banning of the two Soviet magazines *Moscow News* and *Sputnik* provides one recent indication of this. The explanation for banning these publications, given first in a *Granma* editorial entitled "An Unavoidable Decision Consistent With Our Principles," reflects, if nothing else, the paternalism inherent in the Revolution's attitude toward Cuban youth. In denouncing those in the Soviet Union who "deny the guiding role of the Party and demand a multiparty system, advocate the free market, exalt foreign investments, have rediscovered popular participation and question internationalism and solidarity aid to other countries," the editorial stressed that

> We now lament the negative consequences noticeable as a result of the dissemination among us of these distortions, confused ideas and fabrications. . . . With pain and bitterness we have had to confront the consequences of this confusion, of all these ideas, in young people who have been poorly informed in terms of ideology and history, a state of affairs for which we are responsible. (*Granma Weekly Review*, August 13, 1989, 9)

This statement *must* raise questions about the leadership's view of Cuban youth, and about its faith in young people's abilities to sort out their thinking with regard to a revolution which now has thirty-year roots. The attempt to exclude ideas seems, at best, a futile way to influence people's thinking, or to correct for weaknesses in the Revolution's own mechanisms of socialization. At worst, it underlines the paternalism that has always characterized, to a greater or lesser degree, the top leadership of the Revolution, and most particularly Fidel.

This same deeply ingrained vein of paternalism feeds the Revolution's seemingly unquenchable need to channel, and thereby contain and control. With youth, as with virtually all other aspects of life on the island, the Revolution seeks somehow to encompass any form or arena of potential rebellion or protest within itself, in effect to coopt it before it escalates. Thus, for instance, cognizant of the fact that popular music has been throughout the world a vehicle and mouthpiece for youthful expression and protest, it has tried to incorporate new musical trends into celebrations of the Revolution itself. On the occasion of the April 1990 celebration of the "Day of the Youth," army helicopters flew over Havana inviting young people to "come dance lambada and reaffirm your commitment to the Revolution." Even the visual accoutrements of youthful rebellion have been adopted and adapted: in recent demonstrations (around events such as the return to Cuban port of the fishing vessel attacked in March 1989 by the United States), headbands worn across the forehead in the style young people have employed in the past few decades all over the world in protest demonstrations (most recently, they form part of our image of Chinese students occupying Tienanmen Square) were handed out to be worn bearing declarations such as *"Yo me quedo"* (I am staying here) or *"Cuba sí"* (Cuba, yes).

Given this drive to grasp within itself and to contain, the terrain of civil society closes down, and the mildest forms of youthful expression have the potential of escalating, or being made to escalate, into signs or proof of antagonism unacceptable to the leadership and branded as such. Further, it plays directly into what the Cuban-American sociologist Nelson Valdés describes as the "dichotomous terms" which have traditionally characterized Cuban political reality. Valdés writes, with great insight, about the constant reference to "betrayals" in the rhetoric of Cubans:

> The right to competing and distinct political perspectives has not gained acceptance in Cuban politics. Like other social relations, politics appears to be based on total, complete and absolute loyalty—to an individual or a set of "morals." Politics, hence, requires unconditional loyalty, trust and faith. These then become an index of political commitment. . . . Cuba before 1959 was a society filled with discord, with no fundamental community of interests, and could not foster a culture of tolerance and diversity. The revolutionary experience, after 1959, heightened the divergence and the polarization. The political categories of the 19th Century continue to this day, in Cuba as well as in the exile community. (1992: 220)

The degree to which the leadership is willing to release its grasp and is able to move beyond this rigid dichotomy in judging individual activity and expression will measure, at least in part, its ability to continue.

Reform and the Bureaucracy

Cuba faces perhaps a more immediate dilemma, one which has plagued its socialist system since its early years. It must deal, in some way, with an ever-mushrooming bureaucracy whose interests and existence militate against change or reform of any sort. The source of this swelling bureaucracy is clear to the Cubans: like much else in the Rectification Campaign, at least at first, Fidel pinpointed the SDPE as the personification of the villain:

> In 1973, there were 90,000 administrative personnel in the country and by 1984 the figure had risen to 250,000. In other words, prior to the imple-

mentation of the SDPE and the reforms, we had only 90,000 administrative personnel and now we have two and one half times that many. (*Granma Weekly Review*, July 6, 1986, 2)

The idea, now broadened to encompass political as well as economic entities, is that the source of the "bastard class" is the institutional structures which were copied from their Soviet counterparts during the 1970s. These models are not understood as Stalinist in nature, but they are seen as involving the most negative aspects of Soviet socialism, and as enshrining a political elite which is not composed of "the best and the brightest" but rather—and particularly at the intermediate level—the most compliant and the most career oriented, and therefore the most conservative. This elite is seen as the most stubborn bulwark against effective change. Rectification, within these parameters, becomes, at least on paper, a virtual coup d'état against the enshrined party and state bureaucracy.

There are several fundamental issues which such an interpretation raises, or at least does not resolve. First, and once again, it points to Fidel as the solution. Fidel as the initiator of the coup against the inherently antidemocratic bureaucracy is once again seeking to resolve societal problems through personalistic measures. Fundamentally antidemocratic, paternalistic means are thus being used to combat antidemocratic formations in a cycle of actions and reactions that repeat, over and over again, the pattern of Cuban revolutionary history since 1959.

But perhaps equally critical here is what the Cubans are ignoring in tracing the source and nature of bureaucracy in Cuba to the error of having mistakenly borrowed bad models from other countries. What they forget is the long history of bureaucratic strangleholds which have, at critical moments, enmeshed the Revolution, even during periods in which "capitalist methods" had been most thoroughly rejected. Moreover, forgotten as well is the Revolution's equally long failed track record in dealing with these strangleholds. The top leadership has seemingly always understood, or at least sought to deal with, bureaucracy as a matter of numbers. This continues to be true in the present crisis; thus Fidel's announcement, in September 1990, that:

We must reduce by 80% the office workers in those agricultural enterprises, 80%! Yes, this must end once and for all. And those who keep asking for reports to be filled out, let them beware because we'll see to it that wherever there are 100, less than 20 will be left; and not only there but in the rest of the country as well, less than 20! No one knows the amount of people who have ended up in the offices. (*Granma Weekly Review*, October 14, 1990, 3)

The figures are dramatic, and will become increasingly dramatic as Cuba fights its way through its "special period in peace," a virtual state of war without physical battles into which the Rectification period elided in September 1990. In part, they are dictated by the nature of the current crisis and, most particularly, the need to cut back on public transport to save energy, as well as the pressing shortage of raw materials to keep industry functioning, and of agricultural labor, given the current drive for food self-sufficiency. But nonetheless, the methodology is achingly familiar. In the absence of a deep-reaching analysis of the roots of the problem, not only now but over the whole span of the Revolution, even the most severe number chopping is inevitably doomed to failure.

THE FOURTH PARTY CONGRESS: DEMOCRATIC OPENINGS?

To what degree did the Fourth Party Congress held in October 1991 address, resolve, or even move toward resolving these political issues? It is hard to be very optimistic. Cuba is in dire economic straits. They were spelled out in grim detail by Fidel in December 1991: of the US$3,763 billion in imports agreed to with the Soviet Union in that year, only US$1,673 billion arrived.[10] Given the breakup of that country, the dissolution of the Council for Mutual Economic Assistance (COMECON) (which accounted for 85% of Cuba's trade turnover in 1988), and the termination of Soviet aid, the immediate economic future looks even bleaker (Zimbalist, 1993: 142).

It is largely in this context that Cuba made operative its "special period in peacetime" in September 1990. The "special period" encompasses a range of policies seeking, first, to foster self-sufficiency in food consumption through an intensive development of land, involving modernized irrigation and drainage, and the resettlement of surplus urban residents; second, the rationalization of scarce resources through the reintroduction of widescale rationing and a severe cutback in the consumption of oil and energy resources; third, the movement toward what is, in effect, a mixed economy, through an all-out effort to locate sources of hard currency by encouraging foreign investment in the form of joint ventures, profit and production sharing, and even entities which are 100 percent foreign owned;[11] and fourth, reforms in management and work process which will ease Cuba's reentry into the world economy.[12]

But it is the politics of the "special period" that concerns us in this chapter, and here, I would argue, there would have been a severe crisis even if the dramatic events which destroyed the Soviet Union and Eastern Europe from 1989 to 1991 had never occurred. This crisis had everything to do with the absence of democracy in the structures of decision making, and the ramifications of a system which, in practice, allowed those in charge the freedom to act (or not act) without having to answer to anyone. That is, the system was not working in its own terms.

Preparatory meetings to the Party Congress, held across the island during the summer of 1990, give some indication of the extent of the problems. At the base level, party meetings were opened in the hope of involving not simply party members, but all the workers in a given enterprise. What emerged from these meetings was a litany of complaints about ridiculous inefficiencies, horrifying and stultifying bureaucratic strangleholds and procedures, and a harsh critique of the institutions which were to be the means by which people participated in the decisions which affected their lives. The accounts of these meetings seemed to echo, in some respects, the kind of outpouring that followed upon the failure of the harvest in 1970. And in the echoes are the edges of their potential limits. The solution which by its very repetition found its way to the center of every discussion, be it about a workplace or a political institution, seemed to be decentralization.

The issue of decentralization raises practical, historical, and ideological questions. In a practical sense, the stress on decentralization in the political sphere comes into conflict with the need, during the "special period," for centralized direction of economic policies. (This is probably the reason that, by the time of the Party Congress, the issue of decentralization had faded from the rhetoric of discussion.) Moreover, decentralization is not a new concept in Cuba: indeed, and perhaps ironically given the current critique of the 1970s, it was a word very much at the heart of the 1970 discussion. The institutionalization policies enacted in the wake of those discussions demonstrate with great clarity that decentralization, in and of itself, is not a solution.[13] Decentralization is not a synonym for democratization, nor, for that matter, is increasing participation.

In the political arena, the congress initiated, within clearly defined boundaries, certain potentially dramatic changes. In the Communist Party, there has been an attempt to streamline the top layers by eliminating the Secretariat as well as the "alternate member" status in the Politburo and Central Committee. Further, direct secret ballot elections will now be the rule for selection to membership and appointments to committees at all levels. But perhaps most important, the congress marked the possibility of deep-reaching shifts in the nature of the party, and specifically the nature of its membership. One indication of this was the 53 percent turnover in Central Committee membership, evidence of the leadership's efforts to incorporate new faces and, particularly, younger people. The party seems to be moving in the direction of becoming a far more mass organization, more rooted within Cuban traditions—a *partido criollo*, heir to the organizational legacy established by Martí—rather than to international models. Already, its membership numbers 600,000 (a proportion of the population enormously in excess of that in the Communist Party in the former Soviet Union), 60 percent under the age of forty-six. The congress's official elimination of atheism as a requirement for membership constitutes one further step in the direction of, at a minimum, a more inclusive membership.[14] But Cuba will remain a one-party state: Fidel makes this crystal clear in his recent denunciations of multiparty systems as "imperialism's great instrument to keep societies fragmented."[15] Nor is it clear, in the end, that the decision-making structure will, in practice, be much altered or that the Cuban leadership's call for democracy within the party will bear much fruit: history has demonstrated, in both capitalist and socialist societies, the difficulties in maintaining, as one Cuban analyst put it, a party structure that is *"unido pero no uniforme"* (united but not uniform). And, of course, the international pressures upon Cuba to close down upon the second half of this formula (as well as the traditions of the Revolution itself, and of the heritage upon which it draws) are and will be immense.

Indeed, no form of nascent opposition outside the party will be tolerated. The leadership's harsh (and, many observers might argue, given their size and following, extremely foolish) treatment of the tiny human rights groups which have begun to form in the country underscores its confiscation of the political arena.

The politics of the "special period" must inevitably further pressure for intensified measures against even mild expressions of dissent. While war footing is never a good setting anywhere for the civil rights of individuals, in this context it provides a renewed justification for an already existing tendency in Cuba. The leadership's recent de facto banning of the Cuban Film Institute (ICAIC) film *"Alicia en el Pueblo de las Maravillas"* ("Alice in Wonderland"), as well as its attempts to organize what it calls "rapid response detachments" to meet vaguely defined internal disturbances, gives an ominous indication of what the immediate future holds.

The second set of major changes within the political sphere involves a substantial revamping of the governmental system, Popular Power, which at present, as one Cuban friend put it, is "neither popular nor powerful." Popular Power was established on the local or municipal, provincial, and national levels in 1976; [16] since that time, expectations that it would provide a genuine forum for full popular discussion of the nation's present and future direction have faded, in the light of its limited jurisdiction, and its inability (particularly in Havana, where 30% of the population lives) to resolve problems even within this jurisdiction. Indeed, disenchantment with the system was so widespread that Popular Power was one of the two most criticized institutions during the nationwide discussions prior to the Party Congress. In the summer of 1990, a series of articles in the weekly magazine *Bohemia* gave some sense of the depth of discontent with Popular Power: 40 percent of those surveyed indicated that they felt they played no role in the governing of their country, and registered their lack of confidence in their local delegate.[17]

The reforms proposed by the Party Congress and adopted, in part, by the National Assembly at its July 1992 meeting would alter some of the structures of Popular Power, and in this sense, they hold a degree of promise. They fail, however, to alter fundamental aspects of the system, and therefore must be regarded as highly limited. First, province-level delegates and national deputies will now be elected by direct popular vote. Formerly, these representatives were chosen by municipal-level delegates (who were directly elected). However, the form in which this decision was embodied in the November 1992 Electoral Law limits both its potential impact and, indeed, popular perception of it as a reform altogether. Candidates for provincial and national assemblies will not be nominated, as are municipal candidates, from the base. Rather, they will be proposed by candidacy commissions, and selected by the various municipal assemblies, which will put forth as candidates exactly the number needed to fill available slots. The electors' right to directly choose will be limited to their ability to vote for none, some, or all of these candidates (each of whom must receive at least 50 percent of the vote in order to be elected).[18] In essence then (and despite Fidel's heated assertions to the contrary),[19] the recommendation of the 1991 Party Congress for direct elections from the base of provincial and national Popular Power delegate/deputies has been encapsulated in a system which channels choice, applying to it qualitative controls which effectively negate the "directness" of the electoral process, and essentially recreate, albeit in an altered form, the old indirect system of elections in all its essentials.

Second, the term of provincial assembly delegates will be extended to five years. Third, consideration was given to clarifying and enhancing the power of municipal-level delegates. Proposals made at the Party Congress to extend delegates' terms in office from two and a half to five years (in order to allow them to build up some degree of know-how and expertise) and to professionalize them (in order to allow them to focus their attention full-time upon the districts they represent) were, in the end, rejected by the National Assembly. But executive committees, which, because they operated continuously, had in many municipalities effectively replaced the assemblies as the governing bodies, were eliminated in their current form. They will be replaced by a committee no longer made up of elected delegates, but rather appointed by each assembly and therefore clearly subordinate to that assembly. The reform is intended to underline the purely administrative nature of the executive committee and the sovereignty of the assembly itself as the single governing body. To reinforce the subordinate and purely administrative nature of the new executive committee, the president of each assembly will serve, as well as the committee's president.

Fourth, the late 1980s popular council experiment (a kind of intermediary between the neighborhoods and the municipal assemblies, whose purpose is to respond in a more rapid and flexible manner to local problems, using largely local resources to do so) was hailed as a great success and has been extended across the island. Some 900 are now in operation.

And fifth, the party as party will no longer participate in nominating candidates for the provincial and national assemblies.[20] Here, what is being acknowledged, in a limited fashion, are the problems arising from the manner in which the party is interwoven into the structure of Popular Power. But this hardly begins to address the chief ambiguity and perhaps the major factor undermining the authority of Popular Power as an independent institution of popular government: that is, the fusion of party and state. The extreme overlap of party and state is succinctly captured by the fact that virtually every National Assembly deputy is a party member: the leadership does not recognize this overlap as in any way problematic. This single fact underscores one of the major unresolved dilemmas which will, then, continue to haunt the Revolution.

CONCLUSION

The problems illuminated here remain dauntingly clear. They involve, above all, the fragility of the terms of discussion and debate, and of the spaces for organized expression of ideas.

My point is not that there are no bases or roots upon which to draw in molding a renewed popular dialogue, neither elicited from the center, nor charted or confined by it. To the contrary, and despite the fracturing of the intelligentsia in the early 1970s, and fifteen years of virtual silence around key issues of socialism while official Marxism-Leninism ossified further, these roots do exist. They were planted firmly in the early revolutionary period and were watered and nourished (although in the end extinguished) by the promise or potential of other key moments of crisis and transition. Paradoxically, and as a direct result of the dire economic crisis gripping Cuba, there has been an opening to the outside world not simply in economic terms, but in intellectual and political terms.

But movement toward a more expansive plane of discourse promised, most recently, in the 1990 "Call" to the Fourth Party Congress is, of course, tentative: it has been expanding and contracting in a fashion uneven enough to make the final outcome—even given the renewed declarations of imminent demise echoing from Washington and Miami—by no means certain. This unevenness is shadowed by multiple threats. On one side, there is the seemingly ever-present thread of paternalism in the Revolution: its instinct to channel and control, which has at other moments reined in, narrowed, and effectively contained the terrain of what is acceptable. On the other side, and with a terrible and tragic irony, there is the continuing U.S. obsession with the Cuban Revolution, and its intensified attempts to strangle it by isolating it and forcing others to act in like manner—a policy, we might note, which has been, for thirty-three years, nothing if not counterproductive.

NOTES

1. The phrase "actually existing socialism" is taken from Rudolf Bahro's book, *The Alternative in Eastern Europe* (London: New Left Books, 1978).

2. See *New York Times* editorial, December 11, 1989, A22.

3. George Fauriol, on "NBC Nightly News" (July 27, 1989).

4. Tad Szulc, on "NBC Nightly News" (July 27, 1989).

5. "All Things Considered," National Public Radio (August 1, 1989).

6. *Granma Weekly Review*, November 12, 1989, 4. Fidel's words, in context, were as follows: "Now there are two types of socialists, two types of communists: good and bad ones, as defined by imperialism. . . . Those who do not submit to imperialism . . . they call inflexible. Long live inflexibility!"

7. Among the published articles, see, in particular, Gerardo Timossi, "Cuba: Una Agenda Diferente Para Los Cambios," and Fernando Martínez, "El Socialismo Cubano: Perspectivas y Desafíos." Both are in *Cuadernos de Nuestra América* vol. 7, no. 15 (July–December 1990).

8. Published in English under the title *Fidel and Religion* (New York: Simon & Schuster, 1987).

9. For the Cuban account of these trials, see *Vindicación de Cuba* (Havana: Editora Política, 1989). For a journalistic examination which raises some of the critical and unanswered questions, see Julius Preston's "The Trial That Shook Cuba," in the *New York Review of Books* vol. 36, no. 19 (December 7, 1989): 24–31. See also Janet Habel, *Cuba: The Revolution in Peril* (London: Verso Books, 1991): chap. 7, 177–199, and Andres Oppenheimer, *Castro's Final Hour* (New York: Simon & Schuster, 1992): part I, 17–163.

10. *Granma International*, January 12, 1992, 3. For a detailed account of what arrived, and didn't arrive, from the Soviet Union in 1991, see Fidel Castro, "Los Problemas de Nuestra Pais Solo Los Puede Resolver la Revolucion" (Speech to the Fourth Party Congress) in *Bohemia* vol. 83, no. 43 (October 25, 1991): 26–30.

11. *Economist Intelligence Unit, Country Report: Cuba* no. 3 (1991): 20.

12. Andrew Zimbalist, "Teetering on the Brink: Cuba's Current Economic and Political Crisis," *Journal of Latin American Studies* vol. 24, part 2 (May 1992): 411.

13. For a discussion of the 1970s institutionalization process, see "Cuba: the Institutionalization of the Revolution," in *Cuban Studies/Estudios Cubanos*, particularly articles by Valdés and Dominguez in vol. 6, no. 1 (January 1976): 1–66, and by Pérez-Stable in vol. 6, no. 2 (July): 31–72; Frank Fitzgerald, "A Critique of the 'Sovietization of Cuba' Thesis," *Science and Society* no. 42 (Spring 1978): 1–32; Rhoda Rabkin, "Cuban Political Structure: Vanguard Party and the Masses," in *Cuba: Twenty-five Years of Revolution*, ed. Sandor Halebsky and John M. Kirk (New York: Praeger, 1985): 251–269; and Halebsky and Kirk, *Transformation and Struggle: Cuba Faces the 1990s* (New York: Praeger, 1990), particularly articles by Pérez-Stable and Bengelsdorf.

14. See "Resoluciones del IV Congreso del Partido Communista de Cuba," *Granma* (daily), October 23, 1991, 3, as well as accounts of discussions of the party at the congress, in *Granma* (daily), October 15–19, 1991.

15. "Address to the National Assembly," *Granma International*, December 22, 1991, 1.

16. For accounts of the Popular Power system during its fifteen years of operation, see Archibald Ritter, "The Organs of People's Power and the Communist Party: The Nature of Cuban Democracy," pp. 270–290, in *Cuba: Twenty-five Years of Revolution*, ed. Halebsky and Kirk; B. Jorgensen, "The Interrelationship Between Base and Superstructure in Cuba," *IberoAmericana: Nordic Journal of Latin American Studies* vol. 13, no. 1 (1983): 27–42.

17. *Bohemia*, July 6 and 20, 1990.

18. See *Granma International*, November 8, 1992, 2.

19. See Fidel's remarks to the National Assembly, ibid., 4.

20. See "Resolución Sobre el Perfeccionamiento de la Organizacion y Funcionamiento de los Órganos del Poder Popular," in *Granma* (daily), October 23, 1992, 5.

12

Haiti: Prospects for Democracy

Kenneth I. Boodhoo

Haiti, the richest colony in the New World in the seventeenth century; the second country in the Western Hemisphere to gain its independence; the first black republic in the world, remains the hemisphere's basket case, both in terms of its economic situation and the persistence of dictatorial rulership. And, while much of the world continues its march toward democratized political systems, Haiti, after flirting with such ideas for a brief while in 1990, returned to its roots of military dictatorship supported by elite interests.

The violent overthrow of Jean-Bertrand Aristide's government was the sixth change of government in Haiti in as many years. Yet, this change was fundamentally different from the others in that President Aristide was elected by an overwhelming majority of Haiti's electorate in what was generally accepted as a free and fair election—probably the first such election in the country's almost two-hundred-year history. To that extent, the Aristide government, in the eyes of the majority of the Haitian population, and in terms of international recognition of the regime, was the first legitimate government of the country since Jean-Claude Duvalier was driven from power in early 1986.

This chapter provides a brief overview of the structure and function of the Haitian state since the nineteenth century, and makes a preliminary assessment of the prospects for democracy in contemporary Haiti.

CLASS, COLOR, AND AUTHORITARIAN RULE IN THE NINETEENTH CENTURY

The debate over the structure and function of the state in Haiti did not begin with the violent process leading to the election of Jean-Bertrand Aristide in 1990. Nor did it begin with the fall of Jean-Claude Duvalier in early 1986. Indeed, that debate began in 1806, just two years after independence was proclaimed. At that time, Henri Christophe, a black man from the north, and Alexandré Petion, a mulatto from the south, led each side in a civil war, resulting in the de facto division of the country. The debate continued even more intensely from 1986 until 1990, and after the brief hiatus of the Aristide government, continues today. Why is it that the citizens of Haiti have been unable to achieve a consensus on the nature of its political system, and why, especially, has it been so difficult for democracy to take root in Haiti?

The answer to both questions can be found firstly in how issues of color and class have determined social relations, and consequently influenced the political dynamics of Haitian society for its almost two-hundred-year history. It can be found secondly in how those in control of the state have perceived its purpose and function in terms of the acquisition of wealth and domination over the society.

To be sure, *La question de Couleur* emerged just as the Haitian state was born from the bloody independence struggle. The bastion of black power was Haiti's north under the leadership of black Jean Jacques Dessalines. When the south, led by mulatto Petion, rebelled against perceived northern domination, the two sides clashed, resulting in Dessalines's death. With Christophe assuming control over the north, battles with the south continued, leading to the division of the country between 1806 and 1820.

Yet the division of the country was not based only on the dispute over color. The structure and function of the state were contested with equal intensity. In general, the north supported a powerful central government which would maintain the plantation agricultural system, making use of the now freed slaves. The south, on the other hand, favored a more liberal political and economic system including the dismantling of the large plantations and the eventual establishment of peasant agriculture. The state, as a consequence, would have a more limited role than as anticipated in the north. Under mulatto general Jean-Pierre Boyer not only was Haiti reunified but domination over Hispaniola continued until 1844.

With the demise of the plantation system by the second half of the nineteenth century, the bourgeoisie (predominantly mulatto) needed to develop new methods for the acquisition of wealth. Unable, or unwilling, to become engaged in industrial activities, and with agriculture steadily moving into the hands of the peasant farmer, the bourgeoisie turned to marketing and trading. Eventually, they came to control the export of agricultural raw material, especially coffee and sugar, and the import of consumer goods and other supplies.

In order to be able to assert complete hegemony over Haiti's economic system, the bourgeoisie understood the necessity of controlling the political system. Of equal importance was the need to develop linkages with the hinterland to assure control over the supply of agricultural raw material. Therefore, control over the state and the development of class allegiance with their counterparts in the hinterland greatly influenced the structure of the political system and class alignment in the society for the next century. Most importantly, the evolving political and economic relationships of the 1800s gave rise to the structures of poverty endured by the majority of Haitian people until today.

The structure of poverty had its basis in the class divisions which became more clearly demarcated during the second half of the nineteenth century. These divisions, of course, determined who controlled surplus and therefore profit. The first to develop was the dichotomy between the growing urban sector and its rural counterparts. Ultimately, the rural dwellers would refer to the capital as the "Republic of Port-au-Prince." Within each area was the rise of sharp class divisions.

The dominant group in the urban sector was the mulatto bourgeoisie. Yet as the century progressed some blacks became participants in this group. The group included the propertied class, senior state officials, the commercial sector, and the leaders of the Roman Catholic church. Represented in smaller numbers were professionals, senior military officers, and lower-ranking members of the clergy.

The divisions were equally sharp in the countryside and especially in the port cities of Aux Cayes, Jeremie, Jacmel, and Gonaives. Here the bourgeoisie included the small merchants and the large landowners. The commercial class in the city met the rural producers only through the middle man: the rural merchant or the buyer who negotiated the prices for the raw material and transported it to Port-au-Prince or other ports. The commercial elite hardly came face-to-face with the peasant producers. When the United States entered as the occupying force in 1915, its policies exacerbated class divisions and perpetuated the authoritarian state.

While control over the state permitted the bourgeoisie the authority to organize and regulate all commercial activities for their benefit, it further permitted office holders to develop fiscal and taxing policies to finance their activities. Further, those sectors that proved lucrative could be privatized for personal benefit. Thus Michel-Rolph Trouillot has noted "a cornerstone of that system was a fiscal policy that persistently siphoned off the meager resources of the peasantry, so that the peasantry came to denounce the state while having no control over it" (1990: 59).

From the early nineteenth century, customs revenues became the major source of the state's finances, with import and export duties (the latter especially upon coffee) being the major contributor. In 1810, for instance, the customs department contributed 73 percent of all government revenues. By 1842 this had increased to about 90 percent. Import and export duties peaked at 98.2 percent of state income by 1881, falling slightly to 95 percent by 1909 (ibid.: 61). While the peasant coffee producer was made to carry the burden of the export tax, the entire society paid the cost of import duties, since they were passed on to the consumer as higher prices. Thus no one, especially among the masses of the poor, could escape this system of extortion established by the state.

With the need to control the apparatus of government in order to regulate commerce, impose a system of revenue collection, and administer privatized sectors for personal profit, it stands to reason that those in power would be most unwilling to abdicate rulership in the face of vague notions of a democratized system. Indeed, the system in place encouraged the perpetuation of authoritarian rule, which meant, firstly, that alignment with the military (the source of legitimized force) was necessary to maintain control, and, secondly, that political change would be instituted primarily by violent means.

While alignment with the military served obviously to consolidate authoritarian rule on many occasions, it served a more insidious function—the appearance of rulership by blacks (since many of the military leaders were black) while true power resided with the mulattoes who "advised" such leadership. In the nineteenth century this practice became known as *politique de doublure* (rulership from below). Thus, in the mid-1800s, four black generals successively assumed the presidency, each for relatively brief periods. The common element among these four presidents was their manipulation by the mulatto group, who, while appearing to meet the demands of the majority black population, nevertheless maintained ultimate control over the state.

IMPLICATIONS OF U.S. OCCUPATION

Asserting that Haitians "were immature and not yet ready for democracy," the United States imposed a high commissioner, responsible to the U.S. president (Dupuy, 1989: 139). Alex Dupuy (ibid.: 132) has noted that "no laws, regulations or budget proposals could be enacted by the Haitian government . . . without prior approval by the High Commissioner." A new constitution, drafted by the then secretary of the navy, Franklin D. Roosevelt, designed obviously to promote U.S. interests, was imposed upon the country. The authoritarian structure was further promoted by the refusal of the United States to permit elections for a Haitian president—even though that office during the occupation was primarily a titular one.

Contradicting a century-old policy of Haiti, the new constitution permitted foreign ownership of land and property, setting the stage for the attempted reintroduction of the plantation system. This was done to encourage U.S.

investment, partly out of the U.S. conviction that the peasant farming system could not develop into a competitive export economy. Additionally, the taxation system was overhauled and new taxes introduced. Those taxes placed upon the production and consumption of alcohol and tobacco had a particularly adverse impact upon peasant producers and small distillers and merchants, but reflected the class interests of the occupying forces.

In order that a stable climate for foreign investment be maintained, the United States abolished the country's original army, replacing it with a U.S.-trained modern military and police force. The dominant role given to this force, especially with regard to its policing functions, would, over the next fifty years, create a group extremely adept at controlling the broad civilian population, and especially when aligned with the bourgeoisie, with the ability to dominate the society for its own interests.

With the United States aligning itself with the mulatto bourgeoisie during the occupation, favoring the latter with the senior civilian and military positions, it is not surprising that this relationship served to perpetuate mulatto domination after the occupation ended in 1930. Consequently, for the next fifteen years, Haiti was ruled successively by two mulatto presidents: Sténio Vincent (1930–1941) and Elie Lescot (1941–1946). The only difference between the two regimes, it has been stated, was the extremes to which the latter went in favor of the mulattoes (see Dupuy, 1989: 146). Lescot practiced color discrimination in all aspects of social life. Color became the primary criterion for appointment. Mulatto social clubs practiced discrimination based upon color. Further, cultural norms of the poor black masses were denigrated, and practitioners of the popular belief system, voodoo, were persecuted. As a consequence, it is not surprising that the black population of Haiti has looked upon the post-1946 period as one of a new independence, for that date marks the transition of rulership in Haiti from the mulattoes to the blacks. However, it must be emphasized that until the election of Aristide in 1990, black rulership reflected the interests of the bourgeoisie rather than of the black lower class.

THE RISE OF BLACK NATIONALISM

Contributing to the rise of black consciousness and the demand by blacks for participation in the political process was the rise of a small, yet politically significant, black middle class during the 1940s. Limited educational opportunity had provided an avenue for social mobility especially among some urban blacks. In greater numbers, therefore, were bureaucratic, administrative, and managerial positions occupied by blacks, solidifying their middle-class status. The ensuing competition for job opportunities with the mulattoes spilled over into the political arena.

Contributing to the political socialization of the black middle class was the development, in the postoccupation period, of various organizations, including political parties and trade unions, articulating the interest of the blacks. Probably of most lasting significance was the intellectually oriented *Indigeniste* movement led by Jean Price-Mars and Antenor Firmin. Linked to the international movement which promoted "Negritude," the Indigeniste movement argued for the legitimacy of the black perspective in national affairs. It was supported by a literary group which viewed Haitian life as a unique blend of African and French strands, making for a Creole culture which should be permitted the opportunity to develop. Race for them meant more than a biological category; it was also social and cultural (Nicholls, 1977: 163).

A more radical wing of the Indigeniste movement developed during this time. The *Griot* group, as it was termed, actually had its inception in another called *les Trois D* (Luis Diquoi, Lopimer Denis, and François Duvalier). While incorporating the ideas of Price-Mars, the Griot group, emphasizing the African roots of Haiti, demanded, for instance, that voodooism should be central to Haitian life. To that extent, they harshly criticized the Roman Catholic Church for introducing an alien religion into their culture. The answer to Haiti's problems, they argued, required the transfer of political power to the "authentic" representatives of the black majority and a reorganization of the society to reflect African institutions and values (Dupuy, 1989: 148). It does appear, therefore, that the color/class conflict between the mulattoes and the blacks was, at this time, redefined as an issue of race.

It was in this environment of rapidly rising black consciousness that the 1946 elections were held. Among the eight major presidential candidates, all but one were black. Dumarsais Estime, a member of the black bourgeoisie and a lawyer from the north, emerged as the winner. This was seen as a victory for black nationalism and for the increasing role of the black middle class. In order to broaden the base of his regime, Estime included in his first cabinet Daniel Fignole from the Peasant Labor Movement (Mouvement Ouvrier Paysan [MOP]) group and François Duvalier of the Griot. A mulatto, André Rigaud of the Popular Socialist Party (Parti Socialiste Populaire [PSP]), was placed in the commerce ministry. Yet this exercise in compromise quickly failed. Rigaud resigned from the cabinet within a few months, and his mulatto PSP became the formal opposition to the Estime government.

Until Estime was overthrown by a military coup in 1950, his government reflected the interests of the black bourgeoisie and the black middle class. Much more effort was directed toward competition with the mulatto elite concerning the benefits of holding office than toward serving the needs of the predominantly poor black population. Indeed, the class interests of the Estime regime transcended interests based upon race and color.

Colonel Paul Magloire, who had led the coup against Estime, became the leading candidate for the presidency. While appearing as a popular choice of the majority black population, he was, in fact, the compromise candidate acceptable to the mulattoes, the Roman Catholic Church, big business, and the army. With this broad elite support, and with his acceptance by the masses on the basis of color, Magloire won the presidency, instituting a period of authoritarian rule.

Brought into office with broad-based support, and in spite of favorable international economic conditions, Magloire steadily found himself alienated from his base. His autocratic rulership style, corruption, and use of the office to enhance personal well-being all contributed eventually to his downfall. By 1956, unable to secure an extension of his presidential term of office, Magloire, like so many other Haitian leaders before him, went in exile, setting the stage for the commencement of the Duvalier era.

THE DUVALIERS' DICTATORIAL DYNASTY

The dictatorial dynasty of the Duvaliers had begun in 1957 when François Duvalier, the father of Jean-Claude, won a corrupt election accompanied by widespread Duvalierist violence. Having positioned himself as a *noiriste* in order to obtain power, once in office Duvalier was willing to employ whatever means were necessary in order to consolidate his domination over all aspects of civilian and military life. Within two years, the legislature had become a mere puppet of the president. Force was used as a most efficient method of control. By 1964, having neutralized the two major parties which challenged his domination—the army and the church—Duvalier eschewed all pretensions of a movement to democracy by declaring himself president-for-life and appointing his son Jean-Claude to be his successor upon his death. Jean-Claude assumed the presidency, at age eighteen, upon his father's death in 1971, maintaining that office until he was flown into exile after popular uprisings in early 1986.

The Duvaliers hardly pretended to support a democratic political system. And even though from time to time fraudulent elections were held, and even if some of the formal institutions of a democratic system, including parliamentary assemblies, were maintained, the Duvaliers continued in the tradition of authoritarian rule—even refining it in terms of the role of coercion and the centralization of decision making.

François Duvalier skillfully manipulated the majority black population through nepotism, the use of religious symbols, and when those failed, by the use of force. Yet he was equally successful in manipulating the mulattoes, in the name of the black nationalist movement. In the final analysis, while he ruled in the name of the black majority, to the degree that he aligned himself with any group, it was with the black bourgeoisie.

Jean-Claude, who "inherited" the presidency, according to the cynical 1964 constitution, was much less successful than was his father in balancing the political pressures arising from the smoldering class and color problems. Assuming the office at age eighteen, he was obviously unable to command the respect of his subordinates as did his father. To that extent, it does appear that especially during the early days of his rule, his mother served as the true power behind the throne. But even as he matured he did not develop the necessary political skills. Moreover, Haiti's social system has experienced slow but steady transformation since the 1950s.

Primarily as a consequence of the efforts of private voluntary organizations, elementary and eventually some secondary education opportunities became available to the poor, especially since the 1950s. By the 1960s the impact of the Medellin conference of Catholic church leaders, with its new theology of liberation directed to the poor, began to be experienced in the Catholic school system in Haiti. As importantly, since the 1950s, the monolithic presence of Roman Catholicism in Haiti has been steadily undermined, first by the encroachment of primarily U.S.-based Protestant groups, and eventually by Duvalier himself, who elevated the practice of voodoo to new heights, while openly warring with the Catholic clergy. Thus, not only was the status of the traditional church in the society seriously threatened, but just as significantly, new ideas, especially the notion of conscientization, introduced by younger members of the priesthood, ultimately began to impact upon the lives of the rural poor. The activities among some groups of rural peasants are instructive of the challenge to the traditional order.

In Haiti, agricultural output, both for domestic consumption and for export, is produced largely by the rural peasantry. Historically, however, control over the marketing structures, especially for the export of this produce, has been dominated by members of the urban elite and their agents in the rural towns. Consequently, the surplus from this production has accumulated to the latter. It is a system for the extraction of wealth from the peasantry that steadily developed over a century. As Trouillot has emphasized, "The nation met its masters only through intermediaries, and only at points of exchange" (1990: 81).

Until the 1960s, the limited worldview of the rural peasant permitted him to accept an economic arrangement that fundamentally was unjust, and maintained him in a system of poverty. However, since that time the twin factors of education and conscientization encouraged the rural peasantry first to understand and then to organize in resistance to external interests. The programs of one organization, the Diocese-Supported Institute for Adult Education (Institute Diocesain d'Education des Adultes [IDEA]), designed to educate and mobilize the rural peasantry, have been well catalogued by Robert Maguire (1984).

The work of IDEA is centered in the town of Le Borgne in Haiti's northwest peninsula. IDEA was established in 1973 as an institute for peasant leadership training, with the specific focus of encouraging the peasantry to promote development at their level. With this training these leaders or *animateurs* return to their communities to encourage the development of grassroots ideas among their fellow villagers. In the first twelve years of its existence IDEA trained approximately 450 to 500 leaders, who themselves have established over 1,000 small village groups seeking to promote development.

The rise of organized activity among the rural peasantry must present a challenge to those seeking to perpetuate the old order. For it is inevitable that as the former comes to understand some of the root causes of his poverty, he will attempt to promote efforts to combat it. One such effort is gaining control over the marketing of the agricultural output. This must bring the peasant into confrontation with traditional marketing structures seeking to protect their own interests. This confrontation goes to the core of Haiti's development and political problems, for control over surplus denies the opportunity for rural development while concentrating power at the center. A similar challenge is being raised by high school students against the traditional political structures that dominate the society.

Many credit the rebellion by high school students as the catalyst that eventually led to the downfall of the Duvalier government in 1986. Most of the student leaders of this movement attended Catholic high schools in the north at Gonaives and at Jérémie in the south, and were taught by younger priests imbued with the idea of liberating the poor. This movement gained national impetus when in November 1985 three students from the Immaculate Conception high school in Gonaives were killed by the military. Students across the country were galvanized into action, and with organizational skills provided from Gonaives and Jérémy, coordinated national protest was begun. This encouraged participation from the broader masses of the population, and even though confrontation with the military persisted, the widespread nature of the civil unrest ultimately contributed to the resignation of Jean-Claude Duvalier. This was a most unique event in Haitian history, because for most of the country's history the state has been employed to suppress the society, yet another factor impeding the development of democracy in Haiti.

But what perhaps eventually hastened the downfall of Jean-Claude Duvalier was the reemergence of the mulattoes to their original position of being the power behind the presidency. This was initiated when Jean-Claude married mulatto Michele Bennett, resulting in the employment of the state by the nouveau riche Bennett family for the accumulation of private wealth. Michele's own spending habits and lavish lifestyle, surrounded by a sea of despair and depravity, quickly became legend in an increasingly hostile society. By early 1986, the Duvalier family fled Haiti as the civil uprisings reached an unprecedented scale.

FROM DUVALIER TO ARISTIDE

Between March 1986 and Aristide's election in December 1990, five different governments sought to administer the affairs of the country, each protesting that its major desire was to move the country toward democracy. Indeed, under internal and external pressure, a new constitution was completed in 1987 and overwhelmingly approved in a national referendum, which paved the way for the much-anticipated general elections of November 29, 1987. Yet that day will forever be remembered as one of the bloodiest in a country with a bloody history. For as Haitians excitedly queued to cast their ballots for the first time, between thirty to fifty were brutally murdered by machine gun fire, orchestrated by some elements within the army with the support of the Duvalierists. The military promptly canceled the election and assumed control over the state. In early 1988, in an apparent attempt to earn international recognition, they staged an "election" which was boycotted by over 90 percent of the populace and most of the political leaders. Leslie Manigat was declared president, but as he attempted to curb the power of the military, he was promptly driven from office in less than one hundred days. The coup's leader, General Henri Namphy, was himself overthrown by Lt. General Prosper Avril a few months later.

When Avril assumed office in September 1988 he claimed that he wanted to be viewed by history as the man who had worked for the establishment of an irreversible democracy in Haiti (*Miami Herald*, September 30, 1988, 14A). He wanted to be remembered as the one who saved Haiti from anarchy and dictatorship. Yet together with these public protestations, Avril consolidated his power and extended his grip over the country. He was also not beyond employing the state to enrich his family. While his term in office was slightly longer than those of the leaders coming immediately before him, he too was driven from office in March 1990, having faced widespread popular uprisings and intense pressure from the United States.

These nationwide uprisings, together with coordinated activity among popular political leaders, marked a significant departure from much of the country's political history. More of the energy of Haitian opposition politics has been expended in the infighting among these leaders than in cooperative activity against the state. For much of Haiti's history, at least until 1985, overwhelming coercion by the state, through its various and effective instruments of suppression, had stifled popular discontent from the ordinary people.

Under the new constitution, the resignation of Avril should have elevated Chief Justice Gabriel Austin to head of state. Yet opposition to the status quo from the general population and political leaders coalesced into the Group of 12 and objected to Austin's close alignment with the military and traditional leadership. Displaying remarkable initiative and imagination, the Group of 12 selected the only female member of the court, Justice Ertha Pascal-Trouillot, complying at least with the spirit, if not the letter, of the constitution. On this rare occasion, the military, presumably under pressure from the United States, acceded to the demands of the civilian population. Haiti appeared to be at the turning point toward democracy. For the first time it seemed that the demands of the broader population had transcended those of the coalition of ruling elites and the military.

That Haiti was at a turning point was emphasized by President Pascal-Trouil-lot, who, in her acceptance speech, declared her most fundamental task was to guide the country toward free elections in the shortest possible time (*Miami Herald*, March 14, 1990, 14A). Yet within days after an election panel was nominated in May 1990, violence from those traditional sources opposed to free elections, especially the Duvalierists and some elements of the military, again began to sweep across the country. But on this occasion the perseverance of the Council of State, the advisory group to the president, the electoral council, and, ultimately, substantial involvement of international actors led to elections for the president and the national parliament, fixed for December 1990.

The international community, led by the unprecedented involvement of the United Nations, determined that Haiti would take the first and important step toward democracy, that is, the holding of national elections. The United Nations financed a team of observers, including security advisors, to facilitate this process. The OAS provided practical assistance for registration and voting procedures. Individual European and Latin American states provided other tangible forms of aid. Ultimately, Jimmy Carter, as chairman of the Council of Freely Elected Heads of Government, brokered arrangements between the military and the provisional government.[1]

Amidst continuing violence intended to destabilize the electoral process, machinery for the elections was put into place and public campaigning contin-ued. Election day was December 16, 1990 and a massive voter turnout gave Jean-Bertrand Aristide 65 percent of the popular vote. Addressing the nation from the balcony of the presidential palace, on Inauguration Day, February 7, 1991, President Aristide told the thousands assembled that "it took us 200 years to arrive at our second independence," and while "at our first independence we cried 'Liberty or Death!' we must now shout with all our strength, 'Democracy or Death!'" (*New York Times*, February 8, 1991, A3).

Little did President Aristide realize how prophetic his inaugural address would prove, and how soon. Since the president was overthrown in the October 1991 coup, it has been estimated that upwards of one thousand civilians have been killed by the army, roving bands of army members, or Duvalierists. Most of those killed have been people from the urban poor who attempted to demonstrate support for Aristide during and following the coup. Haiti's experi-ment with democracy, therefore, lasted a brief eight months. Many would concede, however, that Aristide himself tended to demonstrate some dictatorial tendencies.

Aristide soon realized that victory in the general elections was a much easier task than administering the affairs of the state. On the one hand, he inherited a governmental apparatus riddled with corruption and inefficiency, and largely unable to meet the demands of an increasingly desperate population. Yet Aristide did not help himself by the generally low quality of cabinet members he chose. On the other hand, he faced a business and elite class almost totally united in opposition to his rule, because for the first time, Haiti was faced with a government whose primary interest was meeting the needs of the poorer classes. Traditionally, the state has served as the instrument of the elite and the military to suppress and extort from the ordinary people.

Frustrated by the uncooperative attitude of the elite, confronted by an empty treasury, pressured by the desperately poor for alleviation of their pressing needs, Aristide increasingly employed rhetoric, especially directed against the elite and the perceived Duvalierists. Such was his final speech on his return from the U.N. General Assembly meeting in late September 1991. He told his audience, again from the steps of the national palace:

> Now whenever you are hungry, run your eyes in the direction of those people who aren't hungry. Whenever you are out of work, turn your eyes in the direction of those people who can put you to work. . . . Whenever you feel the heat of unemployment . . . whenever you feel the revolt inside of you, turn your eyes in the direction of those with the means. Ask them why not. (*Haiti-Observateur*, October 9–16, 1991, 7)

Later in his speech he alluded to the instrument of death popularized in South Africa—the burning tire placed around the neck of a potential victim, and now incorporated into Haitian protest. About this, he continued, "What a beautiful tool! What a beautiful instrument . . . it is pretty, it has a good smell!" (*Haiti-Observateur*, October 9–16, 1991, 7). The next day President Aristide was overthrown in a coup and flown into exile. Haiti's first serious attempt at the introduction of democracy came to a sudden and violent end. At an internationally brokered meeting on July 3, 1993, Haiti's military leader, Raoul Cedras, and exiled President Aristide signed an agreement which would return the latter to office on October 30, 1993. These latest developments are positive but inconclusive.

BEYOND ARISTIDE: PROSPECTS FOR DEMOCRACY

Haiti is today the poorest nation in the Western Hemisphere. By any measure of poverty, Haiti's statistics are depressing. Its per capita income of approximately US$300 is one-half that of its neighbor, the Dominican Republic, and one-third of Jamaica's. And even so, Haiti's formal per capita income is inflated by the presence of an exceedingly wealthy but tiny minority. With an infant mortality rate of 120 per thousand, Haiti's rate is ten times that of Barbados, and its literacy level of about 30 percent is by far the lowest in the region (Goodwin, 1990: 110, 114, 116). It is clear from the foregoing that there is limited opportunity for choice in Haiti. In fact, the only choice for over 90 percent of the population is whether they survive or not! And when the issue of survival is reduced to such a basic level, it is clear that Haitians, as human beings everywhere, will do whatever they believe is necessary to ensure their survival. This is not a scenario that permits the development of a democracy. The following illustrations serve to demonstrate the point.

For about two weeks in March 1990, Haiti was essentially without a government, in the intervening period between the fall of Avril and the appointment of Pascal-Trouillot to the presidency. During this time six major food storage warehouses operated by international voluntary organizations were completely looted. The Catholic Relief Services lost 654 tons of food worth more than US$295,000 (*Miami Herald*, March 3, 1990, 6A). CARE reported 1,700 tons of stolen food worth US$825,000. Much of this theft was not by organized bands of thugs, but the poor ordinary people of Port-au-Prince, who took the opportunity provided by the absence of formal authority to obtain food for themselves and for their families. These ordinary Haitians were exercising an urgent choice: the opportunity to obtain food now, when no one administered law and order, rather than wait and hope for a food delivery later—when some might have already died of starvation! Put another way, the poor, having obtained an opportunity, exercised what they thought was their right—to food, without concern for the rights of others. It is this need to survive which reduces the prospect for the building of a democracy. But just as the ordinary people are concerned about survival, so are the Ton Ton Macoutes,[2] and the Duvalierists.

For the twenty-nine-year period of the Duvalier dynasty their supporters acted with impunity. While the Macoutes extorted benefits at the level of the village, those at the top employed the state to benefit themselves. Formally, this was achieved through excessive taxation, but also included nepotism, kick-backs, and control of the contraband trade. The fall of Jean-Claude Duvalier signaled the possible end of the period of privilege. Indeed, by mid-1986, many of the Macoutes had been identified and summarily executed by brutal street justice. Others fled to the interior or hastily left Haiti as their homes were destroyed.

The elections which were called for November 1987 would have finally ended all hope for the Duvalierists, the Macoutes, and some of both located in the military to maintain the status quo. This is the primary reason for the savagery that left about fifty of the electorate dead on that election day. Later, as Jean-Bertrand Aristide arose as the popular candidate of the masses of ordinary people, again the privileged groups felt their interests threatened. And again they responded with violence. Yet as Aristide, during his brief tenure in office, shifted his verbal attack from the Macoutes and the Duvalierists to the business leaders and the others in the elite class, all he achieved was uniting powerful forces against his government, which led, ultimately, to his overthrow. These groups that were united against him saw their privileged position threatened and exercised their choice.

But the determination to survive, whether it is the daily human survival struggle experienced by the masses of the poor, or the equally determined efforts of the previously privileged to maintain the old order, is not the only problem confronting the prospect for democracy in Haiti. As importantly, at least for the past twenty years, Haiti has experienced the struggle of the passing of the traditional society, as the modernization process begins to be experienced. Over the long run, the efforts at modernization, and with them the inevitable democratization of the society, must have positive consequences. Yet before that is achieved, the confrontation between the old, established order and the emerging new one makes the immediate prospect for democracy somewhat dim.

CONCLUSION

Writing on the problem of democracy in the Third World, political scientist Leslie Manigat postulated that "democratization is a three-stage process." The first stage, he suggested, "is embodied in a political system respecting life and basic liberties and human rights." At this stage "competition expresses itself dominantly as a fight." In the second stage "education and development facilitate the harmonious function of democratic institutions." Since power is shared at this stage competition expresses itself as a debate. Finally, when "democracy itself is building a consensual society," the third stage is attained. At this stage conflict is resolved through bargaining and minority views are incorporated in the dialogue. According to Manigat, at this stage, "competition expresses itself principally as a game." He concluded with the assertion that Haiti was ready for stage one.[3]

Indeed, some may hold, the open elections of December 1990, and the fact that the Aristide government held office—however briefly—do mean that Haiti had achieved stage one of Manigat's democratic process. Yet, the violent overthrow of this government, and with it the total usurpation of the basic rights of millions of Haiti's population, obviously means that Haiti has taken a giant leap backward.

The huge backward step is clearly a consequence of the refusal of the country's elite, supported by the army, to accept Haiti's vast majority of the underclass as having equal rights, and therefore as equal partners, in the country's political system. Haiti's elite has historically viewed the majority poor as objects to be exploited, not as subjects in a shared political system. Once the majority are maintained as objects, the interests of the elite remain supreme. In the late eighteenth century, the majority slave population pursued their interests by means of a long and violent revolution. Hopefully this round of a similar struggle can be concluded more peacefully.

NOTES

1. For details of the implications of Carter's policy while serving as U.S. president, see K. Boodhoo, "Realism vs. Idealism in U.S.-Haitian Relations," *Caribbean Affairs* vol. 1, no. 4 (October–December 1988): 55–57.

2. The Ton Ton Macoutes were Duvalier loyalists who acted as political cadres, secret police, and instruments of terror in Haitian society during and after the Duvalier era.

3. See Leslie Manigat, "Challenges Confronting Third World Democrats," *Vision* vol. 1, no. 2 (May 1989): 7. Washington: Center for Strategic Studies.

13

Democratization and Foreign Intervention: Applying the Lessons of Grenada to Panama and Nicaragua

Pedro A. Noguera

The election of Ronald Reagan in 1980 marked the renewal of an actively interventionist strategy on the part of the United States toward the Caribbean. Whereas the Carter administration had allowed its advocacy of human rights to influence its foreign policies, and thereby resulted in a reduction of U.S. military activities abroad,[1] the election of Ronald Reagan brought a return to the approaches utilized in the past. Under Reagan, the policy of containment, previously utilized by the Truman and Eisenhower administrations to justify efforts to halt the spread of communism, now became referred to as the Reagan Doctrine, and was the new guiding principle for most foreign policy matters.[2]

The adoption and application of the Reagan Doctrine resulted in a substantial increase in U.S. military, economic, and political intervention into the affairs of the smaller states south of the border. Justification for this change in policy was based upon the relative increase in political activity within the region, which the United States deemed threatening to its interests. The revolutions in Grenada and Nicaragua, the growing insurgencies in El Salvador and Guatemala, and the development of political and economic ties between Jamaica and Cuba were all seen as challenges to U.S. hegemony in the region.

A strategy of intervention and destabilization, similar to the pre–World War II gunboat diplomacy, was put into effect throughout the region. This included relatively benign approaches such as the 1982 Caribbean Basin Initiative (CBI), as well as direct military intervention. The motivation for this strategy was to reassert the dominant role of the United States in the political and economic affairs of the region. The 1983 invasion of Grenada was carried out largely as a way of demonstrating Reagan's resolve to utilize military force to remove governments it deemed "unfriendly," and to curtail Soviet and Cuban influence in the region. The low-intensity war waged by U.S.-funded mercenaries known as the Contras, which resulted in the loss of more than 30,000 lives over the course of ten years of fighting, is yet another example. Finally, the December 1989 invasion of Panama, coming after several months of military threats and economic sanctions directed at the regime of General Manuel Noriega by the U.S. government, was the most recent incident of U.S. military intervention in the region.

In all three cases—Grenada, Nicaragua, and Panama—the United States appears to have achieved its objectives. The "unfriendly" regimes in Grenada and Panama were removed through force, and the Sandinista government in Nicaragua was defeated in national elections held in February 1990 following several years of U.S.-sponsored war. In all three cases, the establishment of democratic governments was also a stated objective of U.S. policy. This objective appears to have been achieved with the election of Herbert Blaize in Grenada in 1984, the 1990 election of Violetta Chamorro in Nicaragua, and the installation of the Endara administration in Panama in 1990.

Twelve years after the implementation of the Reagan Doctrine in the Caribbean, with U.S. objectives in the region seeming to have been realized, one question remains: what will be the long-term consequences for the process of democratization of these three countries? Having successfully established these presumably democratic governments, how successful will these governments be in developing democratic institutions and in creating a stable political environment?

In the following pages, I assess the ways in which the legacy of U.S. military intervention has affected efforts to promote democracy. I do so through a study of Grenada in the postinvasion period of 1984–1989. Such an assessment enables us to extract lessons that may be useful for understanding ongoing political developments in Nicaragua and Panama. This assessment is based on three areas that have bearing on the establishment of democracy, namely: (1) the state of the economy in the aftermath of the U.S. invasion, and its relationship to the stability of political institutions on the island; (2) the role played by political parties, with a particular focus on the conduct of the ruling party and the extent to which it has successfully promoted stability and supported democratic values on the island; (3) the impact of the U.S. invasion on regional politics and regional organizations, namely, the Organization of Eastern Caribbean States (OECS) and the Caribbean Common Market (CARICOM).

This analysis is based in part upon data collected during seven months of field research in Grenada from July 1987 to March 1988. During that period, 120 interviews were conducted with Grenadian citizens regarding their attitudes and perceptions of the political changes that had occurred on the island. In addition, thirty in-depth interviews with politicians, labor and community leaders, clergymen, businessmen, and journalists were carried out to obtain an "insider's" perspective on the political changes that have taken place. The data collected from these interviews, combined with my first-hand observations, form the basis of this analysis.

While the situation in each country is unique, and therefore must be analyzed within the context of its own culture and history, the parallels created by the common experience of Grenada's, Nicaragua's, and Panama's subjection to U.S. military intervention make comparative analysis both feasible and necessary. It is for the purpose of identifying the legacies that may be obtained from that common experience that this study was undertaken.

ECONOMIC CONDITIONS AND DEMOCRACY

The practice of democracy in any society is strongly influenced by the state of the economy and by relations between social classes. In societies characterized by a high degree of social inequality, the potential for disorder and instability that can accompany democratic political practices tends to produce governments that are authoritarian. The contradictions that result from combining a political system premised on majority rule with an economic system based on the rule of a minority are often too threatening to order and stability; the practice of democracy simply poses too many risks. Samuel Huntington (1968) and others have found through comparative transnational studies a high correlation between democratic forms of government and economies with a relatively high gross national product and per capita income. Conversely, poorer countries, and even many of those that are considered "nearly industrialized," are less likely to be led by democratic regimes. Wealthier societies are better able to respond to and accommodate the economic demands generated by working-class organizations than poorer nations. In poor nations the power relations that operate in the economy, which are based on the domination of one class over another, are generally replicated in politics. As a result, the primary role of political institutions becomes one of legitimizing this system of inequality, and maintaining existing social arrangements through force if necessary (Olsen, 1970: 35–37).

While the association between economic development and democracy throughout the world is relatively consistent, the English-speaking Caribbean has been the one notable exception to this pattern. On this point Carl Stone makes the following observation:

Most developing countries which achieved independence in the post World War Two period inherited Western European type constitutions. . . . The overwhelming majority of these states have since abandoned that inheritance in favor of military regimes, one-party rule and wide ranging forms of authoritarian rule. The English-speaking Caribbean remains the only area in the Third World where politics based on free elections, multiple parties, and liberal democratic freedoms are still predominant. (1986: 14)

Several scholars have attributed the perpetuation of democratic rule in the West Indies to the legacy of British colonialism (Huntington, 1984; Diamond, 1989; Weiner, 1987), citing the strength of bureaucratic structures created by the British as the most salient contributing factor. Others such as Paget Henry (1985) and Percy Hintzen (1989a) trace the advent of democracy in the Caribbean to the class alliances that were formed during the struggle for independence. In Chapter 1 of this volume, Hintzen argues that in the postcolonial period the middle class utilized the influence it had gained from its leadership within the labor movement of the 1930s to pressure the British into granting independence. As independence drew near and it became clear that the middle class would have to compete with the landed elites for control of the state, nationalism was used as a means to mobilize the lower class to ensure electoral victory. Participation in the political process through political parties and labor unions controlled by middle-class leaders eventually "harnessed lower class mobilization and converted it into regimentation" (see also Hintzen, 1989a: 17). Hence, while democracy has persisted in the region, its form has been restricted by a pattern of middle-class domination that is common throughout the region.

Prior to the revolution in 1979, Grenada followed this pattern of Westminster democracy that prevailed in other parts of the Caribbean. During the period of Peoples Revolutionary Government (PRG) rule, an attempt was made to break with that pattern and to create what the leadership termed a new form of "participatory" democracy. Based in part on the Tanzanian model of African socialism,[3] the PRG sought to create new forms of participation in decision making at both the local and national level. These political reforms were accompanied by a series of social and economic reforms that were intended to raise the quality of living conditions for the rural lower-class majority. Free health and dental care, free primary and secondary education, maternity leave, and the imposition of subsidies on basic foodstuffs were some of the major features of the reform initiative. The PRG hoped that through the adoption of these reforms—the political as well as the socioeconomic—it could establish the legitimacy it would need to maintain popular support and political power.

Since the U.S. invasion in 1984, the state of the economy has been the most important political issue on the island. Evidence of the salience of economic issues can be seen from an examination of the survey results I obtained in 1987. In response to the question "Have your living conditions gotten better or worse during the time that Blaize has been in power?" only 7 percent claimed things had improved, while 73 percent said that they had gotten worse (Noguera, 1989). Despite receiving approximately US$157 million in aid from the United States in the year following the invasion, and approximately US$350 million over the next four years, a majority of the respondents felt that their living conditions had declined. Unemployment, which the PRG claimed to have reduced to 14 percent,[4] had risen to 22 percent according to official estimates in 1988. Despite a substantial improvement in the prices earned on the international market for nutmeg, one of Grenada's leading exports, the balance-of-trade deficit had grown substantially, resulting in significant increases in the cost of living.[5]

Ironically, even as living conditions for the majority of Grenadians seemed to be deteriorating, the government boasted of bringing new prosperity to the island. Pointing to a steady 5 percent growth in the island's GDP for each year since the election of 1984, New National Party (NNP) leaders claimed that "the chains that have bound the spirit of free enterprise and initiative for years have been broken . . . they (Grenadians) are now free, under God, to apply their energies in the direction which the Government has charted. . . . There are evident signs that the country is poised for a tremendous economic take-off" (Noguera, 1989). Perhaps part of the reason for the discrepancy between the perceptions of lower-class Grenadians and those of the government was that economic growth in Grenada had largely been limited to two sectors of the economy—tourism and construction. While some job opportunities were created by expansion in these areas, most of these were either temporary or low-paying.

Shortly after the election, the NNP government began dismantling several of the social services that had been created by the PRG, including free health care, school subsidies, adult education, higher education scholarships, cooperative assistance, house repair loans, and food subsidies. The elimination of these popular programs contributed to the widespread sense that important "economic rights" were being taken away at the same time that the cost of living was increasing.[6]

While the vagaries of the economy in a dependent society such as Grenada make it difficult for any government to assert control over its financial destiny, it is clear that at least part of the blame for the deterioration in economic conditions after 1984 must be placed upon the NNP government headed by Herbert Blaize. A combination of poor planning and administration on the part of the NNP government led to a substantial shortfall in government revenue every year since 1986. In that year, the government enacted major tax reforms that entailed the elimination of all property taxes and imposed a new value added tax (VAT) that was placed on all goods and services purchased on the island. Not only was the tax perceived as extremely regressive by most Grenadian citizens, many of whom had never paid income tax before due to their low incomes, but the government lacked the infrastructure to guarantee collection of the new tax at the time it was adopted.

Partially as a result of this failed policy, the government was later forced to lay off hundreds of public sector employees. Part of the motivation for the large-scale retrenchment in the public sector was a desire by NNP officials to remove sympathizers of the old PRG regime. Even after the 1984 elections, several individuals who held posts in the civil service under the PRG continued to occupy positions in the government bureaucracy and public sector. This included the Grenada Defense Force, where several of the cadets recruited were former Peoples Revolutionary Army (PRA) soldiers.

Adding to the NNP's economic problems was the fact that the large volume of investment from North American entrepreneurs that had been promised in the wake of the invasion, and which was trumpeted as the key to Grenada's future economic prosperity, never materialized. A U.S. toy manufacturer who opened a factory in Grenada shortly after the invasion, and who was identified as a role model for foreign investors, went out of business within a year.[7] While several North Americans have purchased land in Grenada, relatively few new jobs have been created.

Surveys conducted by Farley Brathwaite (1984) and Selwyn Ryan (1984a) during the months following the U.S. invasion clearly indicated that there was a popularly held perception that a substantial increase in foreign aid, particularly from the United States, would flow to the island. Both found in separate surveys that this belief was directly related to Grenadian support for the U.S. invasion and the U.S. military presence on the island in the months that followed. The promise of U.S. aid to Grenada was largely responsible for the NNP's success in the 1984 elections once it became clear during the campaign that Blaize and the NNP were favored by the United States.[8] Expectations were high that the future would be prosperous, and many Grenadians even believed that Grenada could join the United States as the fifty-first state.[9] However, as the living conditions of lower-class Grenadians declined, disappointment soon turned to anger, and the bulk of that frustration was directed at the regime in power— Blaize and the NNP.

Many Grenadians realized that the island's misfortunes were not solely due to the NNP's mismanagement of the economy. Eventually it became obvious that there would be no continuous flow of aid to Grenada, either directly from the U.S. government or from the private sector. In fact, officials at the U.S. embassy in Grenada explained to me quite clearly that it was the goal of the U.S. State Department to gradually reduce the level of U.S. aid sent to Grenada until it was comparable with the amounts received by other islands in the region. The budgetary supplements that were provided to the Grenadian government in 1986 and 1987, in order to assist it in meeting its recurrent expenses, were certainly going to be discontinued according to officials at the U.S. embassy. Moreover, the United States had no plans of even retaining an embassy on the island once its lease expired at Ross Point Inn, the previous site of its operations.

The combined effects of financial mismanagement and a reduction in U.S. aid resulted in considerable dissatisfaction toward the NNP government. The victory of the National Democratic Congress (NDC) in the March 1990 elections was perhaps the clearest indication of popular disapproval with the policies of the NNP government. In 1987 and 1988, when I was conducting interviews on the island, there were already clear indications that popular resentment toward the government was growing due to the country's economic problems. This quote from a fifty-seven-year-old seamstress from the village of Birchgrove, St. Andrews, is indicative of many of the attitudes I encountered during the course of the research:

> Right now life is very hard for the poorer persons in Grenada. Blaize and them don't give a damn about what is happening to we. But I should have known that would be true, because Blaize never did care about the poor. Every day prices is going up, and now them want us to pay the VAT. It's like we ain't have no rights here no more. (Noguera, 1989)

While dissatisfaction with the state of the economy did not lead to the downfall of the government, it is clear that it was a major factor contributing to the breakup of the NNP coalition and the dismissal of Blaize as political leader of the party while still serving as prime minister; a display of party disunity which was highly uncharacteristic of most Westminster-style democracies. In the following section, I explore further the connection between the state of the economy and the behavior of the island's political parties.

INFIGHTING AND INCRIMINATIONS: THE NEW POLITICS OF DEMOCRACY IN GRENADA

As was true in the case of Nicaragua and Panama, the U.S.-backed regime in Grenada was a coalition government, comprised of political parties which previously competed with one another in the electoral arena. The NNP was created through direct U.S. intervention as a result of a conference of centrist political parties held on Union Island in August 1984. Fearing that competition between four to five centrist parties would result in the victory of former prime minister Eric Gairy's Grenada United Labour Party (GULP), the United States facilitated the creation of the coalition that selected political veteran Herbert Blaize as its political leader and candidate for prime minister. Key ministerial positions were to be distributed to leading members of the other parties after the election as a way of appeasing the disparate interests of the parties involved.

Despite the haste with which it was brought together, the NNP succeeded in defeating Gairy by a margin of three to one, and gained all but two of the seats in the Parliament. Though Gairy and his supporters raised objections over the way in which the elections were handled, claiming that the United States had tampered with the process, the coalition government was sworn into office pledging that love of country would enable the parties' leaders to overcome their differences and retain their unity.

However, such promises were relatively short-lived. Within a year, members of the coalition began making accusations against one another of corruption and dishonesty. Two of the more prominent members of the government,

George Brizan and Francis Alexis, who had previously been in the leadership of different parties, began to openly challenge the government's commitment to fulfilling its campaign promises. By 1987, six of the major figures in the coalition left their posts in government and took on the role of leading the opposition to the ruling NNP under a new name—the National Democratic Congress (NDC).

As a result of this maneuvering, politics on the island began to resemble a full-fledged political campaign although elections were not scheduled to be held for another three years. Politicians from the three major competing parties, GULP, NNP, and NDC, began to frantically position themselves in relation to the various constituencies on the island. Party conventions were held with great fanfare and stories featuring political gossip filled the pages of the local tabloids. Politicians from neighboring islands were brought in to demonstrate the regional support possessed by each of the parties. Increasingly, all actions undertaken by the government took on a partisan character, and were portrayed in that light by the local media.

The split between Blaize and the NDC supporters was perhaps even less dramatic than the revolt against Herbert Blaize which occurred two years later. Led by the politically savvy minister of communication and works, Dr. Keith Mitchell, the membership of the NNP voted to remove Herbert Blaize as leader of the NNP while he was still serving as prime minister. Leading a rebel faction within the party, Mitchell argued that Blaize's poor health and inflexibility on policy matters had caused a loss of confidence toward the government among the population.

Mitchell's strategy appeared to presume that once Blaize was removed from party leadership, a no-confidence vote on the government could be passed in Parliament, which would force the governor general to call for early elections. However, Brizan and the NDC were unwilling to cooperate with the no-confidence vote called for by Mitchell, who they feared might be the immediate beneficiary of early elections. Instead, Mitchell was removed by Blaize from his post in government. With less than four months before the scheduled elections, Herbert Blaize died, and the mantle of prime minister was turned over to his deputy, Ben Jones.

The party infighting within the NNP commenced shortly after its electoral honeymoon ended and had a profoundly unsettling effect upon the populace. Having experienced the overthrow of the PRG, the execution of Prime Minister Maurice Bishop, and the U.S. invasion, there was considerable cynicism among Grenadians toward politicians generally, and an overwhelming desire for a period of political peace and stability. In my interviews with Grenadian citizens in 1987 and 1988, a strong sense of distrust toward politicians of all stripes was common among the respondents. Twenty-three percent of the respondents I interviewed told me that they would not vote in the next election. The reason most typically given was that politicians could not be trusted. The following quote from a sixty-two-year-old farmer from the village of Birchgrove, St. Andrews, was typical of the views expressed:

We Grenadians have had enough of these politicians. You can't believe none of them. All them does want is power, and they will do anything to get it. Look at Bishop and Coard. One minute dem is comrades, the next minute Coard having Bishop murdered. Then you watch this here government. Come election time them saying them all together. When the election over is a whole nother thing. You just can't believe a word that dem say. (Noguera, 1989)

The political infighting which followed shortly after the 1984 elections served to contribute toward the feelings of distrust and disappointment expressed here. Very few of the Grenadians I interviewed could have been characterized as apathetic or unconcerned about politics on the island. Most were extremely knowledgeable and informed about political issues but had become cynical of the machinations of local political leaders. The comments expressed by this forty-three-year-old nutmeg worker from Gouyave reflect this frustration:

We Grenadians have been through enough already. We have seen war and violence on this peaceful little island, and we just can't take no more of that. The onlyest problem we still have here is these damn politicians. You just can't believe what dem say. One minute dem is working together, the next minute dem is fighting one another. The people of Grenada have had enough of these polytricks. What we need now is a break from all of that madness. (Noguera, 1989)

Unfortunately, the break from the intrigue and conflict which have characterized Grenadian politics for the last several years may not yet be at hand. The victory of the NDC in the March 1990 elections, under the leadership of former Interim Council head Nicholas Brathwaite, came without the majority needed to control the Parliament. This has required new coalitions to pass legislation between politicians who have a fairly recent history of bitter conflict and acrimony.

To what extent should Grenada's conflict-ridden political situation be attributed to the invasion? Given that the kind of political infighting that has recently characterized Grenadian politics is common to other nations in the Caribbean, and elsewhere, it may not be reasonable to affix blame on the U.S. invasion. However, it is clear that the political vacuum in government created by the invasion opened the door for the political conflict which has ensued hence. While some might argue that it was the revolution of 1979 and the authoritarian nature of the Gairy regime which are the true precursors to the current political uncertainty, both of those were genuinely Grenadian in origin, while the invasion of 1983 was not. Moreover, since at least one of the explicit goals of the U.S. invasion was to restore democracy to Grenada, then it seems fair to evaluate the long-term process of democratization using this goal as our criterion.

THE IMPACT OF THE INVASION ON REGIONAL POLITICS

The 1983 U.S. invasion of Grenada produced substantial changes in the political environment of the Anglophone Caribbean. Not only was the leftist government of the New Jewel Movement (NJM) eliminated in Grenada, but the possibility of its ideological influence spreading to other Caribbean nations was also substantially curtailed. The spread of the revolution's political influence, which the United States argued was a mere cover for a more sinister military threat from the Soviet Union, had served as a primary justification for the U.S.-led assault on Grenada. The smaller states of the eastern Caribbean were particularly concerned that the leftist takeover which had occurred with such ease in Grenada might be repeated on neighboring islands. The possibility that the Bishop government might be successful in implementing some of its ambitious projects for social and economic development and reform, and might therefore be seen as an alternative model, made the threat emanating from Grenada all the more significant.

Given the paranoia of some of Grenada's neighbors toward the revolutionary government, it is not surprising that the execution of Maurice Bishop by members of his own party was seized as an opportunity for U.S. military intervention. Bishop's execution provided the United States with justification for the assault with near unanimous approval from governments in the region. The Reagan administration had begun to publicly express its concerns about the ideological orientation of the NJM government as early as 1980. Military operations carried out on islands in the region, attempts to undermine the PRG's efforts to solicit foreign aid for development projects, and threats of U.S. hostility from representatives of the Reagan administration characterized U.S. policy toward the revolutionary government in Grenada from 1979 to 1983. There is also substantial evidence now that the invasion itself had been planned well before October 25.[10] It is reasonable to conclude therefore that the split in the leadership of the ruling party, followed by the execution of Bishop and his allies within the government, were merely convenient excuses for the action rather than independent causes.

The immediate result of the U.S. invasion for the region was increased polarization within CARICOM, with those members of CARICOM who opposed the invasion becoming at odds with those who participated or lent their support. Efforts by the United States to exclude Trinidad and Tobago, Guyana, Belize, and the Bahamas (because they opposed the invasion) from the trade benefits of the CBI were immediately put into effect.[11] In this way, the United

States attempted to demonstrate that it had the means to reward those that went along with its policies, as well as the ability to punish those that did not. It is also worth noting that in all but three of the countries that opposed the U.S. action, there was a change in government within a year of the invasion. While the Pindling administration was able to win reelection in the Bahamas, accusations of complicity with drug traffickers were leveled at the prime minister by U.S. authorities during the campaign.

In addition to punishing the dissenters, many of the political parties in the region that supported the invasion became much more openly aligned to U.S. political interests in the region. Several of the more conservative parties joined a formal alliance with conservative political groups in the United States known as the Caribbean Democratic Union (CDU). From 1983 to 1988, the CDU provided ideological and political support to conservative political parties in the region. It was not uncommon for members of the CDU to attend party conventions sponsored by one of their members in an attempt to demonstrate their mutual support. This was particularly true when one of its member parties appeared to be experiencing problems, as was often the case with the New National Party in Grenada, which CDU activists attempted to bolster when the party was beset by factionalism and attacks on its leader Herbert Blaize.

For the Caribbean left, the impact of the U.S. invasion of Grenada was devastating. Several political parties, labor unions, and civic organizations had developed ties with Grenada during the four-and-a-half years of PRG rule. A number of intellectuals and technocrats throughout the region had been attracted to the island by the government's willingness to experiment with economic and social reforms, and several had chosen to relocate there to use their talents and skills in support of the revolution. Many hoped that the island could become an alternative model of development which could demonstrate the possibility of greater social equality and economic progress simultaneously. The abortion of this experiment left many leftists in the region demoralized, and in some cases, with their backs to the wall at home. The collapse of the revolution and the triumph of U.S. interests throughout the Caribbean created new opportunities for the right to attack much of what the left had represented in Caribbean politics.

The elections of George Bush in 1988 and Michael Manley in 1989 have substantially weakened the significance of the ideologically based political alignments in the Caribbean. Previous efforts to isolate those governments and parties which opposed the U.S. invasion have largely ceased. The absence of Ronald Reagan and Edward Seaga as symbolic figureheads of conservatism for the region deprived the alliance of the ideological leadership which once held it together. The polarization which characterized relations between CARICOM nations, based upon the stand they took toward the U.S. invasion, has been diminished by a renewed drive toward regional cooperation, particularly in the areas of trade and technology.

To a large extent, the move away from polarization is directly related to the present U.S. ambivalence toward the Anglophone Caribbean. In the absence of a perceived communist threat, the mini-states of the Caribbean lose much of their strategic importance to U.S. foreign policy interests. The CBI, which never achieved much of what was originally promised, has not been replaced by new economic overtures toward the region. For the moment, assistance with U.S. efforts to stop the flow of drugs is the only significant ongoing demonstration of interest by U.S. policy makers in the region. Economic development and support for democracy and humanitarian aid have once again become back burner issues.

FUTURE PROSPECTS OF DEMOCRACY IN GRENADA, NICARAGUA, AND PANAMA

Several years have now gone by since the U.S. invasion of Grenada, and already the memory of that incident has become remote for most Americans. Questions are no longer raised by the U.S. Congress concerning the effects of the invasion on the island's economy, nor is the concern with the practice of democracy in Grenadian society as relevant today as it was ten years ago to U.S. policy makers. Occasionally boosters of the Republican Party mention what they term "the triumph over communism in Grenada" to generate support for their candidates and causes, but even on those occasions the country and its people are far less important than what it is believed the United States accomplished there.

Even less time has elapsed since the invasion of Panama, but the U.S. media and U.S. politicians have already lost interest in that country as well. The fact that thousands of Panamanians are still homeless, and that Panama City remains in shambles, is of little concern. There is still no accurate counting of Panamanian citizens killed during the invasion, and deliberations over compensation to Panama for rebuilding the country have been treated as just one of many requests for foreign aid for which Democratic legislators are demonstrating increasing intolerance. Even the case of the notorious general Manuel Noriega, the man whose apprehension became the declared motive of the intervention, received little publicity during his trial on drug trafficking charges.

Nicaragua continues to receive considerable attention in the United States, largely because the Sandinistas remain a force to be reckoned with in Nicaragua. Their challenge to "govern from below" appears to have been given meaning, as civil servants throughout the country have gone on strike to call for wage increases in response to currency devaluations by the new government. The ongoing possibility of armed conflict between the Contras and the Sandinista-controlled military was yet another factor that made the situation in Nicaragua continue to be of interest to the Bush administration and the U.S. media. Thus far, President Clinton's election has had no effect on U.S. policy toward Nicaragua.

However, should Nicaragua's warring factions ever work out a lasting strategy for reconciliation, it is more than likely that Nicaragua too will become a nonissue for most Americans. Poor developing nations struggling to overcome underdevelopment are largely unimportant to the United States these days unless they hold some strategic significance to U.S. economic or military interests. Since the fall of the Soviet Union, it appears as though the United States will have its way in the Caribbean region, and the Western Hemisphere generally.

Yet, while U.S. interests in Grenada may appear to be secure for the time being, the situation in Nicaragua and Panama remains more precarious. In the aftermath of the U.S. invasion, supporters of the defunct PRG have been in complete disarray. NJM supporters still remain bitterly divided over the split that emerged between the Bishop and Coard factions of the party. Moreover, the newly created Maurice Bishop Patriotic Movement, headed by Terry Maryshow, appears to be poorly organized, and proved unable to mount an effective campaign in the elections of 1984 and 1988. Even though there is substantial evidence of support for the leadership of Maurice Bishop and the policies and programs of his government (Noguera, 1989 and Brathwaite, 1984), many Grenadians appear unwilling at the present to support or vote for those who claim to carry the banner of that legacy. The disorganization of the Grenadian left is one factor that has made it possible for the United States to implement its gradual withdrawal of military and monetary aid within a relatively short period of time.

However, while the left may be disorganized in Grenada the same is clearly not the case in Nicaragua. Since losing the February 1990 election, the Sandinistas have continued to operate as an effective political force within the country. They remain the largest and most well-organized political party, and enjoy a strong base of support in several important trade unions and among many small farmers as well. Aside from the Sandinistas' strength, there is also the reality of the Unified Nicaraguan Opposition's (UNO) weakness. The fourteen political parties that make up UNO range from communists to former Contra leaders, and within days of the electoral victory there were already clear signs of dissension within the ranks. Vice-President Virgilio Godoy, leader of the Liberal Party, has begun to openly challenge President Chamorro. Though US$300 million in aid to Nicaragua was approved by the U.S. Congress in 1991, there are no guarantees of similar levels of aid in the future. Decline in U.S. interest in Nicaragua combined with divisions within the ruling party appear likely to lead to political instability in the future.

In Panama, supporters of the deposed general Noriega have not yet organized into a significant political force in the country. Yet, there are already signs of fierce opposition toward the Endara government within the country. In May

1990, Guillermo Endara's party headquarters were bombed. According to several observers, racial tension, which was common during the 1960s, appears to have surfaced again in the low-income areas of Panama City, which suffered the greatest losses in terms of lives and property during the invasion. This is particularly true in areas such as Chorrios, a largely black, low-income area where Noriega based his headquarters prior to the invasion, and which was destroyed during the U.S. assault. Like Nicaragua, Panama is no longer regarded as a priority for U.S. aid by many U.S. legislators, although it recently received US$420 million, far short of the US$2 billion originally requested by Endara. The unreliability of future U.S. support, combined with the fact that a majority of the countries within the Organization of American States have refused to recognize the Endara government, leaves the future of the regime in doubt.

The rapid decline in U.S. interest toward countries it has invaded or destabilized will in all likelihood have tremendous bearing upon the democratization process which unfolds in those countries. Politicians who link their political fortunes to the hope of ongoing U.S. aid may have difficulty retaining power once it becomes clear that their friendship to the United States, as measured in dollars, was only short-term. Populations that are led to believe that U.S. intervention is a guarantee of U.S. financial support, as so many seemed to have believed in Grenada, Nicaragua, and Panama, are likely to be disappointed. Should the lack of U.S. support be combined with further deterioration of living conditions, disappointment is likely to produce greater frustration and, ultimately, political unrest.

The uncertain futures of the regimes presently in power in Grenada, Nicaragua, and Panama reflect the tension which often exists between political order and democracy. In carrying out their pledges to restore democracy, the three regimes have necessarily had to open up the possibility for their political opponents to organize and exploit the failures of government. The relative fragility of the regimes, combined with the economic uncertainty confronting all three nations, makes the need for order and social peace all the more important to those in power in the months and years ahead.

However, one of the consequences of U.S. intervention has been that popular expectations of substantial improvements in living standards would be brought about within a relatively short period of time. As individuals and groups grow frustrated with the pace of progress, it is likely that they will demonstrate their frustration in ways that contribute to the political and economic uncertainty of the country. Undoubtedly, there will be expectations among the populace that the practice of democracy in Grenada, Nicaragua, and Panama will entail more than the mere holding of elections. Particularly in Grenada and Nicaragua, there is a widespread sense among the population that their political rights extend beyond civil liberties and include rights to land, employment, housing, health care, and education. It may well be that the price of stability in these countries will be ongoing negotiations with the opposition, particularly the trade unions, to work out compromises over austerity programs and national policies.

Democratization in these three countries will, therefore, entail the formulation of a new "social contract" between the governed and the governors. It will involve a recognition that the price of social peace and political order is compromise among the various organized interest groups in the three countries. It will require those who lead to acknowledge that the state is not the only agency capable of exercising power in society. The ability to disrupt and destabilize is also a form of power, and as such, those who have the capability to do so must either be repressed or treated as partners in governance.

The only alternative to constructing this new social contract is to erect authoritarian forms of government. In Grenada, it appears unlikely that this will occur. The new National Democratic Congress government, headed by Brathwaite, appears committed to the practice of democracy within Grenada's Westminster tradition. However, Nicaragua and Panama have no democratic traditions to base their new forms of government upon. Both share a history of political violence, dictatorship, repression, and military rule. The prospects for democracy in these two countries may therefore be more remote.

Undoubtedly, challenges to U.S. interests in the region will spring up again as they have historically; it is unlikely that either a smooth path to prosperity or the status quo will prevail for long. However, while in the recent past the Reagan and Bush administrations have used containment of communism as a justification for military intervention, new rationales will have to be created in the future. Whether acts of intervention are carried out under the guise of combating drugs or undertaken, as they were in the past, as a means of protecting U.S. financial interests, it is likely that they will occur again.

Despite the unclear future outlook of the Caribbean region, there remain important lessons from Grenada which can be applied elsewhere, particularly to nations that have been subjected to U.S. intervention. It is clear that democracy as a political system cannot be imposed by one country upon another through military means. It may indeed be possible for a powerful state to forcibly remove the government of a smaller or weaker state from power, sponsor elections, and see to it that a regime which suits its interests is installed. However, a democratic political system, which has historically been understood to mean more than the mere holding of elections, cannot be imposed externally.

The ingredients of democracy, such as political parties, an independent media and judiciary, and, perhaps most importantly, an atmosphere of tolerance must develop indigenously. While leaders and organizations may look externally for support, both before and/or after coming to power, they must rely upon their ability to appeal to the electorate if they are to be successful in their bids for power and in their efforts to retain it. Democracy requires that the electorate maintain a degree of trust in those who administer the reins of government. Invariably, attaining this trust may be contingent upon some assurance that the needs and minimal expectations of the majority can be satisfied. In essence, democracy rests upon legitimacy, and legitimacy can only be obtained and retained when a population has confidence that its basic needs can and will be met.

What this means is that democratic forms of government and economic underdevelopment exist in antagonistic relationships. Widespread poverty, uneven development, economic decline, or stagnation can all serve to undermine the prospects for democracy. This will undoubtedly be true for Nicaragua and Panama. For both countries, the road to democracy, political stability, and economic development will be a difficult one. It is clear that the willingness of the United States to intervene and to expend great sums of money to remove governments of which it did not approve will not be equivalent to its support for democracy and development in the aftermath of its intervention. These tasks will become the responsibilities of Nicaraguan and Panamanian leaders. Assessing how they fare in carrying out these tasks is a subject which will merit future study and observation.

NOTES

1. See *U.S. Relations with the Caribbean and Central America* (Washington: Bureau of Public Affairs, 1979).

2. The Reagan Doctrine was essentially a policy which aimed at subverting communist governments through support for armed insurgents or economic isolation.

3. For a discussion of the New Jewel Movement's interests and ideas on participatory democracy and the influence of the Tanzanian model, see Manning Marable, *African and Caribbean Politics* (London: Verso Press, 1987): 210.

4. According to a 1982 World Bank Report on Grenada, the Grenadian government had reduced the rate of unemployment to 14 percent. Official government estimates of unemployment in 1988 ranged from 22 to 25 percent.

5. In 1985, the Grenada Nutmeg Cooperative Association negotiated a formula for setting the price of nutmegs on the world market with Indonesia. Grenada produces 30 percent of the world's nutmeg, and Indonesia produces the remaining 70 percent. In the years following the formation of the nutmeg cartel, prices rose substantially, and earnings for nutmeg farmers rose 28 percent over the next three years.

6. The NNP government attempted to maintain some of the more popular reform programs set up by the PRG, such as the teachers' college and the adult literacy program. In such cases, it changed the name and management of the agencies as a way of demonstrating that there was new leadership. In other cases, programs were eliminated either because the government could no longer bear the cost (e.g., house repair loan program, free dental and medical services) or because it was ideologically opposed to the program itself (e.g., the cooperative support agency [NACDA] and the agency that monitored food subsidies [MNIB]).

7. In February 1983, *60 Minutes*, a CBS news program, featured a story about a U.S. toy manufacturer who had developed a toy factory in Grenada and employed several Grenadians. The efforts of the U.S. businessman were heralded as the model for future economic development in Grenada which would rely upon private sector investment rather than direct aid from the U.S. government. Within six months of the news broadcast, the toy company went out of

business, and the company's owner was charged with misuse of government loans which had been made available to him to assist in starting the enterprise.

8. Though the official U.S. position was that it would stay out of the election in 1984, its preference for the NNP was made known in a variety of ways. The National Endowment for Democracy, a conservative private foundation based in the United States, consulted with the NNP throughout the campaign. The U.S.-backed CDU (Caribbean Democratic Union) also openly endorsed Blaize and the NNP. Finally, in an interview with the *Grenada Voice* (July 7, 1984) the U.S. ambassador to Grenada, Loren Lawrence, made it clear that "we (the U.S.) will be out of here very fast if a fairly elected honest government is not put into place."

9. According to a poll conducted by the *New York Times* (October 29, 1983) 87 percent of all Grenadians interviewed expressed interest in seeing Grenada become the fifty-first state.

10. In several of the military maneuvers carried out by the United States in the eastern Caribbean prior to the Grenada invasion (Ocean Venture '81 and '82, Readex '83) there were mock invasions of islands which intended to symbolize Grenada. In addition, in an article printed in the November 12, 1983 issue of the *Seattle Times* it was reported that three weeks prior to the U.S. invasion of Grenada, U.S. Army Rangers staged a mock invasion in which they captured an unused airstrip. The similarity between the war game and the actual military operation carried out on October 25 did not go unnoticed by the newspaper.

11. The major criticisms of the Caribbean Basin Initiative were that (1) the direct aid component provided less than 10 percent of what the region needed to cover its balance-of-payment shortfall; (2) it concentrated most of its provisions on the Central American nations, namely, El Salvador, Honduras, and Costa Rica; (3) it occurred with a simultaneous reduction in U.S. contributions to multilateral agencies (e.g., Caribbean Development Bank) serving the region; and (4) the free trade proposals were never fully implemented due to opposition from U.S. labor unions and the Democratic-controlled Congress.

14

Problems and Prospects for the Survival of Liberal Democracy in the Anglophone Caribbean

Selwyn Ryan

The Anglophone Caribbean has been regarded by many as an exception to the generally held view that democracy has not been able to take root in the newly independent states of Africa, Asia, and Oceana. Whereas military intervention, coup d'états, and prolonged civil war have been the norm in most of Africa, Asia, and Latin America, these have been largely absent in the Anglophone Caribbean where, for the most part, power has been won or lost in the voting booths. Grenada (in 1979) was the first exception to this truth, but that event was seen to be so atypical that it literally traumatized the peoples of the region. These things were not supposed to happen in the calypso islands.

In July 1990, the myth of exceptionalism was again punctured, this time by a band of African Muslims who stormed into Trinidad's parliamentary chambers and its lone TV station, guns ablazing, and held the prime minister, seven cabinet ministers, and several other parliamentarians and communications workers hostage for six tension-filled days. There were many in Trinidad and Tobago, and in the region, who saw the events of July 27 through August 1 as an "aberration," something which was completely outside the Caribbean political tradition.

Caribbean political leaders were horrified at this development, which they saw as a threat to themselves, and in statement after statement, emphasized that political change in the Caribbean had to be effected through the time-tested method of the ballot as opposed to the bullet. As they told Prime Minister A. N. R. Robinson in a joint statement issued from the Caribbean Common Market (CARICOM)

An earlier version of this chapter appeared in *Caribbean Affairs* vol. 4, no. 1 (January–March): 43–60.

summit meeting in Kingston, "We deplore and roundly condemn the terrorist action in a collective expression of our deep concern for . . . the threat to democracy, stability and constitutional government, both in Trinidad and Tobago and within the rest of the community" (*Trinidad Guardian*, August 6, 1990). Jamaican prime minister Michael Manley saw the event as a "shameful blot on Caribbean history." Eugenia Charles, the prime minister of Dominica, angrily condemned the attempted coup as "nonsense." The prime minister of Barbados, Erskine Sandiford, for his part, declared that "Barbados supports democratic government, and where such governments are overthrown or threatened by illegal means, we will not support it" (ibid.). Charles Carter, minister of foreign affairs of the Bahamas, remarked that the armed uprising in Trinidad had "sent shock waves through the entire region, an area which is known as one of the finest examples of democratic institutions that exist in the world. . . . It was regrettable that its record could be spoilt by a small fringe militant group acting on its own and against the interest of the total society" (*Trinidad Guardian*, July 30, 1990). President Desmond Hoyte of Guyana, whose government has been widely accused of rigging elections and using force and fraud to stay in power, also joined in the chorus of condemnation. As Hoyte declared:

> The Government of Guyana unequivocally condemns as being completely unacceptable in Caricom the attempt to overthrow the Government of Trinidad and Tobago by force of arms and endorses completely the statement issued by Caricom Foreign Ministers in Jamaica denouncing the attempted coup. The Government of Guyana considers the attempted coup to be an undesirable departure from the traditions of constitutional government which is part and parcel of the political culture of the Commonwealth Caribbean. (*Trinidad Guardian*, July 30, 1990)

Cheddi Jagan, the Marxist-oriented leader of Guyana's leading opposition party, the Peoples Progressive Party (PPP), likewise went on record as opposing the actions of the Jamaat al Muslimeen. Jagan declared:

> Resort should have been had to institutional mechanisms, including free and fair elections, which Trinidad and Tobago enjoyed to deal with what appeared to be a crisis in the politics of accountability. Whatever might have been the gravity of the situation or the degree of provocation, the PPP finds unacceptable the methods employed to overthrow a legally elected government. (*Trinidad Guardian*, July 30, 1990)

Before assessing the general crisis currently facing democracy in the Caribbean, it may be worthwhile to first identify the factors which made that democracy appear to be unique in the ex-colonial world.

EXPLAINING CARIBBEAN EXCEPTIONALISM

Patterning After British Models

With the exception of Dominica, Guyana, and St. Vincent, the countries in the English-speaking Caribbean have no remaining indigenous populations of any significance. The ancestors of almost the entire contemporary population were "transplants" from Europe, Africa, Asia, or parts of the Americas, who were brought in various forms of servitude to work on European-controlled sugar plantations or in activities which serviced those plantations. With but few exceptions, particularly in Guyana and Trinidad and Tobago, to which large numbers of peoples from the Indian subcontinent were brought as indentured laborers between 1846 and 1917, the early arrivals were mainly of African provenience. This element has been progressively and systematically stripped of much of the core cultural values with which they came. They were deracinated and forced to accept the political value systems of the colonial elite. In time, force gave way to conscious emulation and mimicking. This they did with remarkable success. As Erna Brodber observes with respect to Africans in Jamaica:

> With the universal understanding that they had no alternative ethic, Africans intent on social mobility were more totally socialized into European ways than any group. The heirs in Jamaica of British culture, it is not surprising that educated blacks have carved out a place for themselves in the upper echelons of the university, the church and the civil service. (Brodber, 1989: 61)

Most Afro-Caribbean blacks patterned their political aspirations and practices on the Westminster model, in some cases becoming more slavishly British than the British. They, in fact, became "Afro-Saxons."[1]

The political culture of the Caribbean people was also formed by the traditions of the regionally loved game, cricket, which, unlike soccer, was a sport for English gentlemen. The rules of cricket, which stressed proper form and fair play, were assumed to apply to the pursuit of politics. There were certain things one simply did not contemplate, let alone do. Thus, if the criteria which are usually associated with Westminster-style democracy are used—a competitive party system, free and fair elections, the concept of a loyal opposition, a neutral bureaucracy, free-wheeling interest groups, a free press, recognition of the rule of law, and an independent judiciary—the countries of the English-speaking Caribbean would be found near the top of any comparative chart which ranks countries on a democratic-authoritarian continuum.

In terms of their political belief systems, most of the critical elites of the region hold fast to the view that notwithstanding its imperfections, the majoritarian British political model is superior to all others. With few exceptions, they firmly reject both the presidential system which exists in the United States and Latin America, and the consensual model which is the norm in most of Europe and which uses various forms of proportional representation. They have also not been attracted to the one-party models which were once the norm in most of Africa. Indeed, brainwashing about the superiority of the British system was thorough. What the St. Lucian-born, Nobel Prize-winning economist and political theorist, the late Sir Arthur Lewis, had to say about the leaders of the new states of Africa would have applied with greater force to Caribbean political elites. As Lewis noted:

> The new states would have fared better if they had not had to assume that British . . . ideas were superior to all others. . . . As it is, they will need much un-brain-washing before they grasp their problems in true perspective. (Lewis, 1965: 55)

These political values and predispositions were buttressed by the economic system which obtained in the years just prior to independence and which was carried over into the postindependence period. That system was patterned on the Fabian welfare state model inherited from the British Labour Party government in the post–World War II era. That system involved, inter alia, a close link between the trade union movement and the Labour Party. In most of the Caribbean countries, Trinidad and Tobago being the only exception, the leaders of the leading trade union movements became the political leaders of parties which led their countries to independence, full of promises as to what they would do by way of welfare for the masses when the political kingdom was won. The newly independent states thus became a vast dispensary of patronage in terms of jobs, houses, free secondary and university education, scholarships to go abroad for further study, improved health facilities, contracts, and much else that the masses believed were denied them under the colonial system. Labor accepted the logic of capitalist profitability in exchange for a sustained rise in living standards for their members, access to the corridors of power and influence, and the exercise of political rights.

Politics and Patronage

The political system thus became an arena in which rival political and trade union elites promised the "moon" and sought to outbid each other to dispense patronage to their followers. As Michael Manley well described it:

> In populist politics the moon is promised by the politicians, and democracy consists of making a choice between competing sets of promises which are dangled temptingly every four or five years. The system is the very

antithesis of a process of participation and mobilization. Nowhere is the person enlisted in the service of a national enterprise which is understood and believed to be worth great effort. In the end, therefore, the act of political choice involves, say, the casting of a vote which is not a commitment of the self to an activity. Instead, it is an act which expresses the expectation of a benefit, which will somehow come in spite of oneself, through the effort of a faceless authority known as the government. In due course, the expected package of benefits will be insufficiently realized. It will not occur to the voters that this may partly be the result of their own lack of involvement. However, it will be enough to guarantee that a rival set of promises will get the nod next time. (Manley, 1987: 268–269)

For the first decade after independence, the resources and opportunities available to most Caribbean states made it possible for populist-style democratic systems to be maintained. Given the worldwide expansion of trade and commerce, resources were available in the form of investment inflows into the tourist industry, into the mining enclaves of Trinidad and Tobago (oil) and Jamaica and Guyana (bauxite), in the banana industry in Jamaica and the Windward Islands, and for a while in the sugar industry. Investment in import-substituting industries also attracted both foreign and local investment which helped to provide jobs in the modern sector, which in turn helped to absorb some of the many who were leaving the rural areas in search of opportunity and betterment in the urban sector. Investors were induced to locate in the islands by generous tax holidays, import duty exemptions on plant and raw material, rapid depreciation allowances, the provision of factory shells at peppercorn rentals, subsidized utility rates and infrastructure, and protected domestic markets, as well as assistance in marketing traditional products internationally and regionally. Both labor and capital were thus part of the patronage system. This populist/corporatist formula formed an essential pillar of the democratic system.

The ability of the state, and by extension the political parties controlling the state, to service its clientele was greatly assisted by inflows from various metropolitan countries in the form of aid, price supports, and preferential access for sensitive labor-intensive commodities such as sugar and bananas. The recruitment of farm and domestic labor by the United States and Canada, and the massive migration to Britain in the 1950s and 1960s, and to the United States and Canada in the 1970s and 1980s, also helped to sustain the system. Migration helped to drain much of the potential belligerence that might have exploded in the system if escape was not possible. Migration also meant that remittances were available to sustain families who were left behind.[2]

The statist system was so structured that the elites of both labor and capital had a vested interest in its maintenance. Trade unions had something to offer their new members while capitalists accepted the welfare state as a sine qua non for the maintenance of social and industrial peace. The pattern, as it applied to Jamaica, was well expressed by Carl Stone in his essay "Power, Policy and Politics in Independent Jamaica":

> Both parties, the Jamaica Labour Party and the People National Party . . . had more features in common than differences over the period between the 1940s and the 1960s. What they share is a belief that the state should provide aid and welfare to the poorer classes through social policies and public spending programmes; a view that the state should provide overall economic policy leadership for the private sector and assume a central role in promoting economic development through state funded projects; a perception of the need for some state regulation of the economy in the national interest; a broadly held consensus that the state must provide social services for the citizens and economic services and infrastructure for those engaged in production through social reforms and legislation; and a common commitment to political patronage whereby scarce benefits that flow from government policies and expenditure (jobs, housing, contracts, etc.) are allocated to party supporters.
>
> To a large extent, this push toward wide ranging social policies designed to benefit the poorer classes was facilitated by the rapid growth and diversification of the Jamaican economy over the period between 1950 and 1970. This economic expansion provided the income base from which an enlarged role for the state in social and economic services to the poor could be financed. (Stone, 1989b: 21–22)

Much of what Stone has said in relation to Jamaica also applied to Barbados, St. Vincent, St. Lucia, and the other island states of the Caribbean. There were, however, subtle differences in Trinidad and Tobago and Guyana, where racial pluralism gave a different character to competitive party politics, and in Grenada and Antigua, where the leader of the mass parties (Eric Gairy in Grenada and the Bird family in Antigua) sought to construct personalist or familist regimes which subverted the formal constitutional mechanisms inherited from Westminster.

As Paget Henry writes of Antigua:

> The practice of clientelism was based on an exploitative privatization of public offices and the discriminatory use of their power and resources. Generally, positive resources such as jobs, recognition of civil rights, speedy services, protection of union rights, cheap access to land, etc., have been passed from these offices to supporters via the patronage machine. At the same time, negative resources such as the state's ability to repress, to fire, to deny civil rights, to weaken unions, etc., have passed to opponents through the victimization machine. The setting into motion of

these machines were the primary processes responsible for the structural ambiguities and authoritarian practices that characterized the Antiguan political system throughout this period. Practices such as party manipulation of the police, the judiciary and the civil service, the arbitrary denial of civil rights, the attempts to curtail the freedom of expression, to eliminate opposing parties and unions can all be related to the operating of these machines in the interest of holding on to state power. (1991: 26)

In the case of Trinidad and Tobago, the two main political parties drew their principal support from the African and East Indian communities, which were roughly equal in size. Race and not class constituted the principal political fault line in these societies. The Peoples National Movement (PNM) had its center of gravity in the African community and the Democratic Labour Party (DLP) in the East Indian community. While both parties remained firmly committed to the Westminster formula, the distribution of the population by area and the manner in which the electoral constituencies were demarcated helped the PNM to remain in power continuously from 1956 to 1986. In spite of the frustration which it experienced as a result of its failure to win power through the ballot box, the DLP and its successor, the United Labour Front (1976), nevertheless remained firmly committed to constitutionalism and the parliamentary process. The opposition nevertheless accused the PNM of using the resources of the state to guarantee the support of the Afro-Trinidadian community. Jobs, subsidized housing, scholarships, appointments to the civil service and other public sector organizations, and loans for business ventures were said to be given primarily to Afro-Trinidadians who came to regard the state as a compensatory instrument for communal advancement.

These allegations were challenged by the Afro-Trinidadian community, which denies that it was the principal beneficiary of state largesse, though it felt that it ought to have been, since the East Indian community and the European, Chinese, and Portuguese minorities were dominant in the private sector.[3] In the Afro-Trinidadian view, equilibrium in the society required that Africans be dominant in the bureaucratic and security sectors, since, if the economic dominance enjoyed by the East Indians were to be coupled with political and bureaucratic dominance, the stability of the system would be threatened. Blacks, it was said, would never accept displacement from the space which was "theirs" by prescription and might be tempted to resort to strategies which would destabilize the society.

The example of Guyana in the early 1960s was seen by many as a warning of the potential problems that could result from the concentration of political and economic power in the same hands. In Guyana, the Afro-Guyanese community, which constituted 31.3 percent of the population in 1970, was dominant in the bureaucratic and security establishments while the Indo-Guyanese, who constituted 50.2 percent, were dominant in agriculture and commerce. The East

Indian majority, concentrated as it was in the plantation sector (rice and sugar), was essentially a rural population while the African, European, mixed, and oriental elements were concentrated in the two urban centers of Georgetown and New Amsterdam.

The superimposition of the rural-urban dichotomy on the racial cleavage helped to intensify the intransigence of party politics in Guyana and to give it its peculiar quality. It meant that any government dominated by East Indians would be rurally based and would have to seek to maintain its power in the "jaws" of the African heartland, so to speak. The fact that the latter group, for historical reasons, was dominant in the public service and the protective services also meant that any government which had its power base in the Indo-Guyanese community would encounter resistance, if not outright sabotage, from Afro-Guyanese. Such a government would, in all likelihood, be considered illegitimate even if legal. This, in fact, happened to the PPP in the early 1960s. A similar difficulty emerged when the Peoples National Congress (PNC), a party which had its center of gravity in the Afro-Guyanese community, came to power in 1964. The PNC encountered resistance from the East Indian-dominated sugar industry, which produced a considerable proportion of Guyana's agricultural income and which provided a great deal of its commercial services.

The two major ethnic communities were thus in a position to inflict a great deal of political and economic damage on the national community, all of which made effective governance difficult. The Afro-Guyanese and the Portuguese fragments were apprehensive as to what would happen to them economically if the Indo-Guyanese were allowed to control the state apparatus. They felt that if the latter were "on top" they would not allocate resources fairly and that the Afro-Guyanese would be marginalized and displaced from areas which they controlled in the public sector. They were thus prepared to condone the unfair and unethical political strategies put in place to frustrate such a development. Assisted by the British and U.S. governments, which were concerned about the Marxist and Soviet connections of PPP leader Cheddi Jagan, the PNC and the Portuguese-based United Force (UF) endorsed a system of proportional representation, which was specifically engineered to deny the PPP the political power that it would have enjoyed if the first-past-the-post electoral system was used.[4]

Numerous reports have established that the leaders of the PNC used every political trick in the book—proxy voting, padded electoral lists, fraudulent overseas voting, violence and intimidation by the security forces, involvement of the army in the voting process—to maintain itself in power. The constitution and the judiciary were also manipulated toward this end. Nationalization of large sectors of the economy, including the foreign-owned sector, was also used to weaken the opposition and enlarge the quantum of resources available to the state for dispensation to the Afro-Guyanese community, to whom it was made clear that economic well-being and security was inextricably tied to the maintenance of the PNC in power. Given the economic collapse in Guyana, some Afro-Guyanese are beginning to question the wisdom of that choice. Many are of the view that contrary to what they expected, the paramountcy doctrine of the PNC only brought them greater impoverishment.[5]

Appearance and Reality

What the foregoing analyses indicate is that despite formal resemblance to Westminster or Schumpetarian canons of democracy, the political systems of the Anglophone Caribbean leave a great deal to be desired in terms of how they operated in the postindependence period, although they were considered exemplary models of democratic propriety. It is true that no political parties or pressure groups were outlawed or repressed; that elections were competitive and, with the exception of Guyana, largely free and fair; that no army ever seized formal power; and that expenditure on the military was infinitesimal by comparison to states in Latin America, Africa, and Asia. It is also true that the judiciary was never frontally intimidated or ignored, though one could cite cases where subtle pressures were brought to bear on judges in critical political cases.

Adherence to these institutional and procedural forms has, however, been ritualistic and concealed a reality that was quite different, a reality that was masked by artificial prosperity. Radical critics, in fact, point to several incidents or system features which give an entirely different picture of Caribbean democracy. There have been numerous examples of the ruling elites using vigorous repression when serious challenges were made to dislodge them from power in the interest of the broad masses. In the case of Jamaica, there were riots in 1959, 1963, 1965, 1968, and more recently in 1991. The riots in 1968, variously called the "Rodney riots" or the "black power riots," were regarded as system-threatening and harshly put down. Speaking of these incidents and the response of the establishment to them, Brodber opined that they were indications of the "continued disgruntlement of black people as a group despite constitutional changes." She remarked:

> Events leading up to the Rodney riots do suggest though that despite the location, the colour and the nationality of the new authorities, they were just as scared as the British had been of coalitions of black people. It is difficult to see the exclusion in the late 1960s of Malcolm X's autobiography and the works of Stokely Carmichael, and the very banning of Walter Rodney, in any other light. The post-Independence period therefore still saw the rulers afraid of the black masses and the latter angry and alienated. (1989: 62)

Brodber also noted that there has been a substantial increase in the incidence of social and political violence in recent years. In 1980, there were 889 deaths related to political gang warfare. Drug-related gang warfare had, in fact, become politicized. As she concluded:

> This behaviour is a direct outcome of the constitutional changes that occasioned the establishment of the political parties and the trade unions and brought to the mass of black people the notion that those who held power could be forced by combined action to share it. This concern with power-sharing and the use of violence as a strategy toward this end are not abnormal in a newly independent country. Jamaican political culture seems, however, to have remained unusually close to this option so that social violence now resides within the culture as planned action, as well as the spontaneous reaction it had formerly been. (ibid.)

Trinidad also saw many challenges to the political authority system in the postindependence period. In the 1965–1973 period, there were significant confrontations between the ruling party and radical trade unionists and intellectuals who, inspired by dependency theory, black power, Cuban communism, one or other of the varieties of socialism, or theories of guerilla warfare, challenged the system, forcing the authorities to respond with the full might of the legal and security apparatus. The most significant confrontation came between March and April 1970 when thousands of protesters, mainly black, marched up and down the island, shouting "black power" and "power to the people." The crisis also involved an army mutiny and an attempt by a Sandhurst-trained element of that army to march to Port of Spain to link up with the street protesters in an attempt to seize political power. Prior to July 27, 1990, the 1970 "black power" revolution was the gravest political crisis which Trinidad and Tobago had to face since the achievement of independence in 1962. Following a declaration of a state of emergency on April 21, 1970, hundreds of military and other radicals were detained and charged for treason and sedition. Draconian legislation was subsequently put on the statute books to deter future challenges to public order (Ryan, 1972).

The "black power" challenge was followed by an attempt on the part of idealistic youth to resort to guerilla strategies to destabilize the post-1970 "restoration" of PNM rule. Confrontations between the radical youth and the authorities led to the deaths of fifteen persons, three of whom were policemen. Many feared that constitutional government à la Westminster was in danger of collapse. The report of the government-appointed Constitution Commission captured the mood of the period very well. As it complained:

> the survival of constitutional and parliamentary politics is being challenged as never before in Trinidad and Tobago. Many believe that the institutionalized channels of constitutional politics no longer respond unless there is some dramatic gesture of confrontation such as a "sick out,"

a "go slow," a boycott or a march to Whitehall to see the Prime Minister. Some groups have called on citizens to consider withholding the payment of taxes. Secondary school children have begun to adopt strategies of confrontation and non-negotiable demands. Others have carried this belief into even more extreme action by resorting to armed confrontation. The society has painfully to adjust itself to stories of shoot-outs, killings and woundings, of early morning searches and of widespread public fear of victimization by one side or the other. There is danger that we may become insensitized by exposure to the human tragedy in the situation and accept this state of affairs as part of our political culture. Violence breeds violence. Violence or the fear of it invariably tends to make the citizen more receptive to strong police and military procedures. As the process of conflict escalates, traditional civilian, legal and constitutional procedures are short-circuited in favour of more "efficient" methods of law and order. Although all social change involves a measure of conflict, no democracy can long survive in the midst of unrestrained political violence. (*Report of the Constitution Commission*, 1974: 5)

The crisis of July 27, 1990 can in many respects be seen as a continuation of the 1970–1973 crisis, which in a sense had merely been "postponed" because of the OPEC crisis and the new oil wealth, which served to mop up the widespread discontent of the late 1960s and early 1970s.

CONTEMPORARY CHALLENGES TO CARIBBEAN DEMOCRACY

The Caribbean has always been an area characterized by political and economic crises of one sort or another. The region has been threatened by natural disasters (hurricanes, earthquakes, floods), by international strategic rivalries, economic dislocation consequent upon the collapse of external markets for its staples (sugar, citrus, cocoa, bananas, bauxite, petroleum), or the activities of political buccaneers whether operating from within the island communities or originating outside the region.

The question has often been asked as to why democracy has survived in the Anglophone Caribbean when it has failed in most developing nations in spite of the fact that the islands have had to face many of the crises that enfeeble democracy elsewhere. Carlene Edie, Jamaican author of the recently published *Democracy by Default: Dependency and Clientelism in Jamaica* (1991), argues that the key to the riddle lies in the manner in which the elites in the region have operated a regime of clientelism. Edie agrees that the notion that the political systems of the Anglophone Caribbean are tropical replicas of the Westminster model is fallacious.

Form and Substance

Edie argues that although the forms of democracy in the Caribbean resemble those in Western democracies, the substance is significantly different, subverted as it is by a host of internal and external socioeconomic and political factors. The crucial fact in these countries is the poverty of the masses and their need for basic resources that are the "gift" of the elites who manage the state. Given this need, the masses have become clients of parties which compete for control of the representative institutions of the political system and the state apparatus. A necessary condition for the flourishing of clientelism is the absence or the fragility of legal institutions which are supposed to guarantee individual security, status, and welfare. Where there is a reserve army outside the factory gate waiting to take jobs held by those inside, the role of politicians and power brokers who can intercede on behalf of the dispossessed becomes crucial. According to Edie, clientelism has two dimensions, domestic and international. In its domestic dimension, the links in the chain of dependence include leaders of political parties, nonelected power brokers in the party, municipal councillors, party activists who interface directly with the masses, managers of public sector institutions who have discretion as to whom to employ or what resources are to be dispensed to whom, and trade union leaders. As was indicated above, trade union leaders and their formal links with political leaders are crucial to the patron-client relationship in the English-speaking Caribbean.

Elites in the domestic private sector are also critical links in the clientelistic relationship. The native private sector needs state resources and protection to survive and prosper and knows that it has to give in order to get. It also has a vital interest in minimizing its tax liability. Self-interest, and not altruism or good corporate citizenship, thus provides the motive for the many tributes which it pays to political parties. The private sector also has a vested interest in the predictability of the environment in which it functions and above all in political order. One thus finds private sector firms paying bills for political parties at election time and in between elections as well. Clients themselves, they also function as patrons for major competing political parties in the region.

In Edie's view, the most crucial link in the clientelistic chain lies abroad since, in the final analysis, it is the metropole that is the real source of the sinews of political warfare. When resources from this arsenal are forthcoming in the form of either investment or aid, the indigenous elites find it easier to satisfy their own economic and political needs, and those of their clients.

Applying the analysis to Jamaica in the 1980s, Edie argues that both Reagan and Castro sought to function as international patrons. It was, however, an unequal battle:

> The resources Reagan transferred to Seaga were far greater than those
> Castro transferred to Manley. In return, both Manley and Seaga gave

ideological support to their patrons in the ideological battle between "imperialism" and "anti-imperialism" in the Western Hemisphere. The patron-client chain has become more complex, as the "super" patrons are now foreign, with no cultural ties to the local society. More of the resources of the domestic economy are now being siphoned off for international actors as well as for the ruling middle class and its allies, thus leaving even less for those at the bottom of the ladder. (Edie, 1991: 80)

Manley's defeat in 1980 was seen as a function of the PNP's inability to find the wherewithal to service its clientelistic relationship effectively. No patronage, no votes! Seaga in turn was defeated in 1989 because the IMF-driven free market policies which he sought to put in place reduced or eliminated the state resources required for clientelist patronage. Seaga's policies, which sought to compress the state, also led to a breakdown of the patronage relationship among the Jamaica Labour Party (JLP), the state, the private sector, and the middle and lower classes. Once the state lost its capacity for patronage, its dependent clients mobilized against it. Manley's decision to continue Seaga's policies after winning the 1989 elections created a crisis which contributed to the current delegitimization of the political system and to widespread cynicism and hopelessness.

However, Edie is of the view that "dual clientelism" served Jamaica well in terms of the role which it played in keeping the political and social system from flying apart. Whatever its defects, clientelism helped to lubricate the clashing gears of the social system. To borrow a phrase from the English analyst Walter Bagehot, it is clientelism and not the constitution that was the real "buckle" or "hyphen" which has successfully linked the various parts of the system together and which make it "work." In her view, the clientelist paradigm provides some insight into the question as to why Jamaican society hangs together at all, and why it does not suffer the sort of systemwide political upheavals which have been seen in Trinidad and Tobago.

Difficulties in Establishing Genuine Democracy

The system, however, fails in that it makes genuine economic development or democracy difficult. It divides the masses, who are coerced by their need to compete for scarce resources. This has made mass mobilization for developmental tasks difficult, if not impossible. It has also made it difficult for "correct" economic policies, whether socialist or liberal capitalist, to be pursued since the system is hostile to the sustenance of "economic markets." And, as Manley himself has agreed, the political formula fosters a tendency to emphasize consumption rather than production. Moreover, the system enables the middle classes and their international allies to neutralize the working class and their leaders, to maintain control over the political system, and to appropriate the lion's share of such material resources as are available. What has flourished in Jamaica, therefore, is not true democracy, but a bastard form. As Edie concludes:

> Jamaica boasts of having competing parties, an open news media, a free and impartial judicial system, and four and a half decades of continuous constitutional government. For these reasons, the democratic characterization of the party system has generally been accepted by students of Jamaican politics, despite the fact that substantial deviations from the requirements for democracy have been acknowledged.
>
> The myth is that there is a symbiosis between the formal institutions of democracy and democratic practice. The existence of political parties, frequent elections, and representative bodies does not guarantee representative government. Indeed, Jamaican democracy has been undermined because the formal democratic organizations have been transformed into an instrument of regimentation. This regimentation (disguised as democratic participation) legitimizes the political system and hides its true nature. The conditions have thus been created for domination by those in control of the formal "democratic" organizations. (1991: 47–48)

The competitive nature of clientelism in Jamaica has, however, prevented the emergence of one-party dominance and has allowed "democracy" to survive by default. In Edie's words, "Dual clientelism, which seems inherently authoritarian and is linked with such in most developing nations, has the opposite effect on Jamaica. In the Jamaican case, dual clientelism prevents authoritarianism by dispersing resources; democracy, as a result, survives by default" (ibid.: 7).

Edie's (1991) and Stone's (1980) applications of the clientelist model to Jamaica can be applied to the rest of the Anglophone Caribbean. The current economic crisis in the region is, however, serving to undermine the system. All the islands in the region are now experiencing a severe debt crisis. The need to repay mountains of debt imposes severe limits on the ability of treasuries to maintain adequate social services and essential infrastructure. According to Robert Pastor and Richard Fletcher (1991), Jamaica had to use 40 percent of its US$1.6 billion in export revenues in 1989 to service its debt. This burden has to be borne at a time when official aid and private investment inflows are at their lowest. Net external transfers to the Caribbean rose from US$542 million in 1978 to US$81,142 million in 1982. Thereafter it has fallen steadily, and in 1988 was of the order of US$15 million. Transfers from the United States fell from a high of US$353.5m in 1984 (in the aftermath of the intervention in Grenada) to a low of negative US$44.5 million in 1988 (Pastor and Fletcher, 1991: 108).

Given the constraints posed by the U.S. budget deficit; competing demands for funds to rehabilitate Panama, Nicaragua, and Eastern Europe; the need to combat the drug problem in Peru, Colombia, and other parts of Latin America;

and the new demands generated by the crisis in the Middle East, it is highly unlikely that the Caribbean region, once the recipient of some of the largest aid flows on a per capita basis in the developing world, will continue to be considered an area of priority for U.S. and European official assistance. The formal ending of the Cold War will also impact negatively on the predisposition of U.S. and European aid agencies to provide much by way of official transfers, which in the past went a long way to subsidize the expenses involved in funding the activities of many Caribbean states. The Caribbean is now not only economically insignificant. It has also become strategically insignificant.

Compounding this problem is the fact that prices for agricultural staples have been falling steadily at a time when, because of the power of lobbies, preferential access arrangements are either being reduced in scope or being eliminated altogether (sugar, bananas, etc.). Economic constraints and a slowing of growth in the developed world have also had negative consequences for agricultural commodities, minerals, and other goods which have hitherto found outlets in North America or Europe, to say nothing of the prices which they will fetch in such markets. These constraints have also reduced the flow of tourists, especially from North America, which is the principal "staple" for most of the islands of the Caribbean. If economic crises drive up interest rates, it will also impact negatively on the ability of Caribbean states to service their debt and finance their import needs. Should oil prices go up rather than down, the "scissors crisis" (continuous cuts throughout the society, e.g., laying off workers, cuts in imports, reducing energy use, etc.) will become much worse.

For strategic reasons, the United States introduced the Caribbean Basin Initiative (CBI) in 1983 and made it permanent in 1990. It is, however, now widely agreed that the CBI's impact has not been as significant as expected. As one recent study concluded:

> The U.S. International Trade Commission evaluated the program's effectiveness from 1983–88 and concluded that "overall, levels of new investment in beneficiary countries in the region remain disappointingly low." The CBI stimulated non-traditional exports and had a net positive impact on the economies of the region, but that impact was quite small. Two analysts estimated that the annual trade creation due to the CBI ranged from $164 million to $267 million, less than the annual cost of the simultaneous reduction in the region's sugar exports. (Pastor and Fletcher, 1991: 105–106)

That study also estimated that between 1982 and 1989, the countries of the Caribbean region as a whole lost about US$1.8 billion in potential revenue as a result of the crisis. The CBI hardly made a dent in the loss.

The economic threats facing the Caribbean are aggravated by a new threat, that posed by the international drug lords, who think nothing of corrupting official elites at the highest levels (ministers, police officers, magistrates, soldiers). These new buccaneers have shown that they are also willing to "purchase" countries or enclaves therein for use as transshipment points for "white gold." Antigua, Dominica, the Bahamas, the Turks and Caicos Islands, Jamaica, and Trinidad and Tobago have all been targets for their penetration. The activities of these new criminal elites not only debilitate the youth of the country and aggravate violent crime already seriously affected by the evaporation of economic opportunity, but delegitimize members of governments and officials in the protective services who are seen to be either soft on drug lords or suspected of being on their payroll.

Continued emigration of skilled manpower is also a severe constraint on development. According to one estimate, some 25 percent of the population of the English-speaking Caribbean now lives in the United States, Canada, and the United Kingdom. The loss of skilled and entrepreneurial manpower is said to exceed the positive effect of remittances, even when this assumes critical proportions as in Guyana, where "barrel" remittances now keep most families physically afloat.[6] U.S. and Canadian immigration laws, which make immigration easier for people with skills and investable capital, also aggravate the problem.

The key question of the 1990s, therefore, is whether Caribbean states, faced with the enormous weight of these burdens, will survive in any way which resembles what they looked like in the past three decades. Will liberal democracy survive the onslaught of these new horsemen of the apocalypse?

Many Caribbean political elites have expressed pessimism. Jamaican prime minister Michael Manley, in a reflective and somewhat pessimistic mood, indicated that he had now come to believe that social ethics had little to do with international economic relations and that survival was the principal concern of actors in the international political arena. He had come to believe that it was virtually pointless to appeal to the conscience of man. That was the environment of reality within which Caribbean decision makers must now function. Not to appreciate that was to live in a dream world. Manley also noted that in the modern world of the competitive global corporations, the national state as one knew it had become increasingly irrelevant. Caribbean policy makers, he insisted, now had to dismantle the "log jammed" state and replace it with a more "cost effective" alternative which emphasized decentralization and deregulation.

Manley, in fact, expressed concern as to whether or not competitive politics as one knew it in the Caribbean, with all its tribal dimensions and its commitment to party alternation after one or two terms, could survive in the new international economic environment, where it had becoming increasingly difficult for party elites to find revenues to keep their followers satisfied. The attempt to do so in the past by borrowing had led to many policy "errors" which served to mortgage future generations. In Manley's view, the politics of distribution had to give way to a new kind of politics which emphasized growth, a politics in which hard choices had to be made as to which groups would be fingered to generate that growth, and which groups would have to suffer as a result of those choices and strategic priorities.

The critical problem is whether the Caribbean masses, weaned as they have been on state-dispensed patronage, will accept choices which have been made as beneficial to their long-term interest, or whether they would opt for radical alternatives which continue to promise them the moon. The events of July 27, 1990 in Trinidad and Tobago provide some indication as to what could become the norm in the Caribbean. The age of innocence may indeed be over.

We might do well to end with the warning of the late Professor Gordon Lewis, given in an address delivered in Trinidad as early as 1984:

> What is the nature of that Caribbean world, as you my dear young brothers and sisters enter in for better or for worse? The world of your grandparents was shaped by the labour riots and the disturbances that swept throughout the area, including Puerto Rico, between 1934 and 1938. Your parents were shaped by the decade of independence of the 1960s, including the West Indies Federation. You, today, as the third generation, enter a new world which will be shaped irrevocably by the grim events of October 1983 in Grenada. It is a new world of new and accumulated violence.
>
> West Indians have always assumed that things like *coup d'etat, golpe de estado*, individual dictatorships, are only things that happened in Haiti or Cuba or Santo Domingo. Today Grenada tells us that it is different. The Gairy regime showed us that the Latin American habit of the caudillo could enter the English-Speaking Caribbean. March 1979 told us that the Latin American habit of the coup d'etat could enter the Commonwealth Caribbean. And October 1983 showed us that the habit of political assassination and organized mass murder as weapons of political advancement and the struggle for power can also in their turn enter the English-Speaking Caribbean. It is as if the age of West Indian innocence has finally passed away. (*Trinidad Express*, August 18, 1991)

NOTES

1. The term was first used, or at least popularized, by Lloyd Best, who used it somewhat derisively to describe older black Caribbean elites who were firmly wedded to Victorian value systems.

2. Jamaicans and other West Indians were moving in large numbers to the United States, Cuba, Panama, Venezuela, Aruba, and Curacao before the major trek to the United Kingdom and Canada began in the 1960s and 1970s. In 1986, 20,000 immigrant visas were granted to Jamaicans seeking to enter the United States.

3. Afro-Trinidadians believe that East Indians benefited more from PNM rule than did Africans. In a survey conducted by the author in 1989, fifty-five percent of the Indians

interviewed felt Africans had greater access to job and promotional opportunities in the public sector while 10 percent felt Indians had better opportunities. Forty-six percent of the Africans felt that Indians had better opportunities while only 12 percent felt Africans were the principal beneficiaries. Cf. my "Social Stratification in Trinidad and Tobago" in *Social and Occupational Stratification in Trinidad and Tobago*, ed. Selwyn Ryan (St. Augustine, Trinidad: Institute of Social and Economic Research (ISER), University of the West Indies, 1991): 65–66.

4. Cf. my forthcoming "Structural Adjustment and the Ethnic Factor in Trinidad and Guyana," chapter prepared for forthcoming book being published on behalf of the World Peace Foundation. Cf. also Caribbean Conference of Churches, *Official Report of a Goodwill and Fact Finding Mission to Guyana* (September 30–October 5, 1990).

5. Many Afro-Guyanese now feel that with the collapse of the state sector and the renewed emphasis being given to the private sector they have and will become progressively poorer than the Indo-Guyanese, who have a head start in trade and can also feed themselves. As the executive secretary of the Federation of Independent Trade Unions of Guyana remarked in a discussion of Guyana's Economic Recovery Program (ERP):

> The Afro-Guyanese, in the main, has emerged basically as a wage and salary earner. The Indo-Guyanese, on the other hand, gravitated to the land and later to commerce and manufacture. It is here that the ERP is fraught with danger. The entire program is premised on wage restraint and the determination of prices by the market forces. It follows, therefore, that it is the Afro-Guyanese that will be making most of the sacrifices and receiving the least of the gains . . . the unequal distribution of the benefits that is sure to follow . . . is of serious concern to the Federation for which I speak. (Seminar, University of Guyana, August 1989)

6. Barrels full of goods are sent to Guyanese by their families in North America and the Caribbean. The value of the contents of these barrels invariably exceeds the monthly wages of most Guyanese, making it unnecessary for them to work. Some of the goods are consumed while some are sold.

15

Parties and Electoral Competition in the Anglophone Caribbean, 1944–1991: Challenges to Democratic Theory

Patrick Emmanuel

The Anglophone Caribbean has had a long experience of open competition for the election of representatives to their parliaments. This experience began in Jamaica in 1944, when the first general elections under universal, adult franchise were held. Trinidad and Tobago followed in 1946, the Windward Islands (Grenada, St. Lucia, St. Vincent, and Dominica), Barbados, and Antigua in 1951, and soon thereafter, St. Kitts-Nevis-Anguilla and Montserrat in 1952.

This chapter concentrates on the electoral experience of these ten countries, where between 1944 and 1991, there have been 101 general elections. The electoral systems of these countries are all based on the first-past-the-post (FPP) method. Each country is divided up into a number of constituencies and electors cast a vote for one of a slate of candidates, the winner being the candidate receiving the largest number, majority, or plurality of the votes. In the region as a whole, Guyana is the only country in which a system of proportional representation (PR) is in place. Another noteworthy electoral innovation has been the lowering of the minimum qualifying age for voting, from the original twenty-one years to eighteen years. This widening of the electorate has been effected in all countries, mostly during the 1970s. The fundamentals of the electoral systems are outlined in the constitutions of all the countries, including machinery for periodic review and alteration of the numbers and boundaries of constituencies, and the conduct of elections. Over time constituency numbers have been enlarged; the present numbers are reflected in Appendix, Table 7.

The focus of this chapter is on the dynamics of party competition in the electoral arena. The notion and reality of "party" as an instrument of politics had existed in the Caribbean from the 1920s. In this early period, possession of the vote was circumscribed by high property and income qualifications, and the vast majority of the populations were kept outside the orbit of the formal political system. Thus, a fundamental aim of the earliest political parties was the abolition of franchise restrictions and the introduction of full adult franchise.

TRADE UNIONS AND MASS PARTIES

However, the actual basis of the first mass parties was the emerging trade union movement. The legal right to form trade unions had been won several years prior to the right to vote. The harshness of material life being, as always, the most pressing concern, trade unions and trade union leaders became the primary champions of the disfranchised. When the franchise was universalized, trade union leaders fashioned the first major parties as political committees of their unions. It was these organizations, led by Alexander Bustamante in Jamaica, Eric Gairy in Grenada, Vere Bird in Antigua, Robert Bradshaw in St. Kitts, William Henry Bramble in Montserrat, E. T. Joshua in St. Vincent, and Grantley Adams in Barbados, which then dominated in the first general elections.

The differentiation of party systems, involving the creation and success of alternative groupings, took place at different stages from country to country. Jamaica is the most mature case, as its two successful parties were formed prior to the first general elections in 1944. In all the other countries, except Dominica and Trinidad and Tobago, there was only one major party in place at the time of the first elections, with alternatives being created subsequently. For a time, independent candidates provided the major opposition to single effective parties, often with notable success. However, as viable alternative parties emerged, independents waned and are a comparative rarity in the present circumstances. In Trinidad and Tobago, a major mass party, the Peoples National Movement (PNM), was formed in 1955, nine years after the first elections, and in Dominica, the Dominica Labour Party (DLP), the first successful party, first contested in 1961, ten years after adult suffrage was introduced there. As the regional data will show, there are twenty-four parties which have won elections in the ten countries combined, but there are significant differences between countries in the members of individual successes and the patterns of alternation.

The approach of this chapter is decidedly empirical and comparative. Caribbean political science has long been characterized by sweeping theoretical and ideological generalization often devoid of empirical referents. In economic, social, and political terms, the region is assumed to be homogeneous, to the point that individuality is either unknown or ignored. The consequence is that comparative political science scarcely exists in and about the region. An easy, and unfounded, assumption of uniformity has resulted in the underdevelopment of comparative empiricism, analysis, and theory construction. Thus, political theory is the poorer for this, and this essay is offered as a step toward correcting this unfortunate mistake.

PARTIES AND PARTY SYSTEMS

The data presented on the distribution of votes and seats over time in the several countries constitute the basis on which an effort can be made to identify "systemic" characteristics of the structure and dynamics of electoral competition. This effort requires some elaboration of notions of "party" and "system" as they are applied here.

The term "party" refers to an association of people under a specific name whose primary purposes are the achievement and exercise of governmental power. In the Anglophone Caribbean, the established means for achieving power are success in regularly held elections. Typically, a political party is characterized by:

1. Leadership, of an individual or collective kind;
2. Structure or organization, which may combine features of charisma or rational-legality;
3. Ideology and programs as espoused from time to time;
4. Life-span or durability, in terms of the capacity to subsist or, alternatively, to disappear or be absorbed into a new or other existing organism;
5. Electoral performance, as measured by the numbers of elections contested, the numbers of candidates nominated, votes received, and seats won.

The record shows that the Caribbean experience encompasses stable macroparties of short duration and no success. Caribbean parties have also varied considerably with respect to the possession of personal and institutional charisma, levels of formal and informal organization, and the ideological bent of policies proclaimed and actualized.

In its stricter sense, the term "system" has been applied to refer to a stable pattern of interacting parts. More usually, however, its political science usage has taken in any set of actors and activities, stable or unstable, manifesting themselves in the political arena. In this study, my application of the term raises the following empirical questions:

1. At any point in time, how many competing actors (parties and independent candidates) are engaged?

2. Is there *alternation* in office among parties, that is, a pattern of success and defeat for specific major ties, or does change take place in an unpatterned fashion?

3. Over time, are there changes in the major actors, for example, by way of the demise of old parties and/or the formation of new ones?

The following paragraphs analyze the data on the basis of these relevant specifications and queries. Given the focus of the paper, no attention will be paid to quality of leadership or to organization, ideology, and program. The data concern 101 general elections in ten countries, contested by 133 parties and 2,911 candidates, including independents. The record shows that all the countries have had the experience of large, successful parties and of small, transient unsuccessful groupings (microparties). The total number of parties, large and small, that have contested in general elections in all the countries to date is revealed in Appendix, Table 8.

Most of these parties have really been tiny cliques which have put forward small numbers of candidates at one general election and disappeared shortly afterward. A few small parties lasted longer and were able to win seats and influence for a time. Ninety-one of the 101 elections were won by political parties, while in the remainder no party won a majority and postelection coalitions and realignments ensued. In all there are twenty-four successful parties, that is, parties which won elections and formed governments on one or more occasions. Appendix, Table 9 shows comparatively the sequence of party victories and coalitions for all ten countries.

There are five countries in which elections have been won only by political parties, that is, where there was no need for coalitions involving parties and/or independents. These are Jamaica, Barbados, St. Lucia, Antigua and Barbuda, and Montserrat. Of these five, there are four in which only two parties have won, the exception being Montserrat, in which four parties have been victorious. Appendix, Table 10 shows the frequency of party victories in these countries.

There are five other countries in which two or three parties have been successful, but in which on a few occasions no party had won and some form of postelection coalition was required. Appendix, Table 11 shows the frequency of party victories and coalitions in those countries.

Jamaica is a unique case in that at the time of its first elections (in 1944), both its major parties already existed and commenced a period of electoral competition, broken only once, in 1983, when the Peoples National Party (PNP) boycotted the elections. In Barbados, the Barbados Labour Party (BLP) first faced minor challenge from two small parties, the Electors' Association and Congress Party, until the DLP entered the fray in 1956. The Grenada United Labour Party (GULP) of Grenada faced no organized opposition until the Grenada National Party (GNP) began contesting elections in 1947. But GNP has been relatively unsuccessful with only one victory, in 1962, participation in a coalition (1957–1961), and a successful merger (NNP, 1984–1989). Since the breakup of that alliance, GNP has been renamed The National Party (TNP). In St. Lucia, the People's Progressive Party (PPP) provided fairly strong but unsuccessful opposition to the Labour Party, which won the first four elections. Major two-party competition really began in 1964 with the formation of the United Workers Party (UWP). In St. Kitts-Nevis, the Labour Party held sway from the beginning, against ineffective challenges from microparties and independents. But with the first challenge of the Peoples Action Movement (PAM) in 1966, the tide began a slow turn which brought about first a coalition defeat of Labour by PAM and the Nevis Reformation Party (NRP) in 1980, and subsequently PAM majorities in 1984 and 1989. Effective alternative party challenge came to Montserrat in 1970 after the Labour Party had won all five previous elections. The new Progressive Democratic Party (PDP) defeated the Montserrat Labour Party (MLP) in 1970, after which the old victor became defunct. The resulting party void was filled by the Peoples Liberation Movement (PLM), which contested first against PDP in 1978, and won two more elections until its defeat by the New Progressive Party (NPP) in 1991. Antigua and Barbuda's turn to experience a major challenge to the historically supreme Labour Party also took some time in coming. It was not realized until 1971, when the Progressive Labour Movement (PLM), formed in 1968, was able to mete out the first and so far only general election defeat suffered by the Labour Party. PLM, however, has since disappeared and a new challenger has appeared at the most recent elections in the form of the United National Democratic Party (UNDP).

In the above seven cases, there was at least one (in Jamaica, two) major party in place at the first general elections. All of these except the MLP continue to exist although at this time only two, Antigua's Labour Party and Jamaica's PNP, are in office.

In our remaining three cases, none of the parties which were to become successful existed on the occasion of the first general elections held. In the case of St. Vincent and the Grenadines, the first elections were won by a loose and short-lived grouping styled the Eighth Army of Liberation. However, by the second elections, in 1954, the Peoples Political Party (PPP) was formed, and won against independents. Then, by the third elections in 1957, the St. Vincent Labour Party (SVLP) entered. Elections between 1957 and 1972 were marked by competition between these two major parties, following which the PPP went into decline and has not contested since 1979. The new dominant party in St. Vincent and the Grenadines became the New Democratic Party (NDP), which first contested in 1979, and defeated the Labour Party in 1984 and 1989. St. Vincent and the Grenadines, and Montserrat, then, are the two countries in which former successful labor-based parties, PPP and MLP, have become defunct.

Trinidad and Tobago experienced its first major-party formation in 1955 when the People's National Movement (PNM) was created. Previously, several factions contended, with the Butler Party being the most successful. The PNM won all six elections between 1956 and 1981, gaining majority Afro-Trinidadian and Tobagonian support in a context of Afro-Indian pluralism. It was not until 1986, when efforts to forge an Afro-Indian alternative were successful, that the National Alliance for Reconstruction (NAR) dealt PNM its first and so far only electoral defeat. Since then, however, a section of the NAR led by Basdeo Panday, the former United Labour Party (ULF) leader, has broken away from the NAR and formed the United National Congress (UNC). Thus, at this juncture there appear to be three major-party forces in Trinidad and Tobago: NAR, PNM, and UNC.

Finally, at the other end of the scale of party formation, Dominica stands apart in that at the first elections there were no organized political groups in place. Thus, independent candidates held sway not only in 1951 but in the second and third elections, in 1954 and 1957 respectively. Efforts at party organization bore fruit after 1957 when the Dominica Labour Party came into being. The DLP won its first four contests, between 1961 and 1975, its principal opponents being first the Dominica United Peoples Party (DUPP) in 1961 and 1966 and then the Dominica Freedom Party (DFP), which began its electoral challenge in 1960. After two unsuccessful efforts, the DFP defeated the DLP in the last three elections: 1980, 1985, and 1990.

In the 1990 elections, however, there was a factor at work which portends the reorganization of Dominica's party system. The new United Workers' Party (UWP) replaced DLP as the major parliamentary opposition force, winning six seats to DLP's four. At present, there are three major players in Dominica's electoral arena: DFP, UWP, and DLP.

THE DEGREE OF ALTERNATION

The data show that in the ten states there have been variable sequences of alternation in office among the successful political parties. "Alternation" is typically used to denote a regularity of replacement in office among parties, especially two specific parties.

The record indicates that twenty-four parties have won elections, with another, Grenada's NDC, just short of success but able subsequently to form a government. The patterns of alternation and in several cases the absence of it are as follows:

1. Jamaica: Jamaica evinces a regular pattern of alternation with each of its two major parties, from the inception, enjoying two terms and then losing out to the other.

2. Barbados: Alternation in the case of Barbados is evident, but not as neatly so as is the case in Jamaica. The DLP won three terms (1961–1971) successively after the BLP's two at the beginning. Then,

however, BLP won two (1976–1981) followed by two more to the DLP (1986–1991).

3. St. Lucia: Regularity of alternation begins to weaken with the experience of St. Lucia, where four SLP terms were followed by three UWP, then one SLP, and recently three UWP. Of course, SLP-UWP rivalry began at the fifth general elections, held in 1964.

4. Grenada: There were two occasions on which GULP was unsuccessful in the eight elections between 1951 and 1976, that is, in 1956 and 1962. Since then the NNP party alliance and NDC have both triumphed over Labour.

5. Antigua and Barbuda: Here the pendulum has swung only once against the ALP, with the lone victory of PLM in 1971. For most of the time opposition parties in Antigua and Barbuda have varied, with PLM contesting only three elections with full slates of candidates in Antigua.

6. Montserrat, St. Vincent and the Grenadines, St. Kitts-Nevis, and Dominica: These four states are cases where instead of alternation strictly speaking, there has been a succession of winning parties, with previous incumbents unable thus far to regain office.

In Montserrat, five terms of the MLP were followed by two terms of PDP, and then three terms of PLM, which has recently been defeated by the new NPP. Similarly, in St. Vincent and the Grenadines, but for the PPP-Mitchell coalition of 1972–1974, the sequence has been PPP three terms, SVLP three terms, and NDP two terms. These are multiparty sequences, whereas St. Kitts-Nevis and Dominica are two-party affairs. In the former case, six terms of SKLP were followed by a PAM-NRP coalition and then two PAM victories. (The maintenance of the PAM-NRP coalition is necessitated by PAM's one-seat majority in both of the last two elections as well as the political requirements of a fragile federalist compact.) Dominica's pattern is one in which four DLP terms have been followed by three DFP successes. Trinidad and Tobago manifests a slightly different course of party success. There, following initial coalitions, six straight PNM victories have been followed by a recent success by the NAR party alliance. Future developments, as indeed in all other cases, are unforeseeable.

THE DISTRIBUTION OF VOTING LOYALTIES AND SEATS

An important feature of the political system in general and the party system in particular is the distribution of votes and seats going to parties and independents, over time. Douglas Rae (1971) distinguished an electoral party system in terms of the distribution of votes and a parliamentary party system as indicated by the distribution of seats won. Because of the absence of proportional representation, winning parties in the Caribbean have, except in a few cases, received higher percentages of seats than of votes. In some instances a party has won all the seats, but the losing groups have captured an appreciable share of the popular vote. Generally, the distribution of votes evidences a political pluralism which is not reflected in the allocation of seats. This structural characteristic has often led to calls for the introduction of some system of proportionality in Caribbean elections.

Appendix, Tables 12 to 21 show how votes and seats have actually been spread in the outcomes of the elections under scrutiny.

The dominance of the Antigua Labour Party (ALP) in Antigua and Barbuda in the early period is shown in the very high share of the votes it received. However, by the fifth elections, won by PLM, the winning-party share declined and then rose again, but not to the levels of the 1950s and 1960s. The strength of opposing parties has built up over the entire period. There were four occasions on which the winning party won all the seats, but there was also one, the sixth, in which the winner received fewer votes than the opposition combined (but mainly PLM) (see Appendix, Table 12).

Montserrat shows greater balance in the division of voting loyalties. Opposition candidates received a low of 30 percent, in the first elections, and on three occasions, in 1955, 1987, and 1991, have received more votes than the winning party. Winning-party support was highest in the first elections, and since then has fluctuated between 43 and 65 percent: there have been three occasions in which a party won all the seats, with opposition voting at 30, 35, and 38 percent successively (see Appendix, Table 13).

In St. Kitts-Nevis, the Labour Party's greatest triumph came in the first elections, when it received 85 percent of the votes. But its support fell sharply afterward, although 1961 and 1975 were good years. In the seventh elections (1980), when Labour first lost, PAM and NRP together polled 56 percent of the votes with Labour receiving the remainder (44%). There were three occasions on which the winning party polled less than 50 percent of the votes, Labour once and PAM twice. In the cases of PAM, the party, in an understanding with NRP, did not sponsor candidates in Nevis. And at the time of the coalition, the distribution of seats was PAM three, NRP two, and Labour four (see Appendix, Table 14).

Except for 1966 and 1985, winning-party vote share has never been particularly high in Dominica, and there have been three instances of winning parties receiving fewer votes than the combined opposition. In step with this, opposition strength has always been high, the lowest standing at 35 percent and surpassing 50 percent on three occasions. The usual disproportionality of vote and set shares obtains. In cases where more than one opposition group contests, the disproportion tends to be widest. But at no time have all seats in Dominica gone to one party (see Appendix, Table 15).

In Grenada shares of votes going to winning parties have been over 50 percent on all but one occasion: 1954. In 1957 three parties, GULP, GNP, and

PDM, won two seats each and independents won the other two. Then, in 1990, NDC won seven of the fifteen seats with 35 percent of the vote, while GULP won four, NNP two, and TNP two. Combined opposition voting has been high, with a low of 36 percent in 1951 and a high of 54 percent in 1954, the 1990 outcome being exceptional in that no party won a majority of seats. There was no instance in which a party won all the seats (see Appendix, Table 16).

St. Lucia's record is one of strong popular support for losing parties. Labour improved its standing in 1957 and 1961, after modest showings in the first two elections. But when serious two-party competition began with the entry of UWP from 1964, winning-party shares fluctuated between 52 and 58 percent. As is usually the case, there was the element of disproportionality in seats won, except for the results in 1987, when on both occasions there was exact correspondence of shares of votes and seats. An outstanding instance of disproportionality occurred in 1982 when PLP and SLP won one seat each with 27 percent and 17 percent of the vote respectively (see Appendix, Table 17).

In St. Vincent and the Grenadines, the Eighth Army of 1951 was not a really coherent party association on any reasonable minimal standard. The PPP was the first such party, but fell just short of a majority of the vote on the three occasions on which it won seat majorities, varying from 51 to 69 percent. Votes cast for other parties (and independents) have been at a high level in St. Vincent and the Grenadines. In two elections, when opposition vote share was 30 percent (1951) and more recently, 34 percent (1989), the winning party won all the seats (see Appendix, Table 18).

The experience in Barbados has been one in which winning-party support has been fluctuating over the forty-year period. The shares dropped after 1951, rose after 1961, declined again from 1976, then rose in 1986, and further declined in 1991. Between 1951 and 1966, it must be remembered, the electoral system involved dual membership and dual voting; but from 1971 it has been a system of single membership and single voting in each constituency. There have been three instances in which winning-party support has been at 50 percent or less. Opposition vote support has been high and so has been the share of seats, except in 1986 (see Appendix, Table 19).

In Jamaica, the winning party's vote share has been in the majority in all but three cases: 1944, 1949, and 1962. In 1983, the elections were boycotted by the PNP whereupon the Jamaica Labour Party (JLP) won all the seats (fifty-four seats unopposed and the remaining six in contests against minor interests), receiving 90 percent of the votes cast. Opposition strength has always been considerable, 1983 of course excepted. But, in elections of 1976, 1980, and 1989, the share of opposition seats has tended to be lower than previously (see Appendix, Table 20).

Between 1956 and 1986 when there were party victories in Trinidad and Tobago, there was one occasion (1956) in which the victor's support was below 50 percent of the votes cast. The case of 1971, like Jamaica's 1983 elections, was one in which other major parties boycotted. PNM won eight seats unopposed and twenty-eight against minor competition. With the exception of 1971, opposition voting has been considerable, and so have been opposition seat victories, with the additional exception of 1986 (see Appendix, Table 21).

When the data are looked at regionally the following findings are noticed. There are twelve occasions on which a party won all the seats, this outcome occurring in six of the ten countries. It has happened four times in Antigua and Barbuda, three times in Montserrat, twice in St. Vincent and the Grenadines, and once each in St. Kitts-Nevis, Jamaica, and Trinidad and Tobago. Second, the factor of disproportionality between vote and seat shares was most acutely manifested on twenty-four occasions when the party winning a majority of the seats received 50 percent or less of the total votes. This represents 24 percent of the 101 general elections. The apparent unfairness of this disproportionality must be considered in light of the fact that winning parties, and losing ones as well, did not always contest all seats in general elections. Since party percentage of vote is calculated on the basis of total votes in all constituencies instead of votes cast in contested constituencies, it follows that percentage shares are lower. Consider the recent experience in St. Kitts-Nevis. The Peoples Action Movement won six of the eleven seats, in both 1984 and 1989, and its share of total votes is recorded as 48 percent and 44 percent respectively. However, PAM on both occasions did not contest the seats in Nevis and its share of votes cast in St. Kitts only is 53 percent in both 1984 and 1989. Other factors which may also be featured in these situations are variations in the sizes of constituencies, and the presence of effective third parties as occurred in Dominica and Grenada in 1990.

SCHISM, REALIGNMENT, AND ALTERNATIVE PARTIES

A final aspect of the experience of the instrument of party in the region is the occurrence of intra-party schisms and the consequences in resignations or defections and the formation of alternative political parties. In a number of cases these alternative parties have been quite successful, being able to defeat the older parties out of which new leadership had come. More generally, several candidates contesting more than once have stood for more than one party, including some who also ran as independents. Apart from the experience of successful alternative parties born of defections from older parties, there are also several instances of permutation among a host of unsuccessful politicians appearing in a variety of party sobriquets. The most successful examples of alternative parties formed directly as a result of splits within older parties are the DLP of Barbados and the UWP of St. Lucia. The DLP of Barbados was launched mainly by former members of the older Barbados Labour Party (BLP), including Errol Barrow, later prime minister, J. E. Theodore Brancker, A. E. S. Lewis, J. Cameron Tudor, and Frederick Smith. The new DLP also included Wynter Crawford, subsequently deputy prime minister, who had been the founder-leader of the Congress Party. Among other persons who later joined the DLP were Frank Walcott, the trade union leader, and former Conservative Party figures E. L. Carmichael and W. R. Coward. The new party soon proved its mettle; while winning only four seats in its first electoral contest in 1956, it went on to win majorities in five of the next seven elections—in 1961, 1966, 1971, 1986, and 1991.

St. Lucia's UWP has a somewhat similar provenience. The party was formed by a combination of political figures leaving the Labour Party, with members of the previously ineffective PPP. Actually, at first John Compton and a group of former SLP members had formed a National Labour Movement (NLM) in 1961, which subsequently merged with PPP figures to form the UWP in 1964. The major persons involved in the early UWP were John Compton, Maurice Mason, Vincent Monrose, and the Bousquet brothers from the Labour Party, and George Mallet, Michael DuBoulay, Hunter Francois, and Henry Giraudy from the PPP. The UWP has been very successful electorally, having won five of the six elections held between 1964 and 1987.

A third successful alternative party whose formation is linked to defection and realignment is the New Democratic Party (NDP) of St. Vincent and the Grenadines. The NDP was founded by James Mitchell, a former member of the country's Labour Party and minister of government. Mitchell had left Labour, for which he had won the Grenadines seat in 1966 and 1967, running successfully as an independent in 1972. He then took the opportunity to become premier by allying with the PPP, which, like Labour, had won six seats in the 1972 elections. Then when the coalition (Mitchell-PPP) collapsed by 1974, he headed a loose alliance of candidates in the elections of that year, but was the only one victorious. The NDP was formed after the 1974 elections and began its challenge in 1979, when it won two seats. Since then this new party won the elections of 1984 (with nine of the fifteen seats) and 1989 with all fifteen seats. Most of the party's candidates have been new to elections, but it has sponsored candidates originally aligned with PPP (Victor Cuffy and Emory Robertson), United People's Movement (Parnell Campbell and Carlyle Dougan), and Democratic Freedom Movement (E. W. Griffith).

In Antigua and Barbuda, the only party thus far to have defeated the Labour Party has been the PLM, which was a creation of defectors from the ALP, in alliance with opposition interests, unsuccessful up to then, and subsequently. The principal ALP defectors included George Walter, at the time senior official of the ALP's trade union, the Antigua Trades and Labour Union (ATLU), Donald Halstead, Sydney Prince, and Keithlyn Smith. The alliance embraced Robert Hall and other members of the Antigua-Barbuda Democratic Movement (ABDM), and there were also involved other emerging political figures who had not yet been strongly aligned party-wise. The PLM defeated the ALP in 1971, having first shown its promise by winning four seats in a special election in 1968. In 1976, PLM received more votes than Labour but won only five of the seventeen seats, Labour taking eleven and the other taken by an independent (in Barbuda). After that the party waned and broke up, clearing the way for a new round of ALP predominance.

Montserrat's PDP and PLM are the fifth and sixth examples of successful alternative parties whose leadership derived from an established dominant party. The PDP was formed by Austin Bramble, son of William Bramble, leader of the MLP and chief minister. Austin Bramble was a member of the MLP and had won a seat in 1966 on that party's ticket. Joining him in the PDP were former MLP candidates Eustace Dyer and R. G. Joseph, and John Osborne, who was previously leader of the Montserrat Workers Progressive Party (MWPP) and would later form the PLM to defeat the PDP in the last three general elections (1978, 1983, 1987). The PDP won general elections twice, in 1970 and 1973, but since then the next three elections, as seen, were won by PLM, whose leader was previously a PDP candidate. John Dublin was a former PDP winner (1970) who lost as an independent in 1973 and then won for PLM in 1978 and 1983.

The NAR, the only group to have defeated the PNM in Trinidad and Tobago was, as its name indicates, an amalgamation of leaders and senior members of four parties: the Democratic Action Congress (DAC) led by A. N. R. Robinson, the United Labour Front (ULF) headed by Basdeo Panday, the Organization for National Reconstruction (ONR) led by Karl Hudson-Phillips, and the Tapia House Movement (THM) whose leader, Lloyd Best, did not take part in the eventual NAR amalgamation. Robinson, who was selected as NAR leader, was formerly a senior member of the PNM who resigned in 1970, first forming the ACDC (Action Committee of Dedicated Citizens) and later the DAC. Hudson-Phillips was also a senior PNM parliamentarian, who, later than Robinson, also left the PNM and founded ONR. He was appointed one of two deputy leaders of NAR. The other was Panday, who began his electoral career as a candidate of the Workers and Farmers Party (WFP) in 1966 and afterward formed the ULF. The THM had itself contested the 1976 elections separately and in 1981 took part in a loose three-party alliance with DAC and ULF. On that occasion ONR declined alliance and contested on its own.

Apart from Robinson and Panday, other NAR candidates who had contested on different platforms previously were Jennifer Johnson and Pamela Nicholson from DAC; Winston Dookeran, Emmanuel Hosein, John Humphrey, Nizam Mohammed, Kelvin Ramnath, and Trevor Sudama from ULF; Theodore Guerra, Oswald Hem Lee, and Anselm St. George of ONR; and Gloria Henry, Lincoln Myers, and Bhoe Tewarie of Tapia. The NAR's remaining twenty candidates in 1986 were first-timers.

In Grenada there have been four parties which have formed governments in the wake of general elections: GULP, GNP, NNP, and NDC. The GULP is the country's oldest party and the only one to have contested all general elections held between 1951 and 1990. It has always been under the leadership of Eric Gairy. Several politicians over time have defected from GULP but none have become leaders of successful parties. The Grenada National Party, in consequence of its lack of long-term effectiveness against its archrival, GULP, entered into a People's Alliance with the New Jewel Movement (NJM) in the elections of 1976. But the NJM leader Maurice Bishop emerged as opposition leader instead of GNP's Herbert Blaize when the alliance won six of the fifteen seats in those elections. Then in 1984 GNP merged with two new parties, the Grenada Democratic Movement led by Dr. Francis Alexis and the National Democratic Party headed by George Brizan, to form the New National party under Blaize's leadership. Although NNP won the 1984 elections, the party split progressively during its term of office into three groups: first, NDC with Brizan as leader and then Nicholas Brathwaite, The National Party led first by Blaize and then by Ben Jones, and a reduced NNP now led by Dr. Keith Mitchell.

Thus, in the regrouping which occurred prior to the 1990 general elections, the following realignments took place:

1. NDC: five former NNP candidates were now aligned with this party: Alexis, Brizan, Phinsley St. Louis, Kenny Lalsingh, and Tillman Thomas.

2. TNP: from the NNP, this party brought Jones (leader), George McGuire, Pauline Andrew, Alleyne Walker, and Felix Alexander. But it also recruited two former GULP candidates, Michael Caesar and Marcel Peters.

3. NNP: the reconstituted NNP included from among the ranks of the original NNP Mitchell (leader) and Grace Duncan, as well as Winston Whyte, formerly of GULP, UPP, and CDLP, and Winston Fleary, an independent in 1984.

4. GULP: in 1990 GULP's slate of candidates included Dr. Wellington Friday, former senior member of GNP.

Realignment of politicians in Grenada has not been as successful in producing both stable and victorious alternative parties as has been the case in the six countries discussed previously. While the hitherto dominant GULP has been defeated in the last two general elections, the alliances that have done so have been characterized by instability. The NNP of 1984 won fourteen of the fifteen parliamentary seats, but rapidly came apart. In the follow-up, the realignments of 1990 were such as in fact to prevent any party from winning a majority of seats, the outcome being NDC with seven seats, GULP rebounding with four, and two each to NNP and TNP. After the elections realignment has continued. Two GULP parliamentarians sided with NDC, and the two TNP winners also declared support for an NDC-led government; but the TNP leader has since opted out of this arrangement and returned to the opposition benches. Meanwhile, a third GULP representative and one of the NNP's have resigned from their respective parties and sit as independents. On the face of it, therefore, Grenada's parliament at the time of writing is made up of seven NDC representatives supported by two from GULP and one from TNP, making up the government majority, and, in opposition, GULP, NNP, and TNP, one each plus two independents.

In the remaining three states, Dominica, Jamaica, and St. Kitts-Nevis, there has been comparatively little traffic among candidates of major parties, and no case of a successful party being formed on the basis of defection of a leader or leaders from a previously existing major party. The Dominica Freedom Party has sponsored two former Labour Party candidates, Eden Durand and Pat Stevens, while Labour has in turn sponsored Henry Dyer, previously a DFP candidate. Additionally, the new main opposition party, UWP, has incorporated two former Labour candidates in Romanus Bannis and Thomas Etienne. Jamaica's two powerful party rivals, JLP and PNP, have also had little trading of candidates, but most of the little movement that has taken place has been away from the JLP to PNP: B. B. Coke, Edward Fagan, Rose Leon, O. A. Malcolm, and Dr. Winston Williams. In return the record shows only one candidate, Victor Bailey, as having run for PNP and subsequently for JLP. Finally, in the case of St. Kitts-Nevis, the stability of candidacy among major parties has been high as only three candidates have passed among them: Ivan DeGrasse from Labour to PAM, Frederick Parris from PAM to Labour, and Ivor Stevens from PAM to its coalition partner, NRP.

The above discussion has focused on the transit of candidates between major parties only. But it must be recorded that there were several instances of realignment, occurring in a number of ways: independents joining minor or major parties, minor party candidates joining major parties, as well as the reverse of these movements. With some 133 parties having been created in the milieu of ten countries, realignment helped to adjust the relation between supply and demand for electoral candidates. More significantly, realignment, evidencing freedom of association and dissociation, facilitated flexible responses from the party system in diversifying the offerings of leadership and sometimes of program available to Caribbean electorates.

Appendix: Tables

Table 1
Population Census, 1970 (Guyana)

Group	Size	%
East Indians	377,256	51.0
Africans	277,091	30.7
Amerindians	32,794	4.4
Portuguese	9,688	1.3
British	3,976	0.5
Chinese	4,674	0.6
Mixed Races	84,077	11.4
Total	708,636	100.0

Source: Guyana Population Census, 1970.

Table 2
Percentage Support for Parties in Terms of Votes Cast and Percentage Turnout, 1951–1991 (Barbados)

Year	BLP	DLP	Others	Percentage Turnout
1951	53.3	—	46.5	64.6
1956	49.3	19.9	30.8	60.3
1961	36.8	36.3	26.9	61.3
1966	32.6	49.5	17.9	79.3
1971	42.4	57.4	0.2	81.6
1976	52.7	46.4	1.0	73.5
1981	52.2	47.1	0.7	71.6
1986	40.4	59.4	0.2	71.6
1991	43.0	49.8	7.2*	63.0

* Includes votes for the NDP (6.8%)

Source: Duncan, et al. (1978); Emmanuel (1979); Barbados Supervisor of Elections Reports.

Table 3
Representative Government in Grenada, 1837–1950

Year	Population	No. Eligible Voters	% Voting	No. Reps.
1850	7,952*	—	—	—
1856	32,671	229	155	—
1862	—	655	482	—
1869	—	506	512	—
1876	37,684	575	265	8*
1925	66,302	—	—	—
1950	—	—	—	—

* Male population eligible to vote

Source: Compiled from Brizan (1983).

Table 4
Daily Wages in Grenada, 1838–1978

Year	Principal 1: Men	Principal 2: Women, Elderly, Children
1838	0.12	0.08
1938	0.30	0.28
1940	0.34	0.28
1947	0.72	0.60
1950	0.82	0.68
1951–1952	1.20	1.00
1959	1.56	1.40
1974	4.00	3.00
1978	6.80	5.80*
1979	—	—

* Wage changes should be considered against the following: (1) generally, these were subsistence level wages, given that labor was plentiful and unemployment constantly high; (2) in some cases wages kept pace with inflation and the cost of living, in other cases they did not. Consider the following: in the period 1939–1959, the consumer price index rose by 200%; but agricultural workers' wages rose by 360% and 400%, reflecting a rise in real income of 160% and 200% respectively (Brizan, 1983: 271).

Source: Antoine (1984) as cited in Oakes (1988: 137); Brizan (1983)

Table 5
Wage Increases for Agricultural Workers, 1981–1986 (Grenada)

Year	Principal 1: Men	Principal 2: Women, Elderly, Children
1981	8.50	7.50
1983	—	—
1985	10.50	9.50
1986	13.00	12.50

Source: Wage Table, Department of Labour, Government of Grenada, 1989.

Table 6
Budget Deficit and Foreign Exchange Reserves (in m/n Surinamese Guilders)

Year	1980	1988	1990	1991*
Budget Deficit	26.4	495.0	206.0	361.0*
Foreign Exchange Reserves	383.4	15.8	65.0	57.0

* First half of the year

Source: Ministry of Finance.

Table 7
Number of Constituencies, 1991

Country	Constituencies
Jamaica	60
Trinidad and Tobago	36
Barbados	28
Dominica	21
Antigua	17
St. Lucia	17
Grenada	15
St. Vincent	15
St. Kitts-Nevis	11
Montserrat	7

Source: Compiled by Patrick Emmanuel.

Table 8
Number of Political Parties Contesting General Elections

Country	No. of Large and Small Parties
Antigua and Barbuda (1951–1989)	13
Montserrat (1952–1991)	9
St. Kitts-Nevis (1952–1989)	10
Dominica (1951–1990)	12
Grenada (1951–1990)	8
St. Lucia (1951–1990)	4
St. Vincent and the Grenadines (1951–1989)	11
Barbados (1951–1991)	8
Jamaica (1944–1989)	22
Trinidad and Tobago (1946–1986, 1991)	36
Total	133

Source: Compiled by Patrick Emmanuel.

Table 9

Anglophone Caribbean Sequence of Winning Parties

Election	Jamaica*	Barbados	St. Lucia*	Antigua & Barbuda	Trinidad & Tobago	Dominica	St. Kitts-Nevis	St. Vincent & the Grenadines	Grenada	Montserrat
1st	JLP	BLP	SLP	ALP	Coalition	Inds.	SKLP	Eighth Army	GULP	MLP
2nd	JLP	BLP	SLP	ALP	Coalition	Inds.	SKLP	Inds.	GULP	MLP
3rd	PNP	DLP	SLP	ALP	PNM	Inds.	SKLP	PPP	Coalition	MLP
4th	PNP	DLP	SLP	ALP	PNM	DLP	SKLP	PPP	GULP	MLP
5th	JLP	DLP	UWP	PLM	PNM	DLP	SKLP	PPP	GNP	MLP
6th	JLP	BLP	UWP	ALP	PNM	DLP	SKLP	SVLP	GULP	PDP
7th	PNP	BLP	UWP	ALP	PNM	DLP	SKLP	Coalition	GULP	PDP
8th	PNP	DLP	SLP	ALP	PNM	DFP	PAM	SVLP	GULP	PLM
9th	JLP	DLP	UWP	ALP	NAR	DFP	PAM	SVLP	NNP	PLM
10th	JLP	—	UWP	—	PNM	DFP	PAM	NDP	Coalition	PLM
11th	PNP	—	UWP	—	—	DFP	PAM	NDP	—	NPP
No. of Parties	2	2	2	2	2	2	2	3	3	4

* Recent victories by the PNP (Jamaica) and the UWP (St. Lucia) are not recorded in this table.

Source: Compiled by Patrick Emmanuel.

Table 10
Frequency of Party Victories

Country	Party	No. of Wins
Jamaica* (1944–1989)	JLP	6
	PNP	5
Barbados (1951–1991)	BLP	4
	DLP	5
St. Lucia* (1951–1987)	SLP	5
	UWP	6
Antigua and Barbuda	ALP	8
(1951–1989)	PLM	1
Montserrat (1952–1991)	MLP	5
	PDP	2
	PLM	3
	NPP	1

* Recent victories by the PNP (Jamaica) and the UWP (St. Lucia) are not recorded in this table.
Source: Compiled by Patrick Emmanuel.

Table 11
Frequency of Party Victories and Coalitions

Country	Party	No. of Victories	No. of Coalitions
Trinidad and Tobago	PNM	7	2
(1946–1991)	NAR	1	
St. Kitts-Nevis	SKLP	6	1
(1952–1989)	PAM	1	
Dominica (1951–1990)	DLP	4	3
	DFP	3	
Grenada (1951–1990)	GULP	6	2
	GNP	1	
	NNP	1	
St. Vincent (1951–1989)	PPP	3	2
	SVLP	3	
	NDP	2	

Source: Compiled by Patrick Emmanuel.

Table 12

Antigua and Barbuda: Distribution of Votes and Seats in General Elections

Election Year	Winning Party			Other Parties/Individuals Opposition Groups	
	Party	% Vote	% Seats	% Vote	% Seats
1951	ALP	87	100	13	0
1956	ALP	87	100	13	0
1961	ALP	85	100	15	0
1965	ALP	n.a.	100	n.a.	0
1971	PLM	58	77	42	23
1976	ALP	49	65	51	35
1980	ALP	58	77	42	23
1984	ALP	68	94	32	6
1989	ALP	64	88	36	12

Source: Compiled by Patrick Emmanuel.

Table 13

Montserrat: Distribution of Votes and Seats in General Elections

Election Year	Winning Party			Other Parties/Individuals Opposition Groups	
	Party	% Vote	% Seats	% Vote	% Seats
1952	MLP	70	100	30	0
1955	MLP	47	60	53	40
1958	MLP	56	60	44	40
1961	MLP	58	71	42	29
1966	MLP	61	71	39	29
1970	PDP	65	100	35	0
1973	PDP	65	71	35	29
1978	PLM	62	100	38	0
1983	PLM	55	71	45	29
1987	PLM	45	57	55	43
1991	NPP	43	57	57	43

Source: Compiled by Patrick Emmanuel.

Table 14
St. Kitts-Nevis: Distribution of Votes and Seats in General Elections

Election Year	Winning Party			Other Parties/Individuals Opposition Groups	
	Party	*% Vote*	*% Seats*	*% Vote*	*% Seats*
1952	SKLP	85	100	15	0
1957	SKLP	54	63	46	27
1961	SKLP	65	70	35	30
1966	SKLP	44	70	56	30
1971	SKLP	51	78	49	22
1975	SKLP	60	78	40	22
1980	PAM, NRP	56	56	44	44
1984	PAM	48	55	52	45
1989	PAM	44	55	56	45

Source: Compiled by Patrick Emmanuel.

Table 15
Dominica: Distribution of Votes and Seats in General Elections

Election Year	Winning Party			Other Parties/Individuals Opposition Groups	
	Party	*% Vote*	*% Seats*	*% Vote*	*% Seats*
1951		Independents		Independents	
1954		—	—	—	—
1957		—	—	—	—
1961	DLP	48	64	52	36
1966	DLP	65	90	35	10
1970	DLP	50	73	50	27
1975	DLP	49	76	51	24
1980	DFP	51	81	49	19
1985	DFP	57	71	43	29
1990	DFP	49	52	51	48

Source: Compiled by Patrick Emmanuel.

Table 16
Grenada: Distribution of Votes and Seats in General Elections

Election Year	Winning Party			Other Parties/Individuals Opposition Groups	
	Party	*% Vote*	*% Seats*	*% Vote*	*% Seats*
1951	GULP	64	75	36	25
1954	GULP	46	75	54	25
1957	GULP	44	25	56	75
1961	GULP	53	80	47	20
1962	GNP	54	60	46	40
1967	GULP	55	70	45	30
1972	GULP	59	87	41	13
1976	GULP	52	60	48	40
1984	NNP	58	93	42	7
1990*	NDC	35	47	65	53

* 1990 elections were unusual. The NDC victory came without the majority needed to control Parliament. The NDC then had to form coalitions with opposition parties.
Source: Official Election Reports, 1951–1990.

Table 17
St. Lucia: Distribution of Votes and Seats in General Elections

Election Year	Winning Party			Other Parties/Individuals Opposition Groups	
	Party	*% Vote*	*% Seats*	*% Vote*	*% Seats*
1951	SLP	50	63	50	37
1954	SLP	47	63	53	37
1957	SLP	66	88	34	12
1961	SLP	62	90	38	10
1964	UWP	52	60	48	40
1969	UWP	58	60	42	40
1974	UWP	54	59	46	41
1979	SLP	56	71	44	29
1982	UWP	56	88	44	12
1987	UWP	53	53	47	47

Source: Official Election Reports, 1951–1987.

Table 18
St. Vincent and the Grenadines: Distribution of Votes and Seats in General Elections

Election Year	Winning Party			Other Parties/Individuals Opposition Groups	
	Party	*% Vote*	*% Seats*	*% Vote*	*% Seats*
1951	8th Army	70	100	30	0
1954	—	—	—	—	—
1957	PPP	49	63	51	37
1961	PPP	49	67	61	33
1966	PPP	49	56	51	44
1967	SVLP	54	67	46	33
1972	—	—	—	—	—
1974	SVLP	69	77	31	23
1979	SVLP	54	85	46	15
1984	NDP	51	69	49	31
1989	NDP	66	100	34	0

Source: Compiled by Patrick Emmanuel.

Table 19
Barbados: Distribution of Votes and Seats in General Elections

Election Year	Winning Party			Other Parties/Individuals Opposition Groups	
	Party	*% Vote*	*% Seats*	*% Vote*	*% Seats*
1951	BLP	55	63	45	37
1956	BLP	49	63	51	37
1961	DLP	56	58	64	42
1966	DLP	50	58	50	42
1971	DLP	57	75	43	25
1976	BLP	53	71	47	29
1981	BLP	52	63	48	37
1986	DLP	59	89	41	11
1991	DLP	50	64	50	36

Source: Compiled by Patrick Emmanuel.

Table 20

Jamaica: Distribution of Votes and Seats in General Elections

Election Year*	Winning Party			Other Parties/Individuals Opposition Groups	
	Party	% Vote	% Seats	% Vote	% Seats
1944	JLP	41	69	59	31
1949	JLP	43	53	57	47
1955	PNP	51	56	49	44
1959	PNP	55	63	45	37
1962	JLP	50	58	50	42
1967	JLP	51	62	49	38
1972	PNP	56	70	44	30
1976	PNP	57	78	43	22
1980	JLP	59	85	41	15
1983**	JLP	90	100	10	0
1989	PNP	57	75	43	25

* The recent (1993) victory by the PNP is not recorded in this table.

** The PNP boycotted the 1983 elections. The JLP held all sixty seats in Parliament, creating a one-party Parliament for the first time in Jamaica's modern political history.

Source: Compiled by Patrick Emmanuel.

Table 21

Trinidad and Tobago: Distribution of Votes and Seats in General Elections

Election Year	Winning Party			Other Parties/Individuals Opposition Groups	
	Party	% Vote	% Seats	% Vote	% Seats
1946					
1950					
1956	PNM	40	54	60	46
1961	PNM	57	67	43	33
1966	PNM	52	67	48	33
1971*	PNM	84	100	16	0
1976	PNM	54	67	46	33
1981	PNM	53	72	47	28
1986	NAR	66	92	34	8
1991	PNM	45	58	55	42

* In 1971, in response to the calls of the radical opposition, 66% of the population stayed away from the polls. The election was virtually uncontested except by the PNM and a few quickly assembled political parties. For further discussion of the 1971 elections, see Hintzen, 1989a: 84–85.

Source: Compiled by Patrick Emmanuel.

Bibliography

Alm, James. (1988) "Noncompliance and Payroll Taxation in Jamaica," *Journal of Developing Areas* vol. 22, no. 4 (July): 477–496.

Almond, G. and J. Coleman, eds. (1960) *The Politics of Developing Areas*. Princeton, NJ: Princeton University Press.

Amandala. (various dates) Belize City, Belize.

Amin, S. (1976) *Unequal Development*. New York: Monthly Review.

Antoine, Patrick. (1984) *"River Antoine" : An Estate and Its History*. Mimeo. St. Georges, Grenada.

Apter, D. (1965) *The Politics of Modernization*. Chicago and London: University of Chicago Press.

Ayearst, M. (1960) *The British West Indies: The Search for Self-Government*. London: Allen & Unwin.

Baber, Colin and H. B. Jeffrey. (1986) *Guyana: Politics, Economics and Society*. London: Frances Pinter, and Boulder, CO: Lynne Rienner Publishers.

Bahadoorsingh, K. (1968) *Trinidad Electoral Politics—The Persistence of the Race Factor*. London: Institute of Race Relations.

Barbados Economic Report. (1987, 1990) Bridgetown, Barbados: Ministry of Finance.

Barber, B. (1984) *Strong Democracy: Participatory Politics for a New Age*. Berkeley: University of California Press.

Barriteau, Eudine and R. Clarke. (1989) "Grenadian Perceptions of the People's Revolutionary Government and Its Policies," *Social and Economic Studies* vol. 38, no. 3 (September): 54–91.

Barrow, C. and J. E. Greene. (1979) *Small Business in Barbados: A Case of Survival*. Cave Hill, Barbados: Institute of Social and Economic Research (ISER), University of the West Indies.

Beckford, G. and M. Witter. (1980) *Small Garden, Bitter Weed: Struggle and Change in Jamaica*. St. Thomas, Jamaica: Maroon Publishing.

Beckles, H. (1989) *Corporate Power in Barbados: The Mutual Affair*. Bridgetown, Barbados: Lighthouse Communications.

———. (1990) *A History of Barbados*. Cambridge: Cambridge University Press.

Belle, G. (1977) *The Politics of Development: A Study in the Political Economy of Barbados*. Ph.D Diss. University of Manchester.

Benjamin, M. (1990) "Things Fall Apart," *NACLA Report on the Americas* vol. 24, no. 2 (August): 18.

Berreman, G. (1975) "Bazaar Behavior: Social Identity and Social Interaction in Urban India." In *Ethnic Identity*, ed. George De Vos and Lola Romanucci-Ross. Palo Alto, CA: Mayfield.

Bloomfield, L. M. (1953) *The British Honduras–Guatemala Dispute*. Toronto: Carswell Company.

Bobb, Euric. (1983) "The Oil Industry: Impact on the Local Economy. Review 1982/Forecast 1983," *Quarterly Economic Bulletin* vol. 7, no. 1 (March): 94. Central Bank of Trinidad and Tobago.

Bradley, C. Paul. (1960) "Mass Parties in Jamaica: Structure and Organization," *Social and Economic Studies* vol. 9, no. 4 (December): 375–416.

Brathwaite, F. (1984) *The 1984 Grenada Elections*. Cave Hill, Barbados: University of the West Indies.

Brathwaite, L. (1953) "Social Stratification in Trinidad," *Social and Economic Studies* vol. 2, nos. 2–3 (October): 5–175.

Brizan, G. (1983) *Grenada: Island of Conflict—From Amerindians to People's Revolution, 1498–1979*. London: ZED Press.

Brodber, E. (1989) "Socio-cultural Change in Jamaica." In *Jamaica in Independence*, ed. R. Nettleford, 55–74. Kingston: Heinemann Publishers (Caribbean), and London: James Currey Publishers.

Carew, J. (1985) *Grenada: The Hour Will Strike Again*. Prague: The International Organization of Journalists.

Central America Report. (various dates) London.

Chase, A. (1964) *A History of Trade Unionism in Guyana: 1900–1961*. Georgetown, Guyana: New Guyana Company.

Cheltenham, R. L. (1970) *The Political and Constitutional Development of Barbados, 1946–1966*. Ph.D Diss. University of Manchester.

Clarke, Colin. (1992) "Spatial Pattern and Social Interactions Among Creoles and Indians in Trinidad and Tobago." In *Trinidad Ethnicity*, ed. Kevin A. Yelvington. London and Basingstoke: Macmillan.

Coleman, J. and C. Rosberg. (1964) *Political Parties and National Integration in Tropical Africa*. Berkeley and Los Angeles: University of California Press.

Collins, M. (1987) *Angel*. London: The Woman Press.

Dahl, Robert A. (1971) *Polyarchy: Participation and Opposition*. New Haven, CT: Yale University Press.

Davies, O. (1986) "An Analysis of the Management of the Jamaican Economy: 1972–1985," *Social and Economic Studies* vol. 35, no. 1 (March): 73–110.

Davies, R. (1990) "Gorbachev's Socialism in Historical Perspective," *New Left Review* no. 179 (January-February): 5–28.

Davis, N. (1988) "Debt Conversion: The Jamaican Experience," *Social and Economic Studies* vol. 37, no. 4 (December): 151–170.

Davis-Pierre, M. (1975) *House of Assembly Dominica, Procedure Working Methods*. Rouseau, Dominica: Government Printing Office.

Despres, L. A. (1967) *Cultural Pluralism and Nationalist Politics in British Guiana*. Chicago: Rand McNally.

———. (1975) "Towards a Theory of Ethnic Phenomena." In *Ethnicity and Resource Competition in Plural Societies*, ed. Leo A. Despres. The Hague: Mouton.

Deutsch, K., ed. (1963) *Nation-Building*. New York: Atherton Press.

De Vos, G. (1975) "Ethnic Pluralism: Conflict and Accommodation." In *Ethnic Identity*, ed. George De Vos and Lola Romanucci-Ross. Palo Alto: Mayfield.

Diamond, L., J. Linz, and M. Lipset, eds. (1989) *Democracy in Developing Countries: Latin America*. Boulder, CO: Lynne Rienner Publishers.

Downes, A. (1986) "Barbados Today: An Economic Analysis of Barbados, 1981–1986." In *Political Barbados*, ed. S. Price. Bridgetown, Barbados: Letchworth.

Du Bois, W. E. B. (1949) *Color and Democracy*. New York: Harcourt Brace.

Duncan, N. (1986) "The Barbados General Elections, 1986," *CARICOM Perspective* no. 35 (April–June).

———. (1989) "Third Parties," *The New Bajan* (March).

———. (1991) "The State, Nationalism and Security: The Case of the Anglophone Caribbean." In *Conflict, Peace and Development in the Caribbean*, ed. Jorge Rodriguez Beruff, J. Peter Figueroa, and J. Edward Greene, 241–258. London: Macmillan.

Duncan, Neville, G. Danns, P. Emmanuel, and J. Cole. (1978) *Barbados 1976 General Elections Public Opinion Survey*. Cave Hill, Barbados: Institute of Social and Economic Research (ISER), University of the West Indies.

Dupuy, A. (1989) *Haiti in the World Economy*. Boulder, CO: Westview Press.

Eaton, G. (1975) *Alexander Bustamante and the New Jamaica*. Kingston: Kingston Publishing.

Edie, C. (1986) "Domestic Politics and External Relations in Jamaica under Michael Manley, 1972–1980," *Studies in Comparative International Development* vol. 21, no. 1 (Spring): 71–94.

———. (1989) "From Manley to Seaga: The Persistence of Clientelism in Jamaica," *Social and Economic Studies* vol. 38, no. 1 (March): 1–36.

———. (1991) *Democracy by Default: Dependency and Clientelism in Jamaica*. Boulder, CO: Lynne Rienner Publishers.

Emmanuel, P. (1978) *Crown Colony Politics in Grenada, 1917–1951*. Cave Hill, Barbados: Institute of Social and Economic Research (ISER), University of the West Indies.

———. (1979) *General Elections in the Eastern Caribbean: A Handbook*. Cave Hill, Barbados: Institute of Social and Economic Research (ISER), University of the West Indies.

Emmanuel, P., F. Brathwaite, and E. Barriteau. (1986) *Political Change and Public Opinion in Grenada, 1979–1984*. Cave Hill, Barbados: Institute of Social and Economic Research (ISER), University of the West Indies.

Enloe, C. H. (1973) *Ethnic Conflict and Political Development*. Boston: Little, Brown and Company.

Evenson, D. (1990) "Channeling Dissent," *NACLA Report on the Americas* vol. 14, no. 2 (August): 27.

Everitt, John C. (1984) "The Recent Migrations of Belize, Central America," *International Migration Review* vol. 18, no. 2 (Summer): 319–325.

Farley, R. (1954) "The Rise of the Peasantry in British Guiana," *Social and Economic Studies* vol. 2, no. 4 (March): 87–103.

Fried, M. (1956) "The Chinese in British Guiana," *Social and Economic Studies* vol. 5, no. 1 (March): 54–73.

Girvan, N. (1971) *Foreign Capital and Economic Underdevelopment in Jamaica*. Mona, Jamaica: Institute of Social and Economic Research (ISER), University of the West Indies.

———. (1978) *Corporate Imperialism: Conflict and Expropriation*. New York: Monthly Review Press.

Girvan, N. and R. Bernal. (1982) "The IMF and the Foreclosure of Development Options: The Case of Jamaica," *Monthly Review* vol. 33, no. 9 (February): 34–60.

Girvan, N., R. Bernal, and W. Hughes. (1980) "The IMF and the Third World: The Case of Jamaica, 1974–1980," *Development Dialogue* (2): 113–155.

Glasgow, R. (1970) *Guyana: Race and Politics Among Africans and East Indians*. The Hague: Martinus Nijhoff.

Gomes, A. (1954) *Hansard* December 10, 690.

Gonsalves, R. (1970) *The Role of Labour in the Political Process in St. Vincent, 1935–1970.* Unpublished M.Sc. Thesis. University of the West Indies. Kingston, Jamaica.

——— . (1977) "The Trade Union Movement in Jamaica." In *Essays on Power and Change in Jamaica*, ed. Carl Stone and A. Brown, 89–105. Kingston, Jamaica: Jamaica Publishing.

Goodwin, Paul B., ed. (1990) *Global Studies: Latin America*, 4th ed. Guilford, CT: Dushkin Publishing.

Gramsci, A. (1971) *Selections from the Prison Notebooks*. London: Lawrence and Wishart.

Granma. (daily) March 16, 1990, 5. Havana, Cuba.

Granma Weekly Review. (various dates) Havana, Cuba.

Grant, C. H. (1976) *The Making of Modern Belize: Politics, Society and British Colonialism in Central America*. Cambridge: Cambridge University Press.

Harker, T. (1991) "Caribbean Economic Performance: An Overview." Paper presented at the Third Conference of Caribbean Economists, Santo Domingo, Dominican Republic, July.

Harris, D. (1977) "Notes on the Question of a National Minimum Wage for Jamaica." In *Essays on Power and Change in Jamaica*, ed. Carl Stone and A. Brown, 106–115. Kingston, Jamaica: Jamaica Publishing.

Harris, N. (1986) *The End of the Third World*. Harmondsworth, England: Penguin Books.

Harris, P. B. (1976) *Foundations of Political Science*. London: Hutchinson.

Hass, E. (1958) *The Uniting of Europe: Political, Social and Economic Forces*. Stanford, CA: Stanford University Press.

Heine, J., ed. (1990) *A Revolution Aborted: The Lessons of Grenada*. Pittsburgh, PA: University of Pittsburgh Press.

Henry, P. (1985) *Peripheral Capitalism and Underdevelopment in Antigua*. New Brunswick, NJ: Transaction Books.

——— . (1990) "Social and Cultural Transformation in Grenada." In *A Revolution Aborted: The Lessons of Grenada*, ed. Jorge Heine. Pittsburgh: University of Pittsburgh Press.

——— . (1991) "Political Accumulation and Authoritarianism in the Caribbean: The Case of Antigua," *Social and Economic Studies* vol. 40, no.1 (March): 1–38.

Hintzen, P. (1981) *Capitalism, Socialism and Socio-Political Confrontation in Multi-Racial Developing States: A Comparison of Guyana and Trinidad*. Ph.D. diss. Yale University.

——— . (1989a) *The Costs of Regime Survival: Racial Mobilization, Elite Domination, and Control of the State in Guyana and Trinidad*. Cambridge and New York: Cambridge University Press.

——— . (1989b) "Arthur Lewis and the Bourgeois State." Unpublished paper presented at the Caribbean Studies Association XVI Annual Conference, Bridgetown, Barbados, May.

Hintzen, P. and R. Premdas. (1983) "Race, Ideology and Power in Guyana," *Journal of Commonwealth and Comparative Politics* vol. 21, no. 2 (July): 175–194.

Hintzen, P. and M. Will. (1988) "Biographic Entries on Leaders of the Anglophone Caribbean." In *Bibliographical Dictionary of Latin American and Caribbean Political Leaders*, ed. R. J. Alexander. Westport, CT: Greenwood Press.

Howard, M. (1987) *Income Tax Reform in Barbados: 1977–1987*. Barbados: University of the West Indies.

――――. (1988) "The Gorbachev Challenge and the Defense of the West," *Survival* vol. 30, no. 6 (November–December): 483–492.

Hoyos, F. (1973) *Builders of Barbados*. London: Macmillan.

――――. (1978) *Barbados: A History From Amerindians to Independence*. London: Macmillan.

Huggins, Martha K. (1978) "U.S.-Supported State Terror: A History of Police Training in Latin America," *Crime and Social Justice* nos. 27–28: 149–171.

Huntington, S. (1968) *Political Order in Changing Societies*. New Haven, CT: Yale University Press.

――――. (1984) "Will More Countries Become Democratic," *Political Science Quarterly* vol. 99, no. 2 (Summer): 193–218.

Hyde, Evan X. (1969) *Knockin' Our Own Ting*. Belize City: Cubola Productions.

Industrial Stabilization Act 1965, *Laws of Trinidad and Tobago*, Act no. 8. Port of Spain, Trinidad: Government Printer.

Jamadar, P. A. (1975) *The Mechanics of Democracy: Proportional Representation in First-Past-the-Post*. Port of Spain, Trinidad: Imprint Caribbean Ltd.

Jamaica Daily Gleaner. June 1, 1987. Kingston, Jamaica.

Jamaica Parliament. Budget Debate, 1986/87. Kingston: Jamaica Information Service.

Jamaica Weekly Gleaner. (North American Edition, various dates) Ontario, Canada.

Jefferson, O. (1972) *The Post-War Economic Development of Jamaica*. Mona, Jamaica: Institute of Social and Economic Research (ISER), University of the West Indies.

John, K. (1971) *Politics in a Small Colonial Territory: St. Vincent, 1950–1970*. Ph.D Diss. University of Manchester.

Kagarlitsky, B. (1987) "The Intelligentsia and Changes," *New Left Review* no. 164 (July–August): 5–26.

Karch, C. (1979) *The Transformation and Consolidation of the Corporate Plantation Economy in Barbados, 1960–1977*. Ph.D Diss. Rutgers University, New Brunswick, NJ.

Kaufman, M. (1985) *Jamaica Under Manley*. London: ZED Books.

Kirton, G. (1977) "A Preliminary Analysis of Imperialist Penetration and Control via the Foreign Debt: A Study of Jamaica." In *Essays on Power and Change in Jamaica*, ed. Carl Stone and A. Brown, 72–88. Kingston, Jamaica: Jamaica Publishing.

Kornhauser, W. (1959) *The Politics of Mass Society*. Glencoe, IL: Free Press.

Kunsman, C. (1963) *The Origins and Development of Political Parties in the British West Indies*. Ph.D Diss. University of California at Berkeley.

Kwayana, E. (1991) *Walter Rodney*. Wellesley, MA: Calaloux Publications.

Labour Beacon. September 7, 1991, 1–2. Belize City, Belize.

Lacey, T. (1977) *Violence and Politics in Jamaica, 1960–1970*. Manchester, England: University of Manchester Press.

Laguerre, J. G. (1983) "The General Elections of 1981 in Trinidad and Tobago," *Journal of Commonwealth and Comparative Politics* vol. 21, no. 2 (July): 133–157.

Lauren, P. G. (1988) *Power and Prejudice: The Politics and Diplomacy of Racial Discrimination*. Boulder, CO, and London: Westview.

Lent, John A. (1982) "Mass Media and Socialist Governments in the Commonwealth Caribbean," *Human Rights Quarterly* vol. 4, no. 3 (Fall): 371–390.

Lewin, M. (1988) *The Gorbachev Phenomenon: An Historical Interpretation*. Berkeley: University of California Press.

Lewis, G. K. (1968) *The Growth of the Modern West Indies*. New York: Monthly Review Press.

――――. (1987) *Grenada: The Jewel Despoiled*. Baltimore: Johns Hopkins University Press.

Lewis, W. Arthur. (1965) *Politics in West Africa*. London: Allen & Unwin.

Lipset, Seymour Martin. (1959) "Some Requisites of Democracy: Economic Development and Political Legitimacy," *American Political Science Review* vol. 53, no. 1 (March): 69–105.

Looney, R. (1987) *The Jamaican Economy in the 1980s: Economic Decline and Structural Adjustment*. Boulder, CO: Westview Press.

MacDonald, S. (1986) *Trinidad and Tobago: Democracy and Development in the Caribbean*. New York: Praeger.

Maguire, R. (1984) "Strategies for Rural Development in Haiti." In *Haiti Today and Tomorrow*, ed. R. Foster and A. Valdman. Landham: University Press of America.

Manigat, L. (1989) "Challenges Confronting Third World Democrats," *Vision* vol. 1, no. 2: 7. Center for Strategic Studies, Washington, DC.

Manley, M. (1982) *Jamaica: Struggle in the Periphery*. London: Third World Media.

————. (1987) *Up the Down Escalator: Development and the International Economy—The Jamaican Case*. London: Andre Deutsch.

Maritime Areas Act. (1991) Belmopan: Belize Government Printery.

McAfee, K. (1991) *Storm Signals: Structural Adjustment and Development Alternatives in the Caribbean*. Boston: ZED Press.

Miami Herald. (various dates) Miami, Florida.

Munroe, T. (1972) *The Politics of Constitutional Decolonization in Jamaica, 1944–1962*. Mona, Jamaica: Institute of Social and Economic Research (ISER), University of the West Indies.

Nascimento, C. A. (1974) "The Transferability of the Concepts of Media Ownership and Freedom." Paper presented at a seminar on "Communications and Information for Development in the Caribbean Area." University of Guyana, Georgetown, May 16.

Nath, D. (1950) *A History of Indians in British Guiana*. London: Published by D. Nath.

National Bi-Partisan Commission Explains the Maritime Areas Bill and Recent Developments Between Belize/Guatemala. (1991) Belmopan: Belize Government Printery, October.

Nettleford, R. (1989) *Jamaica in Independence*. Kingston: Heinemann (Caribbean) Ltd.

New Belize (a publication of the government of Belize). June 1968, 3; October 1983, 86. Belmopan: Belize Government Printery.

New York Times. (various dates) New York, NY.

Nicholls, D. (1977) *From Dessalines to Duvalier*. London: Cambridge University Press.

Noguera, P. (1989) "The Basis of Regime Support in Grenada from 1951–1988: A Study of Political Attitudes and Behavior in a Peripheral Society." Ph.D Diss. University of California at Berkeley.

Oakes, E. (1988) "Grenada Under Occupation: U.S. Economic Policy, 1983–1987," *Rethinking Marxism* vol. 1, no. 3 (Fall): 131–157.

Obeyesekere, G. (1975) "Sinhalese-Buddhist Identity in Ceylon." In *Ethnic Identity*, ed. George De Vos and Lola Romanucci-Ross. Palo Alto: Mayfield.

Olsen, M. (1970) *Power in Societies*. New York: Macmillan.

Orellana, M. R. (1987) "In Contemplation of Micronesia: The Prospects for the Decolonization of Puerto Rico under International Law." *The University of Miami Inter-American Law Review* vol. 8, no.2 (Spring): 457–490.

Oxaal, I. (1968) *Black Intellectuals Come to Power*. Cambridge, MA: G. K. Hall and Schenkman.

Palacio, Joseph O. (1990) *Socioeconomic Integration of Central American Immigrants in Belize*. SPEAR Reports 2. Belize City: Cubola Productions.

Pastor, R. and R. Fletcher. (1991) "The Caribbean in the Twenty First Century," *Foreign Affairs* vol. 70, no. 3 (Summer): 98–114.

Pateman, C. (1970) *Participation and Democratic Theory*. Cambridge: Cambridge University Press.

Payne, A. (1981) "Seaga's Jamaica After One Year," *World Today* vol. 37, no. 11 (November): 434–440.

————. (1988) *Politics in Jamaica*. London and New York: C. Hurst and St. Martin's Press.

————. (1991) "Jamaican Society and the Testing of Democracy." In *Society and Politics in the Caribbean*, ed. Colin Clarke, 1–30. New York: St. Martin's Press.

Paz, Octavio. (1982) "Latin American Democracy." In *Democracy and Dictatorship in Latin America*, ed. Octavio Paz, 5–18. New York: Foundation for the Independent Study of Social Ideas.

Phillips, F. (1985) *West Indian Constitutions: Post-Independence Reform*. New York: Oceana Publications, Inc.

Premdas, R. (1972) *Voluntary Associations and Political Parties in a Racially Fragmented State*. Georgetown, Guyana: Department of Political Science, University of Guyana.

————. (1973) "Competitive Party Organizations and Political Integration in a Racially Fragmented State: The Case of Guyana," *Caribbean Studies* vol. 12, no. 4 (January): 5–35.

Proto, Felix. (1989) *The Guadeloupe Region as it Stands*. Basse Terre, Guadeloupe: Guadeloupe Region Regional Council, Republic of France.

Pryor, Frederic. (1986) *Revolutionary Grenada: A Study in Political Economy*. New York: Praeger.

Pye, L. and S. Verba, eds. (1965) *Political Culture and Political Development*. Princeton, NJ: Princeton University Press.

Rae, D. (1971) *The Political Consequences of Electoral Laws*. London and New Haven, CT: Yale University Press.

Ragatz, Joseph. (1972) *The Fall of the Planter Class in the British Caribbean*. New York: Octagon Books.

Report of the British Guiana Commission of Inquiry on Racial Problems in the Public Service. (1965) Geneva: International Commission of Jurists.

Report of the Commission of Enquiry into Subversive Activities in Trinidad and Tobago. (1965) House Paper No. 2. Port of Spain, Trinidad: Government Printer.

Report of the Constitution Commission. (1974) Chairman, Sir Hugh Wooding. Port of Spain, Trinidad: Trinidad and Tobago Printing and Packaging Ltd.

Report on the General Elections 1961–1965. (1965) Port of Spain, Trinidad: Government Printery.

Richards, N. H. (n.d.) *The Struggle and the Conquest: Twenty-Five Years of Social Democracy in Antigua*. St. John's, Antigua: Workers Voice Printery.

Rodríguez, J. L. (1990) "Los Cambios en la Politica Economia y Los Resultados de la Economia Cubano, 1986–1989" (Performance and Change in the Cuban Economy, 1986–1989), *Cuadernos de Nuestra America* vol. 7, no. 15 (July–December): 69–70.

Romalis, C. (1969) *Barbados and St. Lucia: A Comparative Analysis of Social and Economic Development in Two British West Indian Islands*. Ph.D Diss. Washington University, St. Louis, MO.

Ryan, S. (1972) *Race and Nationalism in Trinidad and Tobago*. Toronto: University of Toronto Press.

————. (1984a) "The Grenada Question: A Revolutionary Balance Sheet," *Caribbean Review* vol. 13, no. 3 (Summer): 7–9, 39–43.

————. (1984b) *Grenada Political and Social Outlook*. St. Augustine, Trinidad: St. Augustine Research Associates.

————. (1989) *Revolution and Reaction: Parties and Politics in Trinidad and Tobago, 1970–1981*. St. Augustine, Trinidad: Institute of Social and Economic Research (ISER), University of the West Indies.

————. (1990) "The Restoration of Electoral Politics in Grenada." In *A Revolution Aborted: The Lessons of Grenada*, ed. J. Heine, 265–290. Pittsburgh, PA: University of Pittsburgh Press.

Sanders, A. (1969) "Amerindian Attitudes and Integration," *New World* vol.1, no. 1 (January): 1–22.

Sartori, G. (1965) *Democratic Theory*. New York: Praeger.

Schumpeter, Joseph A. (1950) *Capitalism, Socialism, and Democracy*. New York: Harper and Row.

Searle, C., ed. (1984) *In Nobody's Backyard: Maurice Bishop's Speeches, 1979–1983*. London: ZED Press.

Security and Intelligence Bill, with Explanatory Notes. (n.d.) Belmopan: Belize Government Printery.

Segal, D. A. (1992) " 'Race' and 'Color' in Pre-Independence Trinidad and Tobago." In *Trinidad Ethnicity*, ed. K. A. Yelvington. London and Basingstoke: Macmillan.

Segal, R. (1967) *The Race War*. New York: Bantam.

Sherlock, P. (1980) *Norman Manley*. London: Macmillan.

Shoman, Assad. (1987) *Party Politics in Belize, 1950–1986*. Belize City, Belize: Cubola Productions.

Singham, A. (1968) *The Hero and the Crowd in a Colonial Polity*. New Haven, CT: Yale University Press.

Sloan, John W. (1989) "The Policy Capabilities of Democratic Regimes in Latin America." *Latin American Research Review* vol. 24, no. 2: 113–126.

Smith, T. E. (1973) *Elections in Developing Countries*. Westport, CT: Greenwood Press.

Spearhead. (various dates) Belize City, Belize.

Stephens, E. H. and John D. Stephens. (1987) *Democratic Socialism in Jamaica*. Princeton, NJ: Princeton University Press.

Stewart, T. (1991) *Debt Crisis in the Periphery as Manifestations of the Continuity of Imperialism Thesis: The Specificity of the Industrializing Commonwealth Caribbean*. M.Phil. Thesis. University of the West Indies, St. Augustine.

Stone, C. (1974) *Electoral Behaviour and Public Opinion in Jamaica*. Kingston, Jamaica: Institute of Social and Economic Research (ISER), University of the West Indies.

———. (1977a) "Worker Participation in Industry—A Survey of Workers' Opinions." In *Essays on Power and Change in Jamaica*, ed. Carl Stone and A. Brown, 182–202. Kingston, Jamaica: Jamaica Publishing.

———. (1977b) "Tenant Farming Under State Capitalism." In *Essays on Power and Change in Jamaica*, ed. Carl Stone and A. Brown, 117–125. Kingston, Jamaica: Jamaica Publishing.

———. (1980) *Democracy and Clientelism in Jamaica*. New Brunswick, NJ: Transaction Books.

———. (1982) "Seaga is in Trouble," *Caribbean Review* vol. 11, no. 4 (Fall): 4–7, 28–29.

———. (1986) *Class, State and Democracy in Jamaica*. New York: Praeger.

———. (1989a) *Politics Versus Economics: The 1989 Elections in Jamaica*. Kingston, Jamaica: Heinemann Publishers (Caribbean) Ltd.

———. (1989b) "Power, Policy and Politics in Independent Jamaica." In *Jamaica in Independence*, ed. R. Nettleford, 19–54. Kingston: Heinemann Publishers (Caribbean) Ltd. and London: James Currey Publishers.

Stone, C. and A. Brown, eds. (1977) *Essays on Power and Change in Jamaica*. Kingston, Jamaica: Jamaica Publishing.

Thomas, C. Y. (1983) "State Capitalism in Guyana: An Assessment of Burnham's Co-operative Socialist Republic." In *Crisis in the Caribbean*, ed. Fitzroy Ambursley and Robin Cohen, 27–48. New York: Monthly Review Press.

———. (1988) *The Poor and the Powerless: Economic Policy and Change in the Caribbean*. New York: Monthly Review Press.

Thorndike, T. (1985) *Grenada: Politics, Economics and Society*. Boulder, CO: Lynne Rienner Publishers.

Tinker, H. (1977) *Race, Conflict and the International Order*. London: Macmillan.

Trimberger, E. K. (1978) *Revolution From Above: Military Bureaucrats and Development in Japan, Turkey, Egypt, and Peru*. New Brunswick, NJ: Transaction Books.

Trinidad Guardian. (various dates) Port of Spain, Trinidad.

Trouillot, M. (1990) *Haiti: State Against Nation*. New York: Monthly Review Press.

Valdés, N. (1992) "Cuban Political Culture: Between Betrayal and Death." In *Cuba in Transition: Crisis and Transformation in the 1990s*, ed. S. Halebsky and J. Kirk, et al. Westport, CT: Westview Press.

Watson, H. (1986a) "The 1986 General Elections and Political Economy in Contemporary Barbados." Department of Political Science, Howard University.

———. (1986b) "Imperialism, National Security, and State Power in the Commonwealth Caribbean: Issues in the Development of the Authoritarian State." In *Militarization in the Non-Hispanic Caribbean*, ed. Alma H. Young and Dion E. Phillips, 17–41. Boulder, CO: Lynne Rienner Publishers.

Weber, M. (1958) *From Max Weber: Essays in Sociology*. Translated, edited, and with an introduction by H. H. Gerth and C. Wright Mills. New York: Oxford University Press.

Webster, Bethuel. (1968) *Draft Treaty between the United Kingdom of Great Britain and Northern Ireland and the Republic of Guatemala Relating to the Resolution of the Dispute over British Honduras*. Belize City, Belize: Government Printer.

Weiner, M. (1987) "Empirical Democratic Theory." In *Competitive Elections in Developing Countries*, ed. Myron Weiner and Evgun Ozbuden. Washington, DC: American Enterprise Institute.

Weiskoff, R. (1985) *Factories and Food Stamps*. Baltimore: Johns Hopkins University Press.

West India Royal Commission Report. (1945). Her Majesty's Stationery Office. Cmd 6607. London.

Will, M. W. (1972) *Political Development in the Mini-State Caribbean: A Focus on Barbados*. Ph.D Diss. University of Missouri.

Williams, E. (1969) *Inward Hunger: The Education of a Prime Minister*. Chicago: University of Chicago Press.

Worrell, D., ed. (1981) *The Economy of Barbados, 1946–1980*. Bridgetown, Barbados: Central Bank of Barbados.

Yelvington, K. A. (1992) *Trinidad Ethnicity*. London and Basingstoke: Macmillan.

Young, Alma H. (1970) "Ethnic Politics in Belize." *Caribbean Review* vol. 7, no. 4 (April): 32–36.

———. (1986) "The Central American Crisis and Its Impact on Belize." In *Militarization in the Non-Hispanic Caribbean*, ed. Alma H. Young and Dion E. Phillips, 139–157. Boulder, CO: Lynne Rienner Publishers.

———. (1991) "Peace, Democracy and Security in the Caribbean." In *Conflict, Peace and Development in the Caribbean*, ed. Jorge Rodriguez Beruff, J. Peter Figueroa, and J. Edward Greene, 3–21. London: Macmillan.

———. (1992) "Political Parties of Belize." In *Political Parties of the Americas 1980s to 1990s*, ed. Charles Ameringer, 77–87. Westport, CT: Greenwood Press.

Young, Alma H. and D. Phillips, eds. (1986) *Militarization in the Non-Hispanic Caribbean*. Boulder, CO: Lynne Rienner Publishers.

Young, Alma H. and Dennis H. Young. (1988) "The Impact of the Anglo-Guatemalan Dispute on the Internal Politics of Belize," *Latin American Perspectives* vol. 15, no. 2 (Spring): 6–30.

Zimbalist, A. (1993) "Hanging on in Havana," *Foreign Policy* no. 92 (Fall): 151–167.

Zoll, D. A. (1974) *Twentieth Century Political Philosophy*. Englewood Cliffs, NJ: Prentice-Hall.

Index

About the Editor and Contributors

CARLENE J. EDIE, from Jamaica, is Associate Professor in the Department of Political Science at the University of Massachusetts at Amherst. Her various contributions to journals have focused on the relationships among external dependency and domestic clientelism, party politics, and electoral processes in Jamaica, and comparative problems of socialism and rural development in Tanzania and Jamaica. She is the author of *Democracy by Default: Dependency and Clientelism in Jamaica* (1991). Her articles can be found in journals such as *Social and Economic Studies*, *Journal of Development Studies*, *Studies in Comparative International Development*, and *Journal of African Studies*.

CAROLLEE BENGELSDORF is Professor of Politics and Feminist Studies at Hampshire College in Amherst, Massachusetts. She has written numerous articles and presented papers on the state and society in socialist nations, contemporary Cuba, and women in Cuba. She is the author of *The Problem of Democracy in Cuba: Between Vision and Reality* (1993).

KENNETH I. BOODHOO, from Trinidad, is Associate Professor in the Department of International Affairs at Florida International University. His major publications have focused primarily on the Anglophone Caribbean, and his articles have appeared in journals such as *Caribbean Review*, *Caribbean Studies*, and the *Journal of Caribbean Studies*. He is the author of *Eric Williams: The Man and the Leader* (1986). He has contributed chapters to H. Michael Erisman, ed., *The Caribbean Challenge* (1983); and A. Young and D. Phillips, eds., *Militarization in the Non-Hispanic Caribbean* (1986).

NEVILLE DUNCAN, from Jamaica, is Senior Lecturer in the Department of Sociology and Government at the University of the West Indies (Cave Hill, Barbados). He is Dean of the Faculty of Social Sciences, University of the West Indies (Cave Hill, Barbados). He has published numerous articles on Barbados and the Anglophone Caribbean, focusing especially on issues of economic development, political behavior, electoral processes, and national security. He contributed a chapter to J. Rodriguez Beruff, J. Peter Figueroa, and J. Edward Greene, eds., *Conflict, Peace and Development in the Caribbean* (1991) . He is the author of *The Vincentian Elections, 1974* (1975), *Public Finance and Fiscal Issues in Barbados and the OECA* (1989), and *Barbados 1976 General Elections Public Opinion Survey* (1978) with G. Danns, Patrick Emmanuel, and J. Cole.

PATRICK EMMANUEL, from Grenada, is Senior Research Fellow at the Institute of Social and Economic Research (Eastern Caribbean) at the University of the West Indies (Cave Hill, Barbados). His current research interests include Caribbean government, elections and party systems, political integration, and ideology. He is the author of *Crown Colony Politics in Grenada, 1917–1951* (1978), *General Elections in the Eastern Caribbean* (1979), and *Approaches to Caribbean Political Integration, Elections and Party Systems in the Commonwealth Caribbean, 1944–1991* (1991), and co-author of *Political Change and Public Opinion in Grenada, 1979–1984* (1986). His articles have appeared in journals such as *Social and Economic Studies* and the *Bulletin of Eastern Caribbean Affairs*.

ROSARIO ESPINAL, from the Dominican Republic, is Assistant Professor in the Department of Sociology at Temple University, Philadelphia, Pennsylvania. She has been a faculty fellow at the Kellogg Institute for International Studies at the University of Notre Dame, and a guest fellow at the Latin American Center, Oxford University. She has published widely on the subject of democracy and electoral processes in the Dominican Republic. Her articles have appeared in journals such as *Bulletin of Latin American Research, Journal of Latin American Studies,* and *Electoral Studies.* She is the author of *Autoritarismo y democracia en la Política Dominicana* (1987).

CARMEN GAUTIER-MAYORAL, from Puerto Rico, is Director of the Social Science Research Center, University of Puerto Rico, and Secretary-Coordinator of the Caribbean International Relations Working Group of the Latin American Council for the Social Sciences. She is the author of *Poder y Plebiscito: Puerto Rico en 1991* (1990) and *Puerto Rico en la Economía Política Del Caribe* (1990). She has also published articles on Puerto Rico in *Caribbean Affairs* and *Caribbean Review.*

PERCY C. HINTZEN, from Guyana, is Associate Professor and Chair of the Department of Afro-American Studies at the University of California at

Berkeley. He is the author of *The Costs of Regime Survival: Race Mobilization, Elite Domination and Control of the State in Guyana and Trinidad and Tobago* (1989). His articles on race, ethnicity, and political economy have appeared in *Social and Economic Studies*, *Journal of Commonwealth and Comparative Politics*, and *Journal of InterAmerican Studies and World Affairs*.

PEDRO A. NOGUERA is Assistant Professor in the School of Education at the University of California at Berkeley. For the past several years, his research has been focused on political change in the Caribbean and Latin America. He has done research in Grenada in 1982 and in 1987, as well as research on the political consequences of migration in Central America, with extensive field work in Belize and El Salvador. He has recently completed a manuscript entitled *The Imperatives of Power, Regime Survival, and the Bases of Regime Support in Grenada*. He has also contributed an article on mass literacy as a political strategy to the *International Journal of University Adult Education* (Fall, 1992).

RALPH R. PREMDAS, from Trinidad, is Professor in the Department of Government at the University of the West Indies (St. Augustine, Trinidad). He held teaching positions at the University of Guyana, University of California at Berkeley, University of Ife, Nigeria, and McGill University. He is currently serving as a U.N. consultant on ethnicity and development. He is the author of over thirty publications on Guyana including *Racial Politics in Guyana* (1973), *Communist Politics in Fiji* (1978), and *The Costs of Ethnic Conflict in Guyana* (1992), and is the editor of *Ethnic Conflict in the Caribbean* (1992).

SELWYN RYAN, from Trinidad, is Director of the Institute for Social and Economic Research at the University of the West Indies (St. Augustine, Trinidad). He has written numerous articles, monographs, and books on politics in the Anglophone Caribbean, especially Trinidad. He is the author of *Race and Nationalism in Trinidad and Tobago* (1972), *Revolution and Reaction: Parties and Politics in Trinidad and Tobago, 1970–1981* (1990), and *Social and Occupational Stratification in Trinidad and Tobago* (1991).

BETTY SEDOC-DAHLBERG, from Suriname, is the former Dean of the Faculty of Social Sciences at the University of Suriname. She is currently a Visiting Professor of Planning and Policy at the University of Florida at Gainesville. She is the editor of *The Dutch Caribbean: Prospects for Democracy* (1989).

DESSIMA WILLIAMS, from Grenada, was Ambassador from Grenada to the OAS and United Nations, 1979–1983. She is currently the Jacob Ziskind visiting Associate Professor of Sociology at Brandeis University, Waltham, Massachusetts. Her research, teaching, and writing focus on U.S. foreign policy, development, women, and gender studies.

ALMA H. YOUNG is Professor of Urban and Public Affairs and Director of the PhD Program in Urban Studies at the University of New Orleans, Louisiana. She is currently a member of the Visiting Committee for the Political Science Department at the Massachusetts Institute of Technology. She was President of the Caribbean Studies Association and former editor of the *Caribbean Studies Newsletter*. She is the co-editor of *Militarization in the Non-Hispanic Caribbean* (1976) and a regular contributor to *Latin America and Caribbean Contemporary Record*. Her research and writings have focused on comparative urbanization and political developments in the Anglophone Caribbean, especially in Belize.